Future of Business and Finance

The Future of Business and Finance book series features professional works aimed at defining, describing and charting the future trends in these fields. The focus is mainly on strategic directions, technological advances, challenges and solutions which may affect the way we do business tomorrow, including the future of sustainability and governance practices. Mainly written by practitioners, consultants and academic thinkers, the books are intended to spark and inform further discussions and developments.

More information about this series at http://www.springer.com/series/16360

Caren Brenda Scheepers · Sonja Swart

Change Leadership in Emerging Markets

The Ten Enablers Model

 Springer

Caren Brenda Scheepers
Gordon Institute of Business Science
University of Pretoria
Sandton, South Africa

Sonja Swart
Executive Development
University of Stellenbosch Business School
Sandton, South Africa

Eaton Business School
Westford Education Group AAL Taawun
Sharjah, United Arab Emirates

ISSN 2662-2467   ISSN 2662-2475   (electronic)
Future of Business and Finance
ISBN 978-3-030-40845-9   ISBN 978-3-030-40846-6   (eBook)
https://doi.org/10.1007/978-3-030-40846-6

This Springer imprint is published by the registered company Springer Nature Switzerland AG.
The registered company address is: Gewerbestrasse 11, 6330 Cham, Switzerland

Foreword

This book arrives at a prescient time because management and leadership education is in a state of flux. The relevance of business school education and the flagship MBA degree are under the spotlight. While this trend began from within the field of business and management education, engaging leading scholars like Henry Mintzberg, Sumantra Goshal, Jeffrey Pfeffer and Christina Fong, it is increasingly being echoed on the outside with headlines like the 'MBA Disrupted' from publications like the UK-based *Economist*. In this book, Caren and Sonja provide an example of how academics and practitioners can collaborate to create a bridge between theory and practice, thereby responding to Karl Weick's *relevance gap*. The result is an illustration of how, as famously expressed by Kurt Lewin, "there is nothing so practical as a good theory."

Having worked with Sonja in my time as a financial services business executive and with Caren, now a budding academic, I am grateful that they have combined their efforts to respond to the call to fill the gap between theory and practice by integrating pragmatic steps-based change frameworks grounded in the literature to develop a useful and relevant leadership change framework. Their leadership change framework is distinguished by enablers, which they use to illustrate how leaders can influence processes of transformational change in organisations located in what they define as emerging market contexts. The authors' inclusion of neuroscience enhances our understanding of how behaviour change functions. It is a welcome integration of the neuroscience knowledge to change leadership. They invoke the seminal work by Kurt Lewin who 70 years ago argued that behaviour is a function of individual choice and the environment in which such individuals operate, thereby inviting scholars to study leadership in context. An invitation to focus on context as much as on individual choice was largely ignored until the *Leadership Quarterly* article titled *"Toward a Contextual Theory of Leadership"* by Richard Osborn, James Hunt and Lawrence Jauch was published.

Caren and Sonja draw on leadership literature, empirical evidence as well as practical analogue and digital tools to argue and illustrate that, when pursuing transformational change, while the role of top management team leadership is necessary, it is not sufficient. The sufficiency rule is fulfilled by incorporating the role of leaders broadly distributed throughout the organisation because transformational change requires the buy-in of the organisation as a whole. This has serious implications for both scholars and practitioners interested in leadership in emerging markets, as described by Caren and Sonja, because it draws greater attention to the underexplored idea of distributed leadership in organisational studies as opposed to the focus on top management literature and practices, especially on how leadership distributed throughout the organisation influences the implementation of strategies aimed at transformational change.

Caren and Sonja focus simultaneously on leadership roles and process-based organisational change to deftly broaden the content of organisational change leadership. In addition to visioning and inspiring, they argue that change leadership must encourage and model ongoing communication, participative decision-making and the minimising of resistance and maximising effectiveness of complex environments. In so doing, the authors respond to the criticism of atomistic business and management education and advance leadership roles and process-based organisational change literatures and practices.

This book provides a literature-based pragmatic approach to transformational change leadership that should draw the attention of those who are sceptical of business management and education. Caren and Sonja are commended for undertaking the task of reimagining the role of leadership in contexts that desperately need leaders, broadly distributed, to stand up and be counted as their organisations respond to disruptive changes both endogenously and exogenously caused. By so doing, they contribute to giving meaning to leadership scholarship—responding to a call by scholars like Joel Podolny, Rakesh Khurana and Marya Besharov. In my opinion, failure to lead with purpose in this time of seismic changes in business and society will have disastrous consequences. Caren and Sonja have not failed to lead in these disruptive contexts, neither should we.

Gordon Institute of Business Science   Morris Mthombeni
University of Pretoria
Sandton, South Africa

Preface

Growing up in South Africa during apartheid and living through the transition while being young adults allowed us to experience transformational change first-hand. Having been exposed to several changes in our cultural milieu, our personal lives as well as in the corporate environment, we realised we had a story to tell and lessons to share.

We were fortunate to be part of organisations early on in our careers that were brilliant at developing people and exposed us to international change management and diversity thinking in the late 1980s when it was not yet a hot topic.

The change leadership domain attracted us from our first exposure, and we had an attachment to the science ever since. At personal, professional levels and even as parents, we have been studying, living and breathing the issues of leadership and change for the last twenty-five years.

The field of neuroscience added to our fascination with the domain, since understanding the way our brain functions assisted with understanding why change is so difficult and how we can enable the change process. Therefore, we included elements of neuroscience. It thus facilitates a greater understanding and depth of the domain.

We had the privilege of sharing this model with more than four thousand managers over the last nineteen years. They were generous in providing feedback and improvements that improved the model. Through many iterations and practical applications, the model now goes to print. We realise that it will still evolve but are sharing it with you in its current format. We are confident that it will assist in integrating your ideas and offer a framework or model that will make leadership of change easier in our emergent economies. We are making practical exercises available to you in the online toolbox and reflection questions toolbox on the Springer website.

Sandton, South Africa   Caren Brenda Scheepers
9 August 2019   Sonja Swart

Dedications

Thanks to:

The peer reviewers for their valuable feedback and time.

Leaders who trusted us with their stories around change.

Organisations who contracted our business coaching and consulting services.

Dr Morris Mthombeni, Interim Dean, Gordon Institute of Business Science, University Pretoria, for the excellent foreword to the volume.

From Sonja:

A special thank you to the following people without whom I could not have completed this book.

- To University of Stellenbosch Business School, Executive Development for allowing me to be part of their virtual faculty team since 2001. They enabled me to teach change management and leadership courses to managers and executives from a wide range of public and private organisations all over Africa.
- To Eaton Business School who gave me an opportunity to be a visiting lecturer and to engage with managers and executives from all over the globe.
- To my husband, my partner of 30 years, who loves me unconditionally and whom I love dearly. You allowed me the time and space to work and write without worrying about the day-to-day duties of being a mother and wife.
- To my children, Berns and Nix, you are my life and you bring me my greatest joy.
- To my mother, you are my soul mate and a true role model of how to live a meaningful life.
- To Ray Topp, you gave me my big break and a life-changing opportunity to move from statistical consulting to change management consulting. You were my first and most significant teacher.
- To so many colleagues, clients and learners who helped me grow and learn. You were all in my mind while writing this book. To those of you who contributed to this book, read manuscripts and gave me sound and invaluable advice: A special thank you to Michelle Malherbe, Hans Kuilman, Jenny Leclezio, Liesl De Villiers and Steyn Heckroodt.

- I also have very dear friends who supported me emotionally and lovingly. Alida, Dalene, Elana, Glaudine, Francé, Hannelie, Helga, Lizette L, Lizette V, Madeleine and Wesley, you fill my life with joy and I love you all very dearly.
- Hilette, Werner, Michaela, Elgar, Dalene and Melinda thank you for helping me with the graphic art.
- Caren, without you this book would never have been possible. I admire you more than you will ever know. Thank you, thank you, thank you. For your patience, encouragement and support. You are a phenomenal writer, consultant and friend.
- And then finally. . . .

Dear Source
So far beyond my understanding
Thank you for this beautiful life
Thank you for our bright and brilliant brains
Bless the readers of this book
And the effort that it took
You alone know how it will go
In your hands I leave it now

From Caren:

I dedicate this book in the loving memory of my mentor, Dr Mandla Adonisi, who supported my growth in organisational development and inspired my interest in strategy formulation and implementation.

A special thank you to the following people without whom I could not have completed this book.

- To my husband, thank you Marius for our 35 years of partnership and your support for my writing projects.
- To my children, Darius and Clarisse, you are the blessings in my life.
- To my parents and in-laws, thank you for showing me the virtue of Christian values.
- To friends who made life's lessons easier to learn through your emotional support.
- To Dr Morris Mthombeni, thank you for your support as the Executive Director: Faculty and Interim Dean, Gordon Institute of Business Science. Your insight into both the strategy and organisational development disciplines is an inspiration. We value your ability to integrate theory and practice in your leadership role on several boards and in your teaching.
- To so many co-authors, colleagues, clients and students, I appreciate your support and valuable teaching moments that we shared. This book is for you.
- To various institutions, University of the Free State, University of the Witwatersrand, The Academy of Management, University of Cape Town, Graduate School of Business, University Stellenbosch Business School and University of Pretoria, Gordon Institute of Business Science, for introducing me to the Scholarship of Teaching and Learning.

- To Sonja, my colleague and friend for 20 years, without you this book would never have been possible. I admire your optimism, dedication and perseverance more than you will ever know. Thank you! I am proud of your development as scholar and value our partnership. I am grateful for our journey over the last seven years in co-authoring this volume.

  To my Source, Jesus Christ, thank you for Your Grace and Mercy to me, Your servant.

Endorsements

"How do you manage change where it is most difficult? Scheepers and Swart bring their rich experience from emerging economies to address this fundamental question. Based on neuroscience, the Ten Enablers Model provides a practical approach to leading transformations at multiple levels—individual, group, team, department and organisation. In this book, the authors' contextual perspective to the change leadership field is useful for academics and practitioners alike".

—**Prof Bella L. Galperin**, *Professor of Management, Senior Associate Director, TECO Energy Center for Leadership, The University of Tampa, Department of Management, John H. Sykes College of Business, Tampa, Florida, USA*

"It is rare to find a management book that so effortlessly intertwines sensible and practical perspectives, thoroughly well-researched new cases, a contextual sensitivity and genuine research. In this new book on change leadership, Caren Scheepers and Sonja Swart have achieved exactly this. Particularly valuable is the consistent threads throughout the book of practice notes, neuroscientific perspectives, emerging markets perspectives and a strong evaluation bent. This book should be a staple of management education and is a welcome and valued addition to the cannon of excellent managerial writing to have sprung from the African continent over the past years".

—**Prof Gregory Lee**, *University of the Witwatersrand Business School, Johannesburg, South Africa*

"Managing change is a personal and professional requirement for a life well lived, a life in which we are able and willing to take stock of what serves and what hinders people and organisations and then have the courage and the skills to change what is necessary. *Change Leadership in Emerging Markets* is a fantastic companion to those leading change at whatever level combining the neuroscience, the academic thinking and the practical to provide a navigational aid to those leading change in emerging markets and organisations. The 10 Enablers Change Toolbox is as relevant for personal change as it is for organisational or societal change".

—**Dr Heather Cairns-Lee**, *Affiliate Professor of Leadership, IMD, Switzerland*

"On occasion, business leaders struggle to put theory into practice. Similarly, the classroom is often the space wherein the comment is made that what we teach in theory is too far removed from practice. This challenge is beautifully addressed and eloquently solved by the authors in an almost perfect plait of solid research and applied science. They go toe to toe with conventional change wisdoms (Lewin and Kotter) to highlight and contrast what is needed in the emerging market change leadership field. As such, the publication carries both academic standing and business appeal. It reads like a story everyone can relate to. The authors create comfort in the early stages of the publication, setting the stage for the key success factors to enable change as they move seamlessly between organisation, theory and framework and the individual. Bringing neuroscience into the equation in order to set the stage for addressing the ego, and its role in the success or failure of change, is a brilliant move. It places "the individual, versus team, versus organisational goals theme" right in the middle of what change is all about. And then, in the final instance, the authors achieve what so many others fail to accomplish—they take the theory to practice. In a simple to follow yet soundly researched and effectively tested model, they leave the reader with ten change enablers. These enablers beautifully complement that what the organisation aims to achieve on a strategic level. With this fusion of change management into the strategic space, the authors give change management leadership ability the focus it deserves as an enabler, not just for achieving change, but for successfully implementing and achieving strategy".

—**Prof. Steyn Heckroodt,** *Harvard Business School Publishing Moderator and Professor in Strategy and Leadership, University UAE, Dubai*

"It is timely for books on key leadership topics to address the context leaders lead in. This book does exactly that—it pairs world-class research and practice on contemporary change leadership and puts in the context of emerging markets which are by their nature less stable, but at the same time, offer exciting opportunities to leapfrog conventional methods. In a time of ongoing change and transformation, new approaches are needed that are more inclusive, systemic and future-focused. Caren and Sonja are masters in their field and help us think anew about the ongoing and ever-increasing disruption and complexity we face as leaders and change practitioners. The inclusion of neuroscience is a welcome addition to how behaviour change really works—something that has been overlooked in many change interventions over the years. Ego mastery is another welcome and interesting inclusion which highlights the importance of leadership and culture in the process of sustainable change. Helping us with new mental models and challenging our current assumptions, as well as providing us with great practical tools, is a great way forward in this field".

—**Marianne Roux,** *Consulting Director and Professor of Practice, Monash Business School, Melbourne, Australia*

"Reading this book makes one very aware of its significant contribution to the discourse (spoken or written) on leadership and the context of its application, which by its nature suggests change. What excites me most about the book is that it starts its application journey with ethos. It is not only an important base and point of departure, but it is as equally difficult place to start due to the cultural and personal value systems embodied in any ethos. The reader becomes aware of how the ethos informs everything else that follows, and one cannot help but wonder and become sensitive about the impact of ethos on the outcomes of complex adaptive systems. The authors ought to be commended for their courage to tackle the mercurial concepts of leadership and change and how they cleverly make us witnesses of their experiences. Their combined scholarly and practical approach makes it an authentic read as they, at various points, almost invite criticism, to see differently, which is excellent if we want to maintain a high standard of discourse on the things that have a daily impact on our personal lives and our society. It offers different lenses to look at the leadership universe. This is of value to the practitioner and the scholar. Well done".

—**Frik Landman**, *CEO, Stellenbosch Graduate Institute, Stellenbosch, South Africa*

"This is a serious book, and worthy of serious consideration. It is an astonishing combination of the wisdom of the two authors who have managed to combine their collective wisdom in a coherent and rich document. I have known Sonja for more than 2 decades and can credit her with my foundation knowledge in change management. She is a profound thinker, and what I learnt from her continues to be the essence of my approach to change, both in my formal job and now in my consulting practice. This book is testament to the development of her thinking, mastery of her topic and ability to partner with another leading professional and academic in Caren. The book begins with classic change management models such as John Kotter, and then expands from there, culminating in the Ten Enablers Model. The 10 enablers are easy to remember and provide a holistic and inclusive approach incorporating the latest academic research on the topic. The enablers are described in relation to a different but relevant emerging markets including China, Russia, Brazil and South Africa adding further depth to the offering. Of particular interest is their take on leadership mastery and effective communication, highlighted against the backdrop of the latest thinking in neuroscience. The inclusion of very practical tips and tricks for change practitioners and leaders makes this essential reading for any professional who is serious about sustainable transformation in these turbulent times".

—**Jenny Leclezio**, *Partner and Co-founder of Shine Relationship Consulting, Petervale, Johannesburg, South Africa*

"In times of rapid change leaders need to transform their organisations to ensure continued success. *Change Leadership in Emerging Markets* provides a comprehensive framework of 10 enablers which allow transformation without disruption. The use of neuroscience provides a unique lens to enhance learning and improve chances of success. Of particular interest is the fact that the tools presented are agnostic of leadership style and hierarchy. This is an essential workbook for those seeking to understand how to implement change better. The insights may also find application in personal development".

—**Dr Leon Vermaak**, *Head of Insurance, Standard Bank Group, Johannesburg, South Africa*

"In *Change Leadership in Emerging Markets: The Ten Enablers Model*, the authors encapsulate modern wisdom from multiple disciplines on the specific factors that support change leadership, with consideration of the distinct nature of the emerging market context. The book not only delves into intrapersonal factors that enable change leadership, but by incorporating contextually relevant cases and literature from disciplines such as strategy or neuroscience becomes relevant to any business manager in this context. What is particularly useful about the book is that it structures an extensive array of topics relating to change management very well in terms of its theoretical foundation as well as its practical value. It therefore gives foundational insights of change leadership in this context based on principles of leadership, change frameworks and complexity theory, but then takes the reader on a journey to understand what they can practically do to lead change. The usefulness of this book extends to instructors of change leadership as it offers reflection exercises and tools that can be used equally in classrooms and for self-directed learning. A person who works through this book will have a thorough understanding of the core principles of change leadership and will gain useful and comprehensive insights to lead change in emerging market contexts".

—**Dr Charlene Lew,** *Senior Lecturer, Gordon Institute of Business Science, University Pretoria, Sandton, South Africa*

"This text offers refreshing insight into the field of change leadership. The authors build skilfully on traditional change management theory and integrate it into one coherent and comprehensive model. By referencing emerging market economies to illustrate key principles, the writers advance our understanding of change leadership contexts. Highly relevant for those working in State or corporate environments, the reader is provided with a practical, systematic process to follow that includes an understanding of both ego mastery and of neuroscience to support the individual internal shifts required by actors involved in any change process. Combining solid research, case study summaries and many practical tools, this text offers a rich resource to leaders, change practitioners and individuals who live and work in a constantly evolving world".

—**Dr Sarah Riordan,** *Organisational Psychologist, Integrated Development Solutions, Cape Town, South Africa*

"Are you aware of the challenges that could be posed to your organisation by the 4IR, yet find that your company is stuck in 'baby boomer' technologies and processes? Then this book is for you! This is the definitive book for all of us who need to introduce change in our organisations, whether private or governmental.

Clearly stating the most common misconceptions in leadership and change, the authors base their findings on extensive research covering leadership, change management and the impact of neuroscience on the change management environment. As a result of their very informative research they have developed a powerful change management approach called the Ten Enablers Model. The details of each of the ten enablers for change management implementation are supported by a vast array of examples of their application in practice. With its roots firmly based in emerging markets, this is an essential book for all of us who are engaged in or intend to introduce change in any organisation (private or governmental)".

—**Hans Kuilman,** *Director, Kindeng Consulting, Johannesburg, South Africa*

Contents

About the Authors

Caren Brenda Scheepers is an Associate Professor in Contextual Leadership, Organisational Development and Change and Strategic Implementation of the MBA programme at the Gordon Institute of Business Science (GIBS), University Pretoria, South Africa. She holds a PhD in Psychology and is a Professional Credentialed Coach with the International Coaching Federation. She has authored and co-edited books, numerous academic journal articles and case studies. She has been consulting on several large-scale organisational development interventions in international consulting environments and served as an internal management consultant in the financial services industry.

Sonja Swart has been an independent change consultant, running her own change management practice, Sonja Swart Change Consulting, since 2000. She consults on a variety of areas, namely executive coaching, design and implementation of change processes, design and implementation of people performance and development strategies, team effectiveness workshops and conflict resolution workshops. Sonja is involved in lecturing at the Eaton Business School in the United Arab Emirates, as well as the University of Stellenbosch Business School Executive Development (USB-ED) in South Africa.

Part I

Theoretical Background

Orientation to Change Leadership

1.1 Domain of Change Leadership in Emerging Markets

Welcome to Change Leadership in Emerging Markets! We invite you to join us on this journey.

Fasten your seat belt and enjoy reading, while we guide you through milestones to assist in your leadership of change.

We invite you to consider a specific change process that you are leading, supporting or consulting on. Apply the thinking in this volume to your challenges and decision-making. May you put as much effort in the planning of the **process** of change as in the **content** of the strategic solution that you intend to implement.

We designed the volume in two parts: the first three chapters in Part I focus on an introduction and an academic positioning of the change framework. The practical application follows in Part II. For academics, scholarly practitioners or students who are interested in a theoretical foundation, Part I would be relevant. For those of our readers who would like to use the book as a practical tool to implement change, Part II would be the focus.

The capacity to lead change is pivotal in enhancing corporate competitiveness (By, 2005; O'Reilly, Caldwell, Chatman, Lapiz, & Self, 2010; Surty & Scheepers, 2019). Often, organisations have adequate strategic orientation to meet challenges in a radical, turbulent environment. Nonetheless, the actual capacity within the organisation to implement strategic objectives is often lacking. In this regard, this volume centres less on which strategic direction would be best, as this type of **content** would feature in the "Strategy" discipline. The focus here is instead on **the process** of strategy formulation, adaptation and implementation, as well as on getting buy-in, pacing and sequencing change to manage resistance.

Most change processes that we encountered were discontinuous and rarely ran smoothly. Huge variations existed with regards to the scope of change, where large scope usually pointed to transformation with magnitude of complexity and long timelines, spanning years and sometimes decades.

© Springer Nature Switzerland AG 2020
C. B. Scheepers, S. Swart, *Change Leadership in Emerging Markets*, Future of Business and Finance, https://doi.org/10.1007/978-3-030-40846-6_1

We observed over the years that generally, organisational transformation processes aligned with macro-environmental factors, have become more radical, complex and uncertain, especially, for example sociopolitical and technological changes. Strategic change has been the subject of attention in strategy and organisational theory for some time (Fiss & Zajac, 2006). Changes could be proactive or reactive. Unfortunately, literature contains abundant empirical evidence of change interventions that failed to meet their performance goals (Owen & Dietz, 2012), due to, amongst other reasons, inadequate leadership of people in managerial roles, coordination that was unsuccessfully implemented, and insufficient training and inadequate information systems in place to measure the change.

This volume furthermore centres on how active involvement and participation during the change process enable commitment and ownership. In this sense, it supports an Organisational Development (OD) value system, where OD is defined as "a *system-wide application and transfer of behavioural science knowledge to the planned development, improvement, and reinforcement of the strategies, structures, and processes that lead to organization effectiveness*" (Cummings & Worley, 2015, p. 2). In contrast, Cummings and Worley (2015, p. 3) emphasise that pure "*Change management focuses more narrowly on values of cost, quality and schedule*". As such, all OD interventions involve change management, but change management may not involve OD. Burke's chapter in Cummings (2008, p. 14) concurs that OD definitions include one or more of these common terms: "*planned, applied behavioural science; system-wide; improving an organisation's capacity for change and development*". Burke further adds that "*most OD practitioners conform to some mode of open systems thinking*" (in Cummings, 2008, p. 16). Likewise, in this book, we endeavour to offer an open systems framework to change leadership in the context of emerging markets.

To define the span of this volume, we are convinced that transformation involves paradigmatic change and as such, the scope is transformational and not only small-scale changes. Kuntz and Gomes (2012) define the process of transformational change in organisations as a radical process, requiring full redefinition of organisational goals and values and adapting to the dynamic needs of both internal and external customers. For smaller-scale changes, organisations could follow some of the steps but it may not be necessary to go through all the steps.

OD interventions generally involve processes where building capability to change is part and parcel of the change intervention. This transfer of skill would enable the organisation to utilize the skills that were transferred during the change to change in future on its own. An OD intervention would typically disrupt the status quo, in order to increase the effectiveness of the organisation.

Emerging market researchers like Al-Ali, Singh, Al-Nahyan, and Sohal (2017, p. 723), observe that "change management entails a systematic approach to managing change that deals with people and resources". These scholars describe "change-oriented leadership" that has a positive and significant direct effect on planned change. We concur that leadership has a significant impact on the successful implementation of change and thus this volume has been called "Change Leadership" to describe a change-orientation in leadership that systematically plans the change, while considering the people and resources involved. We agree with Carter (2008) who declares that effecting change involves more than traditional change management in his article titled, *Successful Change Requires More Than Change Management*. For instance, controlling or coordinating the change process is required in a way that enables people to adapt to change in a positive way.

We would recommend that leaders consider the intervention that would cause the least disruption to the organisation. Large-scale transformation typically requires dedicated resources and effort that could take an organization away from current focus areas and could lead to a decline in present customer service levels. As a result, leaders must ensure that the transformation effort is truly necessary prior to embarking on this journey.

Researches in the nineties observed that in studying change, one may focus on the content, determinants and results of strategic change, or the process and the role managers play in the strategic process (Rajagopalan & Spreitzer, 1997). The classical work of Kouzes and Posner (2012), originally in 1996, emphasised that the role of leaders in effecting change is envisioning the change, energising the organisation to change and enabling the change to take place. Likewise, the focus of this volume is the role of leaders in effecting the change. Since we are behavioural scientists, we are particularly interested in the behaviour change that is required during these processes, in line with Heifetz, Linsky, and Grashow (2009), who declared that people cannot make the adaptive leap necessary to thrive in a new environment without learning new attitudes, values and behaviours.

The focus of this volume is on ten enablers for change success. It addresses the role leaders need to play in creating a successful change outcome. It starts with **Enabler 1, Ethos** in which a stable, ethical foundation is created upon which the change process can be built. The next enabler, **Enabler 2, Ego Mastery** addresses the need for change leaders to be self-aware, master their egos, stay centred and balanced and remain congruent with the purpose of the change throughout the change process. Next, change leaders are encouraged to explore their environment (**Enabler 3, Explore**) with the aim of finding opportunities that will enable their organisations to respond creatively and uniquely to the challenges in the environment (**Enabler 4, Eureka Moments**). Effective change leaders are able to translate these opportunities into powerful, inspirational visions that can be communicated to the organisation in ways that will enable these opportunities to be realised (**Enabler 5, Envisioning**). The next step in the process is to **Engage (Enabler 6)** all stakeholders by getting them to buy into the change and agree to implement the change. In **Enabler 7, Embark**, the focus is now on starting the change process, by setting and agreeing goals. In **Enabler 8, Execute** the focus is on delivering the goals that will move the organisation towards the achievement of the vision. In **Enabler 9, Evaluate**, change leaders are encouraged to review the change process, to identify ways of improving in future and share lessons learnt. The last enabler, **Enabler 10, Exit**, suggests leaders have the courage and confidence to step aside when the time has come for them to hand over the baton to a new leader who can lead the next change process.

Our intention is to offer practical guidelines on transformation on an individual level, group or team, departmental and organisational level. Therefore, the model we provide can be utilised on these levels and in Part II we will offer guidelines, as well as examples for practical application.

In this volume, the authors define emerging markets according to the MSCI Emerging Markets' Index (for quick reference see: https://www.msci.com/market-classification). The list of emerging markets includes in the Americas: Brazil, Chile, Columbia, Mexico and Peru. In Europe, Middle East and Africa: Czech Republic, Egypt, Greece, Hungary, Poland, Qatar, Russia, South Africa, Turkey and United Arab Emirates (UAE). In Asia: China, India, Indonesia, Korea, Malaysia, Pakistan, Philippines, Taiwan and Thailand.

1.2   Research Method

Ethical clearance had been obtained from the University of Pretoria, after submitting an interview schedule and description of methodology of the research towards this volume. The authors personally interviewed leaders in the domain to gain primary data on "Change Leadership in emerging markets". These leaders had been chosen based on their extensive consulting experience in the field of change and/or leading change, especially in emerging markets. It was a convenience sampling method, seeing that these interviewees had been part of the authors' network and previous consulting and publication projects. To a lesser extent, snowball sampling was used as several interviewees referred other leaders to be interviewed.

As practitioners, the authors had the privilege to conduct business consulting and leadership coaching over the last 30 years. We have combined experiences of over 55 years in this field in numerous industries, such as manufacturing, fast-moving consumer goods, automotive, logistics, Non-governmental (non-profit) Organisations (NGOs) and financial services. Most of our exposure was in Southern Africa, some in North, West and East Africa and Western Europe. Recently, our exposure included other emerging markets, for example Mauritius, India, China, Brazil and several of our interviews represented these countries.

The authors have also been lecturing in the field of Leadership, Organisational Development and Transformation, Change Management and People Management over the last 20 years on Middle, Senior and Executive level at companies' academies, Business Schools' Academic (Master's Business Administration) and Organisation Specific Programmes. The authors gained anecdotal data from various emerging markets through interactions in the classroom and through delegates' individual and syndicate assignments.

Consequently, the authors consulted theoretical frameworks, based on the sound body of knowledge in the Leadership, Organisational Development and Strategy disciplines. This book endeavours to investigate how the cases of several Southern African organisations and other emerging markets are managing change in the turbulent socioeconomic and political contexts. As such, this book used Interpretivism as research philosophy, since it sought to shed light on the complexity of strategic change leadership in various organisations. Using the literature review, consequent models and interview data were used as lenses through which organisational change processes could be examined and studied.

Saunders and Lewis (2012) state that the Interpretivism philosophy is particularly relevant to the field of organisational behaviour and development. This study thus reports on case studies that were conducted, positioned in the research paradigm of Interpretivism. Babbie and Mouton (2001, p. 643) declare, "Interpretivism aims at interpreting or understanding human behaviour, rather than explaining or predicting it". The research followed a phenomenological research methodology approach to fieldwork and in-depth case reflection and analysis (Yin, 2003, 2015), from the researchers as an insider's perspective (Mouton, 2001). Observations were interpreted to build conceptual frameworks (Babbie & Mouton, 2001) of effective Change Leadership.

A comprehensive literature review was conducted on strategic change, leadership, OD and change management, and its relevance to this study. Following from the literature review, the study offers the broad learning points in conceptual frameworks of "Change Leadership" by quoting current authors in the Leadership, OD and Change Management fraternity. In each chapter to follow, a summary is offered of this review.

1.3 Practical Application

Our departure point in this volume is that you are either a leader of a team of executives, senior managers or of a team of department heads. You may also be a leader of a team of specialists. You might be a practitioner or scholar in the field of Organisational Development or a consultant or business coach in this domain. The worksheets have been intended that you may ponder on the questions and utilise them in your strategic planning or implementation planning sessions. They are designed to stimulate your thinking and preferably you would involve other resources, such as your team members or ideally other departments within your organisation to contribute. May your quest to find these answers benefit you, others and your organisation. As we improve institutions, we improve communities and societies and ultimately the world.

We would like to encourage consultants and coaches to work with "the organisation in the mind of the leader" (Hougaard & Carter, 2018). For example: What are their working definition of an organisation? How do they describe their areas of responsibility? What are the boundaries in their own mind of where their responsibility starts and ends? How is this influencing their effectiveness?

The literature reviews, analyses, assessment tools and recommendations are shared in each chapter to enable effective transformation journeys. The reflection questions offered in the discussion of each leadership role could be used as a starting point and would need to be adapted to address the research objectives of the specific organisation. As such, this volume could be viewed as a report of our experiences and conceptual frameworks extrapolated from these research outputs to enable more effective change leadership.

We discuss several case studies in which the principles in this volume had been implemented with various levels of success. We mentioned the organisation's name if the case had been written up and the information was available in the public domain, such as websites, books, media and published cases. In some cases, we did not mention the organisation's name or combined information from various cases to render anonymity to the interviewees and their organisations. The next chapter offers an orientation to leadership of change.

References

Al-Ali, A. A., Singh, S. K., Al-Nahyan, M., & Sohal, A. S. (2017). Change management through leadership: The mediating role of organizational culture. *International Journal of Organizational Analysis, 25*(4), 723–739. https://doi.org/10.1108/IJOA-01-2017-1117

Babbie, E., & Mouton, J. (2001). *The practice of social research.* Cape Town: Oxford University Press. https://www.oxford.co.za/book/9780195718546-practice-of-social-research

By, R. T. (2005). Organisational change management: A critical review. *Journal of Change Management, 5*(4), 369–380. https://doi.org/10.1080/14697010500359250

Carter, E. (2008). Successful change requires more than change management. *Human Resource Management International Digest, 16*(7). https://doi.org/10.1108/hrmid.2008.04416gad.005

Cummings, T. G. (Ed.). (2008). *Handbook of organizational development.* Los Angeles: Sage. https://books.google.co.za/books?hl=en&lr=&id=VTOi1wmzQM4C&oi=fnd&pg=PA1&dq=Cummings,+T.+G.+(Ed.).+(2008).+Handbook+of+organizational+development.+Los+Angeles:+Sage.&ots=TaW8YunX0N&sig=K4SFOBX1B7xTJyjAqG3fUuPkuCE#v=onepage&q&f=false

Cummings, T. G., & Worley, C. G. (2015). *Organization development & change* (10th ed.). Cincinnati, OH: South-Western College Publishing. https://www.loot.co.za/product/thomas-cummings-organization-development-and-change/lszv-2176-g370?referrer=googlemerchant&gclid=CjwKCAjw5vz2BRAtEiwAbcVIL_49WYGXAaU1mrKBwWHl3ZZBiQ72sHG5Qwv5JACp9vKcDEEphNuZKhoCKWQQAvD_BwE&gclsrc=aw.ds

Fiss, P., & Zajac, E. (2006). The symbolic management of strategic change: Sensegiving via framing and decoupling. *Academy of Management Journal, 49*(6), 1173–1193. Retrieved from https://www.scholars.northwestern.edu/en/publications/the-symbolic-management-of-strategic-change-sensegiving-via-frami

Gomes, E., Angwin, D., Peter, E., & Mellahi, K. (2012). HRM issues and outcomes in African mergers and acquisitions: A study of the Nigerian banking sector. *The International Journal of Human Resource Management, 23*(14), 2874–2900. https://doi.org/10.1080/09585192.2012.671509

Heifetz, R. A., Linsky, M., & Grashow, A. (2009). *The practice of adaptive leadership: Tools and tactics for changing your organisation and the world.* Boston, MA: Harvard Business Press. https://www.hks.harvard.edu/publications/practice-adaptive-leadership-tools-and-tactics-changing-your-organization-and-world

Hougaard, R., & Carter, J. (2018). *The mind of the leader.* Boston: Harvard Business School Press. https://store.hbr.org/product/the-mind-of-the-leader-how-to-lead-yourself-your-people-and-your-organization-for-extraordinary-results/10153

Kouzes, J. M., & Posner, B. Z. (2012). *The leadership challenge: How to make extraordinary things happen in organizations.* New York: Wiley. https://www.amazon.com/Leadership-Challenge-Extraordinary-Things-Organizations/dp/1119278961

Mouton, J. (2001). *How to succeed in your master's and doctoral studies: A South African guide and resource book.* Pretoria: Van Schaik Publishers. https://www.vanschaik.com/book/4e95949a91b0f

O'Reilly, C. A., Caldwell, D. F., Chatman, J. A., Lapiz, M., & Self, W. (2010). How leadership matters: The effects of leaders' alignment on strategy implementation. *Leadership Quarterly, 21*(1), 104–113. https://doi.org/10.1016/j.leaqua.2009.10.008

Owen, K. O., & Dietz, A. S. (2012, October–December). *Understanding organizational reality: Concepts for the change leader.* Sage Open, 1–14. https://doi.org/10.1177/2158244012461922. Retrieved from http://journals.sagepub.com/doi/pdf/10.1177/2158244012461922

Rajagopalan, N., & Spreitzer, G. M. (1997). Toward a theory of strategic change: A multi-lens perspective and integrative framework. *Academy of Management Review, 22*(1), 48–79. https://doi.org/10.5465/AMR.1997.9707180259

Saunders, A., & Lewis, P. (2012). *Doing research in business and management: An essential guide to planning your project.* Essex: Pearson Education Limited. https://www.amazon.com/Doing-Research-Business-Management-essential/dp/0273726412

Surty, S., & Scheepers, C. B. (2019). Moderating effect of environmental dynamism on the relationship between leadership practices and employee response to change. *Management Research Review.* https://doi.org/10.1108/MRR-03-2019-0094

Yin, R. K. (2003). *Case study research* (3rd ed.). Thousand Oaks, CA: Sage. https://www.academia.edu/32420108/Yin_Case_Study_Research_Design_and_Methods

Yin, R. K. (2015). *Qualitative research from start to finish.* New York: Guilford Publications. https://www.guilford.com/books/Qualitative-Research-from-Start-to-Finish/Robert-Yin/9781462517978

Leadership of Change

2

2.1   Traditional Change Models

In their textbook, *Organizational Behaviour* (2015, p. 566) Robbins and Judge describe planned change as *"change activities that are intentional, and goal orientated."* Kurt Lewin offers a classic three-step model of a change process. Lewin (1951) advises that successful change in organisations should follow these three steps: unfreezing the status quo (involving moving away from equilibrium by overcoming pressures of individual resistance and group conformity), movement to the desired end state and refreezing the change to make it permanent.

Lewin argues that the driving forces directing behaviour away from the status quo have to be increased, whereas the restraining forces, which hinder movement away from equilibrium, have to be decreased. He furthermore advises companies to move quickly through the change. To sustain the change over time, the change must be refrozen, without it, the change will be short lived. This phase will stabilise the driving and restraining forces.

Another traditional model is Kotter's eight steps (Kotter, 1996), which he formulated from large samples of companies that had gone through change processes and were unsuccessful implementing these changes. The typical mistakes organisations make are, for example, not to create a sense of urgency for the need for change (step 1); failing to create a coalition that could manage the change process (step 2); failing to formulate a vision (step 3) and to communicate the vision and strategy (step 4); or to remove obstacles that could impede the achievement of the vision (step 5); not providing short-term or quick wins and achievable goals (step 6); not consolidating improvements, and making adjustments (step 7); finally not anchoring the changes in the organisation's culture (step 8).

Traditionally, Action Research (AR) has also been used to bring about planned change. It is a change process that is based on the systematic collection of data and selection of a change action. It offers a scientific methodology for managing planned change. The five steps in action research include diagnosis, analysis, feedback, action and evaluation. The change agent is usually an outside consultant playing a

© Springer Nature Switzerland AG 2020   11
C. B. Scheepers, S. Swart, *Change Leadership in Emerging Markets*, Future of
Business and Finance, https://doi.org/10.1007/978-3-030-40846-6_2

role in the diagnosis, analysis and offering feedback on findings. It is problem focused and offers focused action to resolve the problems and it reduces resistance, since employees are engaged in the process.

As Chap. 1 explained, organisational development (OD) is a collection of change methods that are built on humanistic, democratic views that endeavour to improve organisational effectiveness and employee well-being.

Appreciative Inquiry is a specific type of OD approach that accentuates the positive and identifies the unique qualities and special strengths of an organisation on which members can build to improve performance.

This book relates to the OD type of process model of change, where there are steps to follow and employees' involvement is sought through several communication and training opportunities. The Ten Enablers Model will illustrate this in Part II of the book.

2.2   Leadership During Change

2.2.1   Orientation to Leadership During Change

In this section, we offer an orientation to our positioning on change leadership. It commences with highlighting a couple of misconceptions, with clarifications of the departure points on change leadership in this volume.

In his classic book, *The Wealth of Nations* (1776), Adam Smith presents the traditional view that markets lead themselves to efficient outcomes. However, a contrary modern view is represented by Riane Eisler, who declares in her book *The Real Wealth of Nations* (2008):

> I saw that in our inextricably interconnected world none of us has a secure future so long as hunger, extreme poverty, and violence continue unabated. I saw that present economic systems are despoiling and depleting our beautiful Earth... (Eisler, 2008, p. 2).

We support Eisler's (2008) view to consider social and environmental issues too. However, we observed that market conditions and failure to perform financially indeed regularly precipitated change processes, as described by Pretorius and Holtzhauzen (2008). Nonetheless, we luckily also notice that many change processes are undertaken to transform organisations to be responsive and adaptable to social and environmental issues. For example, many organisations have worked tirelessly to recover environmental damages while others have spent huge amounts of money educating their employees and supporting their surrounding communities in various ways. The change processes in this volume thus refer to commercial as well as social and environmental objectives, as described in the triple bottom line construct of Elkington and Hartigan (2008). It would be an erroneous assumption that changes are always undertaken in response to financial issues. Social and environmental issues might also be relevant.

We next present misconceptions about top management's role in change leadership.

2.2.1.1 Misconception 1: Only Top Management Counts in Change Leadership

We dispute the notion that only top management counts in change leadership for the following reasons.

Admittedly, Kuntz and Gomes (2012) emphasise that senior leadership have the power to prompt cultural change, as they set the purpose and direction of the organisation. Gill (2007) emphasises that change should not only be managed, suggesting planning, organising, directing and controlling, but must be led. Leadership in this sense involves vision, strategy and support for a culture and values supporting the vision (Surty & Scheepers, 2019). We concur. Therefore, our focus is here on leadership roles in change processes. Leadership is indeed about establishing direction, aligning people, motivating and inspiring and producing long-lasting change (Holbeche, 2007). Leadership in this regard, refers to roles being played, generally by those in managerial positions that can affect change.

However, we and our interviewees have witnessed people without positional power, such as those not in managerial positions, playing an influencing role. This influence of people throughout the organisation, would constitute leadership, seeing that we support Northouse's (2001) definition of leadership as being about influence towards achieving goals. In this instance, goals relate to change objectives. It implies that leadership is not necessarily linked to hierarchy.

Nonetheless, we observed that top management's leadership is crucial in bringing about successful change processes, in line with other researchers' opinions, such as Burke (2008) and Owen and Dietz (2012). Uhl-Bien, Marion, and McKelvey's (2007) seminal work declares that leadership is a function of diverse agents and their interaction. We concur with this view as it also relates to the post-heroic view of leadership. Proponents of the post-heroic view, such as Alimo-Metcalfe and Alban-Metcalfe (2005), went further by referring to the previous heroic view of a single leader, specifically to white western male managers. Consequently, they called for leadership studies in more inclusive diverse settings. The study underlying this volume is an answer to this call as it purposefully includes emerging markets' leaders in the sample.

Kuntz and Gomes (2012) agree that effective change management depends on strong leadership, as instituting change is difficult. They define change leadership as significantly altering an organisation's goals, values, vision and methods of serving its internal and external clients. It will ensure the future success and survival of the organisation (Kuntz & Gomes, 2012). Dixon, Meyer, and Day (2010) similarly emphasise a need for strong leadership to drive change. Nonetheless, "leadership qualities are needed throughout the organisation" (Collier & Esteban, 2000, p. 207).

Even though the role of top management is emphasised here, the role of these leaders in involving the other levels is important. Martins and Terblanche (2003, p. 65) describe, for example, that it is crucial for employees to understand the vision and mission and "... the gap between the current situation and the vision and mission, to be able to act creatively and innovatively...". One of our interviewees offered an explanation of the link to creativity, "Our Deputy Chairman's clear direction and belief in me, assisted me in allowing my creativity to flow freely".

We therefore, advocate a focus on leadership that cascades down and through the organisation.

2.2.1.2 Misconception 2: Change Leadership Mainly Involves Formulating Purpose and Content of Change

We disagree with the opinion that change leadership mainly involves purpose and content of change, as follows:

In the 1990s, Rajagopalan and Spreitzer (1997) indeed advised that the theory of strategic change can be divided between two schools of thought, the content school that focuses on the determinants and results of strategic change, and the process school which analyses the role managers play in the strategic process. In this volume, we advocate for a process school of thought, where leaders' roles in especially roll-out and implementation of change are in view. This aspect relates to the first misconception, where only top management counts in this process. As such, change leadership certainly involves more than only formulating or directing the content of the change.

For example, other roles in change leadership entail communication. Agboola and Salawu (2011) likewise advise that the reasons for the change are communicated adequately, with management treating employees as partners who can assist in facilitating the change process. We argue accordingly that involvement of employees, even during the initial planning phase, would increase chances of successful implementation. Barrett (2002) also emphasises that more meaningful communications can enable employees at all levels to be informed about, as well as understand the organisation's change strategy, ensure less resistance and more support from employees.

Unfortunately, while management regularly invests a significant amount of money into the planned change, little is invested in communicating, training and follow-up. Wittig (2012) in her article *Employees' reaction to Change*, illustrates how factors such as communication, participation in decisions and impact on their role influence this reaction. Nelson (2005) also emphasises that the influence on employees' roles is a deciding factor in their attitude towards change. For example, the insecurity around losing a job or even guilt when not being affected by downsizing, could trigger a change in behaviour.

The work of Denise Rousseau (2004) on the psychological contract is relevant here. Scheepers and Shuping (2011), indicate that organisational changes influence this contract. Van der Westhuizen, Scheepers, and Kele's (2018) study on the influence of the breach of the psychological contract on employee engagement, indicates that times of turmoil and disruption require proactive management of this psychological contract. Keenan, Bixner, Morieux, and Powell (2009) likewise promote an action plan to minimise the decline in productivity and increase in turnover, by managing the social contract. Bamford and Forrester (2003) advise managers accordingly to consider creating a workforce that will identify change, take ownership and implement change, rather than the traditional approach of plan and instruct. It is about them creating an environment that is conducive to experimentation and risk-taking.

The importance of paying attention to this "softer" side of change leadership is similarly illustrated by Bovey and Hede (2001), who identify employee resistance as a possible contributing factor to the failure of change. Interestingly, Beer and Nohria (2000) advise organisations to utilise expert consultant resources in this regard. Oreg and Berson (2011) find that leaders' personal characteristics have a profound effect on follower's reactions to change. Their facilitation of the change process assists followers in dealing with the difficulties during a change process. Lines, Selart, Espedal, and Johansen (2005) in their turn, identify a relationship between organisational change and trust in management, for example the level of trust influences change and change in turn, affects the level of trust. For one of our interviewees, establishing trust with the employees from the acquired company posed more difficult than expected. He said, "It took time to build trust with the new employees and everything I said and did were under scrutiny". In the published case study on a post-acquisition integration process, the leadership of the culture change is highlighted (Scheepers & Sita, 2016). We thus argue that more than content of change is involved when leading change and that change leaders should thus focus on the cultural aspects during these processes.

2.2.1.3 Misconception 3: Only the Transformational Leadership Style Is Relevant in Change Leadership

We do not agree that only the transformational leadership style is relevant in change leadership, due to the following arguments.

Admittedly transformational leadership is a leadership style that is regularly mentioned in relation to levels of trust, as the study of Vingers and Celliers (2006) claims. A discussion on leadership would of course be incomplete without reference to the contemporary views of Bass (1990) on transformational and transactional leadership. Four behaviours of transformational leadership are relevant to leading change: idealised influence, individualised consideration, intellectual stimulation and inspirational motivation. McKnight (2013) similarly emphasises transformational leaders who induce a sense of purpose and momentum amongst their employees when going through a strategic change. In a constantly changing environment, these types of leaders have the charisma, influence and adaptability to successfully implement change through creating a combination of high expectations and rewards linked to the achievement of the vision of the organisation.

Transactional leadership, in turn, entails exchanges and transactions, specifying roles and implications in change. Vingers and Cilliers' (2006) research indicates that successful change can only be offered by transformational leaders. We contend that various leadership styles could be required during the different phases of change processes, for example the transactional leader's style of contingent rewards is also relevant. Van Wart and Kapucu (2011) concur that leadership requires different competencies based on different situations. Interestingly, innovation in leadership was pointed out by Pellissier (2012) as a distinguishing factor, in addition to technological innovation, to remain competitive in a turbulent environment.

Strandholm, Kumar, and Subramanian (2004) explore two options that management can adopt, a market-oriented approach or an efficiency-based approach, depending on whether they are risk takers or risk averse. It is of key importance to align the change strategy with the business strategy of the organisation and for the top management team to possess the characteristics best suited to the environment of the organisation. Alignment is furthermore required between organisational levels and decision-making approaches involved in strategic change (Nyström, Höög, Garvare, Weinehall, & Ivarsson, 2013). In addition to these studies, we would highlight that alignment is required across organisational silos, in addition to alignment across levels in the organisation. An example of this alignment is Nedbank's Area Collaboration effort, where Business Banking and Retail Banking worked together towards a change vision of an integrated offering (Scheepers, Oosthuizen, & Retief, 2016). As one of our interviewees commented, "I go out of my way to enable collaboration across silos in the bank to achieve our vision". Another interviewee emphasised that "our leaders have to live the value of collaboration towards the common good". A leadership approach that is particularly relevant for encouraging collaboration across silos is the Complexity Leadership construct of Uhl-Bien et al. (2007) and Contextual Leadership as described by Osborn and Marion (2009) and Kutz (2008). For these reasons, we contend that more than one leadership style is relevant during organisational change processes.

2.2.1.4 Misconception 4: In Complex Contexts of Emergence Leadership Is Obsolete

We disagree that complex contexts make leadership obsolete, for the following reasons.

Complexity science offers a framework for understanding the dynamics of the VUCA (volatile, uncertain, complex and ambiguous) environment of business. Scholars like Weberg (2012) acknowledge the relevance of natural biological systems for understanding organisational dynamics. Complex Adaptive Systems (CAS) in Health Care, for instance, do not follow rational, predictive patterns; instead, a change in one part of the system would have an influence on another distant part, without a direct cause-and-effect causal relationship, due to the interdependent relationships in these systems (Edgren & Barnard, 2012; Weberg, 2012). For example, Weberg (2012, p. 268) laments that "... a major contributing factor for these issues is that outdated leadership practices, such as leader-centricity, linear thinking and poor readiness for innovation, are being used in healthcare organisations". Emergence is another characteristic of CAS and as a result, control is not possible like it had been in the traditional bureaucratic organisational forms. Uhl-Bien et al. (2007) declare that the new forms of organisation require more informal entrepreneurial characteristics of leadership.

The question could be asked whether leadership is still relevant, and does it matter in the complex emergent world described above? We would like to answer "Yes" in line with scholars like O'Reilly, Caldwell, Chatman, Lapiz, and Self (2010), who emphasised that leadership matters, particularly in relation to enabling a commitment to change. There are admittedly informal processes and systems that are beyond individual leaders' control and simultaneously, there remain formal organisational processes that must be orchestrated in enabling change processes.

Leadership thus has to focus on both organisational realities and use their judgment when to offer impetus for new ideas, by feeding the organisation and informal groupings with relevant information, as Osborn, Hunt, and Jauch (2002) as well as Arena and Uhl-Bien (2016) described, and when to stand back and allow emergence to happen spontaneously. Once leaders take cognisance of how to implement change processes, they could choose to be agile and flexible in the moment. The most important question leaders could thus ask is, "What is required?", given the particular situation and phase the change process is in, and of course with whom they are interacting.

MacKay and Chia (2013) define unowned events as those at an organisational and environmental level that are beyond anyone's control. The objective of change to organisational strategy is thus to rather cause change through intention (MacKay & Chia, 2013). We would critique frameworks, such as the one of MacKay and Chia (2013) as it assumes an "either/or" notion of control over environmental variables. We could advocate for more subtle control, where the processes and systems to execute change are put in place, per the Ten Enablers Model that will be discussed in Part II of this volume; and due to these parameters being set, leaders could offer inspiration and individualised attention within the framework. Similarly, Walter and Bruch (2010) find that in the military, due to the formalised control system, leaders are more transformational as the transactional performance measurement and reward systems, had been taken care of. We therefore, advocate for creating these systems and processes to offer leaders the space within which they could have the opportunity to focus on the relational and inspirational aspects of leadership.

In this regard, Kumar (2012) declares that managing organisational change is the process of planning and implementing it in a manner that minimises employee resistance and costs; while at the same time maximising the effectiveness of the change effort. This parallel effort described by Kumar (2012), might unintentionally point to the leadership competency within complex emergent systems where more systemic and multidimensional leadership is required that is sometimes paradoxical and thus a dynamic balance between opposite approaches is required.

For these reasons, we argue that leadership—albeit leadership from a collective and not only from individual leaders as in traditional approaches to leadership—is even more relevant in complex times.

2.2.2 Positioning of This Volume's Change Leadership Framework

Our positioning on change leadership in emerging markets could be described by the adage: "Location, Location, Location", to indicate context, for the following reasons.

We subscribe to a systems viewpoint on leadership, where leadership is embedded in context (Osborn & Hunt, 2007; Osborn & Marion, 2009). Already in the 1940s Kurt Lewin authored articles on the application of systems theory to the social sciences (Lewin, 1947). Martins and Terblanche (2003, p. 64) also prefer open systems theory to provide a holistic approach, as it allows, "... the investigation

of the interdependence, interaction and interrelationship of the different sub-systems
. . . within an organisation". This implies that individuals, teams and organisations
are viewed as open dynamic systems. With systems, there are usually input,
throughput and output. For instance, on the organisational level, labour enters the
organisation and several design elements form part of the organisation's throughput,
such as the strategy and structure. As output, the organisation could measure the
financial results and stakeholders' satisfaction.

Liden and Antonakis (2009, p. 1587) report that despite "Lewin's identification
of the importance of context in behavioural research over 70 years ago, leadership
psychology tended to ignore the context". Lewin proclaimed in those early years that
behaviour is a function of person and environment. Consequently, behaviour can
only be comprehensively understood, within the situation in which it is embedded.
Liden and Antonakis (2009, p. 1587) declare in their introductory article to the
special issue in *Human Relations* on "Considering context in psychological leadership research", that "although context has been acknowledged as salient to leadership for decades, only in recent years has empirical research given the context
widespread attention". They perceive Fiedler's (1967) contingency theory as an
early adaptation of Lewin's thesis in which the effectiveness of a leadership style
is dependent on the context.

We thus advocate for a framework that takes leadership further than the traditional perspective of motivating their direct followers to an approach of being in
relationship with followers as well as the larger organisation and ultimately society.
It relates to the Leader–Member Exchange theory of leadership (Uhl-Bien, 2006).

Scholars like Zhang and Rajagopalan (2010) highlight that the challenge and
success in the implementation of strategic change in organisations are situated in
leadership's ability to determine the right scale and scope of strategic change in
relation to the organisation's capacity to absorb change. A quote from an interviewee
demonstrates this intention as follows, "We pace the implementation of our culture
interventions to ensure the organisation is ready to implement them". This ability to
pace implementation and determine the right scale for change, relates to a contingency approach. Accordingly, the most important question leaders could ask in
relation to change is what is required, given the context.

For example, leaders are required to use their judgment in pacing their
interventions. Several of our interviewees mentioned the disruption that change
generally had caused in their organisations. Zhang and Rajagopalan (2010) concur
and describe an inverted U-shaped relationship between strategic change and
organisational performance. At low levels of strategic change, a positive effect on
organisational performance is evident. In cases of high levels of strategic change, a
negative effect is witnessed. These are the types of principles that we deem to be
important for leaders to take cognisance of.

Liden and Antonakis (2009) point out that the difference between Fiedler's
(1967) and House and Mitchell's (1974) approaches is that Fiedler argued that
leaders had to be assigned to positions and situations, fitting their style, where the
other scholars believe that leaders can change their styles to fit the situation.

Scholarly practitioners' work relevant here is Kutz (2008) and Kutz and Bamford-Wade (2013), who found that leaders are able to and should adapt their styles to fit the situation. For example, the study of Kumalo and Scheepers (2018) revealed that different leadership styles are relevant at different phases of a turnaround process in the public service in South Africa; for instance, the transactional style was most relevant when the decisions around the retrenchments and restructuring had to be made and the transformational style was required in the later recovery phase, whereas the authentic leadership style was applied in the transformational phase.

We advocate for leadership to be aligned to what the situation or in this case, organisational change requires, and in cases where a different leadership style is required, that leaders would exit the situation and allow others to lead, as the 10th or final "Enabling" role of Change Leadership in our model suggests.

2.3   Change Frameworks

This section will commence with the orientation to change with definitions to differentiate it from transformation, Organisational Development, Organisational Behaviour and to offer the position of the authors of this volume. The next section will give an overview of the main change frameworks in the literature and an orientation to the one described in this volume.

2.3.1   Orientation to Change Frameworks

Even though a multitude of change frameworks exist in the literature, during the research towards this volume, the interviewees rarely mentioned a change framework or model that they had used to direct their thinking, planning and/or taking action during their change processes. There appears to be a disconnect between academic research and practice of change implementation. Our hope is that this volume addresses this gap by offering a simultaneously theoretically sound and practical application model for practitioners. Literature is inconclusive on several important defining aspects of change and each of the following misconceptions will be discussed, with the positioning of this volume's authors towards the end of each of the sections.

2.3.1.1 Misconception 1: Transformation and Change Are Interchangeable

We do not perceive transformation and change as interchangeable, for the following reasons:

Scholars quoting from philosophers' musings, describe change and transformation as separate entities, for example Palese (2013, p. 191) mentions in relation to Zygmunt Bauman's take on liquid modernity, "...an existence where the need gives way to the desire that dismays men in the constant changes and transformations that affect their lives...". Others, like Kuntz and Gomes (2012) see the process of transformational change in organisations as a radical process at times, requiring full redefinition of organisational goals and values and adapting to dynamic needs of both internal and external customers. Amis, Slack, and Hinings (2004) emphasise that structural changes are normally made when implementing radical change in an organisation. Todd already identified in the late 1990s this radical change type as one of his three types of change. Radical change implies that the organisation is forced to change due to environmental inputs, incremental change is where the organisation needs to change to get in line with the organisation's objectives and continuous improvements are required when incremental improvements are needed. Todd's conceptual framework focuses on key areas such as strategy, politics, people and process (Todd, 1999).

We perceive transformation as usually larger in scope that involves most elements in the organisation, whereas change management usually entails implementing a change process that may be smaller in scope than transformation. A clear distinction could thus be made between transformational business model change and incremental small-scale changes. Change could, for example entail only structural changes or technological changes being implemented. The role of change management during transformation projects is however critical, and external factors can have a significant impact on organisations. Cummings and Worley (2008) indicate that the magnitude of the event is important and that it "is usually triggered by some major disruption to the organisation, such as the lifting of regulatory requirements, a technological breakthrough, or a new chief executive officer" (p. 12). The events would likewise trigger a transformational change, instead of a mere change process. French, Bell, and Zawacki (2005) in their turn, consider strategic change as one of the potential interventions that could be used to facilitate organisational transformations. When changes in an organisation's environment occur, the organisation will potentially undergo transformations either as a proactive measure or as a reactive response to such changes (French et al., 2005).

Kim and Mauborgne (2004) studied organisations in over 30 countries over the past 100 years and found that 86% of new strategic ventures were mere line extensions or incremental improvements from previous ones, while only 14% were aimed at creating new markets or industries and were thus truly transformational. We, therefore, argue that transformation and change are not interchangeable.

2.3.1.2 Misconception 2: Change Management Is Organisational Development

We do not agree that change management is necessarily organisational development, as follows:

In the 1980s, Buller advised that the concepts of organisational development and change management can be applied to mergers and acquisitions and to revive declining enterprises (Buller, 1988). This well-intended guidance of Buller highlights how change management and organisational development are used in the same sentence, without differentiating between the constructs.

The main difference between organisational change and organisational development is their value orientation. Organisational development supports values of human potential, participation and development. Nonetheless, performance and competitive advantage are also pertinent. Change management focuses more narrowly on values of cost, quality and schedule. Boundaries of the field of Organisational Development are hard to define (Cummings, 2008), for example the purpose of a related domain, Organisational Behaviour, is "improving an organisation's effectiveness" (Robbins & Judge, 2007, p. 9). Porras and Silvers' (1991, p. 61) definition for their part, offers insight as follows, "Transformation involves paradigmatic change, whereas organisational development creates a better fit between an organisation's capabilities and its environmental demands".

In contrast, organisational development (OD) interventions generally involve processes where building capability to change is part and parcel of the change intervention, which would enable the organisation to utilise the skills that were transferred during the change to change on its own in future (as mentioned in the introductory chapter, and quoted from Cummings and Worley, 2015). An OD intervention would typically disrupt the status quo proactively in order to increase the effectiveness of the organisation. Bartlett and Ghoshal (1990) point out in their article "Matrix Management: Not a Structure, a Frame of Mind", that the problem is that companies are organisationally incapable of carrying out their sophisticated change strategies. This is where OD could play an important role in enabling implementation, as it endeavours to "align an organisation's strategy, structure, and human resources systems, as well as a fit between them and the larger environment. It includes attention to the technical, political and cultural aspects of organisations" (Cummings & Worley, 2008, p. 791). To most people, change is disruptive because it involves the unknown and is likely to impact anything from work processes to job security (Brenner, 2008). A major theme in the literature is that organisational change can be destabilising for all organisational members, resulting in uncertainty, fear, psychological stress, anxiety and insecurity (Lawlor, 2013). It is the responsibility of the leaders to manage these risks as the organisation undergoes the change event.

These realities point to the importance of introducing organisational development in change processes and thus that change processes are not always organisational development.

2.3.1.3   Misconception 3: Change Frameworks with Steps Are Obsolete as Change Is Continuous

We disagree that since change nowadays is continuous—change frameworks are obsolete for the following reasons.

Organisational environments are characterised by fluctuation, instability and change (Kotter & Cohen, 2002). Change is thus a continuous process, intending to assist the organisation to be more productive, efficient and effective in the execution of their mission (Briody, Pester, & Trotter, 2012). Graetz and Smith (2010) argue similarly that change is not a once off phenomenon, but a continuity continuum which guards against stagnation. Day-to-day incremental improvements are continuously required. Considering this continuous characteristic of change, the question could be asked whether stepwise change models would still be relevant in our modern day and age. Our modern time is described by Bauman (2000) as constant and relentless change. Shin, Taylor, and Seo (2012), on their part, emphasise that the velocity of change has been increasing. Traditional change models and or Organisational Development models include mostly stepwise approaches, as follows:

Burke (2008) declares that one of the most well-known OD models is one of Burke and Litwin (1992). Spangenberg and Theron (2013) consider the Burke-Litwin model in the context of the ever-evolving external environment and the continuous developments to business management. They find that the most important relevance of the model is the linkage and interaction between leadership, the effectiveness thereof, and the external environment (Spangenberg & Theron, 2013). It assists the organisation in mitigating events that pose a threat to an organisation's existence.

Even though Burke (2008) describes Kotter's (1996) well-known eight steps to change as a-theoretical (meaning not based on theory), Cummings and Worley (2015) too, emphasise Kotter's first step of creating a sense of urgency. Vithessonthi (2010) on his part, describes it as follows: due to radical environmental changes, senior managers perceive a greater sense of urgency which leads to a need for change in the organisation's overall strategy. Strategic change is viewed as an outcome of conflicting pressures. Cummings and Worley (2015) propose in their turn, ten commandments for implementing strategic change properly in organisations. For example, they advise analysis of the organisation and its need for change and creation of a shared vision and common direction. They declare that it is important to hang on to those aspects that bring some sort of stability, heritage or anchor to provide continuity amidst change.

Cummings and Worley (2015) also stress that broad-based support throughout the organisation is important, as a change plan which specifies from where the first meetings should be held to the date by which the company hopes to achieve its change goals. They emphasise the importance of enabling structures designed to facilitate pilot tests and new reward systems. Full involvement, communication and disclosure can be potent tools for overcoming resistance. Throughout the change, process leaders should make it a top priority to prove their commitment to the transformation process. An example of continuous change is the learning organisation where the organisation is constantly preparing and practicing change; change is swiftly activated; employees work together in multidimensional teams and learning is assisted as well as rewarded (Holbeche, 2007).

Worley, Hitchin, and Ross (1996) in their turn, describe four steps of change, where strategic analysis involves an analysis of an organisation's external environment, its current strategic objectives, as well as the extent of its effectiveness; the next step includes strategy making, a process that includes the services, products and markets to be focused on in the future and assesses the culture that will either enable or inhibit the change. The actual strategic change design defines how the change process will be accomplished through sequencing and pacing. Allocating resources for support is an important element of the implementation of the change plan. Sometimes the organisation has the strategic orientation to deal with its turbulent environment, however, it lacks the actual capacity due to a lack of strategic change management. Nadler and Tushman (1990), on their part, identify two dimensions of change, i.e. strategic or incremental and reactive or anticipatory, leading to either adaption, tuning, re-creation or reorientation-type changes. This work is a classic, as is the thinking of Weick and Quinn (1999), who typify change as episodic, a divergence of alignment of the organisation; or continuous, which is evolutionary and results in creating continuously improving organisations. In the late nineties (1999) Warren Bennis rightly asked whether we have reached the "end of leadership" and its replacement with diverse creative alliances. It supports the need of leadership to be distributed throughout the organisation, in line with Senge's (1997) views of shared responsibility towards the creation of the organisation's future.

These change frameworks might have been influenced by the high face validity of Lewin's (1947) three-phase model of the 1940s, namely unfreezing, transitioning and refreezing phases. In line with this notion of phases during organisational change, we would argue for a contextualised approach to change during which there could be phases of radical transformational change interventions that would require a planned change project or large-scale programme with distinct phases or steps, and then a phase of evolutionary, continuous change. Admittedly, the competencies that leaders need to have, would differ across these different types of change. For example, enhancing continuous learning in the organisation or also called exploitative innovation, would require different skills than exploring new frontiers such as during explorative innovation, where radical change must be implemented. Ultimately, we recommend contextual ambidexterity, where both competencies are built in the organisation to be executed when and as required, in line with Benner and Tushman's thesis (2015).

We advocate thus for implementing change frameworks in cases where a definite change process is required, where there is a distinct objective and then to supplement that change programme, that consists of various particular change projects, with the continuous improvement change processes. These continuous change processes often involve a change in culture to share information and ensure continuous learning in the organisation, such as the implementation of a learning organisation (Senge, 1990). Nonetheless, the initial implementation of the learning organisation as such, might still take on the phased approach as described in the change framework of this volume, since changing organisational culture is a type of strategic change (Cummings & Worley, 2015) that requires dedication, careful planning and execution. It is thus essential to align the organisational design elements, such as the structure, reward and recognition processes and technology, with the strategic objective of organisational learning.

2.3.2   Positioning the Change Framework of This Volume

Considering our position on leadership is a contextual approach, change too must be contextualised. For example, in leading change, timing is everything. In this regard, Vithessonthi and Thoumrungroje (2011) emphasise that in times of poor performance, strategic change is used to reverse the poor performance, whereas at other times it is a mechanism for continuously improving performance to counteract organisational stagnation or inertia. By (2005) emphasises that implementation of change could be characterised as discontinuous, continuous, incremental, bumpy or even smooth. Nonetheless, as the discussion above illustrated, By (2005) had not incorporated broader perspectives, for example the relative scale or transformational mind shift changes compared to smaller-scale change.

Burke (2008, p. 15) declares that although there is no singular, all-encompassing theory of organisational change, "open systems theory comes the closest". Several other scholars similarly describe change in an organisation as a complex and non-linear process (Newman, 2012; Peón-Escalante, Oliva-López, & Badillo-Piña, 2008). To comprehend this complexity, organisations are modelled as systems or even ecosystems. Peón-Escalante et al. (2008) criticize Lewin's (1951) three-stage model, by acknowledging that it is generic; however, it does not adequately describe organisational development in large complex organisations. They state that at the "point of synthesis, functions striving to optimise their own performance, lead to overall organic integration" and that systems thinking "provides the framework for understanding the managing of interconnections, and gaining insight into the nature of complex systems, as well as testing assumptions about the effect of change upon the system" (Peón-Escalante et al., 2008, p. 36).

The use of systems thinking is thus important when dealing with complex systems. The authors of this volume, in taking a systems perspective, emphasise the external environment in change leadership. This volume thus approaches organisations as Complex Adaptive Systems (CAS), where there are neural-like networks of interacting, independent agents bonded in a cooperative dynamic of non-linear network feedback systems (Uhl-Bien et al., 2007). In line with other authors, the authors of this volume recognise the environment as non-linear, organic and characterised by uncertainty and unpredictability. This environment is thus too dynamic, unstable, unpredictable and complex to be described by simple models of cause and effect (Uhl-Bien & Marion, 2009).

Furthermore, the environment and organisation are interacting in this network of interdependence. Higgs and Rowland (2005) remind us that the context, scope, complexity, timeline and magnitude of the change are all shaped by the leaders in this process. Weberg (2012, p. 275) too, encourages leaders to "... lead at the intersections, through strong networking, ... and fostering conditions for the organisation to quickly adapt...".

This volume pays attention to strategic change. Trinh and O'Connor (2002) highlight, on their part, several types of strategic change, for example product operational capacity, service delivery ethics, change in affiliations with suppliers and supply chain components and change in diversification of services. They advise organisations to engage in strategic adaptation of choosing new sets of core strategies to position themselves better for future viability, whilst conforming to stipulations imposed by the environment. We accede that strategic change involves improving the alignment among an organisation's environment, strategy and organisational design (Cummings & Worley, 2015); and thus, the theoretical underpinnings of this research are in line with the Organisational Development perspective as described above. Without strategic change, organisations would fail to survive or maintain their top performance (Mohrman, Edward, & Lawler, 2012).

The focus of this volume is on the implementation and less on the analytical study of formulating a strategic initiative, in accordance with Roberto and Levesque (2005) who proclaim that strategic initiatives are not analytical studies; they entail the broad implementation of new processes and systems (Roberto & Levesque, 2005). Leadership is a critical component of successful strategic change and throughout this volume we will focus on specific roles of leaders. This complexity in the execution of strategic change exists even more so in emerging markets and the next section pays attention to it.

2.4 Complexity in Emerging Markets' Environments

Leading change takes place within a complex context of the rational (objective facts and figures, such as economical data), emotional (sensitivity around language and identity) and political (geopolitical and political-economic histories) and current realities. Our focus on the emerging markets includes these aspects, as systematically discussed below.

2.4.1 Rational Realities of Emerging Markets

We live in South Africa and acknowledge that most of our examples and case studies are from this emerging market. However, our experience includes travelling to most of these emerging market destinations, either to conduct consulting or executive coaching projects, or for leisure, or combining a leisurely family holiday with some work. Several of our current South African clients are expanding to other emerging markets and through their experiences, we also gained exposure to the enablers and challenges to work in these markets. In addition, we are exposed to several multinational clients who have a footprint in other, if not all, emerging markets. We also reviewed numerous secondary sources on emerging market trends, academic research reports and case studies. Figure 2.1 illustrates the location of the emerging markets covered during this study.

Kelly Alexander, a researcher in the Centre for Dynamic Markets at the Gordon Institute of Business Science at the University of Pretoria, in her interview with us, contributed the characteristics of emerging markets from her research and other authors' references that she quoted from, as follows:

Alexander advises that *emerging markets* is a term that was developed in the 1970s in order to explain the rise of the East Asian Tigers in relation to the then First and Third World. The unique path and rapid expansion of these economies differentiated them from other nations, whose growth was predictable and constrained. The term *emerging markets* is used widely today, with little clarification around what it means and how it is applied.

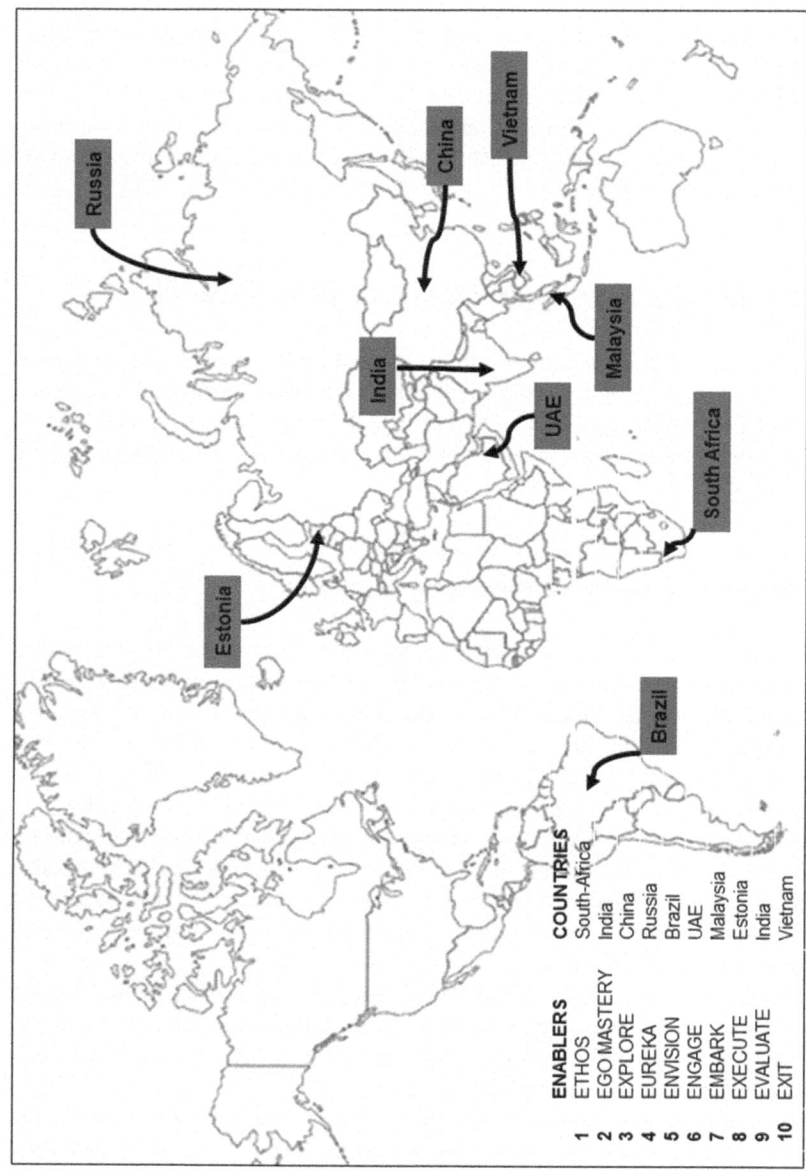

ENABLERS   **COUNTRIES**
1   ETHOS   South-Africa
2   EGO MASTERY   India
3   EXPLORE   China
4   EUREKA   Russia
5   ENVISION   Brazil
6   ENGAGE   UAE
7   EMBARK   Malaysia
8   EXECUTE   Estonia
9   EVALUATE   India
10 EXIT   Vietnam

Fig. 2.1 Emerging markets covered during this study (Authors' own)

A distinction must be made between emerging markets and frontier markets: "frontier markets are generally small, illiquid and risky" according to *The Economist*, "the things that made emerging markets exciting in the 1990s are now found in frontier markets" (The Economist, 2014). According to Ruchir Sharma, the universe of emerging markets include Brazil, Chile, Colombia, Mexico, Peru, South Africa, Morocco, Egypt, China, India, Indonesia, Korea, Malaysia, Philippines, Taiwan, Thailand, Czech Republic, Hungary, Poland, Russia and Turkey.

However, frontier markets include a far greater number of countries and are listed as:

Argentina, Ecuador, Panama, Jamaica, Trinidad and Tobago, Bulgaria, Croatia, Estonia, Latvia, Lithuania, Romania, Serbia, Slovenia, Ukraine, Botswana, Ghana, Kenya, Mauritius, Namibia, Nigeria, Tunisia, Bahrain, Jordan, Kuwait, Lebanon, Oman, Qatar, Saudi Arabia, UAE, Bangladesh, Kazakhstan, Pakistan, Sri Lanka and Vietnam (The Economist, 2014).

According to White and Brown (2014), the initial understanding of emerging markets, namely based on the factors of demographic and economic growth, is no longer sufficient in providing a useful explanation and understanding of emerging markets. White and Brown state that "increasingly other factors are driving performance, shaping development and distinguishing one market from the next. The role of economic, political and social institutions is key to improving competitive performance and overall progress" (2014, p. 3). One of the major criticisms of the term *emerging markets* is that it has become too broad, with too many countries—at diverse stages of development—being viewed together, without differentiation.

White and Brown (2014) discuss the importance of institutional voids. This is a key factor for the research towards the publication of our *Change Leadership in Emerging Markets*, as these institutions shape the way in which business operates and the execution of several change projects mentioned in this book, were influenced by the institutional void. These voids include corruption and government bureaucracy, the skill levels held by the labour force, and stable financial systems, among others. The well-known and respected scholar, Theo Veldsman, in *Talent Management in emerging markets* (Bluen, 2012), explains that emerging markets are typified by the lack of infrastructure and the imbalances between, for example, the skills required in the economy and the educational system that cannot supply in the need. The population growth rate is for instance also too high for the economy to provide employment. These issues of infrastructure are giving more reasons for companies that operate in these emerging markets to get involved in the funding of infrastructure, such as construction of roads. These organisations might also contribute to health care and education and developing skills and offering training to locals (Veldsman, 2012).

The term *emerging markets* is broadly understood and has relevance globally, and thus is still a useful concept and a signifier of meaning. The term *emerging markets* refers to those countries that are in the midst of a transition from a developing to a developed country, although the trajectory is not set, and success is not certain.

The focus on economic growth is key in shaping the way in which development is measured. A country's development is theorised to be attained only through economic development, and "economic progress is a necessary condition for some other purpose, judged to be good" (Rostow, 1959, p. 6). Emerging markets have been defined according to this measure, as they are able to provide high levels of economic growth, and through attracting investment, they, in turn, are able to develop and experience economic growth. It is thought to translate into development for the country more broadly. However, the current volume aims to further the idea of development, to include the role of change leadership to drive economic growth and development. Furthermore, it is assumed that improved change leadership in emerging markets will result in stronger institutions. These rational distinctions between emerging markets and considerations are thus relevant to change leadership.

2.4.2 Emotional Realities of Emerging Markets

Throughout this volume, we point to the emotional sensitivity of our language when referring to emerging markets or historically referred to the "Third World", as if there are "winners" or first and second world and then "thirdly-rated global citizens", called the "Third World".

According to Smith (2003) at the 1955 Bandung Conference, the term *Third World* came to mean the non-aligned states of the world at that time. During the period of the Cold War, the USA (United States of America) and the USSR (Union of Soviet Socialist Republics) were characterised as the First and Second Worlds, respectively. The First World referred to those nations who were democratic and capitalist, while the Second World referred to the nations who were led by "the dictatorship of the proletariat" and were socialist (Smith, 2003). There were, however, a large number of states who were not directly aligned with either party— particularly the newly decolonised and independent states of Africa, and Asia, and although the nations of South America were not initially included in the Bandung conference, they too were later considered part of the Third World (Smith, 2003).

These states were to form a "Third Force", which would resist colonial and imperial objectives, and seek to develop in a manner which was both nationalist and progressive, while maintaining and rebuilding the cultural elements which had been sidelined during colonialism (Smith, 2003). According to Thomas (2000, p. 6), this development was "not necessarily a middle way, but certainly a distinctive, positive force". Therefore the aim was to create a new and alternative vision of development.

Maintaining the use of this term is in our opinion dangerous, since many scholars believe that the idea of the Third World leads to generalisation and a homogenisation of the history of emerging markets. These homogenising assumptions surrounding the term *Third World* must, therefore, be discarded. Third World countries are not homogenous, but rather each has its own cultural practices, different economic strengths and are thus not all classified as "poor". In addition, they have had diverse experiences with globalisation (Smith, 2003). Some countries have managed to maximise the benefits available to them, while others have been further marginalised.

Veldsman (2012) points out that the cultural imperialism attitude of some multinational companies entails that they have an ethnocentric attitude of focusing on doing things like they would have done in their home country. A polycentric attitude is less focused on only the home country's culture, where some positions, especially not the critical functions are occupied by locals. The locals might feel that their culture is perceived as inferior to the home country's culture. A geocentric attitude takes the best of both cultures and builds common goals across the divide of us and them. The authors of this volume would encourage change leadership to consider how a more geocentric attitude could be developed when interacting with people in emerging markets.

Hall (2000) examines the role of globalisation in the construction of identity and highlights three possible outcomes of globalisation. The first of these outcomes is the broadening of the definition of one's culture to include various diverse aspects. This would be as a result of the other influences, which the members of that particular cultural group are in contact with. The second outcome is the strengthening of local identities. This would be in response to the idea that other cultural groups are a threat to the "purity" of their cultural group. Finally, Hall (2000) states that instead of retaining and protecting one's existing identity and salience of their cultural group, new, hybrid identities may be formed.

In 1992, Francis Fukuyama proclaimed "the end of History", stating that democracy and an economic model based on the Western world's reliance on the free market would prevail, based on the failure of alternate models. This was then to be exported to the developing world, creating a cookie-cutter approach to development and progress. Yet, an examination of emerging markets reveals that history has not ended and there remains a conflict within these markets. For other researchers such as Polanyi (Munck, 2004), there is a dual movement between the creation of hegemony (meaning domination or control) and a counter-hegemonic movement. This is evident in the way in which emerging markets attempt to forge an independent development path, seeking new partners and attempting to form new and alternative power blocs. However, they are simultaneously reliant on traditional development partners and the basis of many emerging market economies remains traditional first-world trading partners. In terms of the development path of these countries, Veldsman (2012) observes that the emerging markets regularly leapfrog developed countries on the technology innovation curve, by moving to sophisticated technology without the adoption of less sophisticated technology, such as widespread adoption of mobile technology. The emerging markets thus do not necessarily follow the same development path as the developed countries. In the section below on relevance of change leadership for emerging markets, more perspective will be offered on approaches of OD practitioners that have to be considered when working in these sensitive contexts.

Change leadership includes thus a sensitivity around specific emotionally-laden words to describe the host countries and its citizens. Emotional intelligence is essential for effective change leadership.

2.4.3   Political Realities of Emerging Markets

Leading change within emerging markets requires leadership to understand the political landscape. We often find in our consulting and teaching work that our business leaders are ill-equipped to deal with political realities and regularly refrain from influencing government proactively or to leverage their collective political clout in negotiations. However, especially in the emerging markets, government plays a crucial role. In 2013, Ernst and Young reported that one-fifth of the largest companies in emerging markets were State-Owned Enterprises (SOEs).

Emerging markets are grouped into various regional alliances and change leadership will benefit from taking note of them, especially where there are specific trade agreements in place that might enable or pose a barrier for businesses in these areas. For example, the Southern African Development Community (SADC) offers member countries access to one another's markets.

Furthermore, there is a rise in distinct emerging markets groupings, such as the BRICS (Brazil, Russia, India, China and South Africa) and CIVETS (Colombia, Indonesia, Vietnam, Egypt, Turkey and South Africa). In addition, the Next Eleven (Bangladesh, Egypt, Indonesia, Iran, Korea, Mexico, Nigeria, Pakistan, Philippines, Turkey and Vietnam) are expected to be the countries that could replace BRICS in the hearts and minds of investors (Lawson, Heacock, & Stupnytska, 2007). Therefore, within the framework of emerging markets, there is a disaggregation as investors and operators learn more about individual markets. Veldsman (2012) declares that emerging markets are experiencing fundamental transformation of their foundational layer of norms, values, beliefs and assumptions. There are diverse, competing ideological debates on, for example, socialist versus capitalist economic systems, privatisation versus nationalisation or the role of the state in the economy. Iheriohanma (2011) warns that these uncertainties create fertile ground for corruption and fraud.

Joseph Stiglitz, an economist from Harvard, offers a balanced view in this book, *Globalisation and its discontents* (2002) that opening up international trade has helped many countries grow far more quickly than they would otherwise have done. International trade helps economic development when a country's exports drive its economic growth. Exported growth was thus the centrepiece of the industrial policy that enriched much of Asia and left millions of people there far better off than before. Because of globalisation many people in the world now live longer than before and their standard of living is far better. People in the West may regard low-paying jobs at Nike as exploitation, but for many people in the developing world, working in a factory is a far better option than staying down on the farm and growing rice.

However, it is concerning that the critics of globalisation accuse Western countries of hypocrisy, since they have pushed poor countries to eliminate trade barriers, but kept up their own barriers, preventing developing countries from exporting their agricultural products and so depriving them of desperately needed export income (Stiglitz, 2002).

It is interesting to note the influence of complexity and specifically Complex Adaptive Systems' (CAS) characteristics that played itself out in globalisation. For instance, Stiglitz (2002) advised that the anti-globalisation protests are a result of the connectedness, since links between activists in different parts of the world, particularly those links forged through Internet communication, brought about the pressure that resulted in the international landmines treaty, despite the opposition of many powerful governments.

Veldsman (2012) also warns that multinationals sometimes dominate the emerging market country's economic landscape, due to the vast amount of capital that they invest and as a result, the local companies cannot compete with them. This leads to governments sometimes introducing import barriers. Veldsman (2012) further notes that due to the inequality in the emerging markets and the high Gini-coefficient, multinational organisations have to be cognisant of their role in socio-economic upliftment and community involvement in projects to improve education, health care, etc. "Graduate programmes and bursaries could also play an important role" (Veldsman, 2012, p. 193). It is concerning that emerging markets are often a dumping ground for developed countries' dated technologies that emerging markets then cannot efficiently deploy or maintain. Multinational organisations use the emerging markets to outsource their manufacturing or service sites for subcomponents or services to the developed countries (Veldsman, 2012).

Eisler (2008) emphasises that civil society and governments alike vigorously criticise business practices that cause hunger, ill health and environmental destruction and pollution. Even in the rich United States, working parents are stressed because they have too little time to care for their children (Folbre, 2001). Paul Elkins (1986) in his book *The Living Economy: A new economics in the making*, laments that investment does not bring down unemployment, neither does growth. He proclaims that economics is at an impasse, that its instruments are blunted, and its direction confused.

These outcries represent the disillusionment of people in our modern world and the dangers of inequalities. We are adding our voices to those warning that globalisation has to be considered carefully and consciously. The consequences for the emerging markets, in particular, have to be taken into account in responsible decisions around global expansions. Change leaders have to thus be acutely aware of political repercussions of their implementation of change processes, as an important contextual variable.

2.4.4   Relevance of Studying Emerging Markets for Change Leadership

It is encouraging that renowned OD scholars in the West, such as Anne Litwin, are interested in research in the emerging markets. She authored a seminal chapter on "Global OD Practice: The legacy of colonialism and oppression" in *The NTL Handbook of Organization Development and Change* (2014). She reminds us that OD originated in the West and the values of OD reflect the Western values of individual learning, development, participation and openness and constructively confronting differences. She warns that as Western trained consultants, we must be sensitive to the cultural context in which we are working, even as we ground our work in values that can help create healthy organisations. We would like to add that not only OD consultants, but line managers who are leading change processes, must have insight into cases in which their own value systems might be contrary to the local culture of the host country.

In this regard, Litwin (2007, 2014) refers to the theory of Hofstede (2001) on typifying cultures and warns that when OD scholarly practitioners (or change leaders) promote participation, they need to bear in mind Hofstede's notion of high-power distance cultures (Hofstede & Hofstede, 2005). In these cultures, as represented by some of the cultures in African countries or in Latin America and Asia, with high power distance cultural orientations, people think that leaders know best and are comfortable with leaders making decisions for the group.

Another example is where Western OD consultants (or change leaders) would promote the confrontation and resolution of differences. They need to be careful of cultural orientations of uncertainty avoidance. In these cultures, they do not prefer confrontation and tension and it makes them uncomfortable, such as in the Asian cultures (Trompenaars, 1993). In other situations, when the focus is on the needs and rights of the individuals, OD consultants must be careful of collectivist cultures, that are focused on the needs of the groups, not individuals. It will serve change leaders to be acutely aware of cultural difference frameworks.

Litwin (2014) reminds us that the goal of colonialism was to take control of a country and exploit the resources of the conquered. Colonialists were trying to exterminate native cultures, languages and religions and replace them with those of the colonizers. Colonialism was carried out by expansionist Europeans in building empires: between 1492 and 1850 the Americas were colonized by Portugal and Spain, where indigenous people and languages were brutally displaced in Mexico, Central America and South America. From 1730 to after World War II, Asia, Africa and the Pacific were occupied. By 1914, 85% of the earth were colonized by Europe. Mills (1997, p. 127) describes whiteness not as a colour, but as a set of power relations. Resentment of previous colonizers and their descendants lingers.

Litwin (2014) thus advises that OD consultants and we would add change leaders, rather work with local partners who know the culture, when engaging with a host country and we would add, particularly in the emerging markets. Litwin (2014) reports an example in Nigeria, where training of local leaders all over Northern Nigeria took place. The enabling environment created a focus on reproductive health and created awareness. Over the years, it did not appear as if any change was taking place, but in 2009, a large grant from the British Government Department for International Development initiated work to redesign Nigeria's health system and the country's health system was open to the changes, due to the OD interventions over a long period. This case also illustrated how the OD methods can be adapted in many cultures.

Graetz and Smith (2010) suggest looking at whether models used for organisational change are appropriate for transition economies. They contend that the influence of markets and social interventions and the economy will dictate the use of existing models and might require designing models more apt to a more flexible context. In this regard, research of Chengadu and Scheepers (2017) reveals that in emerging markets, informal relations and contacts were even more important than in developed economies. Other scholars, like Gomes, Angwin, Peter, and Mellahi (2012) found that in the Nigerian banking sectors, pre-merger Human Resource Management practices were perceived to be influenced by existing informal social relationships between managers and owners of merged banks (Gomes et al., 2012).

With regards to other emerging markets, Salim's (2011) exploration of the Emirates Bank and NBD in the UAE's merger, indicated that even though there were initially resistance and hostility towards the merger of the two entities, clear communication and ownership of the strategy, engagement with employees through workshops, detailed work plans touching on job designs and organisation design, stakeholder engagement and leadership commitment, can reduce employee anxiety, lead to adoption of the new culture and successful merger of organisations. In a study in Saudi Arabia, the most important factors identified to play a major role in the implementation of strategic change were: culture, leadership, learning and training (Alhazemi, Rees, & Hossain, 2013).

Scheepers, Swart, Parbhoo and Alexander in Chengadu and Scheepers (2017), emphasise the reliance of leaders in the emerging markets, such as India and China in particular, on informal relations and contacts. Interestingly, scholars in the complexity leadership domain, likewise discovered that in the complex adaptive system, leadership is about influence of others and does not rely on formal authority structure or hierarchy (Lichtenstein & Plowman, 2009). This framework of open complex systems is thus ideal for understanding leadership in the context of emerging markets.

2.5 Conclusion

In this chapter the complexities in emerging markets were highlighted. These complexities are highly relevant to this study on change leadership.

As the macro-environment contextual variables, for example the political, economic, social, technological and environmental issues, become more complex and also uncertain, the organisational change components and processes have to become more complex to match the environmental complexity. In Complexity Theory, the law of requisite complexity dictates that the complexity on the inside must reflect the complexity on the outside. Prof Mary Uhl-Bien from Texas Christian University declared in her presentation to the GIBS MBA students on 18 May 2017, *Complexity must meet complexity*. Uhl-Bien was referring to the scholarly work of Boisot and McKelvey (2011) on Ashby's law of requisite variety or that the variety a system generates must match the environment it finds itself in. This implies that complexity is required of the internal organisational design components, such as the structure, technology, management process, human resource systems and organisational culture. As a result, change leadership has to take note and develop a keen insight into the complexities of these markets to effectively design and direct their organisation's proactive internal adaptation and positioning in these emerging markets.

References

Agboola, A. A., & Salawu, R. O. (2011). Managing deviant behaviour and resistance to change. *International Journal of Business and Management, 6*(1), 235–242. https://doi.org/https://doi.org/10.5539/ijbm.v6n1p235. Retrieved from http://www.ccsenet.org/journal/index.php/ijbm/article/view/7134

Alhazemi, A. A., Rees, C., & Hossain, F. (2013). Implementation of strategic organizational change: The case of King Abdul Aziz University in Saudi Arabia. *International Journal of Public Administration, 36*(13), 972–981. https://doi.org/10.1080/01900692.2013.773036

Alimo-Metcalfe, B., & Alban-Metcalfe, J. (2005). Leadership: Time for a new direction? *Leadership, 1*(1), 51–71. https://journals.sagepub.com/doi/10.1177/1742715005049351

Amis, J., Slack, T., & Hinings, C. R. (2004). The pace, sequence, and linearity of radical change. *The Academy of Management Journal, 47*(1), 15–39. https://doi.org/https://doi.org/10.2307/20159558. Retrieved from https://www.jstor.org/stable/20159558?seq=1#page_scan_tab_contents

Arena, M. J., & Uhl-Bien, M. (2016). Complexity leadership theory: Shifting from human capital to social capital. *People and Strategy, 39*(2), 22–27. Retrieved from http://www.sagewaysconsulting.com/wp-content/uploads/2017/03/ComplexityLeadershipTheory_HRPS_39.2_Arena_Uhl_Bien.pdf

Bamford, D. R., & Forrester, P. L. (2003). Managing planned and emergent change within an operations management environment. *International Journal of Operations & Production Management, 23*(5), 546–564. https://doi.org/10.1108/01443570310471857

Barrett, D. J. (2002). Change communication: Using strategic employee communication to facilitate major change. *Corporate Communications: An International Journal, 7*(4), 219–231. https://doi.org/10.1108/13563280210449804

Bartlett, C. A., & Ghoshal, S. (1990). Matrix management: Not a structure, a frame of mind. *Harvard Business Review, 68*(4), 138–145. Retrieved from https://hbr.org/1990/07/matrix-management-not-a-structure-a-frame-of-mind

Bass, B. M. (1990). From transactional to transformational leadership: Learning to share the vision. *Organizational Dynamics, 18*(3), 19–31. Retrieved from https://www.sciencedirect.com/science/article/pii/009026169090061S

Bauman, Z. (2000). *Liquid modernity*. Cambridge: Polity Press. https://www.worldcat.org/title/liquid-modernity/oclc/44157073

Beer, M., & Nohria, N. (2000, May–June). Cracking the code of change. *Harvard Business Review*, 2–9. Retrieved from https://hbr.org/2000/05/cracking-the-code-of-change

Benner, M., & Tushman, M. (2015). Reflections on the 2013 decade award—"Exploitation, exploration, and process management: The productivity dilemma revisited" ten years later. *Academy of Management Review, 40*(4), 497–514. https://journals.aom.org/doi/full/10.5465/amr.2015.0042

Bennis, W. (1999). The end of leadership: Exemplary leadership is impossible without full inclusion, initiatives and co-operation of followers. *Organizational Dynamics, 28*(1), 71–80. http://thierryschool.be/solar-system/starship-II/artemis/sTabuwuAbra3u.pdf

Bluen, S. (2012). *Talent management in emerging markets*. Randburg: Knowres. http://www.kr.co.za/knowres-publishing-1/talent-management-in-emerging-markets-mobi

Boisot, M., & McKelvey, B. (2011). Chapter 16. Complexity and organization-environment relations: Revising Ashby's law of requisite variety. In P. Allen, S. Maguire, & B. McKelvey (Eds.), *The SAGE handbook of complexity and management* (pp. 280–298). Los Angeles: Sage. https://pdfs.semanticscholar.org/1ccb/760b00c10409064c401bd4b6a53da987e9c2.pdf

Bovey, W., & Hede, A. (2001). Resistance to organizational change: The role of cognitive and affective processes. *Leadership & Organization Development Journal, 22*(8), 372–382. https://doi.org/10.1108/01437730110410099

Brenner, M. (2008). It's all about people: Change management's greatest lever. *Business Strategy Series, 9*(3), 132–137. https://www.emerald.com/insight/content/doi/10.1108/17515630810873366/full/html

Briody, E., Pester, T. M., & Trotter, R. (2012). A story's impact on organisational-culture change. *Journal of Organisational Change, 25*(1), 67–87. https://doi.org/https://doi.org/10.1108/09534811211199600. Retrieved from https://nau.pure.elsevier.com/en/publications/a-storys-impact-on-organizational-culture-change

Buller, P. F. (1988). For successful strategic change: Blend OD practices with strategic management. *Organisational Dynamics, 16*(3), 42–55. https://doi.org/10.1016/0090-2616(88)90035-6

Burke, W. W. (2008). A contemporary view of organisational development. In T. G. Cummings (Ed.), *Handbook of organizational development* (pp. 13–38). Los Angeles: Sage. https://books.google.co.za/books/about/Handbook_of_Organization_Development.html?id=VTOi1wmzQM4C&redir_esc=y

Burke, W. W., & Litwin, G. H. (1992). A causal model of organisation performance and change. *Journal of Management.* Retrieved from http://documents.reflectlearn.org/Offline%20OA%20Models%20and%20Frameworks/BurkeLitwin_ACausalModelofOrganizationalPerformance.pdf

By, R. T. (2005). Organisational change management: A critical review. *Journal of Change Management, 5*(4), 369–380. https://doi.org/10.1080/14697010500359250

Chengadu, S., & Scheepers, C. B. (Ed.). (2017). *Women leadership in emerging markets.* New York: Routledge, Taylor and Francis. Retrieved from https://www.routledge.com/Women-Leadership-in-Emerging-Markets-Featuring-46-Women-Leaders/Chengadu-Scheepers/p/book/9781138188969

Collier, J., & Esteban, R. (2000). Systemic leadership: Ethical and effective. *Leadership & Organization Development Journal, 21*(4), 207–215. https://doi.org/10.1108/01437730010335454

Cummings, T. G. (Ed.). (2008). *Handbook of organizational development.* Los Angeles: Sage. https://books.google.co.za/books?hl=en&lr=&id=VTOi1wmzQM4C&oi=fnd&pg=PA1&dq=Cummings,+T.+G.+(Ed.).+(2008).+Handbook+of+organizational+development.+Los+Angeles:+Sage.&ots=TaW8YunX0N&sig=K4SFOBX1B7xTJyjAqG3fUuPkuCE#v=onepage&q&f=false

Cummings, T. G., & Worley, C. G. (2008). *Organization development & change* (9th ed.). Mason, OH: South-Western Cengage Learning. http://www.mcs.gov.kh/wp-content/uploads/2017/07/Organization-Development-and-Change.pdf

Cummings, T. G., & Worley, C. G. (2015). *Organization development & change* (10th ed.). Cincinnati, OH: South-Western College Publishing. https://www.loot.co.za/product/thomas-cummings-organization-development-and-change/lszv-2176-g370?referrer=googlemerchant&gclid=CjwKCAjw5vz2BRAtEiwAbcVIL_49WYGXAaU1mrKBwWHl3ZZBiQ72sHG5Qwv5JACp9vKcDEEphNuZKhoCKWQQAvD_BwE&gclsrc=aw.ds

Dixon, S. E. A., Meyer, K. E., & Day, M. (2010). Stages of organizational transformation in transition economies: A dynamic capabilities approach. *Journal of Management Studies, 47*, 416–436. https://doi.org/https://doi.org/10.1111/j.1467-6486.2009.00856.x. Retrieved April 16, 2018, from https://www.researchgate.net/publication/46540356_Stages_of_Organizational_Transformation_in_Transition_Economies_A_Dynamic_Capabilities_Approach

Edgren, L., & Barnard, K. (2012). Complex adaptive systems for management of integrated care. *Leadership in Health Services, 25*(1), 39–51. https://doi.org/10.1108/17511871211198061

Eisler, R. (2008). *The real wealth of nations: Creating a caring economics.* San Francisco, CA: Berrett-Koehler Publishers. https://www.amazon.com/Real-Wealth-Nations-Creating-Economics/dp/1576756297

Elkington, J., & Hartigan, P. (2008). *The power of unreasonable people: How social entrepreneurs create markets that change the world*. Boston, MA: Harvard Business Press. https://www.tandfonline.com/doi/abs/10.1080/10495140903550759

Elkins, P. (Ed.). (1986). *The living economy: A new economics in the making*. New York: Routledge & Kegan Paul. https://www.amazon.com/Living-Economy-Paul-Ekins/dp/0415039371

Ernst & Young. (2013). *Global trends 2009*. Cleveland: Ernst and Young Global Management Ltd. https://www.ey.com/Publication/vwLUAssets/EY_Global_review_2013/$FILE/EY_Global_review_2013.pdf

Fiedler, F. E. (1967). *A theory of leadership effectiveness*. New York: McGraw-Hill. https://www.amazon.com/Living-Economy-Paul-Ekins/dp/0415039371

Folbre, N. (2001). *The invisible heart: Economics and family values*. New York: New Press. https://www.amazon.com/Invisible-Heart-Economics-Family-Values/dp/1565847474

French, W. L., Bell, C. H., & Zawacki, R. A. (2005). *Organization development and transformation: Managing effective change* (6th ed.). New York, NY: McGraw-Hill/Irwin. Retrieved from http://www.worldcat.org/title/organization-development-and-transformation-managing-effective-change/oclc/681881822

Fukuyama, F. (1992). *The end of history and the last man*. New York, NY: Free Press. https://www.amazon.com/End-History-Last-Man/dp/0743284550

Gill, R. (2007). Postfeminist media culture: Elements of a sensibility. *European Journal of Cultural Studies, 10*(2), 147–166. https://doi.org/10.1177/1367549407075898

Gomes, E., Angwin, D., Peter, E., & Mellahi, K. (2012). HRM issues and outcomes in African mergers and acquisitions: A study of the Nigerian banking sector. *The International Journal of Human Resource Management, 23*(14), 2874–2900. https://doi.org/10.1080/09585192.2012.671509

Graetz, F., & Smith, A. T. C. (2010). Managing organizational change: A philosophies of change approach. *Journal of Change Management, 10*(2), 135–154. https://doi.org/https://doi.org/10.1080/14697011003795602. Retrieved from http://www.tandfonline.com/doi/abs/10.1080/14697011003795602

Hall, S. (2000). The question of cultural identity. In K. Nash (Ed.), *Readings in contemporary political sociology*. Oxford: Blackwell Publishing. https://www.amazon.com/Questions-Cultural-Identity-SAGE-Publications-ebook/dp/B012D5627O

Higgs, M. J., & Rowland, D. (2005). All changes great and small: Exploring approaches to change and its leadership. *Journal of Change Management, 5*(2), 121–151. https://doi.org/10.1080/14697010500082902

Hofstede, G. (2001). *Cultures' consequences. Comparing values, behaviours, institutions and organisations across nations* (2nd ed.). Thousand Oaks, CA: Sage. https://digitalcommons.usu.edu/unf_research/53/

Hofstede, G., & Hofstede, G. J. (2005). *Cultures and organisations: Software of the mind* (2nd ed.). New York: McGraw-Hill. https://www.amazon.com/Cultures-Organizations-Software-Mind-Third/dp/0071664181

Holbeche, L. (2007). *Understanding change*. New York, NY: Routledge. https://www.routledge.com/Understanding-Change-1st-Edition/Holbeche/p/book/9780750663410

House, R. J., & Mitchell, T. R. (1974). Path-goal theory of leadership. *Journal of Contemporary Business, 3*, 81–97. https://apps.dtic.mil/dtic/tr/fulltext/u2/a009513.pdf

Iheriohanma, E. B. J. (2011). Capacity building, leadership questions and drains of corruption in Africa: A theoretical discourse. *Asian Social Science, 7*(3), 131–138. http://www.ccsenet.org/journal/index.php/ass/article/view/9734

Keenan, P., Bixner, R., Morieux, Y., & Powell, K. (2009). *Managing survivor guilt*. Boston Consulting Group. Retrieved from https://www.bcg.com/documents/file15442.pdf, https://www.bcgperspectives.com/content/articles/people_management_human_resources_change_management_managing_survivor_guilt/

Kim, W. C., & Mauborgne, R. (2004, October). Blue ocean strategy. *Harvard Business Review*, 76–84. Retrieved from https://hbr.org/2004/10/blue-ocean-strategy

Kotter, J. P. (1996). *Leading change.* Boston, MA: Harvard Business Press. Retrieved from http://www.hbs.edu/faculty/Pages/item.aspx?num=137

Kotter, J. P., & Cohen, D. S. (2002). *The heart of change.* Boston, MA: Harvard Business School Press. Retrieved from http://www.hbs.edu/faculty/Pages/item.aspx?num=13479

Kumalo, M., & Scheepers, C. (2018). Leadership of change in South Africa public sector turnarounds. *Journal of Organizational Change Management,* Vol. ahead-of-print No. ahead-of-print. https://doi.org/10.1108/JOCM-04-2017-0142

Kumar, S. S. (2012). Challenges of managing an organisational change. *Advances in Management,* 5(4), 13–15. https://econpapers.repec.org/article/mgnjournl/v_3a5_3ay_3a2012_3ai_3a4_3aa_3a2.htm

Kuntz, J. R., & Gomes, J. F. (2012). Transformational change in organisations: A self-regulation approach. *Journal of Organisational Change Management,* 25(1), 143–162. https://www.emerald.com/insight/content/doi/10.1108/09534811211199637/full/html

Kutz, M. R. (2008, Winter). Toward a conceptual model of contextual intelligence: A transferable leadership construct. *Kravis Leadership Institute, Leadership Review, 8,* 18–31. Retrieved from https://www.researchgate.net/publication/228464894_Toward_a_conceptual_model_of_contextual_intelligence_A_transferable_leadership_construct

Kutz, M. R., & Bamford-Wade, A. (2013). Understanding contextual intelligence: A critical competency for today's leaders. *Emergence, Complexity, Organization, 15*(3), 55–80. https://www.semanticscholar.org/paper/Contextual-Intelligence%3A-A-Critical-Competency-for-Kutz-Bamford-Wade/9360476036b78a85a4179389919c41e6b22e65b8

Lawlor, J. (2013). Employee perspectives on the post-integration stage of a micro-merger. *Personnel Review, 42*(6), 704–723. https://doi.org/https://doi.org/10.1108/PR-06-2012-0096. Retrieved from https://arrow.dit.ie/cgi/viewcontent.cgi?referer=https://www.google.co.za/&httpsredir=1&article=1067&context=tfschhmtart

Lawson, S., Heacock, D., & Stupnytska, A. (2007). Beyond BRICS: A look at the 'next 11'. In *Goldman Sachs, BRICS and beyond* (pp. 161–164). New York: Goldman Sachs. Retrieved from http://www.goldmansachs.com/our-thinking/archive/archive-pdfs/brics-book/brics-chap-13.pdf

Lewin, K. (1947). Frontiers in group dynamics: Concept, method, and reality in social science; social equilibria and social change. *Human Relations, 1,* 5–41. https://doi.org/10.1177/001872674700100103

Lewin, K. (1951). *Field theory in social science.* New York: Harper & Row. https://www.amazon.com/Field-Theory-Social-Science-Theoretical/dp/B000JJ0WN2

Lichtenstein, B. B., & Plowman, D. A. (2009). The leadership of emergence: A complex systems leadership theory of emergence at successive organizational levels. *The Leadership Quarterly, 20,* 67–630. https://doi.org/10.1016/j.leaqua.2009.04.006

Liden, R. C., & Antonakis, J. (2009). Considering context in psychological leadership. *Human Relations, 62*(11), 1587–1605. https://doi.org/https://doi.org/10.1177/001872670934637. Retrieved from http://journals.sagepub.com/doi/abs/10.1177/0018726709346374

Lines, R., Selart, M., Espedal, B., & Johansen, S. T. (2005). The production of trust during organizational change. *Journal of Change Management, 5*(2), 221–245. https://doi.org/10.1080/14697010500143555

Litwin, A. (2007). OD: Dancing in the global context. *OD Practitioner, 39*(4), 11–15. https://annelitwin.com/wp-content/uploads/2014/04/OD-Dancing-in-the-Global-Context.pdf

Litwin, A. (2014). Global OD practice: The legacy of colonialism and oppression. In B. B. Jones & M. Brazzel (Eds.), *The NTL handbook of organization development and change* (pp. 483–497). Hoboken, NJ: Wiley. https://www.wiley.com/en-us/The+NTL+Handbook+of+Organization+Development+and+Change%3A+Principles%2C+Practices%2C+and+Perspectives%2C+2nd+Edition-p-9781118836163

MacKay, B., & Chia, R. (2013). Choice, chance, and unintended consequences in strategic change: A process understanding of the rise and fall of NorthCo Automotive. *Academy of Management Journal, 56*(1), 208–230. https://doi.org/10.5465/amj.2010.0734

Martins, E. C., & Terblanche, F. (2003). Building organisational culture that stimulates creativity and innovation. *European Journal of Innovation Management, 6*(1), 64–74. https://doi.org/10. 1108/14601060310456337

McKnight, L. L. (2013). Transformational leadership in the context of punctuated change. *Journal of Leadership, Accountability & Ethics, 10*(2), 103–112. Retrieved from http://connection. ebscohost.com/c/articles/89867398/transformational-leadership-context-punctuated-change

Mills, C. W. (1997). *The racial contract.* Ithaca, NY: Cornell University. https://www.cornellpress. cornell.edu/book/9780801484636/the-racial-contract/#bookTabs=1

Mohrman, S. A., Edward, E., & Lawler, I. (2012). Generating knowledge that drives change. *Academy of Management Perspectives, 26*(1), 41–51. https://doi.org/https://doi.org/10.5465/ amp.2011.0141. Retrieved from http://amp.aom.org/content/26/1/41.abstract

Munck, R. (2004). Globalization, labor and the Polanyi problem. *Journal of Labour History, 45*(3), 251–269. https://www.tandfonline.com/doi/abs/10.1080/0023656042000257765

Nadler, D., & Tushman, M. (1990). Beyond the charismatic leader: Leadership and organizational change. *California Management Review, 32*(2), 77–97. Retrieved from http://www.hbs.edu/ faculty/Pages/item.aspx?num=3576

Nelson, L. (2005). Managing the human resources in organisational change: A case study. *Research and Practice in Human Resource Management, 13*(1), 55–70. http://citeseerx.ist.psu.edu/ viewdoc/download?doi=10.1.1.733.9589&rep=rep1&type=pdf

Newman, J. (2012). An organisational change management framework for sustainability. *Greener Management International, 57*, 65–75. https://www.jstor.org/stable/pdf/greemanainte.57.65.pdf

Northouse, P. G. (2001). *Leadership: Theory and Practice* (2nd ed.). London: Sage. https:// onlinelibrary.wiley.com/doi/abs/10.1002/%28SICI%291099-1379%28200002%2921%3A1% 3C115%3A%3AAID-JOB5%3E3.0.CO%3B2-C

Nyström, M. E., Höög, E., Garvare, R., Weinehall, L., & Ivarsson, A. (2013). Change and learning strategies in large scale change programs: Describing the variation of strategies used in a health promotion program. *Journal of Organizational Change Management, 26*(6), 1020–1044. https://www.emerald.com/insight/content/doi/10.1108/JOCM-08-2012-0132/full/html? skipTracking=true

O'Reilly, C. A., Caldwell, D. F., Chatman, J. A., Lapiz, M., & Self, W. (2010). How leadership matters: The effects of leaders' alignment on strategy implementation. *Leadership Quarterly, 21* (1), 104–113. https://doi.org/10.1016/j.leaqua.2009.10.008

Oreg, S., & Berson, Y. (2011). Leadership and employees' reactions to change: The role of leaders' personal attributes and transformational leadership style. *Personnel Psychology, 64*(3), 627–659. https://doi.org/10.1111/j.1744-6570.2011.01221.x

Osborn, R. N., Hunt, J. G., & Jauch, L. R. (2002). Towards a contextual theory of leadership. *The Leadership Quarterly, 13*, 797–837. https://doi.org/10.1016/j.leaqua.2009.01.010

Osborn, R. N., & Hunt, J. G. J. (2007). Leadership and the choice of order: Complexity and hierarchical perspectives near the edge of chaos. *The Leadership Quarterly, 18*, 319–340. https://www.sciencedirect.com/science/article/pii/S1048984307000690

Osborn, R. N., & Marion, R. (2009). Contextual leadership, transformational leadership and the performance of international innovation seeking alliances. *The Leadership Quarterly, 20*, 191–206. https://www.sciencedirect.com/science/article/pii/S1048984309000137

Owen, K. O., & Dietz, A. S. (2012, October–December). *Understanding organizational reality: Concepts for the change leader.* Sage Open, 1–14. https://doi.org/10.1177/2158244012461922. Retrieved from http://journals.sagepub.com/doi/pdf/10.1177/2158244012461922

Palese, E. (2013). *Zygmunt Bauman. Individual and society in the liquid modernity.* Cham: Springer. https://www.ncbi.nlm.nih.gov/pmc/articles/PMC3786078/

Pellissier, R. (2012). Innovation in a complex environment. *SA Journal of Information Management, 14*(1), 1–14. https://doi.org/https://doi.org/10.4102/sajim.v14i1.499. Retrieved July 27, 2019, from http://www.sajim.co.za/index.php/SAJIM/article/view/499/594

Peón-Escalante, I., Oliva-López, E., & Badillo-Piña, I. (2008). Methodology for an organisational development process: An integral and sustainable qualitative transformation of complex inter-institutional networks, working on social and environmental problem situations. *Journal of Organisational Transformation and Social Change, 5*(1), 31–44. https://doi.org/10.1386/jots.5.1.31/1

Porras, J. I., & Silvers, R. C. (1991). Organisation development and transformation. *Annual Review Psychology, 42*, 51–78. https://www.annualreviews.org/doi/10.1146/annurev.ps.42.020191.000411

Pretorius, M., & Holtzhauzen, G. T. D. (2008). Critical variables of venture turnarounds: A liabilities approach. *Southern African Business Review, 12*(2), 87–107. https://repository.up.ac.za/handle/2263/7394?show=full

Rajagopalan, N., & Spreitzer, G. M. (1997). Toward a theory of strategic change: A multi-lens perspective and integrative framework. *Academy of Management Review, 22*(1), 48–79. https://doi.org/10.5465/AMR.1997.9707180259

Robbins, S. P., & Judge, T. A. (2007). *Organisational behaviour.* Upper Saddle River, NJ: Pearson Prentice Hall. https://trove.nla.gov.au/work/20179295?selectedversion=NBD28629878

Robbins, S. P., & Judge, T. A. (2015). *Organizational behaviour* (16th ed.). Boston, MA: Pearson. https://www.pearson.com/us/higher-education/product/Robbins-Organizational-Behavior-15th-Edition/9780132834872.html

Roberto, M., & Levesque, L. (2005). The art of making change initiatives stick. *MIT Sloan Management, 46*(4), 53–60. Retrieved from http://sloanreview.mit.edu/article/the-art-of-making-change-initiatives-stick/

Rostow, W. W. (1959). *The stages of economic growth.* London: Cambridge University Press. https://www.ufjf.br/oliveira_junior/files/2009/06/rostow.pdf

Rousseau, D. M. (2004). Psychological contracts in the workplace: Understanding the ties that motivate. *Academy of Management Executive, 18*(1), 120–127. https://www.scirp.org/(S(lz5mqp453edsnp55rrgjct55))/reference/ReferencesPapers.aspx?ReferenceID=1821911

Salim, B. (2011). A study on strategic initiatives and actions taken during a banking merger. *International Journal of Emerging Sciences, 1*(3), 246–259. Retrieved from https://www.researchgate.net/publication/267808562_A_Study_on_Strategic_Initiatives_and_Actions_taken_during_a_Banking_Merger

Scheepers, C. B., Oosthuizen, M., & Retief, D. (2016). Area collaboration at Nedbank: Cultivating culture through contextual leadership. *Emerald Emerging Markets Cases.* https://doi.org/10.1108/EEMCS-05-2016-0066

Scheepers, C. B., & Shuping, J. (2011). The effect of human resource practices on the psychological contract at an iron ore mining company in South Africa. *South African Journal of Human Resources Management, 9*, 1–19. https://sajhrm.co.za/index.php/sajhrm/article/view/302/347

Scheepers, C. B., & Sita, D. (2016). *Allergan SA: Contextual leadership sustaining culture during mergers.* Ivey Publishing, 9B16C044. https://www.iveycases.com/ProductView.aspx?id=82246

Scheepers, C. B., Swart, S., Alexander, K., & Parbhoo, H. (2017). Women's movements in emerging markets. In S. Chengadu & C. B. Scheepers (Eds.), *Women leadership in emerging markets* (pp. 65–104). New York, NY: Routledge, Taylor and Francis. https://www.routledge.com/Women-Leadership-in-Emerging-Markets-Featuring-46-Women-Leaders/Chengadu-Scheepers/p/book/9781138188969

Senge, P. M. (1990). *The fifth discipline: The art and practice of the learning organisation.* New York: Doubleday. https://onlinelibrary.wiley.com/doi/abs/10.1002/hrm.3930290308

Senge, P. M. (1997). Communities of leaders and learners. *Harvard Business Review, 75*(5), 30–32. https://hbr.org/1997/09/looking-ahead-implications-of-the-present

Shin, J., Taylor, M. S., & Seo, M.-G. (2012). Resources for change: The relationships of organizational inducements and psychological resilience to employees' attitudes and behaviors toward organizational change. *Academy of Management Journal, 55*(3), 727–748. Retrieved from https://journals.aom.org/doi/abs/10.5465/amj.2010.0325?journalCode=amj

Smith, A. (1776). *The wealth of nations*. London: William Strahan. https://www.abebooks.co.uk/servlet/BookDetailsPL?bi=30582438515&searchurl=n%3D100121503%26pics%3Don%26sortby%3D1%26tn%3DWealth%2Bof%2BNations%26an%3DAdam%2BSmith&cm_sp=snippet-_-srp1-_-title1

Smith, B. C. (2003). *Understanding third world politics: Theories if political change and development* (2nd ed.). London: Palgrave Macmillan. https://www.macmillanihe.com/page/detail/Understanding-Third-World-Politics/?K=9781137003256

Spangenberg, H., & Theron, C. (2013). A critical review of the Burke-Litwin model of leadership, change and performance. *Management Dynamics, 22*(2), 29. Retrieved from https://www.questia.com/library/journal/1P3-3090433461/a-critical-review-of-the-burke-litwin-model-of-leadership

Stiglitz, J. E. (2002). *Globalization and its discontents*. New York: WW Norton & Company. https://wwnorton.com/books/Globalization-and-Its-Discontents/

Strandholm, K., Kumar, K., & Subramanian, R. (2004). Examining the interrelationships among perceived environmental change, strategic response, managerial characteristics, and organizational performance. *Journal of Business Research, 57*(1), 58–68. https://doi.org/10.1016/S0148-2963(02)00285-0

Surty, S., & Scheepers, C. B. (2019). Moderating effect of environmental dynamism on the relationship between leadership practices and employee response to change. *Management Research Review*. https://doi.org/10.1108/MRR-03-2019-0094

The Economist. (2014, April 5). Wedge beyond the edge: Money is leaving emerging markets for riskier bets at the investment frontier. Retrieved from http://www.economist.com/news/finance-and-economics/21600132-money-leaving-emerging-markets-riskier-bets-investment-frontier-wedge

Thomas, A. (2000). Poverty and the 'end of development'. In *Poverty and development into the 21st century*. Oxford: Oxford University Press. https://global.oup.com/academic/product/poverty-and-development-9780198776260/?cc=us&lang=en&

Todd, A. (1999). Managing radical change. *Long Range Planning, 32*(2), 237–244. https://doi.org/10.1016/S0024-6301(99)00022-9

Trinh, H. Q., & O'Connor, S. J. (2002). Helpful or harmful? The impact of strategic change on the performance of U.S. Urban Hospitals. *Health Services Research, 37*(1), 143–169. https://doi.org/https://doi.org/10.1111/1475-6773.99208. Retrieved from https://www.ncbi.nlm.nih.gov/pmc/articles/PMC1430355/

Trompenaars, F. (1993). *Riding the waves of culture*. London: Nicholas Brealey. https://www.amazon.com/Riding-Waves-Culture-Understanding-Diversity/dp/1857881761

Uhl-Bien, M. (2006). Relational leadership theory: Exploring the social processes of leadership and organizing. *The Leadership Quarterly, 17*(6), 654–676. https://digitalcommons.unl.edu/leadershipfacpub/19/

Uhl-Bien, M., Marion, R., & McKelvey, B. (2007). Complexity leadership theory: Shifting leadership from the industrial age to the knowledge era. *The Leadership Quarterly, 18*(4), 298–318. https://www.sciencedirect.com/science/article/pii/S1048984307000689?via%3Dihub

Uhl-Bien, M., & Marion, R. (2009). Complexity leadership in bureaucratic forms of organizing: A meso model. *The Leadership Quarterly, 20*(4), 631–650. https://doi.org/10.1016/j.leaqua.2009.04.007

Uhl-Bien, M. (2017). *Complexity leadership*. Unpublished presentation to GIBS MBA students on 18 May 2017, at the Gordon Institute of Business Science, University Pretoria, Sandton.

Van der Westhuizen, T., Scheepers, C. B., & Kele, T. (2018). Job satisfaction and organisational support moderating the relationship between psychological contract breach and engagement. *Journal of Economics and Behavioral Studies, 10*(3), 187–202. https://ojs.amhinternational.com/index.php/jebs/article/view/2327

Van Wart, M., & Kapucu, N. (2011). Crisis management competencies: The case of emergency mangers in the USA. *Public Management Review, 13*(4), 489–511. https://www.tandfonline.com/doi/abs/10.1080/14719037.2010.525034

Veldsman, T. (2012). People professionals fit for emerging markets. In S. Bluen (Ed.), Talent management in emerging markets. (Chap. 8), pp. 179–203. http://www.kr.co.za/knowres-publishing-1/talent-management-in-emerging-markets-mobi

Vingers, G., & Cilliers, F. (2006). Effective transformational leadership behaviours for managing change. *South African Journal of Human Resources Management, 4*(2), a87. Retrieved from https://sajhrm.co.za/index.php/sajhrm/article/view/87

Vithessonthi, C. (2010). Resistance to change as issue selling in multinational firms. *Journal of Organisational Transformation and Social Change, 7*(3), 265–284. https://doi.org/10.1386/jots.7.3.265_1

Vithessonthi, C., & Thoumrungroje, A. (2011). Strategic change and firm performance: The moderating effect of organisational learning. *Journal of Asia Business Studies, 5*(2), 194–210. https://doi.org/10.1108/15587891111152348

Walter, F., & Bruch, H. (2010). Structural impacts on the occurrence and effectiveness of transformational leadership: An empirical study at the organizational level of analysis. *The Leadership Quarterly, 21*, 765–782. https://www.sciencedirect.com/science/article/pii/S1048984310001220?via%3Dihub

Weberg, D. (2012). Complexity leadership: A healthcare imperative. *Nursing Forum, 47*(4), 268–277. Wiley Periodicals Inc. https://onlinelibrary.wiley.com/doi/abs/10.1111/j.1744-6198.2012.00276.x

Weick, K. E., & Quinn, R. E. (1999). Organizational change and development. *Annual Review of Psychology, 50*(1), 361–386. https://doi.org/10.1146/annurev.psych.50.1.361

White, L., & Brown, L. (2014). *Dynamic markets: Advancing the notion of emerging markets through an empirical measure of institutions*. Gordon Institute of Business Science, University Pretoria. Retrieved from http://web.isanet.org/Web/Conferences/FLACSO-ISA%20BuenosAires%202014/Archive/ae038518-94df-4e03-84e0-d6252690444d.pdf

Wittig, C. (2012). Employees' reactions to organizational change. *OD Practitioner, 44*(2), 23–28. Retrieved from https://c.ymcdn.com/sites/www.odnetwork.org/resource/resmgr/odp/odp-v44,no2-wittig.pdf

Worley, C., Hitchin, D., & Ross, W. (1996). *Integrated strategic change: How organization development builds competitive advantage*. Reading, MA: Addison-Wesley. https://www.pearson.com/us/higher-education/program/Worley-Integrated-Strategic-Change-How-Organizational-Development-Builds-Competitive-Advantage-Pearson-Organizational-Development-Series/PGM2742.html

Zhang, Y., & Rajagopalan, N. (2010). Once an outsider, always an outsider? CEO origin, strategic change, and firm performance. *Strategic Management Journal, 31*, 334–346. https://doi.org/10.1002/smj.812. Retrieved from http://onlinelibrary.wiley.com/doi/10.1002/smj.812/full

Introduction to Neuroscience and Change

3

3.1 What Is Neuroscience?

The brain is a hugely complex entity and understanding how it functions is the principal objective of neuroscience. Neuroscience is a rapidly emerging field, and the rate of development has increased dramatically in the past decade (Jorgenson et al., 2015). We have learned more about the brain in the last decade than in all the previous centuries combined (NINDS, 2016). Every day new tools are developed and applied to enable a better understanding of the brain.

In this book, we tap into basic and exciting knowledge of this complex field. We in no way pretend to be expert neuroscientists. We are practitioners in the field of organisational change seeking new ways of improving implementation of change. We find the insights in neuroscience and neuro-leadership to be very useful and are sharing this with others who might have a desire to implement change successfully.

Neuroscience (sometimes also referred to as neural science) is the study of the nervous system (the brain and the spinal cord) and its effect on cognitive functions (how we think) and human behaviour (how we behave) (Brazier, 2018; Carmichael, 2013). Neuroscientists focus on the brain and its impact on behaviour and cognitive (thinking) functions. Although the focus of neuroscience might include studying the nervous system when people have neurological, psychiatric and neurodevelopmental disorders, the emphasis in this volume is on the normal functioning of the brain and the nervous system.

Imaging technologies such as positron emission tomography (PET), functional magnetic resonance imaging (fMRI) and quantitative electroencephalography (QEEG) have made it possible for scientists to detect neural connections in the human brain. An increased body of theoretical knowledge connecting the brain (the physical organ) to the mind (our consciousness helping us act, think, feel and perceive) has been developed using advanced computer analysis. These technologies support the study of neuroscience and thus scientists have gained a far more precise view of human nature and behaviour change. These technologies have enabled psychology (the study of the human mind and human behaviour) and neuroscience

© Springer Nature Switzerland AG 2020
C. B. Scheepers, S. Swart, *Change Leadership in Emerging Markets*, Future of Business and Finance, https://doi.org/10.1007/978-3-030-40846-6_3

(the study of the anatomy and physiology of the brain) to be integrated (Rock & Schwartz, 2006).

Neuroscience has become more accessible to the mainstream public and researchers, educators and change leaders. The public at large are rapidly translating the insights gained into practical applications at work to achieve higher levels of performance. Knowledge about how the brain functions gives us a deeper insight into assisting ourselves and the organisations in which we function to optimise performance.

The implications of this new research are particularly relevant for organisational change leaders. It is now clear that human behaviour in the workplace is not as simple as previously thought. It also explains why many leadership efforts and organisational change initiatives fail. Leaders who understand the recent breakthroughs in neuroscience can use this knowledge to lead and influence successful change initiatives. Neuroscience considers the physiological nature of the brain and how it predisposes people to resist change and accept and reject some forms of leadership.

However, the fact that we use science to understand human behaviour does not imply that it can be applied as pure science. There remains a great deal of art in it. Although neuroscience assists us in understanding human behaviour and how to manage change more effectively, we do acknowledge that complicated scientific findings can end up being oversimplified and often misinterpreted. Still, the body of evidence suggests neuroscience has the power to influence how leaders lead, followers follow, how people manage change and how change can be implemented more effectively. Therefore, it is beneficial for us to live with an informed view of the brain. Our experience in leading and coaching change has proved that knowing more about the brain facilitates greater success in communicating and implementing change initiatives.

To improve our understanding of the way in which the brain functions, a basic knowledge of brain concepts is required. This does not imply detailed, in-depth studying of brain anatomy or physiology but rather an overview of how certain parts of the brain function together to deliver certain results. The section, Brain Basics explores this knowledge in more detail.

3.2   How Neuroscience Will Be Used in This Book

As authors of this volume, we believe that neuroscience has a considerable contribution to make to implementing change more effectively. We see it as an exciting and cutting-edge field that can help all stakeholders in the change process deal better with change on a personal, team, organisational and even societal level.

We have therefore decided to research insights on how neuroscience can contribute to each of the ten enablers. For each of the ten enablers, we included a section called *Neuroscience Insights into the Enabler*. This will empower change leaders with knowledge on how knowing the brain can help apply each of the ten enablers with greater success.

We are not claiming to be experts in the field of neuroscience or neurobiology, and this is by no means another volume on neuroscience. Our objective here is primarily to search for knowledge that will enable us to improve the success rate of change projects.

To ensure building blocks are in place to understand the neuroscience insights for each enabler, some fundamental **Brain Basics** will now be discussed.

3.3   Brain Basics

Eagleman (2011) in his book, *Incognito*, provides a beautiful picture of the complexity of the brain. He believes the brain to be the most complex machine ever discovered in the universe. Apart from the fact that the brain consists of hundreds of billions of cells called neurons and glia, each of these cells is as complicated as a city and in each cubic centimetre of brain tissue, there are more connections than there are stars in the Milky Way. Siegel defines the brain as not only what is in the skull, but the extended network of nerves that process complex information in the brain, the intestines and all the other major organ systems of the body (Siegel, 2011).

The brain itself is surprisingly heavy—it weighs between 1.3 and 1.5 kg, yet it is very soft and vulnerable. To protect this vulnerable machine, it is cased inside the skull (called the cranium) and is protected by three membranes (the dura mater, arachnoid and the pia mater). Cerebrospinal fluid (CSF) is found between the outer membranes, around and inside the brain.

The video clip below will give the reader insight into what a brain looks like a couple of minutes after it has been removed from a deceased person. It is not recommended for sensitive viewers.

YouTube Clip: The Unfixed Brain by Suzanne Stensaas

https://www.youtube.com/watch?v=jHxyP-nUhUY

When you open the brain, you will see grey matter. The grey matter is composed mainly of cell bodies or neurons. The neurons are the basic building blocks of the brain, and we have approximately a hundred billion neurons (Arden, 2010). Neurons are brain cells that are in constant connection with other neurons. These connections can be either long-lasting or instantaneous connections that can form and then disperse. Each neuron develops "little arms" called dendrites that receive the messages from other neurons and an axon that sends information away from the cell body. White matter can also be observed in the brain.

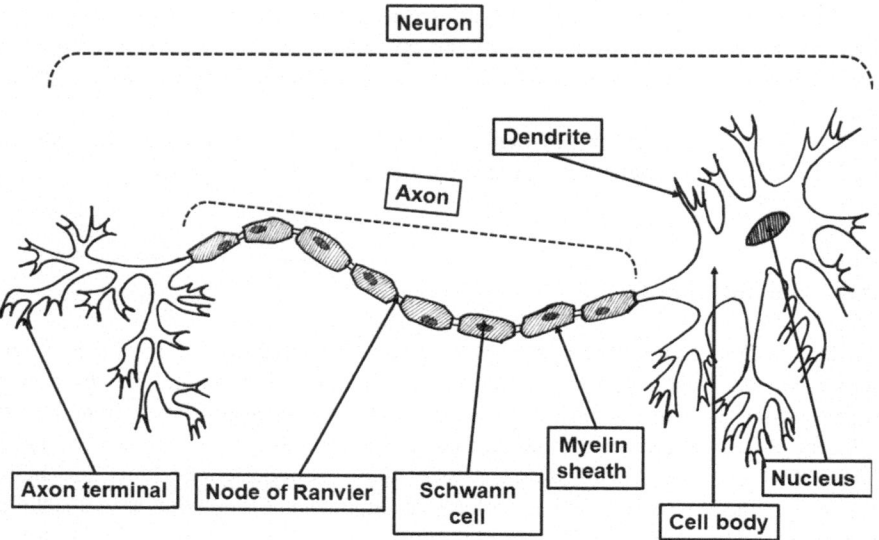

Fig. 3.1 Neuron with axon (Authors' own)

Figure 3.1 represents the neuron and axon that connect neurons with each other.

At the end of each dendrite and axon, is a microscopic gap called a synapse that produces a chemical substance or neurotransmitter that is used to receive or transmit information from one cell to another. The synapse allows communication between neurons. A neurotransmitter is a chemical that relays signals from one neuron to the next (Wanjek, 2014).

Our brain consists of more than one hundred billion interconnected neurons stuffed into a small, skull-enclosed space. It is both dense and intricate. Each of the neurons has ten thousand connections (synapses) linking to other neurons. In the skull portion alone, there are hundreds of trillions of connections linking the various neural groupings into a vast spider-web-like network (Siegel, 2011).

When several neurons interconnect, it is called a biological neural network. To illustrate the complexity of these neural networks it has been estimated that the number of possible combinations of these connections sending information is $10^{1000000}$. The number of atoms in the universe is estimated at 10^{80}.

The good news for us in the field of change is that the brain is not fixed and hardwired but is seen to be quite flexible or "plastic". It is constantly rewired by experiences throughout life (Arden, 2010). The concept of neuroplasticity—the ability of the brain to change throughout an individual's life—radically changed the paradigm that the brain remained static during adulthood after significant development in early childhood. Konorski first used the term *plasticity* in his book *Conditioned Reflexes and Neuron Organization* (Konorski, 1948). Siegel (2006) defines neuroplasticity as the ability of the brain to be altered by focusing attention in constructive ways. The change in neural connectivity induced by experience may be the fundamental way in which psychotherapy alters the brain (Siegel, 2006). Neuroplasticity reveals how the brain's interconnectedness can change throughout a lifespan. Where attention goes, neural firing occurs; where neurons fire, connections are made (Siegel, 2006).

The concept of neuroplasticity offers a massive contribution to those involved in change. We have the power to change the "wiring" in our brains. The idea is that attention is the active ingredient that changes the brain (Rock, 2009a). The power is in the focus. The problem is that attention does not go to one place and stays there. Attention has to be forced. Changing the brain is difficult. Enough effort has to be made to focus your attention in new ways. When you change your attention, you are facilitating self-directed neuroplasticity. Self-directed neuroplasticity is at the heart of real change.

3.4 The Two Brain Systems

Daniel Kahneman in his book *Thinking, Fast and Slow* (Kahneman, 2011) suggests that the brain operates using two systems. The first he calls *the automatic system* and the second, *the reflective system*. System 1 is effortless, subconscious, skilled, associative and fast. System 2 factors abstraction, follows the rules, is self-aware, deductive and effortful. System 1 operates on an always-on basis, makes automatic decisions and reverts to fight, flight or freeze when experiencing a threat. System 2 weighs up options presented by system 1 but makes the final decisions on where attention will be focused. Almost everything we consciously decide on is based on automatic reactions and suggestions fed to us by System 1 (Cooper, 2016).

3.5 Key Parts of the Brain

Brain functions became known to scientists as a result of damage, disease, accidents, operations and neural disorders (Swaab, 2014). The brain is divided into specific parts each performing a unique task, for example processing a specific sound or responding to a threatening experience. Each of these sections is made up of brain cells functioning together. Communication routes for brain cells are created by these cells forming connections with cells in other functional units. Imaging technology can map brain regions responsible for specific functions and behaviours (APA, 2014).

However, we cannot contribute one brain function such as attention, to only one part of the brain because the different parts of the brain operate as a whole system. We have to understand that the brain is a complex system. We will attempt to highlight the core functions of certain parts of the brain to help us understand the workings of this complex system.

The brain is composed of three key parts: **the cerebrum, cerebellum and the brain stem** (Fig. 3.2).

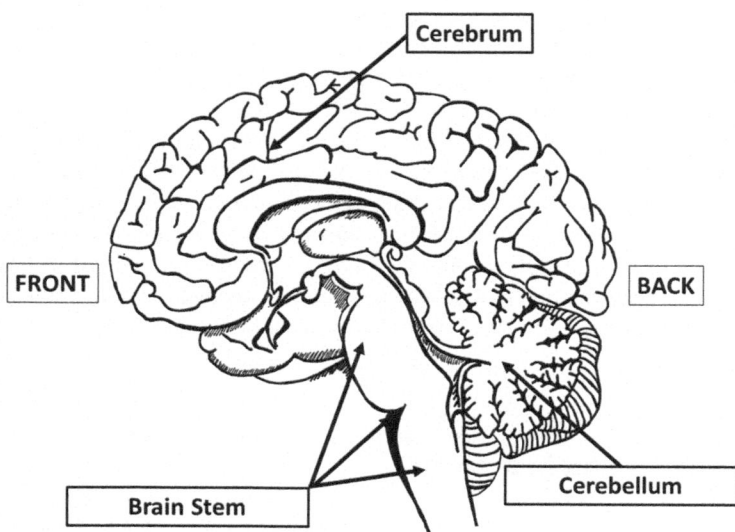

Fig. 3.2 Cerebrum, cerebellum and brain stem (Authors' own)

The **cerebrum** is the largest part of the brain, consisting of two hemispheres (left and right) and is divided into four lobes: frontal, parietal, temporal and occipital. It performs higher functions like interpreting our senses, enable us to talk and reason, feel emotions and learn new things. Figure 3.3 contains the key functions of the different lobes of the brain.

The surface of the cerebrum is called the **cerebral cortex**—the entire wrinkly outer top part of the brain. It consists of the neocortex (90%), the hippocampus and parts of the cingulate cortex. The neocortex contains the **prefrontal cortex (PFC)** in the very front of our brain, behind our forehead, involved in "executive functions" such as planning, goals and actions and the **medial prefrontal cortex (mPFC)**. Siegel (2007) lists the functions of the mPFC as body regulation, attuned communication, emotional balance/affect regulation, response flexibility, empathy, insight or self-knowing awareness, fear modulation/fear extinction, intuition and morality.

The **cerebellum** is located under the cerebrum. Its function is to coordinate muscle movements, maintain posture and balance. The **brainstem** includes the midbrain, pons and medulla. It acts as a relay centre connecting the cerebrum and cerebellum to the spinal cord. It performs many automatic functions such as breathing, heart rate, body temperature, wake and sleep cycles, digestion, sneezing, coughing, vomiting and swallowing. Ten of the 12 cranial nerves originate in the brainstem (Goldberg, 2010).

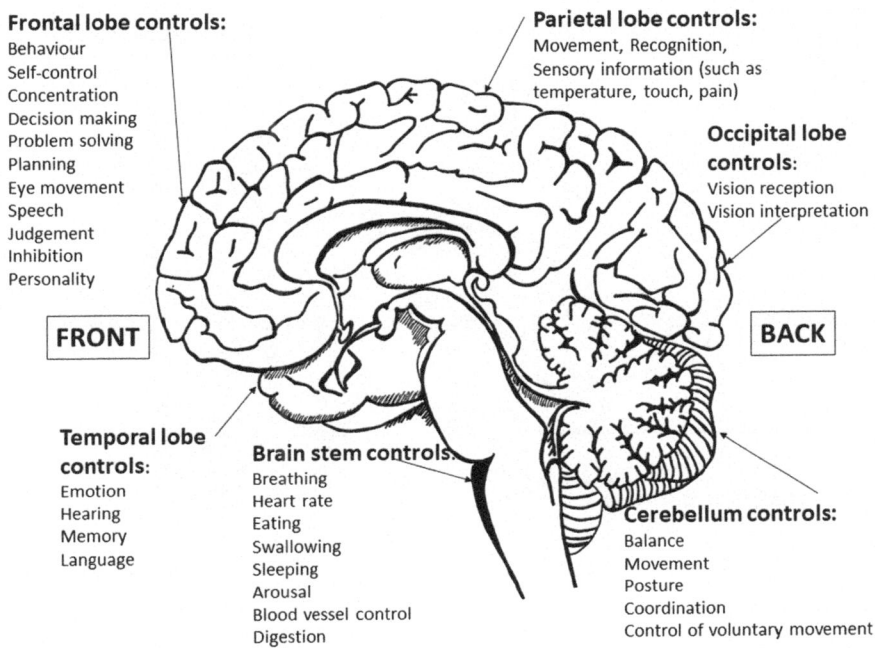

Frontal lobe controls:
Behaviour
Self-control
Concentration
Decision making
Problem solving
Planning
Eye movement
Speech
Judgement
Inhibition
Personality

Parietal lobe controls:
Movement, Recognition,
Sensory information (such as
temperature, touch, pain)

Occipital lobe controls:
Vision reception
Vision interpretation

FRONT

BACK

Temporal lobe controls:
Emotion
Hearing
Memory
Language

Brain stem controls:
Breathing
Heart rate
Eating
Swallowing
Sleeping
Arousal
Blood vessel control
Digestion

Cerebellum controls:
Balance
Movement
Posture
Coordination
Control of voluntary movement

Fig. 3.3 Different brain functions of the lobes (Authors' own)

The brain responds to being hungry, rejected or adopting change with similar neuronal activity (Lieberman et al., 2004).

3.6 The Triune Brain

A model explaining the evolution of the brain was developed in the 1960s by an American physician and neuroscientist, Dr. Paul D. MacLean. In his book *The Triune Brain in Evolution: Role in Paleocerebral Functions* (1990), he explains that the skull holds three brains, each a representation of a stage in the evolutionary process. Although these three brains operate as an interconnected system, each has their specific functions and capabilities. He defined the three parts as the neocortex or neo-mammalian brain, the limbic system or paleo-mammalian system and the reptilian brain (Fig. 3.4).

Although MacLean's model is regarded by some scholars as an oversimplified organising theme, the authors of this volume still believe it has potential because of its simplicity. It enables a framework from which the layperson can attempt to

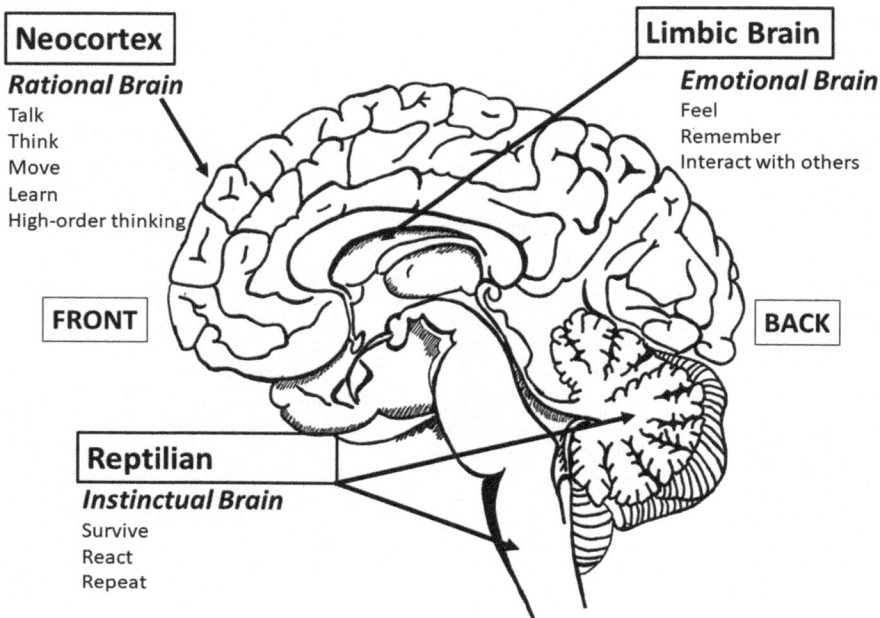

Neocortex

Rational Brain
Talk
Think
Move
Learn
High-order thinking

Limbic Brain

Emotional Brain
Feel
Remember
Interact with others

FRONT

BACK

Reptilian

Instinctual Brain
Survive
React
Repeat

Fig. 3.4 The Triune Brain (Authors' own)

understand the complexity of the brain as an organising system and to manage emotions, learning, focus and change in general.

The limbic system is involved in controlling many of our emotions, storing memories and regulating hormones. It is the centre of our fears and desires and influences our peripheral nervous and endocrine system (Bailey, 2018).

Daniel Siegel in his YouTube clip, *"What is Mindsight?"* states that the function of the Limbic system is to:

- Appraise significance
- Create motivational states
- Create memory systems
- Emotions
- Attachments

YouTube Clip: What is Mindsight? by Daniel Siegel

https://www.youtube.com/watch?v=IKwQuGCPeFk (2 min)
https://www.youtube.com/watch?v=0jwGU7h2HdY (10:38 min)

3.7 Neurotransmitters

Although there are approximately 100 different neurotransmitters and related neurochemicals in the brain (Arden, 2010), the most common neurotransmitters and their functions will now be discussed.

3.7.1 Dopamine

Dopamine is referred to as the reward neuromodulator (Goldberg, 2009) or the chemical of desire (Rock, 2009a). Dopamine is a monoamine neurotransmitter and is one of the most active neurotransmitters in the brain's motivation and reward system. It is interesting to note that solving any problem creates a little rush of dopamine (Rock, 2009a).

Dopamine is also called the *chemical of interest* and is released when the orbital cortex detects something unexpected, such as novelty, or if gratification or reward is experienced. When humans smell food, dopamine is released to increase appetite. Dopamine is more prevalent in the left hemisphere than in right hemisphere (Goldberg, 2009). When something goes well, dopamine is released (Eagleman, 2015).

Dopamine is also responsible for motivating you towards your desired goal. The anticipation of the reward releases dopamine which in turn creates energy to move you closer to the reward. When the reward is finally obtained, another dopamine release is activated (Hampton, 2015).

3.7.2 Serotonin

Serotonin is another monoamine neurotransmitter and has been called the confidence molecule. About 90% of all serotonin in the body is used to regulate intestine movements (King, 2009). It also helps soothe anxiety, depression and mood fluctuations (Siegel, 2011). It is released when we are feeling stressed or when we feel deprived of nurturing. It regulates moods, sleep and digestion (Hanson & Menius, 2009). It is necessary for memory processing and learning.

The molecule serotonin figures in cardiovascular regulation, respiration, circadian rhythm, sleep–wake cycles, appetite, aggression, sexual behaviour, sensorimotor reactivity, pain sensitivity and reward learning (Churchland, 2011).

When you feel significant or important, serotonin is released. The brain then repeats the behaviour that led to feeling significant to maintain the release of serotonin. Your history of gaining significance forms neural pathways leading to repeating the behaviour.

If you're in a good mood, you've got serotonin to thank.
If you're in a bad mood, you've got serotonin to blame (Hampton, 2015).

When serotonin levels are low, it can lead to depression and loneliness. Anti-depressants such as Serotonin-Specific Reuptake Inhibitors (SSRIs) aim at increasing the effect of serotonin (Hanson & Menius, 2009). Serotonin is kept in the synapse for longer than usual periods. A more natural way of producing serotonin is by exposing yourself to sunshine for 20 min per day. The skin absorbs the sun's ultraviolet rays producing vitamin D and serotonin (Hampton, 2015).

3.7.3 Cortisol

Cortisol is released by the adrenal glands during the stress response (Hanson & Menius, 2009). If cortisol levels are raised, the amygdala and the outer shell of the nucleus accumbens (NA) are stimulated. Cortisol further inhibits the hippocampus that could result in a heightened need for reward and gratification. When cortisol is released, it increases blood sugar, it can suppress the immune system, it can help with metabolism and it can decrease bone formation.

Once released into the bloodstream, cortisol triggers strong reactions throughout the entire body, ranging from cardiovascular activity to the immune system and memory formation. Once the threat has passed, cortisol levels drop, and these systems return to baseline levels. However, when stress becomes chronic—as in the case of burnout—the body fails to return to normal, leading to a cascade of potential health problems (Michel, 2016).

3.7.4 Norepinephrine/Noradrenalin

Noradrenalin has been described as the *chemical of alertness and fear*. It underlies the fight-or-flight response and is released when humans feel fearful and alert. The release of noradrenalin can affect heart rate, stimulate the excretion of glucose, sends blood to skeletal muscles, can increase blood flow to the brain and can raise blood pressure. It also induces arousal.

3.7.5 Oxytocin

Oxytocin is a neuropeptide that promotes nurturing behaviours towards children and bonding in couples. It is also associated with closeness and love. Research has shown that men release less oxytocin than women (Hanson & Menius, 2009). It is sometimes called the *cuddle hormone* and is released when humans feel close to someone, loved, attached to someone and when trust and comfort are experienced (Siegel, 2011). Skin-to-skin contact can also release oxytocin.

During research studies conducted on cocaine-using mothers, their oxytocin levels and maternal behaviour showed significantly lower levels than those of non-using mothers. When fathers used a nasal spray to inject oxytocin, they showed significantly more love and affection towards mothers and children. In a study in which participants were required to play an economic game with the objective of winning, those who were administered oxytocin, were found to be more successful as they trusted others more. Oxytocin nasal sprays can now be bought online (Harman, 2015). Oxytocin can be released naturally through social bonding, eye contact, attentiveness or interaction with a pet.

Past events in which trust was broken could result in neural pathways being formed that prevents the release of oxytocin. To change this will require rewriting of new pathways building trust through interaction (Hampton, 2015).

3.7.6 Acetylcholine

Acetylcholine promotes wakefulness, memory and learning, sexual performance, appetite control and release of growth hormones.

3.7.7 Endorphins

Endorphins literally mean "self-produced morphine" as it has an opiate-like chemical structure, masks pain or discomfort, and is associated with the fight or flight response. Endorphins are found in the pituitary gland, other parts of the brain and throughout the nervous system. It helps us survive in emergencies.

Endorphins are released when we laugh, physically exert ourselves, have sexual intercourse and during orgasms. The anticipation and expectation of the release can also lead to a release of endorphins. The smell of vanilla and lavender and eating chocolate has been associated with the release of endorphins.

Table 3.1 provides a summary of the different neurotransmitters.

Table 3.1 Chemicals in the brain

Neurotransmitter	
Dopamine	Chemical of interest
Serotonin	Chemical of confidence
Cortisol	Chemical of stress
Norepinephrine/Noradrenalin	Chemical of excitement
Oxytocin	Chemical of cuddles
Acetylcholine	Chemical of alertness
Endorphins	Chemical of survival

3.8   Brain Principles

The following key brain principles will guide the neuroscience discussion in this book.

3.8.1   Key Organising Principle of the Brain: Minimise Threat, Maximise Reward

As far as can be determined, it seems as though Democritus (460–370 BCE) was the first person to conclude that humans are motivated by either seeking rewards or avoiding pain (Berkman, 2012). The brain's primary function is our survival, and its primary objective is to keep us safe (Gordon, 2000). To survive, a lot of attention needs to be given to sensing potential dangers and reacting quickly and efficiently. When the limbic system in the brain observes something that it might perceive as being dangerous, it lights up far more intensely than when it senses a reward. The stimulation also happens faster, lasts longer and does not fade as quickly (Rock, 2009a). In fact, it has been found that humans scan our environment five times more for threat than for pleasure or reward (Baumeister & Bratslavsky, 2001). That makes us naturally quite negative and explains why being positive is such arduous work. It has been said that we walk towards rewards but run away from threats.

Because we are programmed for survival, the brain seeks to minimise danger and maximise reward. This is the fundamental organising principle of how the brain functions (Gordon, 2008; Rock & Ringleb, 2013). Rock (2009a) coined the term, *the toward and away principle* stating that the brain classifies the world into things that will either hurt you or help you stay alive. The brain is thus determined to minimise danger (an away response) and maximise reward (a toward response).

The brain organises the world into things that will either harm us or things that will help us (Rock, 2009a). Gordon (2008) confirms this when he states that much of our motivation driving social behaviour is governed by an overarching organising principle of minimising threat and maximising reward.

The limbic system scans data streaming into the brain, telling us what to pay attention to and in what way (Rock, 2009a). When a person encounters a stimulus, their brain will tag the stimulus as "good" and engage or "bad" and disengage. The brain has designed this towards and away system as a survival instrument to help us remember instantaneously what is good and bad in the environment (Rock, 2009a) and respond to it immediately.

Toward responses include curiosity, happiness and contentment. Away responses include anxiety, sadness and fear. The limbic system continually makes toward and away decisions. These decisions happen automatically before we are consciously aware of them (Rock, 2009a). The limbic system fires up far more intensely when it perceives danger compared to when it senses reward. It lasts longer, is faster and harder to budge. The *toward* emotions are subtler, more easily displayed and harder to build on.

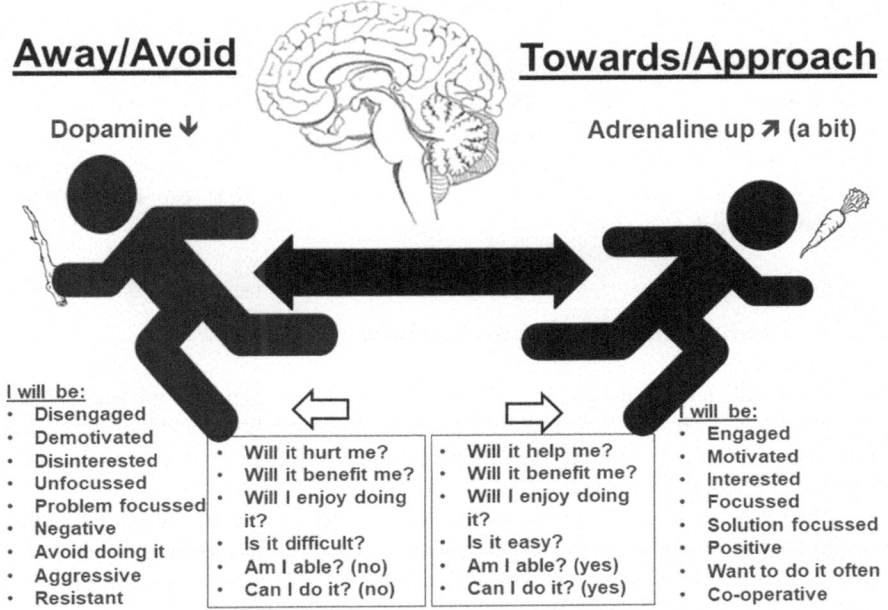

Fig. 3.5 Towards and away organising principle of the brain (Authors' own synthesis based on Rock (2009a))

The avoid-approach response has a dramatic effect on our perceptions, our ability to problem solve, make decisions, manage stress, collaborate with others and be motivated (Rock, 2009a).

Figure 3.5 explains the avoid-approach/away-towards notion discussed above.

Figure 3.5 aims to demonstrate that the brain is programmed to perceive a change as either something it should go towards or run away from. People perceive the change brought to them by change leaders as either a threat or a reward. If they see the change as something that might harm them, or something they might not be able to do, or that it might be too difficult to cope with, they will metaphorically run away from the change and resist it in a number of ways. Change leaders need to get stakeholders to "run" towards the change, i.e. to understand how the change will benefit them and provide resources and skills development to get the stakeholder to want to support the change. The fact that dopamine, the pleasure hormone, decreases when the brain perceives the change as a threat, explains why threats will be avoided. The fact that adrenaline is released when we see the change as something positive, demonstrates why we will have the energy to do what we perceive as something that will serve as a benefit to us.

3.8.2   The Brain as an Error Detector

The brain is also programmed to look out for dangers to prevent threats from the environment. It is continually seeking deviations from the environment as it has come to be expected. The orbital frontal cortex (in close proximity to amygdala—the brain's fear circuit) generates error signals and then involves the anterior cingulate cortex (ACC) and other frontal brain areas to interpret the fear response from the amygdala (Patsenka, 2010).

3.8.3   The Brain Is a Prediction Machine

Uncertainty also triggers alarm bells in our brain. Ambiguity and uncertainty generate threats and fears and force the brain to make predictions. That makes the brain feel in control. Anxiety due to uncertainty weakens cognitive and social functioning (Salati & Leoni, 2017).

To facilitate survival, the brain devotes a lot of attention to predicting what will happen next. From birth, the brain perceives patterns from the outside world, stores these as memories and uses this data to predict what will happen from moment to moment. Hawkins (2004) believes that prediction is the primary function of the neocortex and is the foundation of intelligence.

The following text is an example of how the brain picks up patterns and makes sense of it.

> Olny srmat poelpe can raed tihs.
> cdnuolt blveiee taht I cluod aulaclty uesdnatnrd waht I was rdanieg.
> The phaonmneal pweor of the hmuan mnid, aoccdrnig to a rscheearch at Cmabrigde Uinervtisy,
> it deosn't mttaer in waht oredr the ltteers in a wrod are, the olny iprmoatnt tihng is taht the frist and lsat ltteer be in the rghit pclae. The rset can be a taotl mses and you can sitll raed it wouthit a porbelm.
> Tihs is bcuseae the huamn mnid deos not raed ervey lteter by istlef, but the wrod as a wlohe.

3.8.4   The Brain Prefers Certainty and Routine

Any input into the brain that does not fit a stored pattern is perceived as dangerous for survival and will result in an "away" reaction. Therefore, the brain prefers certainty. Routine actions are stored in the basal ganglia requiring very little energy to be exerted. New, unlearnt behaviours require substantial energy resources, and the brain will prefer not to participate in such behaviours. This is why learning a new skill can be such a challenge. Rock (2009b) believes that uncertainty feels like a threat to one's life.

Change leaders needs to understand that they have to be aware of their words, emotions and conduct during times of uncertainty so prevalent during change processes as it can have an enormous effect on the success of the project. The brain craves information—to make predictions and draw conclusions—to survive. Time spent listening and providing information to stakeholders will never be in vain during times of uncertainty (Salati & Leoni, 2017).

Given the principles mentioned above, is it clear that:

• The brain likes repetition
• The brain likes comfort
• The brain is risk averse
• The brain wants to minimise danger
• The brain loses "it" if it does not use "it"
• The brain dislikes surprises
• The brain likes fun and excitement (as long as it is not a threat)
• The brain likes rewards (as defined by the individual himself)

3.9   Neuroscience and Change

It could be argued that developments in neuroscience have made a significant impact on the field of Change Management, perhaps the most significant since its inception. Now it can be scientifically proven that "one can teach an old dog new tricks" and that "a leopard can indeed change its spots". Rock concurs when he states that "we are at the beginning of a new theoretical framework for change that draws from the science of the brain" (Rock, 2009a, p. 224).

Understanding that the brain is "programmed" to seek homeostasis (the natural movement of any organism towards equilibrium and away from change) and comfort, further helps explain why we find change so difficult. If a complex system (such as the human mind or an organisation) moves too much in one direction, such a system will move with a compensatory movement in the opposite direction (Rock & Page, 2009). Change requires neural pathways to be re-circuited and that requires energy and focus. Only repeated, purposeful and focused attention leads to long-lasting change.

The good news, however, is that the brain is not fixed and hardwired, but is quite plastic and is rewired continuously by experiences throughout life (Arden, 2010; Doidge, 2007). The concept of *neuroplasticity* brought about an understanding that lasting changes to the brain throughout an individual's life course are possible (see Sect. 3.3 above). If the brain can change, then human beings can change, which implies that organisations can change, and even societies can change. It is also a relief to know that the brain reaches its peak in middle adulthood and people can continue to sharpen their brains and even grow new brain cells indefinitely (Arden, 2010).

Now neuroscience can help those of us in the field of change understand why people behave the way they do. It can also rationalise the emotions experienced during the change. This knowledge could lead to a reduction in fear (Rock & Page, 2009). It could also normalise behaviour (Rock & Page, 2009) and increase the rate of success in change implementation.

3.10   Neuroscience and Organisations

Organisational neuroscience (ON) uses neuroscience research and knowledge of how the brain works to expand the general knowledge of management studies and applications. It is useful to managers, trainers, consultants and psychologists (Salati & Leoni, 2017).

ON is an emerging research domain within the field of management that integrates organisational behaviour with neuroscience. Stimulated by recent advances in neuroimaging, ON involves the identification of neural substrates and their functioning as they relate to social-cognitive phenomena in organisational contexts. Although a relatively new approach in management research, ON—also referred to as organisational cognitive neuroscience (OCN)—is rooted in social neuroscience which emerged as a field in the 1980s by integrating the fields of social psychology and neuroscience. A strong complement to organisational behaviour, social neuroscience entails a multilevel approach involving factors both internal to the individual (individual differences, internal mental processes) and external to the individual (environmental factors, organisational contexts) (Passarelli, 2016).

> **YouTube Clip: Neuroscience for Organizational Change by Hilary Scarlet**
>
>
>
> https://www.youtube.com/watch?v=0Wk7p2GTsQo&
> list=PLxgZABW7qme8YNwHzZjIPwiWQgTZZonuN

3.11   Critiques of Neuroscience

In recent years, neurocriticism has become an emerging field with people such as the neurocritic, James Coyne, the neuroskeptic, Raymond Tallis and David Brooks, warning against real neuroscience being used to make false claims in an attempt to enter the pop-psychology arena (Jaffe, 2013).

Satel & Lilienfeld in their book, *Brainwashed: The Seductive Appeal of Mindless Neuroscience* also warn their readers to take care not to see neuroscience as the panacea, being the answer to all life's questions. They state that although brains scans can be valuable, they are highly complex systems and can easily be used to manipulate the truth. They further warn against a narrow, "neurocentric" focus and urge us to remember that there is a myriad of factors influencing our thoughts and behaviour. We also need to be on the lookout for "neuroentrepreneurs", and "over-zealous neuroscientists" who want to claim that neuroscience has the capacity to explain what is going on in our minds (Satel & Lilienfeld, 2013, p. 3).

The authors of this volume agree that the brain is an incredibly complex organ and that many brain regions and structures are involved in many different tasks. We also recognise that scientists are only now starting to explore the vast unknown of the human mind and there is much to be revealed and to learn. We see neuroscience as one of a multitude of disciplines needed as input to understanding the complexity of human behaviour during change. We do, however, believe it is an exciting new field that we want to use to gain insights and help us lead change successfully. We urge our readers to read widely and study continuously to stay abreast of new discoveries and in so doing become lifelong learners in leading change.

3.12   Conclusion

In this chapter, the authors aimed to introduce the reader to the basic building blocks of neuroscience to enable a high-level understanding of the topic and serve as a preparation for the section, *Neuroscience Insights into the Enabler* which will follow in Chaps. 5–14. Basic brain anatomy was discussed, and the most important neurotransmitters and neuroimage technologies were introduced. The section, *Brain Principles* contained the most important ways in which the knowledge of the brain can assist in understanding how humans function during times of change. How neuroscience improves our understanding of change management in organisations was also addressed, and the chapter ends with creating awareness that criticism of the field of neuroscience exists.

References

APA. (2014, August). *Scanning the brain: New technologies shed light on the brain's form and function*. American Psychological Association: Psychology Science in Action. Retrieved July 27, 2019, from https://www.apa.org/action/resources/research-in-action/scan

Arden, J. B. (2010). *Rewire your brain: Think your way to a better life*. Hoboken, NJ: Wiley. https://brainmaster.com/software/pubs/brain/Rewire%20Your%20Brain.pdf

Bailey, R. (2018). The limbic system of the brain: The amygdala, hypothalamus, and thalamus. *ThoughtCo*. Retrieved July 26, 2019, from https://www.thoughtco.com/limbic-system-anatomy-373200

Baumeister, B. F., & Bratslavsky, E. (2001). *Bad is stronger than good*. Cleveland, OH: Case Western Reserve University. https://journals.sagepub.com/doi/abs/10.1037/1089-2680.5.4.323

Berkman, E. T. (2012, November 12). Goals, motivation and the brain. What can neuroscience tell us about how to succeed at our goals? *Psychology Today*. Retrieved from https://www.psychologytoday.com/blog/the-motivated-brain/201211/goals-motivation-and-the-brain

Brazier, Y. (2018, June 26). *What is neuroscience?* Medical News Today. https://www.medicalnewstoday.com/articles/248680

Carmichael, J. (2013, July 16). *The popular science guide to neuroscience*. Popular Science. https://www.popsci.com/science/article/2013-07/popular-science-guide-neuroscience/

Churchland, P. (2011). *Braintrust: What neuroscience tells us about morality*. Princeton, NJ: Princeton University Press. https://www.amazon.com/Braintrust-Neuroscience-Tells-about-Morality/dp/069113703X

Cooper, B. B. (2016). *The two brain systems that control our attention: The science of gaining focus*. Retrieved July 27, 2019, from https://blog.bufferapp.com/the-science-of-focus-and-how-to-improve-your-attention-span

Doidge, N. (2007). *The brain that changes itself: Stories of personal triumph from the Frontiers of brain science*. New York, NY: Penguin Paperback. https://www.amazon.com/Brain-That-Changes-Itself-Frontiers/dp/0143113100

Eagleman, D. (2011). *Incognito: The secret lives of the brain*. New York, NY: Random House. https://www.amazon.com/Incognito-Secret-Lives-David-Eagleman/dp/0307389928

Eagleman, D. (2015). *The brain: The story of you*. Edinburgh: Canongate Books. https://www.amazon.com/Brain-Story-You-David-Eagleman/dp/0525433449

Goldberg, E. (2009). *The new executive brain: Frontal lobes and a complex world*. New York: Oxford University Press. https://www.amazon.com/New-Executive-Brain-Frontal-Complex/dp/0195329406

Goldberg, S. (2010). *Clinical neuroanatomy made ridiculously simple* (4th ed.). Miami, FL: MedMaster. https://www.amazon.com/Clinical-Neuroanatomy-Made-Ridiculously-Simple/dp/1935660195

Gordon, E. (2000). *Integrative neuroscience: Bringing together biological, psychological and clinical models of the human brain*. Amsterdam: Harwood Academic Publishers. https://www.amazon.com/Integrative-Neuroscience-Bringing-Biological-Psychological/dp/9058230554

Gordon, E. (2008). Neuroleadership and integrative neuroscience: "It's about validation stupid!". *Neuroleadership Journal, 1*, 71–80. https://acsg.co.za/sites/default/files/Emde_1_NeuroLeadership-and-Integrative.pdf

Hampton, D. (2015). *How happy happens in your brain: The best brain possible*. Retrieved July 26, 2019, from https://www.thebestbrainpossible.com/how-happy-happens-in-your-brain/

Hanson, R., & Menius, R. (2009). *Buddha's brain: The practical neuroscience of happiness, love & wisdom*. Oakland: New Harbinger Publications. https://www.amazon.com/Buddhas-Brain-Practical-Neuroscience-Happiness/dp/1491518669

Harman, O. (2015). The evolution of altruism. *The Chronicle of Higher Education*. Retrieved July 26, 2019, from https://www.chronicle.com/article/The-Evolution-of-Altruism-/151625

Hawkins, J. (2004). *On intelligence: How a new understanding of the brain will lead to the creation of truly intelligent machines*. New York, NY: Times Books. https://www.amazon.com/Intelligence-Understanding-Creation-Intelligent-Machines/dp/0805078533

Jaffe, D. J. (2013, August 6). Review: Brainwashed: The seductive appeal of mindless neuroscience. *Huffpost*. Retrieved July 27, 2019, from https://www.huffingtonpost.com/dj-jaffe/brainwashed-the-seductive_b_3712860.html

Jorgenson, L. A., Newsome, W. T., Anderson, D. J., Bargmann, C. I., Brown, E. N., Deisseroth, K., et al. (2015). The BRAIN Initiative: Developing technology to catalyse neuroscience discovery. *Philosophical Transactions of the Royal Society B: Biological Sciences, 370*(1668), 20140164. https://doi.org/10.1098/rstb.2014.0164

Kahneman, D. (2011). *Thinking, fast and slow*. New York: Farrar, Straus and Giroux. https://www. amazon.com/s?k=Kahneman%2C+D.+%282011%29.+Thinking%2C+fast+and+slow.+New +York%3A+Farrar%2C+Straus+and+Giroux.&i=stripbooks-intl-ship&ref=nb_sb_noss

King, M. W. (2009). Serotonin. The medical biochemistry page. Indiana university school of medicine. Retrieved December 1, 2009. http://themedicalbiochemistrypage.org/nerves.html#5ht.

Konorski, J. (1948). *Conditioned reflexes and neuron organization*. New York, NY: Cambridge University Press. https://onlinelibrary.wiley.com/doi/abs/10.1002/1097-4679%28195001% 296%3A1%3C107%3A%3AAID-JCLP2270060132%3E3.0.CO%3B2-0

Lieberman, M. D., Jarcho, J. M., Bierman, S., Naliboff, B. D., Suyenobu, B. Y., Mandelkern, M., et al. (2004). The neural correlates of placebo effects: A disruption account. *NeuroImage, 22*(1), 447–455. https://doi.org/10.1016/j.neuroimage.2004.01.037

MacLean, P. D. (1990). *The triune brain in evolution: Role in paleocerebral functions*. New York: Plenum. https://pubmed.ncbi.nlm.nih.gov/17797318/

Michel, A. (2016, January 29). Burnout and the brain. Association for Psychological Science. *The Observer*. Retrieved July 26, 2019, from https://www.psychologicalscience.org/observer/burn out-and-the-brain

NINDS. (2016). *Brain basics: Know your brain*. National Institute of Neurological Disorders and Stroke. Retrieved July 27, 2019, from https://www.ninds.nih.gov/Disorders/Patient-Caregiver-Education/Know-Your-Brain

Passarelli, A. M. (2016). Organizational neuroscience. https://doi.org/10.1093/OBO/ 9780199846740-0076. Retrieved July 27, 2019, from https://www.oxfordbibliographies.com/ view/document/obo-9780199846740/obo-9780199846740-0076.xml

Patsenka, A. G. (2010). *Neuroscience of error detection*. Ph.D. dissertation, Michigan State University. http://35.8.223.68/etd/1425/datastream/OBJ/view

Rock, D. (2009a). *Your brain at work: Strategies for overcoming distraction, regaining focus, and working smarter all day*. New York: HarperCollins. https://www.harpercollins.com/ 9780061771293/your-brain-at-work/

Rock, D. (2009b). *Easily distracted: Why it's hard to focus and what to do about it*. Psychology Today, 4 October 2009. https://www.psychologytoday.com/za/blog/your-brain-work/200910/ easily-distracted

Rock, D., & Page, L. J. (2009). *Coaching with the brain in mind: Foundations for practice*. Upper Saddle River, NJ: Wiley. https://www.wiley.com/en-us/Coaching+with+the+Brain+in+Mind% 3A+Foundations+for+Practice-p-9780470405680

Rock, D., & Ringleb, A. H. (2013). *Handbook of neuroleadership*. Lexington, KY: NeuroLeadership Institute. https://www.amazon.com/Handbook-NeuroLeadership-Dr-David-Rock/dp/1483925331

Rock, D., & Schwartz, J. (2006). The neuroscience of leadership. *Strategy Business, 43*, 72–82. https://www.strategy-business.com/article/06207?gko=f1af3

Salati, M. E., & Leoni, A. (2017). Neuroscience within companies: Some case studies. *Neuropsychological Trends, 21*(1), 23–33. https://www.ledonline.it/NeuropsychologicalTrends/allegati/ NeuropsychologicalTrends_21_Sala.pdf

Satel, S. L., & Lilienfeld, S. O. (2013). *Brainwashed: The seductive appeal of mindless neuroscience*. New York, NY: Basic Books. https://www.amazon.com/Brainwashed-Seductive-Appeal-Mindless-Neuroscience/dp/0465062911

Siegel, D. J. (2006). An interpersonal neurobiology approach to psychotherapy. *Psychiatric Annals, 36*(4), 248–252. https://www.healio.com/journals/psycann/2006-4-36-4/%7B231a1eb0-7230-4ff8-b173-c7f31c6b823f%7D/an-interpersonal-neurobiology-approach-to-psychotherapy

Siegel, D. J. (2007). *The mindful brain. Reflection and attunement in the cultivation of well-being*. New York: W&W Norton & Company. https://www.amazon.com/Mindful-Brain-Reflection-Attunement-Cultivation/dp/039370470X

Siegel, D. J. (2011). *Mindsight: The new science of personal transformation*. New York, NY: Bantam Books. https://www.amazon.com/Mindsight-New-Science-Personal-Transformation/ dp/0553386395

Swaab, D. F. (2014). We are our brains: A neurobiography of the brain, from the womb to Alzheimer's (J. Hedley-Prôle, Trans.). Spiegel & Grau: Random House. https://www.amazon.com/Are-Our-Brains-Neurobiography-Alzheimers/dp/0812992962

Wanjek, C. (2014, September 25). Feeling bummed? How disappointment works in the brain. *Livescience*. https://www.livescience.com/48022-disappointment-brain.html

Part II

Practical Application

The Ten Enablers Model

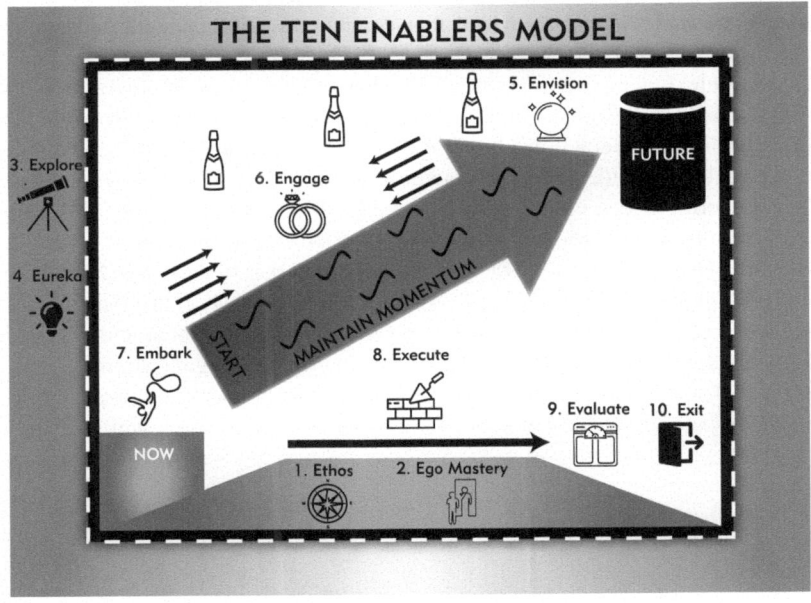

Change is a process which has to be managed.

(Kofi Annan, n.d.)

Electronic supplementary material The online version of this chapter (https://doi.org/10.1007/978-3-030-40846-6_4) contains supplementary material, which is available to authorized users.

4.1   Orientation to the Ten Enablers Model

Given the vast spectrum of information related to change leadership and management and observing the confusion of roles and titles so rife in practice, we decided to develop our own model to explain what is needed to be done in organisations to affect change. In the Ten Enablers Model we explore ten different steps required to bring about successful change. The Ten Enablers Model is the result of collectively spending more than 50 years in practice consulting to and leading a wide variety of change projects, as well as observing what makes some projects successful and what some projects lacked. The model has also been shared with literally thousands of managers and clients who gave feedback and improved the model throughout the years. Many different respondents from all over the emerging market world also added and contributed to the development of this model. We are thankful for these contributions and the collective intelligence which helped us develop this model. We believe it to be a robust framework for enabling change at an individual, team, organisational and societal level and that it integrates the concepts of leadership, management and change.

As the contextual environment in which change takes place in emerging markets are often volatile, messy and chaotic dealing with sometimes difficult workforce and complex leadership interactions, the Ten Enablers Model seeks to provide a holistic approach to dealing with change in emerging markets. It has been used successfully in the Southern African emerging market context, and the authors of this volume believe it can be used with great success in other emerging markets.

The model in its purest form was first introduced as part of a Change Management Course presented by AECI Ltd., South Africa in the late 1980s. It originated from the classic work of Kurt Lewin but was known as the four-box model and was widely used by managers and technical specialists throughout the organisation.

In Fig. 4.1, the horizontal axis indicates that change happens over time, while the vertical axis shows improvement in organisational success (in which ever way

Fig. 4.1 The four-box model (Authors' own adapted from Lewin (1947))

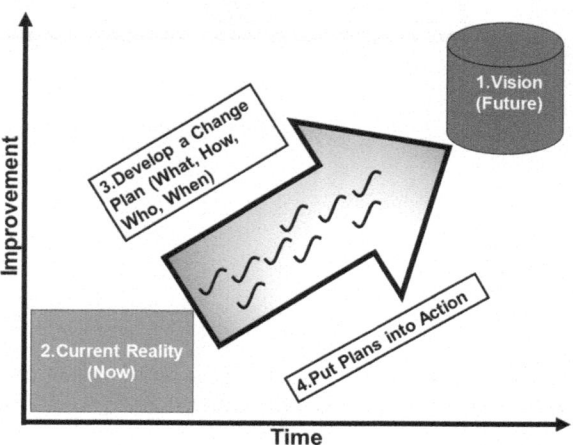

success might be defined by the organisation). In this model, the first step in the process is to ask the question: Where do we want to be? The second box addresses the issue: Where are we currently? The third defines: How will we get there? The "s" curves inside the big arrow indicates a set of integrated drivers or initiatives, each going through their own "s" life cycle. Finally, the fourth step in the process represents the actual actions being implemented after the planning.

Thus, the four steps in this process were defined as:

1. Create a shared vision with meaning (FUTURE)
2. Analyse the current reality (NOW)
3. Develop a change plan (WHAT, WHEN, WHO, HOW)
4. Put plans into actions—implement the change plan (DO IT)

Through the years the model morphed, incorporating additional elements. Many course participants, managers, change leaders, followers and clients applied the model and through iterative enhancements of the model, it has led to the development of the Ten Enablers Model. While the model is presented in this volume as a fait accompli, we regard it as work in progress and we are open to suggestions and improvements to be incorporated in future versions of the Ten Enablers Model. Figure 4.2 explains the model in more detail. Each of the ten essential actions in enabling successful change will now be introduced.

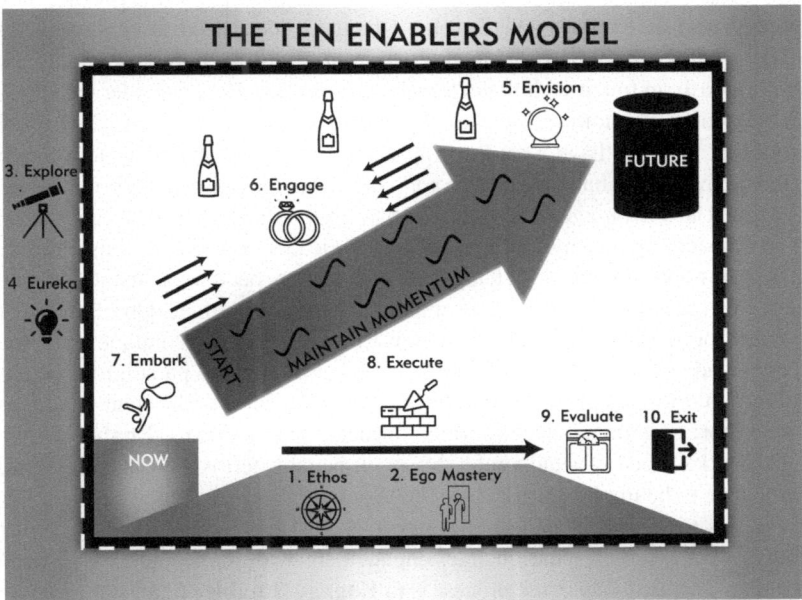

Fig. 4.2 The Ten Enablers Model (Authors' own)

4.2   Introduction to the Ten Enablers Model

The grey outer frame in Fig. 4.2 illustrates the environment or context in which the change takes place, while the white block inside the frame represents the organisation that is embarking on the change process. Note the dotted line separating the external environment and the organisation illustrating the porous nature of the interaction between the two entities.

The starting point of the model is the three-dimensional foundation represented by the trapezium at the bottom of the picture containing the first two elements Enabler 1, Ethos and Enabler 2, Ego Mastery. **Enabler 1, Ethos** is critical as a change process without a stable, ethical foundation could lead to chaos. If the Ethos element is lacking, the change could lead to deterioration with disastrous consequences for the population, with only a few benefiting from the change, while the majority suffers as a result of the change. Examples of these kinds of changes might include the changes brought about as a result of institutionalising Apartheid in South Africa between 1948 and 1994. This enabler will be discussed in detail in Part II, Chap. 5.

The **second enabler** is **Ego Mastery.** We witnessed that those leading and participating in the change process need to manage their intrapersonal well-being. Change leaders must be centred and balanced and be congruent with the purpose of the change. This remains an ongoing, day-to-day process of being self-aware, obtaining feedback and growing. It is only in this state of mind that healthy and productive relationships will be built which will lead to engaged stakeholders and successful change projects.

The next two enablers are to be found on the left-hand side of the picture, namely **Enablers 3 and 4: Explore** and **Eureka**. Change leaders need to be reminded that they exist in a permeable, ever-changing environment. They must be acutely aware and continuously in touch with the external environment. They consider the PESTLE factors (Politics, Economics, Social, Technology, Legislation and Environment) knowing that these all have a critical impact on the organisational system in which they find themselves. Change leaders comprehend that the optimal environment needs to be created to encourage others to identify opportunities for the organisation to flourish. Considering the environment, the change leader now elicits, consolidates and communicates opportunities for change. Change leaders need to persist until a eureka moment (also referred to as an a-ha moment or moment of insight) is found that enables the organisation to react in a powerful, different and unique way to the challenges and opportunities in the environment. Shifting the paradigm mentally is one thing—to bring about the change physically, is an entirely different challenge.

Furthermore, this mind shift has to be translated into a **Vision (Enabler 5)** that is crystal clear, described in detail, preferably in measurable terms with an end target date for the change to be implemented. Once the vision has been created, the reason for the change needs to be formulated, and the cost of the change needs to be calculated. Without a strong case for the change, engagement with stakeholders will be very challenging. The next step in the process is to **Engage (Enabler 6)** all stakeholders, to help understand the rationale of the change, to share the vision with the stakeholders and to get them to experience the a-ha moment. Their commitment to the change is critical as they need to agree to implement the change. Engaged stakeholders operate in effective teams where the sum of the team's output is more than individual efforts.

In **Enabler 7, Embark,** the focus is now on starting the change process as well as setting and agreeing to the goals needed to bring about the change. Change leaders and stakeholders have to understand the current reality, test the change readiness within the organisation and start planning the change in great detail. In **Enabler 8, Execute** the focus is on achieving the goals that will move the organisation towards its vision. It requires attention and persistence ensuring ongoing implementation to close the gap between where we are and where we would like to be. In Enabler 8 actions are managed to ensure movement is enabled and maintained. These actions are illustrated by the large arrow in the model. These steps may involve many ups and downs, but the direction is consistently moving towards the achievement of the vision. The champagne bottles in the graphic represent the small wins which are celebrated when milestones are achieved. The forces for and against the change are also identified and managed. The process in the large arrow follows traditional management steps which are illustrated in Fig. 4.3.

Effective change leaders thus implement this management cycle, to ensure goal delivery against the milestones. Figure 4.3 explains that this process starts with setting SMART (S—specific; M—measurable; A—achievable; R—realistic; T—timely) goals, planning the resources needed to achieve the goals, then monitoring resources, reviewing and evaluating achievement of SMART goals, motivating, coaching for the completion of goals as well as disciplining when goals are consistently not reached. Finally, the process involves the celebration of successes (see champagne bottles in Fig. 4.2) or if required as a last resort, separation. The most significant danger in any change process is falling back into old habits. A good understanding, as well as practice of habit forming and unlearning are required to maintain momentum and ensure sustainable changes.

In **Enabler 9, Evaluate** change leaders are encouraged to review the change process and to identify ways of improving the change process and thus documenting lessons learnt to ensure future change processes do not repeat the mistakes of past change processes.

Fig. 4.3 The management cycle (Authors' own)

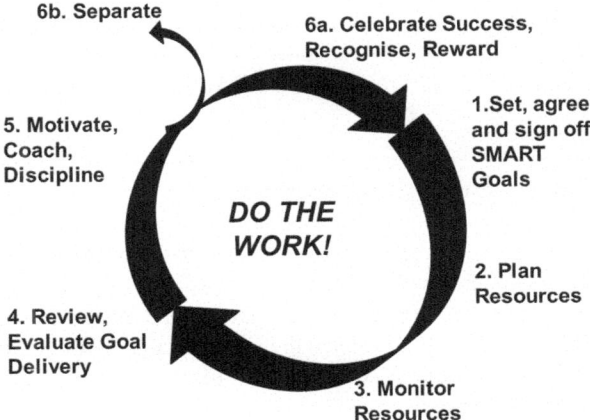

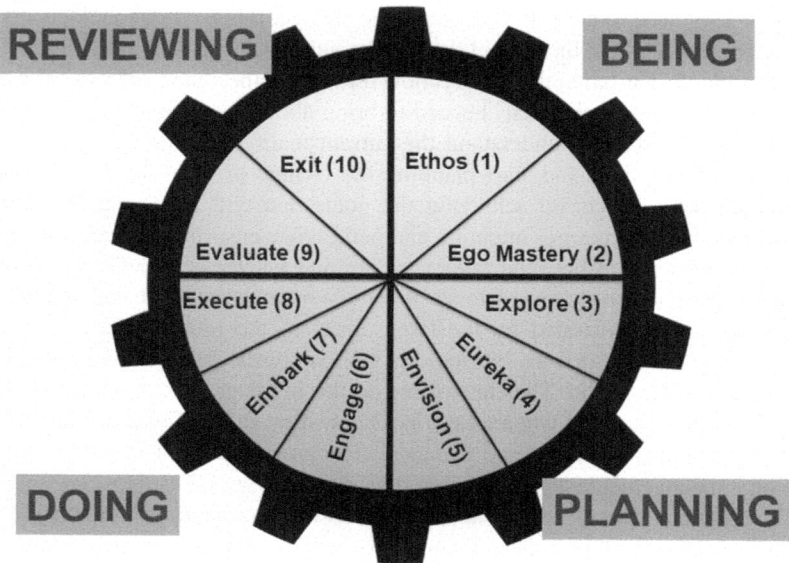

Fig. 4.4 The Ten Enablers Wheel Model (Authors' own)

In the last enabler, **Enabler 10, Exit**, we discuss the fact that change leaders must be competent and confident to step aside when the time is ready to create space for a "new broom". Successors are coached to take over to ensure a smooth transition, and change leaders move on to new opportunities and allow successors to succeed.

For some clients, the illustration in Fig. 4.2 seemed complex, and as a result, we simplified the model. We believe that change is not linear but rather cyclical (Freedman & Ghini, 2010) and therefore developed the Wheel Model to illustrate the cyclical process (see Sect. 4.4). In Fig. 4.4, we divided the ten enablers into four quadrants each representing four states of mind: BEING, PLANNING, DOING and REVIEWING. Some clients still prefer the model used in Fig. 4.2 and therefore, we decided to include both models.

Enablers 1 and 2 are contained in the BEING quadrant, enablers 3, 4 and 5 relate to PLANNING, while enablers 6, 7 and 8 form part of the DOING quadrant and enablers 9 and 10 relate to REVIEWING.

4.3   The Sigmoid Curve

There are a number of sigmoid curves in the big grey transition arrow in Fig. 4.2. The sigmoid curve will be used throughout this volume to illustrate the wave-like nature of change. Charles Handy introduced the sigmoid curve in his book, *The Age of Paradox* (1994). It is called the sigmoid curve because *sigmoid* is the Greek word for "S" and the curve is somewhat "s"-like. Figure 4.5 illustrates the concept. The curve declines during the initial phase of the creation of the "change". This is when there is still a lot of thinking and planning going on. Then the change starts building

Fig. 4.5 Sigmoid curves
(Authors' own adapted from
Handy (1994))

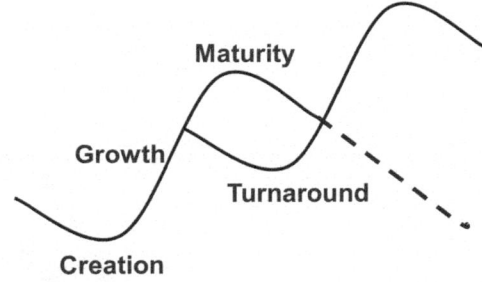

momentum and although it is an uphill battle, it shows forward progression. During the maturity phase, the progress has peaked and now starts declining. This is the time to initiate the next curve, called the turnaround. This would be the best time to "jump" to the next curve. "S" curves are useful as they explain the fact that change goes through phases, and it should be seen as waves that are cyclical in nature.

4.4   Is the Process Sequential?

Although the ten enablers are sequential and numbered from 1 to 10, the steps in the process are not always executed sequentially. We know from experience that no change is strictly linear or follows a tight "paint by numbers sequence" (Freedman & Ghini, 2010). For example, the Ethos (Enabler 1) requires ongoing Ego mastery, the Environment has to be scanned continuously, practising Ethics have to be in place throughout the process. Nonetheless, there is a logic in the sequence of the Ten Enablers, and numbering the enablers makes it easier for the brain to remember them. We consider the process to be more cyclical and we like to apply the metaphor of cogs and wheels. The first wheel or dial turns from one to ten, but because the process is cyclical, it is also possible to return to any enabler in the wheel at any time. As the conclusion of the first change process is reached, we often progress to wheel 2 and start from scratch at Enabler 1. As a result of the lessons learned from change process one, we are propelled forward to the next change process. As one change process follows the other, we continue to move forward. Figure 4.6 illustrates the cog and wheel nature of the enablers.

We also often illustrate the Ten Enablers Model as a spiral or helix. Figure 4.7 illustrates this spiral-like nature of the model.

4.5   Graphic Symbols

We decided to use alliteration in naming the Ten Enablers, because we found that many clients found it useful. In terms of neuroscience, humans find it easier to remember patterns. In addition, we decided to use illustrations to assist our clients in recognising the Ten Enablers. Our visual prompts enable better retention of the Ten

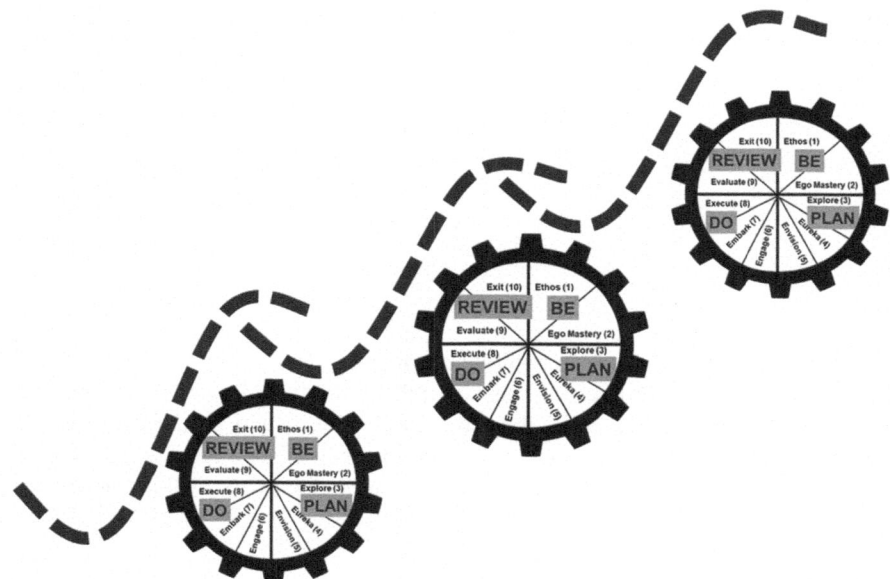

Fig. 4.6 The Ten Enablers cog and wheel model (Authors' own)

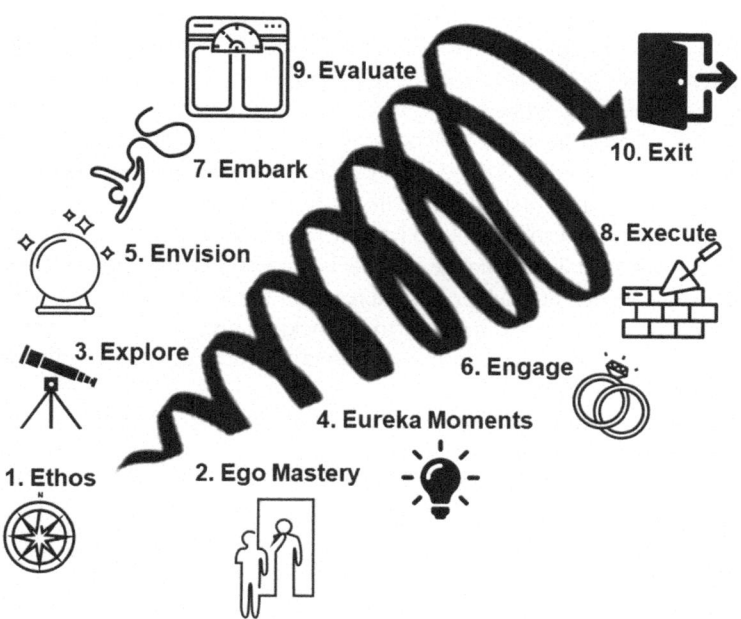

Fig. 4.7 The Ten Enablers helix model (Authors' own)

Table 4.1 The rationale for each figure representing an enabler

Enabler	Explanation of why this symbol was chosen	Symbol
1. Ethos	The compass is a symbol of the moral compass that serves as a guide to move the change in the right direction leading to a better future for the common good.	
2. Ego mastery	The mirror represents being self-aware and managing one's own ego.	
3. Explore	The telescope enables us to explore the "night's sky" (opportunities "out there"). It exposes us to a world that we do not know and might not be able to access. It shows us a multitude of new opportunities.	
4. Eureka	A light bulb is representative of the moment when there is a spark of electricity in the brain and we see things in a new "light" - the eureka moment.	
5. Envision	The crystal ball symbolises the dream we have of the future and seeing it crystalize before our own eyes. We need to look into the future and create a picture of our future reality.	
6. Engage	The engagement ring symbolises commitment to a fundamental change and parties joining together to show their commitment to change.	
7. Embark	Bungee jumping requires courage and facing one's fears letting go of the platform and jumping into the abyss.	
8. Execute	A house is built by laying one brick upon the other. An adhesive is required to make the bricks stick together. Achievement of goals require ongoing action.	
9. Evaluate	The scale indicates a tool used to take objective measures. Where measures are found to be too light or too heavy adjustments are made.	
10. Exit	The door is a symbol of leaving something behind and entering into a new future.	

Enablers. Table 4.1 offers the rationale for each visual representation of the Ten Enablers.

4.6   Tree Metaphor Applied to the Ten Enablers Model

We have also used the metaphor of a tree to assist clients or students in the introduction of the Ten Enablers Model. The illustration below (Fig. 4.8) guides you through the ten enablers starting at the top left corner with **Enabler 1, Ethos**, indicating that sun and water are required for anything to grow. The **second enabler,**

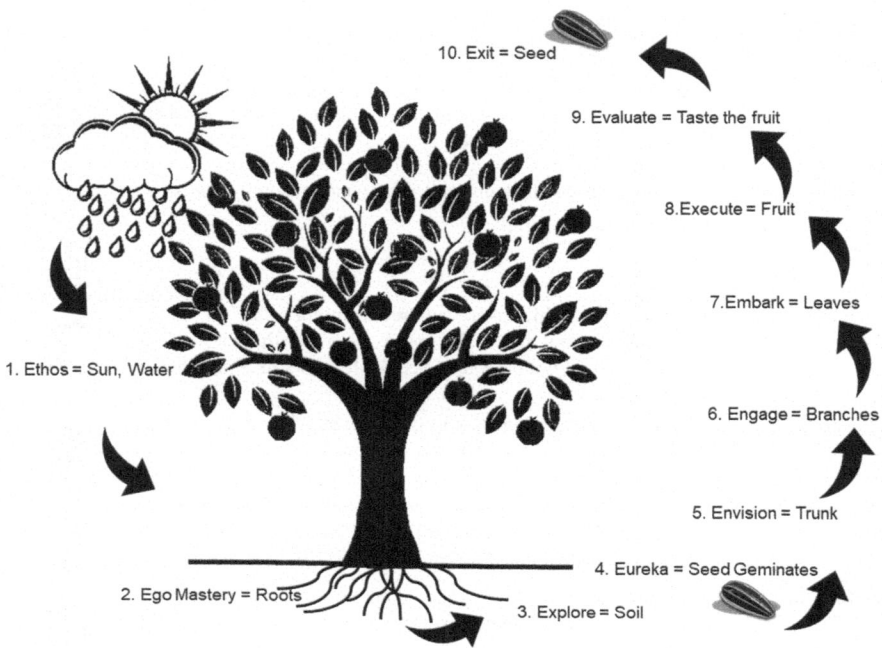

Fig. 4.8 Tree metaphor for the Ten Enablers Model (Author's own)

Ego Mastery, is represented by the roots of the tree. If the roots of the tree are not sturdy and grounded in the soil (signifying **Enabler 3, Explore**), the tree will not survive, no matter how much sun and water it receives. The roots also represent a foundation for everything that will follow. **Enabler 4, Eureka** takes us back to the moment of the birth of the tree—the moment the seed germinated, and it reminds us of the instance when the change was first imagined. Now the trunk follows, and a vision is born **(Enabler 5, Envision)**. The vision is the pillar from which all other branches will flow. Next, the Engagement process **(Enabler 6, Engage)** starts, depicted by the branches. The branches all link back to the vision but spread widely in all directions. The branches now enable the leaves to grow and describe **Enabler 7, Embark**. The fruit on the tree resembles the hard work and symbolises **Enabler 8, Execute**. The only way of evaluating the fruit **(Enabler 9, Evaluate)** is by tasting the fruit. Only once we have tasted the fruit will we know if the challenging work done in Enabler 8 paid off. In **Enabler 10, Exiting**, we return to the seed indicating that the process is cyclical and that time and time again we return to start the process all over (Fig. 4.8).

4.7   Applying the Ten Enablers Model Using a Story

Since story telling is an effective learning method, we applied the Ten Enablers Model to the story of Thandi following her dream....

Thandi believes life is short and every moment needs to be savoured. She loves life and enjoys spending time with her children and her extended family (**1. Ethos**). She has always loved to push herself beyond her own limits (**2. Ego Mastery**). She works hard and plays hard too. She is a positive role model for her children and her extended family. From an early age, she has always loved reading National Geographic and spent hours looking at photographs of distant mountain peaks on faraway continents (**3. Explore**). She recently watched a programme on television about an expedition summiting Everest. She has never climbed a mountain, but lately, it has been surfacing as one of her dreams (**4. Eureka Moments**). As her roots lie deep in Africa, she decided to investigate the possibility of conquering Kilimanjaro. She started investigating packages and costs to conquer the highest mountain in Africa. She realises that this is a dream (**5. Envision**) but if she does not get going, the dream will remain on her bucket list until she kicks the bucket! She also knows a lot needs to be done to fulfil this dream.

Thandi starts by conducting detailed research. What does the mountain look like? How fit does one need to be? How much does it cost? When is the best time to do the trek? Who can help? Who has done it before and what can she learn from them? After thorough research, Thandi takes a long hard look at her own capability. She weighs up whether she has the means, time, energy and persistence to embark on such an arduous journey. She realises that she will need to sacrifice sleeping in, she will have to give up the planned family vacation, no more desserts and wine and a regimented exercise programme would need to be followed through the winter. She does not see herself doing this alone. She finds an expert expedition leader and starts meeting with him to discuss how she will tackle this project. He gives her sound advice and introduces her to others who also plan on summiting the mountain (**6. Engage**). She contacts her friends and enquires who would like to join her on her expedition. She mentions it at her cell group at church and sells the vision to them (**5. Envision and 6. Engage**).

Thandi starts planning in detail (**7. Embark**). She draws up a budget and puts an action plan into place. She plans three mountain climbing excursions for the year ahead, one to the Drakensberg the other two to Table Mountain and the Cederberg Mountain (**7. Embark**). She starts running every day and climbs the steps to the eleventh floor and back every evening before she leaves work. She starts saving money every month (**8. Execute**). She buys her plane ticket and her licences to climb (**8. Execute**). Finally, the day has arrived. She arrives in Nairobi. Her flight to Kilimanjaro is delayed, and she is worried that she might not get to the starting point on time. She adjusts the plan and manages to catch another flight. She is back on track again. She makes it to the starting point in time where she meets her fellow climbers. At first, they are a bit reluctant to get too close, but at the end of day 1, they seem to be a tightly-knit team. They support each other and help wherever they can. The support workers are phenomenal, and Thandi is very impressed with their level of fitness and their positive attitude. The climb is tough, and at the high altitude Thandi suffers a great deal, but she takes it step by step (**8. Execute**). And then finally, she is there! She has achieved her dream, and it feels fantastic. On the walk down, she reflects on what this journey has cost her, but how utterly rewarding it has been. She feels as if she is floating! (**9. Evaluate**).

Thandi is grateful for the opportunity she had to summit Kilimanjaro. She is proud of her achievement, but she realises she needs to find a new goal. She starts investigating going to Everest Base Camp. She encourages her 16-year-old son to join her in climbing Everest in 2020 (**10. Exit**).

Practical Application of the Story

Caren and Sonja experienced the unforgettable journey of climbing and reaching the summit of Kilimanjaro and would like to encourage the readers to take up a challenge such as this one to apply the Ten Enablers.

4.8   Practical Process Flow of the Ten Enablers Model

In the process flow chart illustrated in Fig. 4.9, we would like to introduce the reader to the step-by-step flow of how the model is applied in practice. We believe the value the flow chart adds, is that it depicts on one page how the change process will unfold.

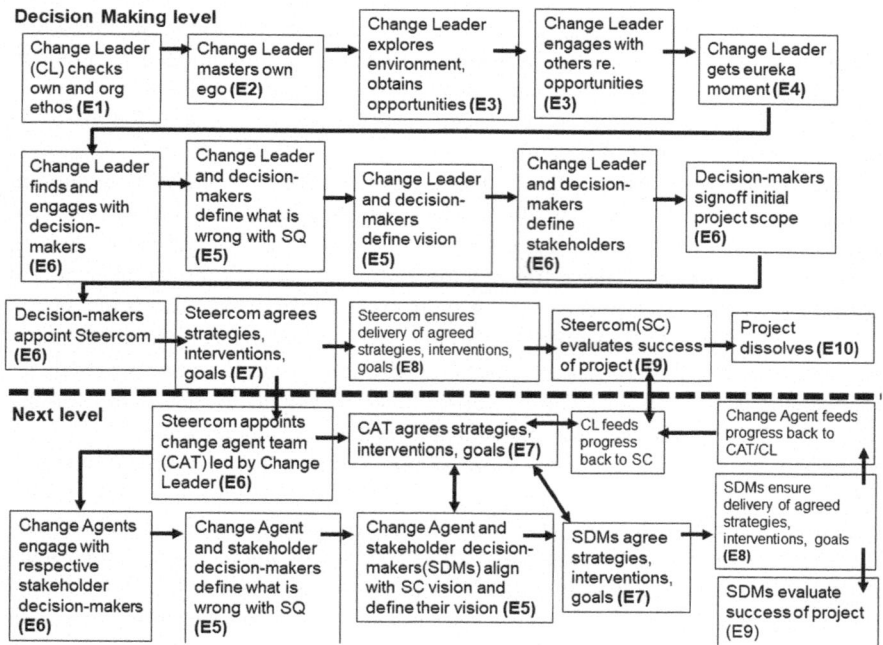

Fig. 4.9 Process flow chart of the Ten Enablers Model (Authors' own). *Org* Organisation, *SQ* Status Quo, *CL* Change leader, *CA* Change Agent, *CAT* Change Agent Team, *SDMs* Stakeholder Decision Makers

The process starts with the change leader (CL) assessing the ethos of the organisation and checking that there is alignment between his ethos and that of the organisation. Next, the change leader ensures his ego is balanced throughout the change process. (We believe that although we label Enabler 2 as Ego Mastery, it is not a once-off step in the process but an ongoing endeavour as the change process unfolds. In fact, it is a lifelong endeavour!) The CL explores the environment to seek opportunities. He engages with others to test his ideas and gains insights from others. While he is investigating opportunities, the CL seeks a moment of insight, also called an a-ha moment or eureka moment, when he "sees" what a different but improved future could look like. Once again, the CL engages with others and tests ideas, builds on the initial "bright" idea and gains more insight. He once again engages with others to determine what the dissatisfaction with the status quo is and what the root cause of the current reality might be. The CL next engages with the decision makers, find a sponsor or sponsors (people with positional power, who will provide backup and support throughout the process) and jointly, they start the process of developing the vision of the future. They also identify the stakeholders, the fears and their desires and needs. The decision makers sign-off on an initial project scope and appoint a steering committee (SC) who are held accountable for the success of the project. The SC next agrees on strategies and interventions and ensures these strategies and interventions are rolled out to its completion. They regularly evaluate the change process and do a final evaluation before the project dissolves.

To enable the change process to be rolled out to the rest of the organisation, the SC appoints a change agent team consisting of change agents representing the stakeholder groups. The change agent team (CAT) led by the change leader (CL) aligns with the SC vision and they agree the strategies, interventions and goals. The change agent engages with the decision makers of his respective stakeholder group, and jointly they define what is wrong with the status quo, align with the SC vision and agree with their strategies, interventions and goals. The stakeholder decision makers are then responsible for ensuring the achievement of these strategies, interventions and goals, they regularly review the success throughout the process and report back to the SC. They conduct a final evaluation once the vision has been attained and the project dissolves.

The CAT team led by the CL have regular meetings where they report on progress made on goals set in the stakeholder groups and recommend adjustments and concerns. The CL feeds this information back to the SC who takes note of the suggestions, makes adjustments and feeds information back to the change team. This process continues until the vision is achieved and the final evaluation is made, after which the CAT dissolves.

4.9   Chapter Layout

The following ten chapters are structured in the following way. First, the reader is introduced to the enabler in a section called *Orientation to the Enabler*, containing a discussion of what the enabler entails and sharing references to relevant current literature. The *Importance of the Enabler* section discusses why this enabler is essential. Next, the *Enabler in Practice* section discusses how the enabler can be applied in practice. Processes, templates, worksheets, tools and tips are provided to facilitate the practical application of the enabler. Next, the *Neuroscience Insights* section explores how neuroscience can assist in implementing each enabler. *Case Studies of How the Enabler is Applied in Emerging Markets* illustrate how the enabler is used in the emerging market context. A set of *Reflection Questions* allows the change leader or his followers the opportunity to measure the extent to which an enabler has been successfully implemented, and finally, the *Conclusion* links the enabler to subsequent enablers.

Reflection Questions Toolbox: Disclaimer
The questions in the *Reflection Questions Toolbox* intend to offer leadership an opportunity for informal self-evaluation, as well as for change leaders to use in generating feedback from their own followers. These measurements are for personal use and we created them as authors to fit with the Ten Enablers Model. These questions are thus not intended to be part of a psychometric test, or a valid and reliable scale or registered 360-degree assessment instrument. The questions could therefore even be altered and customised for change leaders' personal use, which would, of course, influence their reliability and validity. Please note, we thus do not claim the questions to be an evaluation instrument, but merely an opportunity to collect information for use during a change process when implementing the Ten Enablers Model.
The Likert-scale offers five anchor points to decide to which extent the change leader's behaviours would serve the particular enabler. For instance, under the First Enabler, Ethos: The change leader has to evaluate to what extent he aligns the change process with the organisation's values. When the *strongly agree* cell is selected, it implies that the change leader would definitely under most circumstances, align the change process with the organisation's values, whereas if the change leader nearly never aligns the change process to the values, the *strongly disagree* cell will be selected. The other points on the scale would represent, for example, neutral, which implies that in some circumstances the change leader would align values and in other circumstances would not align the change process to the values. Whereas *agree* would represent mostly and *disagree* would represent seldom.

You will notice that a "process map" was developed for each enabler. These "process maps" serve the purpose of guiding the change leader in a step-by-step manner in understanding how to practically make the enabler work. As a summary, we supply the process maps as a set of illustrations (Fig. 4.10). We have found it useful to have all the processes together to serve as a reminder of what fits where and when what needs to be done.

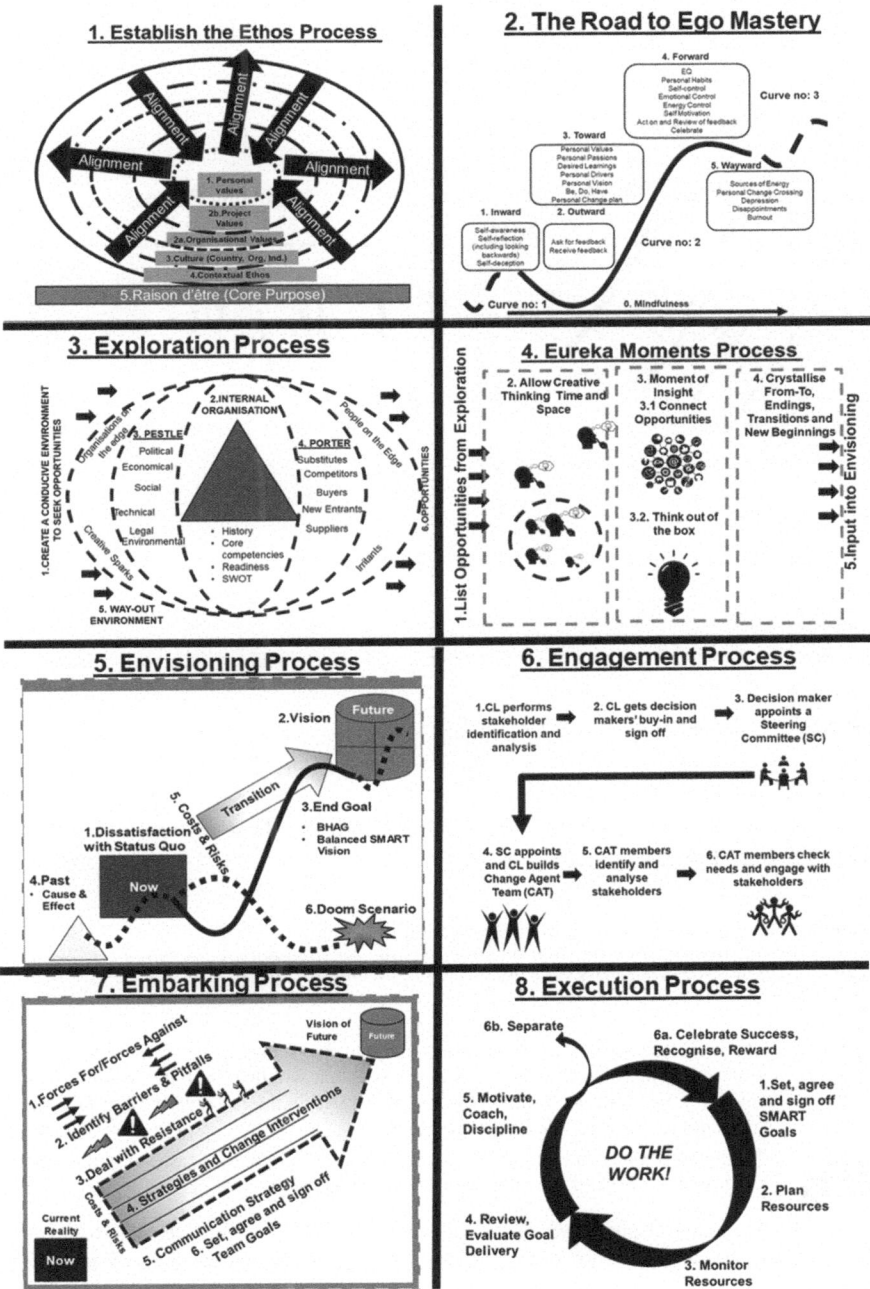

Fig. 4.10 Process maps for each enabler (Authors' own)

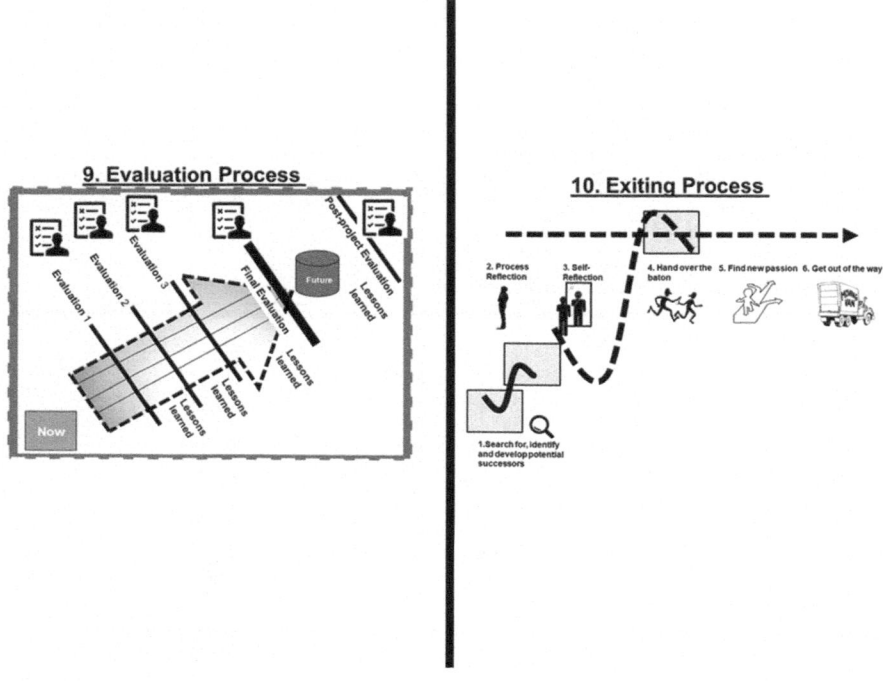

Fig. 4.10 (continued)

In the text, you will encounter the following symbols. These pictures will indicate the following (Table 4.2).

Table 4.2 Explanation of pictures in the application of learning

	The owl represents wise words from the literature
	The tools indicate a template or worksheet that the change leader can use to practically apply the enabler and find answers that will help with implementing the enabler. These tools are available online in *the Ten Enablers Toolbox*.[a] The facilitator could direct change leaders to these exercises
	The gear symbol points to a practical application example of a case study the reader can use to understand how the theory was applied in practice
	The movie clapperboard points to an URL address of a useful video clip that the reader can click on to view a YouTube clip to explain the concept discussed in the text
	The microphone indicates that a podcast is available of a relevant discussion

(continued)

Table 4.2 (continued)

	The magnifying glass is used as a symbol to indicate that an on-line set of *Reflection Questions*[b] is available to assess the change leader's ability to practice the enabler[c]
	The last chapter of this volume, Chap. 15, Conclusion, uses this symbol to indicate that we have arrived at our destination, a milestone has been achieved and that our journey has now come to an end

[a]The Ten Enablers Toolbox can be found online on the Springer website www.springer.com
[b]The Ten Enablers Reflection Questions can be found online on the Springer website www.springer.com
[c]Refer "Reflection Questions Toolbox: Disclaimer"

Tool 1 A Change You Want to Bring About

(This tool can be found online in the Ten Enablers Toolbox on the Springer website www.springer.com)
Before we start this journey, we would like you to identify a change you would like to keep in mind while reading about the Enablers. This will make the journey come alive and add value as it could potentially allow the change leader to have a complete change plan ready after reading the book. Use Tool 1 in the Toolkit to consider a change you would like to bring about in your life, team or organisation.

Our wish is that this journey through the Ten Enablers will be a useful and rewarding endeavour to you.

Let us start this journey. . . .

References

Freedman, J., & Ghini, M. (2010). *Inside change: Transforming your organization with emotional intelligence*. San Francisco, California: Six Seconds Emotional Intelligence Press. https://www.amazon.com/Inside-Change-Transforming-Organization-Intelligence/dp/1935667033

Handy, C. (1994). *The age of paradox*. Brighton, MA: Harvard Business School Press. https://www.worldcat.org/title/age-of-paradox/oclc/28926978?referer=brief_results

Lewin, K. (1947). Frontiers in group dynamics: Concept, method, and reality in social science; social equilibria and social change. *Human Relations, 1*, 5–41. https://doi.org/10.1177/001872674700100103

Reference List for Quotes

Retrieved July 26, 2019, from https://www.brainyquote.com/quotes/kofi_annan_930484

First Enabler

Ethos

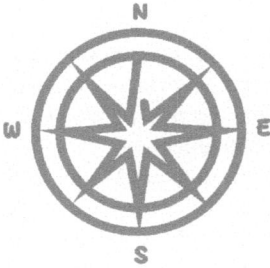

A man without ethics is like a wild beast loosed upon this world.

(Albert Camus, n.d.)

Learning Outcomes

At the end of this chapter, Change Leaders will be able to:

- Jointly identify ethical values required to bring about change
- Ensure alignment of personal values and values underpinning change
- Ensure change agents' behaviour is aligned to agreed values
- Understand different cultural value systems
- Identify contextual ethos

(continued)

Electronic supplementary material The online version of this chapter (https://doi.org/10.1007/978-3-030-40846-6_5) contains supplementary material, which is available to authorized users.

- Identify the core purpose of the project
- Deal with ethical dilemmas
- Lead ethical change processes

5.1   Orientation to Ethos

Ethos is defined in the online dictionary as: "the character or disposition of a community, group, person, etc.; the underlying sentiment or assumptions that inform the beliefs, customs, or practices of a group or society" (http://www.dictionary.com/browse/ethos). We deem ethos essential and thus formulated it as the first enabler. The discussion in this chapter commences with the importance of ethos for change leadership, followed by the current larger societal ethos. The spirit of our time around organisational ethos also receives attention.

Ethos is considered to be the moral compass that will ensure that we do what is right for the greater good. The quote by Harvey Mackay that "*Ethical choices ensure that everyone's best interests are protected. When in doubt, don't!*" (McKay, n.d.) is positioned at the basis of this enabler.

Ethos is positioned in the Ten Enablers Model as the basis from which all other enablers grow. Without the ethos of a change process being in place, the change might be to the detriment of the world in general. As authors of this volume, we advocate that change should only be led from within an ethical framework and where the ethics are not in place, the change should not be undertaken.

This chapter features South Africa as the particular emerging market where ethos requires a contribution to economic growth through job creation for the previously disadvantaged groups. The history of Apartheid is illuminated to offer insight into the country's unique context within which change leadership is embedded.

5.2   Importance of Ethos

Change leadership involves establishing the ethos in the situation, that is assessing the character or beliefs and customs of the people and institution where the change process will be implemented. This is crucial prior to embarking on this change process, because the leaders must continue to live the core values and promote these values of the business. Therefore, leaders should ensure the core assumptions or values are made explicit, as it could offer a compass or direction in terms of true-north and a way of keeping them accountable. The ethos forms a set of ground rules to evaluate whether they are still on the right track. During the turnaround of Nedbank in the early 2000s, Tom Boardman, the CEO at the time, as well as his successor, Mike Brown, said that they wanted to be vision led, but simultaneously values driven, while they had to downsize the organisation and conducted major reorganisation of the business (Scheepers, Maphalala, & Van der Westhuizen, 2014).

Investigating the history of the organisation is essential to understanding the ethos. Kutz (2008) describes hindsight as an important contextual intelligence competence. He emphasises that contextual intelligence is a nuanced ability. For example, the leaders must study the founders' intentions when they started the organisation. What was important to them? What were the driving factors? These drivers might still be underlying assumptions of what would constitute success or demonstrate that the organisation is living its purpose. The formally written vision, mission and values are important here as they usually illustrate the espoused values. The real or lived values are also relevant here to ascertain the ethos of the organisation.

In addition to the initial ethos of the organisation, insight into the recent past is equally important. For example, who were the leaders who had just exited the organisation or had led the previous change processes? What had been the impact of these change processes on the organisation? It links in a circular pattern with the last (10th) Enabler: Exit. Which processes must be exited to embark on this current change process? An example from the interviews on this aspect was the recollections of a change leader when he became CEO of a manganese mine. His predecessor had suffered an illness over a long time, and he had been focussing on establishing a caring family atmosphere in which the attention on hard performance targets had been limited. He reported, "I had to demonstrate that I honoured his legacy and that family values were still important, while I focused the attention on the lower levels of productivity that had to be fixed".

The interviewee mentioned above had to take cognisance of how previous leadership had been perceived as it had created expectations of, for example a patriarchal style of leadership. The context thus places constraints on leadership prototypicality. Likewise, academic literature, for example describes contextual variables that influence whether leadership would be perceived as prototypical (Lord, Brown, Harvey, & Hall, 2001).

A previous research project that the authors of this volume had contributed to, the *Women leadership in emerging markets* book, published by Routledge in New York (Chengadu & Scheepers, 2017), offered several examples of the influence of these contextual variables on leadership. For example, the research underpinning that publication revealed that the expectation of a masculine leadership prototype was even higher in the emerging markets than in the developed economies, because there was a patriarchal system, such as in India, Russia; Brazil; Columbia and China. Women leaders in these environments were generally expected to be agentic, a masculine leadership trait, as explained by Eagly and Johannesen-Schmidt (2001).

A grasp of the contextual ethos is essential. Change leaders are required to perceive the bigger picture or the larger societal ethos, in addition to the immediate organisational ethos. Walsh (1999, p. 59) describes prevalent societal ethos as follows, "Most of us focus on and even become addicted to things like money, possessions, praise and power. Spiritual traditions, all cry out a warning that to obsessively crave such things is to suffer, because they offer only temporary solace, are ultimately unsatisfying, and all too easily distort our values". As the quote illustrates, ethos is described as "our present time".

Palese (2013, p. 191) reveals that, "Zygmunt Bauman is one of the greatest interpreters of our present time, a time which turns into a shapeless mass tending to a constant and relentless change". Our stark materialistic society is described as follows, "The shopping malls seem to be hives or swarms of Bauman, as offering the ideally imagined community: a place where the purpose of purchasing aggregates. Thus, the shopping places offer what no "real reality" outside can give: an almost perfect balance between liberty and security. Within their temples consumers may also find what they were searching outside, uselessly as inexhaustibly: the comfortable feeling of belonging, the reassuring impression of being part of a community" (Bauman, 2000; Palese, 2013, p. 191).

Walsh (1999, p. 13) declares that "ethics are essential. If we live unethically and deliberately hurt others, we also hurt ourselves, because our minds become ridden with guilt and fear". Walsh (1999, p. 52) advises in contrast to our modern lives, "the healthier, more mature motives include desires for truth and justice, kindness and altruism, beauty and the sacred. Plato, the father of Western philosophy, summarised them as the good, the true and the beautiful, calling them higher motives or meta-motives". These meta-motives speak to universal spiritual orientations. Especially in our fast-moving world, these higher ideals are crucial to instil a sense of meaning and purpose in our lives. Nonetheless, our organisations are "nested within a fast-changing global systemic environment" (Collier & Esteban, 2000, p. 207).

An example of the higher goals is the Global UN's Sustainability Development Goals which emphasise opportunities for multi-stakeholder partnerships. For example, goal 17 aspires to strengthen the means of implementation and revitalisation of the global partnership for sustainable development. While partnerships have been used over many years to support sustainable development with public–private partnerships (PPPs) as a particularly common form, they are unfortunately not all successful in achieving their objectives (Van Tulder, Seitanidi, Crane, & Brammer, 2016). Seitanidi and Crane (2009) emphasise that the failure might be attributed to a number of factors, including the specific scope of the partnership, the stakeholders included, the mandate of the partnership and the partnership dynamics and tensions.

5.2.1 The Spirit of Our Time Around Organisational Contextual Ethos

Change leadership needs to role model valued behaviour. Jim Collins found in his *Good to Great* study that organisations with purpose outperform the general market 15 times to one (Collins, 2001). Collins contends that companies cannot rely on the "Hail Mary" strategy or charismatic leader for the long term. Instead, the purpose and values that are supported within the organisation are more important. He furthermore advises communicating, sharing and gaining feedback on the purpose (Collins, 2001). Harvard Professors John Kotter and James Heskett agree in their classic work *Corporate Culture and Performance* (2011). They found that of ten organisations in each of 20 industries, those with a strong corporate culture and purpose, based on a foundation of shared values, outperformed those who did not have it, such as achieving four times revenue growth, created seven times more jobs and realised 12 times more in stock price. Simon Sinek, author of the book *Start With Why* popularised the idea (See his 2009 TED talk—the third most viewed ever TED talk). Sinek advises that defining our 'Why' isn't a new notion, but one worthy of revisiting as a regular practice.

In our post-modernistic society, people are looking for meaning in their lives. Companies could thus benefit from considering the deeper significance of what the organisation is actually involved with. In the last section of this chapter, several examples will be offered of organisations that built sustainability into their DNA or core identity of the business, with positive results in terms of the commitment and engagement of employees.

The societal contextual ethos is shifting towards an expectation for organisations to take more responsibility. Organisations are being accused of abdicating their environmental and societal responsibilities. Business schools are being criticised for not being responsible and are even blamed for executives' deficiencies. This training deficiency is even seen as the culprit for some of the recent corporate scandals (Bendell, 2007). In this regard, Datar, Garvin, and Cullen (2010) suggest that business schools reassess what they teach and rebalance their curricula to develop the values, attitudes, and beliefs that form leaders' worldviews and professional identities.

Luckily, there are 1000 signatories in 100 countries, representing higher education institutions that voluntarily committed to achieving a 2030 vision of realising the sustainable development goals through responsible management education. They adhered to the UN Principles for Responsible Management Education (PRME), stating that as institutions of higher learning involved in the education of current and future managers, they will develop the capabilities of students to be future generators of sustainable value for business and society at large and to work for an inclusive and sustainable global economy (PRME, 2018).

Osborn, Hunt, and Jauch's (2002) concept of contextual leadership broadens the view of leadership as an individual, interpersonal influence to more of a collective influence for managing dynamic systems and interconnectivity extending to the environment. To illustrate the need for the focus on the environment, the case of Exxon's oil spill in 1989 (Taylor, 2014) is relevant. For example, when the Exxon managers were interviewed after their oil spill, they knew the financial value of the crude oil that had been spilled, as well as the value of the cargo and the number of trips the vessel had made, but they could unfortunately not name one of the fish species wiped out by the oil spill.

By, Burnes and Oswick (2012) remind us that we need to highlight the importance of promoting the ethical dimension of change as a means of ensuring that leaders and their followers act in the interest of the many rather than the few. Collier and Esteban (2000, p. 207) declare that "radical change is now the most pervasive feature of organisational life". They developed the concept of a systemic view of leadership appropriate to post-industrial organisations in situations of rapid change. This view of leadership realises that in a post-industrial corporate context, there is "shared responsibility, and this implies shared purposes and a shared commitment to pursue the common good" (Collier & Esteban, 2000, p. 207).

Prior to embarking on a change process, organisations must ascertain what the rules of the game will be during this process. The authors of this volume would encourage leadership to establish an ethos around the involvement of employees during the change process. For example, Cullen, Edwards, Casper, and Gue (2014) too advise giving employees access to the change process through transparent, clear communication and by giving employees a voice. Encouragement of employees to give more input in the change process will decrease uncertainty (Cullen et al., 2014). Scholars like Lewis, Schmisseur, Stephens, and Weir (2006) too, emphasise that the organisation should promote participation and empowerment as the employees will need to feel a part of the change process if they are going to accept change and commit to its objectives. In response to expected resistance, or in an effort to ensure a smooth implementation of organisational change, there are several important strategies for communicating and introducing change initiatives. In the discussion of the later Enablers, these aspects will be returned to. In the discussion of this first Enabler, we highlight that these aspects represent an ethos of participation and inclusion during the change process.

Scholars like Wenger (1998) emphasise that the alignment of leaders and even allegiance to the organisational ethos will enable identification with the organisation and nurture a sense of community. Denis, Lamothe, and Langley (2001) too, suggest that the creation of a collective leadership group, in which members play distinct, but tightly knit and complementary roles, is a critical factor in achieving substantive change. With the current pressure on organisations to take other stakeholders into account, in addition to the emphasis on the shareholder's returns, leadership approaches that include transparency, such as Authentic Leadership (Avolio, Gardner, Walumbwa, Luthans, & May, 2004); Servant Leadership (Greenleaf, 1977) and Stewardship (Block, 1993) have become more dominant.

The research of Amis, Slack, and Hinings (2004) concluded that all the stakeholders are to be consulted and their interests should be considered in a broader context. They found that the initial resistance in the change projects that they had investigated, was caused by various units hoping to retain decision-making authority and initially fearing that they would be stripped of that authority.

Stakeholders are "entities or persons who are or will be influenced by or exert influence directly or indirectly on the project" (Littau, Jujagiri, & Adlbrecht, 2010, p. 29). Stakeholder management has been evolving since Freeman's seminal work in 2010a, which emphasised that an organisation has to manage relationships with all the parties—voluntary or contracted. An organisation should aim at satisfying or exceeding the expectations of its stakeholders without compromising other parties (Garvare & Johansson, 2010). In this regard, other researchers contend that the main function of management is to balance the contradicting demands of the diverse stakeholders and the prosperity of the organisation depends on its ability to meet these demands (Abboubi & Cornet, 2012). Heifetz and Linsky (2002) emphasise that change in patterns of behaviour of several stakeholders is required to meet adaptive challenges in complex adaptive systems. In his article, *Managing for Stakeholders: Trade-offs or Value Creation*, Freeman also focuses on compatibility of stakeholder interests (Freeman, 2010b). Collier and Esteban (2000) highlight that in evolving organisations, also called chaotic situations, purposes, actions and outcomes are never stable, and the "common good thus has itself to be seen as an emergent outcome of systemic leadership" (Collier & Esteban, 2000, p. 210). The original ethos of sustainability focused on the idea of intergenerational equity.

5.3 Ethos in Practice

It is critical to establish the ethos and ascertaining what ground rules and values are non-negotiable before a change is embarked upon. To put ethos into practice, there needs to be an understanding of how ethical standards are formed in change leaders as well as how to establish and maintain a certain ethos during the change process. In addition to a set of clear ethical standards, the purpose has to be determined. *Raison d'être* is a French term to describe one's reason for existence or purpose. Once the reason for the change has been established during Enabler 5, Envisioning, it will need to be aligned with, and tested against the ethos. All intentions, actions, attitudes, behaviours and decisions need to be measured against the moral code, and it should be the guiding light ensuring that the chosen change is to result in a benefit to the majority of stakeholders.

5.3.1 Models Used in Practice

In this section, we share the models we have found useful in practice to understand how ethos is established. We share some classic models we use to assist clients in understanding this enabler, and we introduce models to better understand and remember this enabler.

5.3.1.1 Iceberg Model
The first practical model essential in understanding and ensuring successful change implementation is the classic Iceberg Model. It contributes significantly to an understanding of the Ethos Enabler. This model originated from Sigmund Freud's Iceberg Model of Consciousness developed between 1900 and 1905 (Freud, 1924; McLeod, 2015). In this model, Freud posited that there are three levels of consciousness: conscious, preconscious and unconscious. The invisible, unconscious part of our mind is far more voluminous than the other two parts and exerts a profound influence on our actions and conscious awareness. Our ethics and values are found in this part of our consciousness and drive the above-the-surface behaviour (http://www.wilderdom.com/personality/L8-3TopographyMindIceberg.html).

The illustration below describes these three levels of consciousness (Fig. 5.1).

We find the iceberg model useful because it shows that even though change is often lead from an "above-the-surface" frame of mind, a great deal of what happens during change is really driven by "below-the-surface" issues. If the below the surface issues are not considered, change will not be effective. There is more to change than can be seen with the naked eye. Ethos is a complex concept driven from below the surface but is only visible through actions. Change leaders need to uncover what lies beneath their and others' actions and learn how to align all activities with the desired

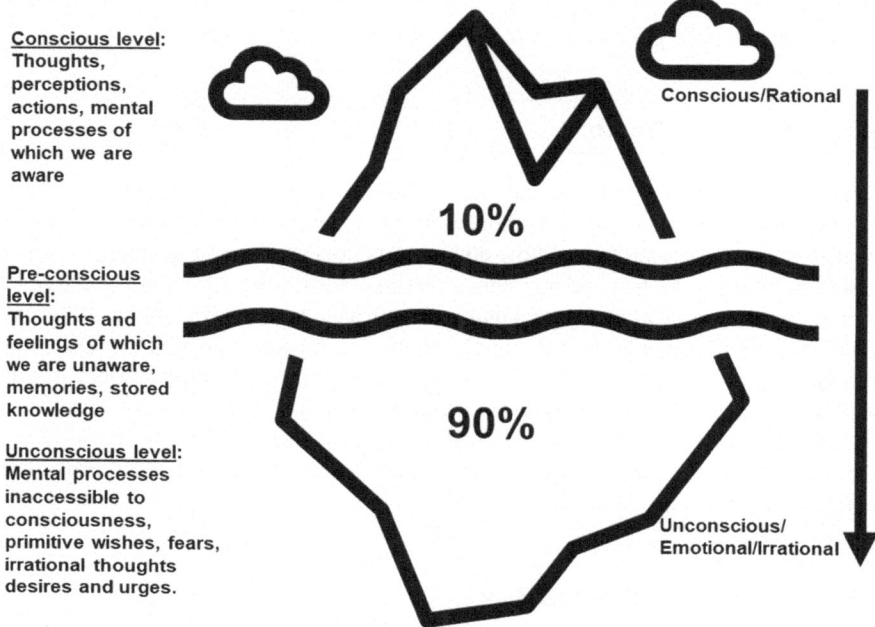

Conscious level:
Thoughts,
perceptions,
actions, mental
processes of
which we are
aware

Conscious/Rational

10%

Pre-conscious
level:
Thoughts and
feelings of which
we are unaware,
memories, stored
knowledge

90%

Unconscious level:
Mental processes
inaccessible to
consciousness,
primitive wishes, fears,
irrational thoughts
desires and urges.

Unconscious/
Emotional/Irrational

Fig. 5.1 Freud's Iceberg Model (Authors' own synthesis, adapted from McLeod (2015) and Freud (1924))

ethos. Without such an alignment there is a danger that the change might be unethical, leading to the long-term detriment of the organisation, society, country or even the planet.

5.3.1.2 Paradigms

Another critical building block facilitating our understanding of the Ethos Enabler is the concept of *paradigms*. The way we view the world is formed from the moment we are born. Parents, family, friends, schools, church, media and society at large influence and extend our view of the world as we grow up. In psychology, the image of the world around us that we carry in our minds consists of a number of mental models. Social cognitive theorists call it schemata, political psychologists and media studies call it frames, scientists refer to it as paradigms and in social studies, they are called social scripts. Other synonyms for a paradigm might be a frame of reference, a worldview, a perspective, or simply: the way we see things.

In this volume, we prefer to refer to the way individuals view the world as *paradigms*. The rationale for this choice is that we believe it to be a useful concept in facilitating the understanding that change is essentially a *paradigm shift*. This will be explored further in Enabler 4, Eureka, when we apply the *From...To* tool (Tool 4.4). The concept of a *paradigm* was first popularised by Thomas Kuhn in his book,

The Structure of Scientific Revolutions (1962) and was defined as a pattern, describing a problem and then working within these boundaries to solve the problem. However, the term is now widely used in other contexts, like the social, marketing and business sciences.

5.3.1.3 Schein's Culture Change Model

Another classic model we believe to be a fundamental building block of change is the Culture Change Model by Edgar Schein dating back to the 1980s. In his book, *Organizational Culture and Leadership*, Schein (1996) defines culture as a pattern of shared basic assumptions that the group learned as it solved its problems of external adaptation and internal integration, which worked well enough to be considered valid. Therefore, these assumptions are taught to new members as the correct way to perceive, think and feel in relation to those problems. Culture is thus the basic tacit assumptions about how the world is and ought to be that a group of people share and that determines their perceptions, thoughts, feelings and their overt behaviour (Schein, 1996). In this model, Schein describes culture as operating at three levels. The first apparent level includes the artefacts that are easy to observe but might be difficult to understand and interpret if you are an outsider. It might consist of symbols, heroes, stories, practices, jargon, habits and even physical arrangements such as buildings, clothes worn and language used. The next level contains the values and beliefs that are not directly observable but can be determined by how people justify and explain what they do. It may include commitments, time and energy spent, what people think and understand to be true and of value. The third level (shared basic underlying assumptions), is so deep-seated that people are unaware of the fact that they make these assumptions. These assumptions are not even questioned or debated. These might include worldviews, philosophies and ideologies.

We have chosen to superimpose the three levels of Schein's model on the Freud Iceberg. The illustration below demonstrates this integration (Fig. 5.2).

If you want to learn more about organisational culture, you will find the following case study of the South African born fast-food company, Nando's very interesting.

Practical Application: Organisational Culture

https://www.ukessays.com/essays/business/management-and-leadership-across-cultures-at-nandos-business-essay.php

5.3.1.4 Multi-layered Model of Self

Building on the Iceberg Model of Freud, and Schein's Culture Model, we developed the following conceptional model representing a multi-layered view of the self.

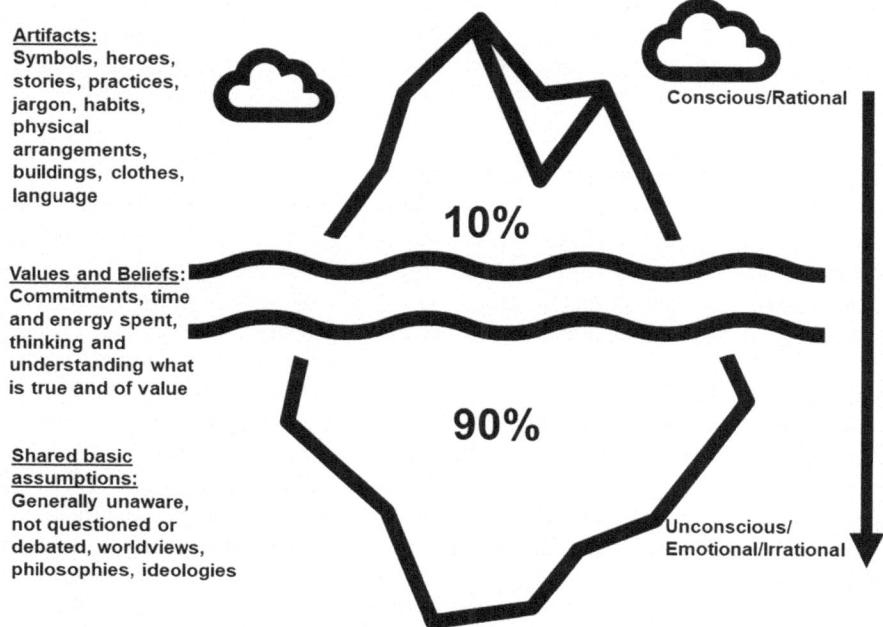

Fig. 5.2 Schein's Three Levels of Culture (Authors' own adapted from Schein (1996))

In Fig. 5.3, the self is seen as consisting of what is visible, cascading down multiple layers to the deepest level of self. Our ethos originates at the deepest levels and becomes apparent in the more visible levels—how we interact with the world and how we choose to show ourselves to the world. This model leads us to the next conceptual model, called the CD model.

5.3.1.5 Compact Disc Model

Combining the models discussed above, we choose to use the metaphor of a Compact Disc (CD) shuttle to explain in simple terms how values drive behaviours, how paradigms are formed and how change leaders can understand their own paradigms and influence others to change their paradigms. The *CD model* will be introduced in this chapter and discussed further in later chapters. The model was developed during the time when CDs were still very popular and used by everyone. With the rapid development of technology, CDs are no longer in vogue, and we foresee the need to update the model soon to accommodate the next generation entrants who do not even understand what a CD is. For now, many of our clients still understand the concept and find it extremely useful.

The CD model describes paradigms as millions of CDs stacked one upon another as in a CD shuttle. Each CD has a number of musical tracks on the disk and every time a stimulus is received through the senses, the CD starts playing a tune in our heads. As the

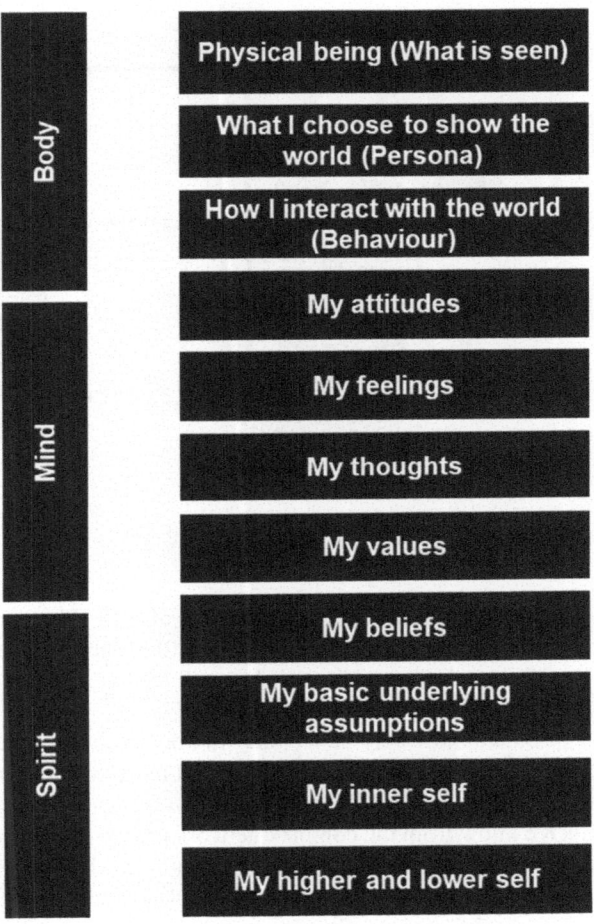

Fig. 5.3 Multi-layered view of self (Authors' Own)

music starts playing we either like or dislike the track. Sometimes we might be neutral towards the stimulus, but most of the time we rapidly judge whether we agree with the stimulus. The CDs are all interconnected and as a result, when one track starts playing it might remind us of other tracks, and then those tunes start playing in our heads.

CDs are stacked according to their level of consciousness and emotive value. Deep-seated emotional paradigms are very difficult to challenge as they are often assumed to be so correct that they are never even questioned and are perceived as the absolute truth. They, therefore, remain at an unconscious level. An example of a deep-seated CD could be one's own sexual orientation or religious beliefs. Higher level CDs are easier to change. They could include physical choices such as fashion preferences or a preferred car brand. Of course, the depth of the CD is entirely dependent on the individual in question and what might be a deep-seated CD for one person, could be a shallow CD for the next person. When there is a substantial emotive response to a stimulus, we can assume the issue is of great value to the person and is therefore at a deep level.

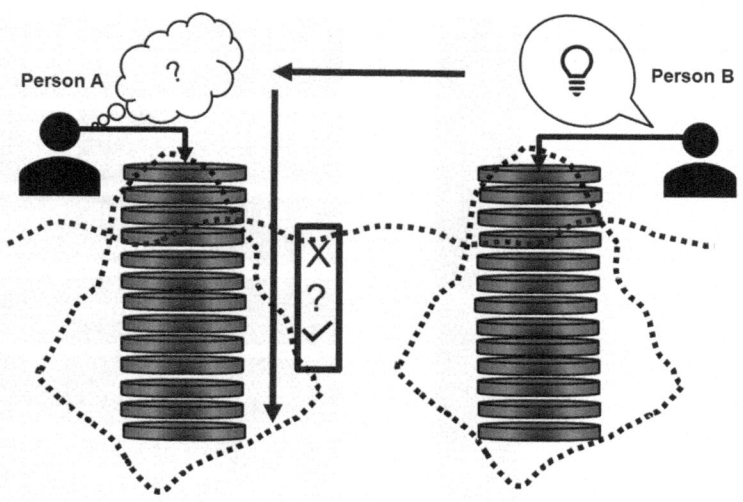

Fig. 5.4 CD Model (Authors' own) (Person B sharing his paradigm with Person A)

Driving the CD shuttle is our sense of self. When anyone dares to challenge or change one of our deep-seated CDs (the ones we hold onto very dearly) or if something of value is discarded, it will lead to a person wanting to protect this CD with his "life".

CDs are intricately linked and wanting to change one CD can trigger other CDs. Not wanting to change one's CD or not understanding others' CDs is the root of all resistance to change, all conflict, all divorces and even all wars.

We know from the complex network of neurons in our brain that this model is an oversimplification of how neural networks work, but the model succeeds in making it easy for others to understand how to lead and manage change.

Figure 5.4 explains the CD model in practice and illustrates two individuals who are interacting. Person B represents the leader and Person A the person he is trying to influence to "buy" his bright new idea or change. While he is communicating with Person A, Person A is accessing his CD shuttle. He is judging the concept at first glance. If the idea Person B is bringing is of benefit to Person A, he might consider buying the idea. If it is not at first glance of value to Person A, he will reject the idea. In change leadership, the change leader needs to understand this dynamic.

The value of the model is that it has the power to assist change leaders in viewing the dynamic from "a distance". If change leaders are taught to consider this dynamic, it gives them perspective. Change leaders can position the change to be of value to others, and they can use the distance perspective to manage their own CDs. When the interaction is "easy", we can be confident we are not working with deep, underlying CDs. When the interaction is complex, we can know for certain we are dealing with deep-seated CDs, and that can often result in an emotional outburst, albeit covert.

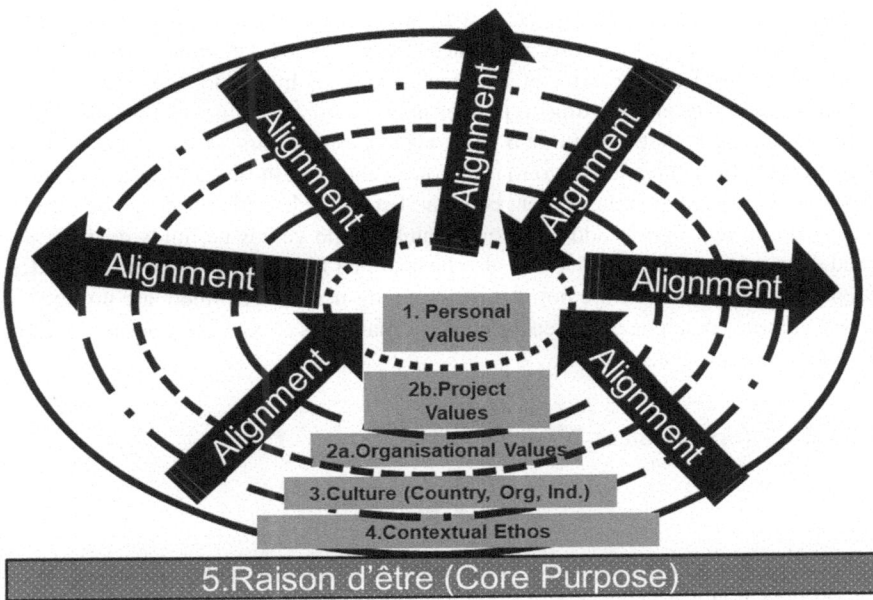

Fig. 5.5 Establishing the Ethos process (Authors' own)

5.3.2   Practical Tools and Templates Used in the Ethos Process

Figure 5.5 illustrates the Ethos establishment process. In the centre of the picture is a circle indicating that the starting point of the Ethos Enabler process needs to be the identification of the change leader's personal values. The clarification of the project and organisational values follow. The country, ethnic group, organisation, team and individual cultures should then be considered, understood and clarified by the stakeholders. It is critical to explore and discuss the broader context. Finally, the purpose of the project needs to be determined and measured against the values and culture of the preceding parties.

5.3.2.1 Personal Values

Without values, there is confusion and chaos. When values disintegrate, everything disintegrates. Health disintegrates, poverty attains dominance over affluence, societies and civilisations crumble. When we pay attention to these values that society has always held sacred, then order emerges out of chaos, and the field of pure potentiality inside us becomes all-powerful, creating anything it desires. (Deepak Chopra, 1998)

Establishing ethos needs to start with the change leader clarifying his own personal values. We, therefore, introduce Tool 1.1, the Personal Values Sheet. This tool is based on the work of Vermeulen (1999). In this tool, we suggest the change leader takes enough time to ponder upon this list of values as this will reveal his moral compass that will guide his actions and behaviours. A list of values have been created to enable a leader to make choices and rank these choices according to importance. We suggest the leader scans the list and select his top ten. The change leader should feel free to add additional values if the values he holds dear are not listed. The wording of the value can also be changed if it works better for the reader. Keep in mind too that we are not making any judgments here—there are no right or wrong values. The choices the leader makes remains his choice and does not need to be justified to anyone.

Tool 1.1 Top 10 Values Template

The online toolbox contains Tool 1.1(a), in which a long list of values is provided that could be used to identify one's own personal values. After reading through the list, the idea is to prioritise the ten values you identify with most and then rank these from 1 to 10. Tool 1.1(b) also contains a template in which the leader can now write up his top 10 values.

In this exercise, it is critical for the leader to be totally honest with himself/herself. The objective is not to necessarily share this information with others, but rather to use this list as an internal compass to help when value-based decisions need to be made. We need to understand that there are two sets of values: those we aspire to and those that are actually in use. The list contains those values that the leader would like to live his life by. He will need to take stock from time to time to see if this list is aligned with the actual values in use. If these values conflict, the change leader will experience dissonance. A feeling of unease will be experienced at a deep subconscious level. It could also be valuable if the change leader asks trusted partners to participate in the process by listing the values, they think the change leader espouses and the actual values according to which he lives.

5.3.2.2 Change Project Values

Collins and Porras define core values as "...the essential and enduring tenets of an organisation. A small set of timeless guiding principles..." (1996, p. 66). We now move onto identifying the core values that will be guiding the change project.

Tool 1.2 Change Project Values Worksheet

Tool 1.2 facilitates the identification of the values that will guide the behaviours, choices, actions and decisions during this project. The change leader can identify these values on his own and then check the list with the steering committee and the change team once they are appointed. These values can also be shared with stakeholders during the engagement process. The list can be adjusted if stakeholders have strong opinions on values that need to be in place.

Practical Application of Values Identification

An example of a list of values agreed to by a change team who consulted us, is included below. Although we strongly recommend values to be limited to five or fewer (for ease of use), this team insisted on an extended list. When a team insists that a more extended list will better guide their behaviours, in our experience, we allow the team to extend the list.

What is non-negotiable?
What do we value above anything else?

Our Values

1. Teamwork
2. Innovation
3. Integrity (incl. honesty, transparency)
4. Excellence (incl. deliver results)
5. Accountability
6. Customer Centricity

5.3.2.3 Cultural Values Dipstick
Based on the work of Hofstede (2001) and Hofstede, Hofstede, and Minkov (2010), we developed the culture values dipstick tool to create awareness of personal culture,

organisational culture or even culture or subcultures in a country. We use it as a discussion tool during meetings where individuals of different cultures need to work together. The tool allows participants to express their opinions of the extent to which each dimension is valued, and then highlight potential areas of conflict during the project. These values can be applied to individuals, teams, organisations, ethnic groups or country cultures.

Tool 1.3 Cultural Values Dipstick

Tool 1.3 offers an opportunity for leaders to plot where they would position the culture of the team. As an example with regards to the individualism or collectivism dimension, the team could choose the one side of the continuum, where people identify themselves in terms of "I" or the other side of the continuum, on the "we" side, or where people identify themselves in terms of the "tribe" they belong to. The instruction is to "Please indicate with a cross on the arrow, the position you consider the … culture to be".

Other dimensions include low versus high position on power distance, uncertainty avoidance, time orientation, gender egalitarianism and assertiveness, etc.

Practical Application of Cultural Values Dipstick

This tool was used during an intervention during which two companies with very different cultures needed to implement a change project. One company was from South Africa, the other from India. The executive team members were each given a copy of the tool and asked to plot where they considered their own culture to be on the arrow as well as the culture of the other team. The South African organisation had a very flat structure with a "healthy disregard for authority" while the Indian organisation adhered to a very hierarchical structure. They used this observation to devise plans to deal with the conflict they experienced during the project.

5.3.2.4 Considering the Contextual Ethos

Insight into the contextual ethos is the hallmark of change intelligence. In establishing the current contextual ethos, reflection is required, and to this end, we have developed a series of specific questions relating to contextual ethos. Tool 1.4 contains these questions.

Tool 1.4 Considering the Contextual Ethos

Tool 1.4 offers the opportunity to consider the contextual ethos. Change leaders can reflect on a set of questions, related to considering the context in terms of what is valued, the spirit of the time, stakeholders, the social impact that the organisation is trying to make, etc.

5.3.2.5 Raison D'être

Collins and Porras (1996, p. 68) define the raison d'être or "reason for being" as "an effective purpose that reflects people's idealistic motivations for doing the company's work. It doesn't just describe the organization's output or target customers; it captures the soul of the organization".

The following worksheet can be used to get an individual, a team, a department, a function or even the total organisation to determine their purpose. Answer the questions in the worksheet and then continue with the five why's process. Collins and Porras (1996) suggest asking oneself five times why it is of importance to you. As you drill down through the repetition of why's, a gradual uncovering of the most authentic and succinct "why" or purpose will emerge. The worksheet in Tool 1.5 offers an opportunity to reflect on this core purpose.

Tool 1.5 Core Purpose Worksheet

Tool 1.5 lists questions such as: What is it that we as a team actually do? What is unique about what we offer? Why does it matter what we do? Ultimately, the purpose statement can be written in the space provided in this tool.

5.3.2.6 When Ethics Go Wrong

In business today, we are constantly confronted with decision-making options. These options can lead us to a fork in the road where we need to make an ethical choice. Before making the ethically "wrong" or questionable decision, we recommend taking time out to consider the following guidelines. Fryer (2007) provides excellent guidelines and using these guidelines, we developed the following template to serve as a tool to assist clients when they are faced with a moral dilemma (Tool 1.6).

Tool 1.6 When Faced with a Moral Dilemma

This tool offers the opportunity to reflect on moral dilemmas, including, "If my mother, father or my trusted partner knew everything I was doing, what would he think and say?"

5.3.3   Implementation Tips for Ethos

Further practical tips that we would like to offer our readers are:

- Build a network intentionally to keep abreast of how the contextual ethos might be changing.
- Build relationships that transcend the workplace.
- Investigate what was intended relative to what actually happened.
- Be interested in others' cultural experiences and background.
- Gain multi-cultural career experiences.
- Test your core values: Why do you believe in these core values and are they truly your values?

5.4   Neuroscience Insights into Ethos

Morality is a matter of biology as much as tradition, religion, or law (Oren Harman, 2015).

There are many different perspectives when it comes to discussing the issue of ethos. The intelligent design movement believes morality is given to man through God's grace and that believers are provided with an abundance of the gift of ethics. Neuroscientists, on the other hand, think our ability to make ethical choices originates from before we are born. As far back as the nineteenth century, Darwin explained in detail how moral awareness developed from social instincts critical for survival (Swaab, 2014). These ethical principles came into existence to promote cooperation and support within social groups, and to enforce a type of social contract whereby rules could be imposed on individuals to benefit the community at large. Altruistic behaviour evolved out of the loving care displayed by parents towards their offspring and was extended to others of the same species to form the cornerstone of human morality.

Our moral values have evolved over millions of years and are based on universal values of which we are unconscious (Swaab, 2014, p. 249). Empathy (the capacity to recognise and share the feelings of others), the basis of all moral behaviour (Swaab, 2014, p. 246) and the key emotion to support right and wrong, develops at a very young age. It seems as though our moral values are hardwired in our brains. It has been found that babies cry in response to other babies crying—not because the noise upsets them, as they cry more in response to human cries than to any different aversive sounds. Children as young as 1 year old are also able to console others in distress (Svetlova, Nichols, & Brownell, 2010). Before they are old enough to have acquired speech, young children (between one and two) show an instinct to comfort family members who are in pain. Newborn babies can copy the mouth movements of adults within an hour after birth (Swaab, 2014, p. 250).

Conditioning by our parents and society also creates neural frameworks that enable us to distinguish "right" from "wrong". Shermer (2011a, 2011b) believes we have evolved a deep sense of right and wrong by emphasising and rewarding reciprocity and cooperation and to diminish and punish excessive selfishness and free riding. He further states that, "On the constitution of human nature are built the constitutions of human societies". The legal system considers children between the ages of 7–15 years (depending on their circumstances) as being able to distinguish between right and wrong. The Roman Catholic Church considers a child of 7 years to be of "an age of reason" when he can participate in his first confession (Begley & Kalb, 2000). Children at the age of 6 years can make moral judgments, from 7 years onwards they start making judgments based on intent. After the age of 8, children start seeking social approval and their brain's judgment circuit, the prefrontal cortex (PFC) approaches maturity. Empathy seems innate, but unfortunately conscience is not (Begley & Kalb, 2000).

5.4.1 Anatomy of Morality

Neurobiological building blocks make up a moral network in our brain. First, brain cells known as mirror neurons, found in the PFC and in other regions of the cerebral cortex, help us learn (largely automatically) by imitation. These cells also react to displays of emotion, like feeling others' pain, i.e. empathy. The PFC plays a significant role when we have to make judgments during moral dilemmas. Individuals with damage to the PFC make these judgments very cold-bloodedly and with impersonal reasoning.

Although essential parts of our moral network are contained in the PFC, it is not only the prefrontal cortex that is involved in moral decisions. Many other cortical and subcortical regions such as the foremost part of the temporal lobe and the amygdala, the septum, the ventral tegmental area (nucleus accumbens) and the hypothalamus also contribute to our moral functioning. These areas are critical for motivation and emotions that underlie ethical conduct. Damage to these areas from either tumours, gunshot wounds or injuries causes delinquent, psychotic and immoral behaviour. Illnesses such as frontotemporal dementia result in antisocial delinquent behaviour such as sexual harassment, assault, robberies, burglaries, hit-and-run crimes and paedophilia. Malfunctional amygdalaes have been found in the brains of murderers and psychopaths, explaining why these individuals rarely express grief or fear.

5.4.2 Values Change Over Time and Depend on Context

Values are complex cognitive and emotional constructs shaped by our significant others, experiences, society and culture. We have values, so we can survive and thrive in a complex world. Values are a critical part of leadership impact and need to be clear to the leader himself and those he interacts with. He needs to be able to articulate these values in such a way that others see them being lived out in his day-to-day actions and notice the alignment between his values and the organisations' values (Swart, Chisholm, & Brown, 2015, p. 54).

Values are not stable over time. Research studies showed that if participants were asked to "think like a trader" when making investment decisions, their physical responses like sweating or increased blood pressure diminished significantly from when they were thinking as themselves. This indicates that the position in which we find ourselves in, will dictate our values. In another study, people were challenged to play a business game. The one game was called the "Wall Street Game" the other the "Community Game". The two games were exactly the same, but participants were unaware of this. Participants were asked to maximise their own returns either through cooperation or cheating. The Community group cooperated at a level of 60% and the Wall Street group only at a level of 30%. In a follow-up study, participants were scanned while playing the same game. Those playing the community game showed strong response in their reward system when they cooperated, while the reward system in the Wall Street group showed intense responses when they maximised their gains. This research suggests that context hugely influences our values (Liberman, Samuels, & Ross, 2004).

According to Pfaff (2015), findings from neuroscience indicate that as human beings we are "wired" to be good, just as we are "wired" to acquire natural language, confirming what Wilhelm von Humboldt already stated in 1792. Von Humboldt intuitively believed that humankind is intrinsically more inclined to benevolence than towards self-serving actions (von Humboldt, 1792). In his book *The Altruistic Brain*, Pfaff (2015) posits that we are born to be good and have the brain circuitry that allows us to be sensitive to what other people are thinking and feeling, to empathise with their suffering, to care about their welfare and to translate that information into compassionate action. Pfaff also argues that we evolved to be altruistic to survive in a hostile world (Pfaff, 2015).

Pfaff (2015) presents a five-step altruistic brain theory (ABT) using neurophysiological and neuroimaging studies where he indicates that: firstly, the central nervous system registers the act you are about to perform even before you have taken the step; secondly, you mentally picture the person who will be the beneficiary of your action; thirdly, your picture of the person you are "saving" merges with your own picture of yourself—you literally see yourself as a beneficiary of your own action; fourthly, neurons in your prefrontal cortex evaluate the emotional consequences of going ahead or not (interaction between the amygdala and the PFC); finally, in the fifth step, if the answer is yes—you act; if the feeling was no—you desist. The default of our brains is to act in ways that are altruistic towards others by choosing others over ourselves.

Wilson (2015) believes that through the ages, human beings realised mutual aid was necessary and self-interest needed to be suppressed to ensure survival. The neural reward-and-punishment system became linked to social practices bonding culture to biology. Our brains have been shaped by thousands of generations of gene/culture evolution (Harman, 2015).

5.4.3 When Ethics Go Wrong

There have been numerous examples of leaders' displaying unethical behaviour: Enron, Madoff, Lehman Brothers and recently Jooste in South Africa (the Steinhoff saga). Swart et al. (2015) state that neuroscience might provide insight as to what lies behind the unethical behaviour. When the brain's energy levels are low, and we are overloaded with conflicting demands, stressed, fearful or experiencing powerful emotions, the PFC cannot cope, and passionate impulses take over. Examples might include toxic personal decisions, extramarital affairs, accepting improper gifts and corruption.

Neuroscience also gives us a glance into the brain to see what happens when we lie. It has been found lying gets easier for humans the more they lie, because lying changes the brain. The amygdala, the part of the brain dealing with emotional responses, is also less active as we continue the lying process.

A study by Garret, Lazzaro, Ariely, and Sharot (2016) shows habitual lying can desensitise us from feeling guilty and make it easier for us to lie in future. Using fMRI scans, Garrett et al. (2016) provide evidence for a gradual escalation of self-serving dishonesty and show that with repetition dishonesty increases. Pujol et al. (2012) further found weak connections in psychopaths' brains affecting their moral reasoning. The structures associated with emotion showed reduced connectivity to prefrontal areas and enhanced connectivity in an area associated with cognition. The video below discusses the biological roots of violence to illustrate these points.

Video Clip: Adrian Raine—Biological Roots of Violence

https://edition.cnn.com/2014/03/26/health/brain-moral-judgments/index.html
(3 min)

5.5   Ethos in the Emerging Markets Context

5.5.1   Case Examples of Ethos in the Emerging Markets Context

In most, if not all of the scholarly work on leadership and change, researchers discuss their theoretical frameworks as if their worldview is exclusively relevant. For example, in the literature quoted above, the systemic leadership perspective had been quoted as relevant to the post-industrial era in the Western world. The question could be asked, Is this frame of reference relevant to the emerging markets?

We certainly concur that in the BRICS (Brazil, Russia, India, China and South Africa) countries, where we had the most exposure; principles of systems thinking are applicable. For instance, in the knowledge economy, less hierarchical command-and-control approaches are indeed exerted. As Collier and Esteban (2000, p. 208) conceptualise "the nature of leadership, not in terms of the person of the leader, not as structurally defined or imposed, but as an ongoing direction-finding process, which is innovative and continually emergent". This notion of leadership as a process fits in the emerging markets' context that is also characterised by high uncertainty and constant change. We thus realise that several constructs in the Western literature could be applied in the emerging markets. However, the question then still remains, how would the constructs be applied to the emerging markets, and which adaptations, elaborations or new contributions would the emerging markets as unique context offer?

In this regard, studies on the influence of national cultures on organisational change management are essential. However, scholars from the Estonian Business School in Tallinn (Ülle Pihlak & Ruth Alas, 2012), who reported on their research titled, "Resistance to change in Indian, Chinese and Estonian organizations", in the *Journal of Indian Business Research*) declare that there is a dire lack of research on the suitability of change management literature from stable Western countries compared to countries in transition, such as India, China and Estonia. Their study revealed that the cause of resistance was mainly fear in Indian and Estonian organisations, but in contrast, in Chinese organisations, it was rather the inertia that increased stress. In India, the stress was mainly caused by leadership problems, and thus communication was essential in this country to combat resistance.

In Estonia, however, the increased workload that accompanied change was particularly difficult. For Estonians, communication, as well as education of the employees, assisted in dealing with the resistance.

HSBC Global Asset Management (2016) considers emerging markets as usually to be in a transitional phase towards developed market (i.e. industrialised) status and in the process of building liquid equity, debt and foreign exchange markets. Casanova and Miroux (2017) on the other hand, emphasise that emerging markets represent underfunded growth opportunities with problems. These problems impede their ability to secure the very funding they need to fully realise their growth opportunities. However, these scholars also describe emerging economies as one of the hallmarks of today's global economy and the dramatic rise of emerging market multinationals (or eMNCs) is a testimony to their growing weight and influence.

Within the broad universe of emerging market countries, the focus of this volume is indeed mostly on the BRICS countries, as defined by Jim O'Neill (2001), formerly of Goldman Sachs. While the countries differ vastly, they provide an insight into each region that they represent. The inclusion of South Africa in 2010, to represent an African perspective is indicative of this broad focus. The BRIC economies (excluding South Africa), represented approximately 23.3% of world GDP (O'Neill, 2001), and approximately two-thirds of world GDP growth in 2008 (The Economist, 2013). Furthermore, the establishment of the BRICS bank indicates that these countries increasingly represent a growing power and an emerging market alternative to the first world development institutions. In this way the BRICS countries highlight the opportunity for new ways of thinking about growth and development and thus provide an interesting lens through which to assess the change leadership models required and those in practice in these markets. BRICS focus, being global as opposed to regional, is key in the importance of selecting this group of economies.

These markets are highly disparate, which has been levelled as a major criticism of the grouping in the past. However, in terms of the research towards this volume, the diversity of the grouping is useful. Table 5.1 highlights a number of indicators, which provide a brief overview of certain aspects of the BRICS economies. Although this is only a snapshot of the economies, it provides some perspective on the strengths of each market. The United States is included for the purposes of comparison with a developed economy. It is evident that each market has unique areas of strengths and weaknesses.

The indicators used in the comparison table consist of:

1. Economic freedom, as presented by The Heritage Foundation, as well as *The Wall Street Journal*, (Miller & Kim, 2015) https://www.heritage.org/index/pdf/2015/book/index_2015.pdf
2. World Economic Forum administrates a Global Competitiveness Report (2014) http://reports.weforum.org/global-competitiveness-report-2014-2015/
3. The Global Innovation Index (2014) https://www.globalinnovationindex.org/content.aspx?page=data-analysis

Table 5.1 Emerging country indices

	1 Index of economic freedom: Country ranking (2015)	2 WEF: Global Competitiveness Report (2014) (144)	3 The Global Innovation Index (2014)	4 Ease of Doing Business Survey (2014)	5 Human Development Index (2014) (187)
Brazil	118	57	61	120	79
Russia	49	53	143	62	57
India	128	71	76	142	135
China	139	28	29	90	91
South Africa	72	56	53	43	118
United States	12	3	6	8	5

4. The ease of doing business survey (2014) http://www.doingbusiness.org/rankings
5. The Human Development Index (2014) http://www.undp.org/content/undp/en/home/presscenter/events/2014/july/HDR2014.html

The comparison table illustrates that China and India rated lowest amongst the emerging markets for economic freedom, whereas Russia ranked the highest of these countries. However, China rated best with regards to their global competitiveness. Russia rated the lowest on the innovation index; whereas China (also on this index), rated best amongst the BRICS countries. South Africa rated the best of these countries with regards to ease of doing business; however, South Africa rated worst in terms of human development, whereas Russia rated highest on this factor.

We travelled extensively to other parts of Africa and surely in rural Lesotho; Namibia, Tanzania, Zambia, Ethiopia, Kenya, Ghana, for example, speaking about a post-industrial era is hardly applicable. Our case study on the Political economy of Malawi, illustrates, for example the difficulty of moving into an industrial era from subsistence agricultural economic realities (Scheepers, White, & Kitimbo, 2017). The Malawian highly family-orientated value system is surely patriarchal in nature and prefers high power distance and a ruler to lead, setting up the emergence of even dictatorial leaders. There are several examples in Africa, where leadership is associated with dictatorship. For instance, Feldstein on behalf of News24 (2017) declares that for decades, Former President Robert Mugabe ruled Zimbabwe in a ruthless manner and over nearly 40 years, he turned the "jewel of Africa" into an economic basket case that has seen inflation of up to 800 percent. Admittedly, these markets are not emerging markets and could be described as frontier markets or underdeveloped economies, but they aspire to enhance the quality of living of their constituents.

We would argue that especially in these environments where the people at the bottom end of the spectrum are most vulnerable, ethos is most relevant. Especially, in situations where family membership in royal families guarantees a leadership position. We furthermore contend that with the turbulence in the emerging markets, ethos is even more relevant in this context. For example, in times of uncertainty, human beings require something stable to hold on to. A set of values that is consistent in the midst of rapid change, offers this stable structure. Change leaders could thus benefit from being clear on what would stay the same, for example their ethos or what they stand for, while they are offering direction towards the change process.

In the next chapters, we will highlight a particular emerging market to offer a more in-depth perspective of changes in a specific country. To provide a particular point of comparison, we will focus our discussion on the historical background of the country as well as highlights or milestones in the quest towards gender equality. We had collaborated on a chapter in Chengadu and Scheepers (2017) on this aspect. For an extensive discussion, refer to the book of Chengadu and Scheepers (2017). In this chapter, a summary will be offered with more emphasis on the historical background, for the purposes of highlighting the waves of change experienced in South Africa. It serves as background to change leaders doing business in South Africa or building alliances with South African companies in other African countries or other emerging markets. All over the globe, President Nelson Mandela is well known and could offer a meaningful discussion point with any South African, since Mandela's presidency was characterised by the successful negotiation of a new constitution, a start on the massive task of restructuring the civil service and attempts to redirect national priorities to address the consequences of apartheid. The ethos of his personal testimony and role model of humbleness is thus relevant to the discussion of this enabler, and the next session pays attention to it.

5.5.1.1 Featuring South Africa as Emerging Market for Application of Ethos

Change leadership in the South African context requires sound hindsight through an understanding of the eventful history of the country to gain sensitivity for the present issues faced in the country. The low human development score in the South African context has been fuelled by the legacy of apartheid. In this regard, Nkomo and Kriek's research (2011, p. 453) indicates that there are relatively unique themes relevant to South African organisations' frame of reference. The years of inequality and neglect of the socio-economic development of a large part of South Africa's population has created "huge challenges for organisations and leadership". Denton and Vloeberghs (2003, p. 85), in addition, emphasise that "the post-election period since 1994, has forced South African managers to handle situations differently".

Prior to 1994, the White minority dominated the South African economy and institutions. Given the depth of the racial and income divides that prevailed for all those years, Dani (2008) declares that the economic redistribution was inevitable. To illustrate South Africa's history, women's empowerment will be discussed as an example of ethos in the section below.

Despite there being many critical turning points in the history of South Africa, one can simplify and divide the transformational change journey into three key phases, the Apartheid Legacy, the struggle against Apartheid and the post-Apartheid era.

The Apartheid Legacy: 1905–1948

The founding of the Women's Christian Temperance Union (WCTU) in 1899 strongly influenced White women's suffrage in South Africa (SAHO, 2011). Similar to Britain, middle-class reformers were key in the women's suffrage movement, since the focus was on influencing legislation. White women were only granted the right to vote in 1930. Unfortunately, due to racial segregation, black women and men were not afforded similar rights until a few decades later (SAHO, 2011). In 1948, the Afrikaner National Party obtained power and formalised the policy of Apartheid, which focused on the segregation of the various race groups within the country.

Charlotte Maxeke founded the first formal women's organisation in 1918. It was known as the Bantu Women's League, and its primary focus was on the resistance of pass laws. According to Ginwala (2002), she was a defining change catalyst in many aspects. The African National Congress (ANC) played a pivotal role in the country's transformation and emancipation since its inception as far back as 1912 (MacKinnon, 2014).

The Struggle Against Apartheid (1950–1994)

As women continued to face many social and economic issues, they started organising themselves within the community to confront various challenges jointly. Wells (1993) further asserts that one of the defining moments in the women's movement was when Federation of South African Women (FSAW) organised some 20,000 women from all racial backgrounds to march to the Union Buildings in Pretoria to present a petition against the carrying of passes by women. This day took place on 9 August 1956 and is celebrated annually through the celebration of Women's Day. The events of 21 March 1960 in Sharpeville where 69 people were shot and killed by police resulted in the formal banning of various political parties including the ANC in 1960.

Politically the Soweto uprising on 16 June 1976 was also a turning point when thousands of students gathered at their schools to participate in a student-organised protest demonstration. While security police tried to disperse crowds, they, unfortunately, ended up killing Hector Pietersen and others who participated in the protest. On 2 February 1990 FW de Klerk, the president at that time, lifted restrictions on the opposition groups. On 11 February 1990, Nelson Mandela a political prisoner, was released after 27 years in prison. South Africa's first democratic election was held in April 1994 and Nelson Mandela was sworn in as President.

Post-Apartheid Era (1994–2018)

After the 1994 election, the Truth and Reconciliation Commission (TRC) was set up in 1995 whose core purpose was to promote reconciliation and forgiveness among perpetrators and victims of apartheid by the full disclosure of truth. In 1996 a new constitution was introduced. In that same year a Commission for Gender Equality was set up in line with the constitution. In Meintjes' view (2012), despite all of the consistent efforts and progress made, the majority of women in South Africa still continue to face discriminatory practices influenced by social norms and gender stereotypes. For example, women with tertiary education earn around 82% of what their male counterparts earn (Moletsane & Reddy, 2010).

Nkomo and Kriek (2011) found in their research that change confronting these South African organisations was embraced, rather than resisted. The leaders perceived the forces of globalisation as driving forces of change. We therefore advise South African organisations to be more competitive to buffer against international competition, making efficiency improvements and streamlining operations. They also need to re-engineer their processes regularly.

According to Zinn (2016), despite South Africa being a top performer with regards to women empowerment amongst the BRIC countries with double the percentage of women directors as compared to China, there is still inadequate representation of women in the Johannesburg Stock Exchange listed corporations. Only 8.79% listed companies have 25% or more women directors (BWASA, 2015). Despite the dramatic shift from apartheid to democracy, the entrenched inequality mindset continues to flourish.

Change leadership in the South African market has to take note of this historical background as well as the current quest of redressing inequality issues. For example, South Africa implemented the Employment Equity Act no. 55 in 1988. It gives preference to previously disadvantaged groups based on race, gender and physical disability. There is thus a huge need for the upliftment of previously disadvantaged groups and to improve the education levels of these groups. Organisations can play a crucial role in offering bursaries and learnerships to these students. In this manner, by adhering to these laws and offering these bursaries, companies are obtaining a license to do business and are perceived as contributing to the local economy and job creation. Against this background, ethos in the South African environment would be to adhere to and contribute to the upliftment of disadvantaged groups to lessen the high inequality, particularly with regards to both race and gender.

5.5.2 Case Examples of Ethos in Emerging Market Organisations

There are several examples of organisations that reformulated their purposes or missions to include sustainability or social impact.

For example, a CEO of an ICT company reframed their information technology service as "We make South Africa work". They use the case of the enablement of card swipes in retail through their services even in the rural areas. Their previous CEO started a culture change process of "ICT with Soul" in which the generally isolated type of work was made more lively and interactive through giving employees a voice and focusing on acknowledging their contributions.

Another example is the published case of Unilever (Scheepers & Van der Veen, 2018), which reported on The Unilever Sustainable Living Plan (USLP) as Unilever's blueprint for achieving their vision to grow their business, while decoupling their environmental footprint from their growth and increasing their positive social impact. The plan sets stretching targets, including how they source raw materials and how consumers use their brands. For example, by 2020, they would have helped more than a billion people take action to improve their health and well-being, as well as enhanced the livelihoods of millions of people as they grow their business. By 2030, their goal is to halve the environmental footprint of the making and use of their products.

Unilever's former CEO, Paul Polman said, "there is no business case for enduring poverty and runaway climate change". Marketline (2017) reports that Unilever is one of the world's largest fast-moving consumer goods (FMCG) companies and offers products across personal care, foods, home care and refreshment categories. Unilever operates in Europe, the Americas, Asia, the Middle East and Africa. It reported revenues of EUR 52,713 million for the fiscal year ended December 2016, with an operating margin of 14.8%.

Another example is the ambition of Philips (2018), who is headquartered in Amsterdam, for 2020: healthy people and sustainable planet. They include sustainability as part of the DNA of the business. Their mission is to improve lives of billions by making the world healthier and more sustainable through innovation. They are setting out ambitious targets for the company's solutions, operations and supply chain. By the end of 2017, Philips calculated that they had improved 2.17 billion lives. Philips' had set ambitious objectives already for 2010, of improving the lives of 2.5 billion people a year; to have 70% of their turnover coming from solutions that meet EcoDesign principles; and 15% circular economy principles; to be carbon neutral in their operations, employing 100% renewable electricity; to recycle 90% of operational waste and send zero waste to landfill; as well as having a collaborative approach with their suppliers to ensure structural sustainable improvements along their supply chain. Philips (2016) is a leading health technology company that generated 2015 sales of EUR 16.8 billion and employs approximately 69,000 employees with sales and services in more than 100 countries.

As part of their Global MBA Elective, we led a group of 20 Gordon Institute of Business Science MBA students in 2017 to Amsterdam and Rotterdam, where we visited the head offices of Unilever and Philips. We experienced how the employees we interacted with from these organisations, were notably proud of these sustainability objectives and they were confident that they would meet the United Nations Sustainability Goals that they had been focusing on. It appeared that their sustainability focus became part of their identity as an organisation.

Organisations must also clarify what they are about or what they stand for. An example of an organisation's purpose is Discovery Ltd., who operates on a key core purpose which is to "make people healthier and to enhance and protect their lives". It delivers on this core purpose through the world's largest scientific, incentive-based wellness solution, engaging more than 5.5 million lives worldwide (Discovery website, n.d.).

While this volume refers mostly to private commercially-orientated companies, public organisations could also benefit from the Ten Enablers Model. In these cases, the mandate from the national, provincial or local government would provide the larger framework within which these public organisations would function. For example, the South African government's agreement on 12 service delivery outcomes generally offers key focus areas of work. Each service delivery outcome has measurable outputs with targets. Each output is linked to a set of activities to achieve the targets and contribute to the outcome. Each of the 12 outcomes has a delivery agreement and, in most cases, involves all spheres of government and also involves various stakeholders outside government.

The Medium-Term Strategic Framework (MTFS, 2014) of government is informed by the electoral mandate and considers how global and domestic conditions may change over time. The basis of the MTSF serves to guide planning and resource allocation across all the spheres of government and to provide direction to national and provincial departments on how to develop their five (5) year strategic plans and budget requirements. The central thrust of the MTSF is to improve the conditions of life of all South Africans and contribute to building a better Africa and a better world. Therefore, government's mission and objectives are to set the country on a higher and sustainable growth path with an expanded and a more diversified economic base.

These strategic priorities include speeding up economic growth and transforming the economy to create decent work and ensure sustainable livelihood as well as massive programmes to build economic and social infrastructure. These ideals could inform the ethos of public organisations, because it emphasises creating a better South Africa, and contributing to a better and safer Africa in a better world. Alignment towards these ideals offers an amazing opportunity to public servants to derive a sense of meaning in their work. It furthermore, offers an opportunity to strive towards the "common good", as described by the classic work of Burns (1978).

In South Africa, the King IV Report on Corporate Governance (Institute of Directors, South Africa, IoDSA, 2016) is the fourth iteration of this report. It consists of revised governance standards and best practice codes. It is aligned with the Companies Act, No. 71 of 2008 as well as the JSE Listing Requirements. In compiling the King IV report, South Africa's role in the constantly changing world was considered, as well as the financial crisis, climate change, population growth in Africa and Asia, as well as technology disruptions.

In the Momentum and Metropolitan merger case study (Scheepers & Swart, 2015), the executives mentioned that "The business case must prevail". This has been a guiding light for them in taking important decisions. Whenever they had to make decisions about which of the two organisations would have the best system and thus was to be kept, or which people were to get which positions, they used this adage as their guidance.

5.6   Measuring Ethos

Reflection Questions Enabler 1: Ethos

Reflection Questions Enabler 1: Ethos, contains a short questionnaire to help you assess the extent to which you are practicing this enabler. You can also ask others to assess you using this instrument.

5.7   Conclusion and Outcome of the First Enabler, Ethos

In this chapter, we paid attention to the First enabler: Ethos. Contextual ethos in the times we live in, our societal ethos, as well as the expectations to organisations, given these environmental factors, were focused on. Specific case studies had been referred to in highlighting the practical application of this enabler, as well as tools and reflection exercises to make it relevant to change processes. Once leadership has paid attention to Contextual Ethos, the Second Enabler must be attended to, namely Ego Mastery.

References

Abboubi, M. E., & Cornet, A. (2012). Towards a dynamic stakeholder management framework for CSR certifications. *International Journal of Business and Social Science, 3*(4), 1–12. Retrieved from http://ijbssnet.com/journals/Vol_3_No_4_Special_Issue_February_2012/1.pdf

Amis, J., Slack, T., & Hinings, C. R. (2004). The pace, sequence, and linearity of radical change. *The Academy of Management Journal, 47*(1), 15–39. https://doi.org/https://doi.org/10.2307/20159558. Retrieved from https://pdfs.semanticscholar.org/e32b/d231c4704c56f43e0a1e2b22f7768507506e.pdf?_ga=2.49413286.187797263.1594145452-914570674.1594145452

Avolio, B. J., Gardner, W. L., Walumbwa, F., Luthans, F., & May, D. R. (2004). Unlocking the mask: A look at the process by which authentic leaders impact follower attitudes and behaviors. *The Leadership Quarterly, 15*, 801–823. http://www.ipcrc.net/LDI/pdfs/sdarticle-unlocking-the-mask.pdf

Bauman, Z. (2000). *Liquid modernity*. Cambridge: Polity Press. https://giuseppecapograssi.files.wordpress.com/2014/01/bauman-liquid-modernity.pdf

Begley, S., & Kalb, C. (2000, March 13). Learning right from wrong: The fragile steps toward a child's understanding that lying, stealing, cheating and hurting are out of bounds. *Newsweek*. https://www.qcc.cuny.edu/socialsciences/ppecorino/medical_ethics_text/Chapter_2_Ethical_Traditions/Learning-Right-From-Wrong.htm

Bendell, J. (2007). World review: The responsibility of business schools. *Journal of Corporate Citizenship, 28*, 4–14. https://www.jstor.org/stable/jcorpciti.17.5?seq=1

Block, P. (1993). *Stewardship: Choosing service over self-interest*. San Francisco, CA: Berrett-Koehler. https://www.amazon.com/Stewardship-Choosing-Service-Over-Interest/dp/1881052869

Burns, J. M. (1978). *Leadership*. New York: Harper & Row. https://www.worldcat.org/title/leader ship/oclc/3632001

BWASA (Businesswomen of the Year Award). (2015). *BWA women in leadership census*. Johannesburg: Business Women's Association of South Africa. Retrieved from http://www. bwasa.co.za/news/bwa-women-in-leadership-census-media-release

By, R. T., Burnes, B., & Oswick, C. (2012). Change management: Leadership values and ethics. *Journal of Change Management, 12*(1), 1–5. https://doi.org/https://doi.org/10.1080/14697017. 2011.652371. Retrieved from https://www.researchgate.net/publication/254307707_Change_ Management_Leadership_Values_and_Ethics

Casanova, L., & Miroux, A. (2017). *The emerging market multinationals report (EMR)*. Emerging Markets Institute (EMI), S.C. Johnson Graduate School of Management, Cornell University. Retrieved from http://www.iberglobal.com/files/2017/Emerging_EMNs_Casanova_Miroux. pdf

Chengadu, S., & Scheepers, C. B. (Ed.). (2017). *Women leadership in emerging markets*. New York: Routledge, Taylor and Francis. Retrieved from https://www.routledge.com/ Women-Leadership-in-Emerging-Markets-Featuring-46-Women-Leaders/Chengadu-Scheepers/p/book/9781138188969

Chopra, D. (1998). *Creating affluence: The A-to-Z steps to a richer life*. San Rafael, CA: Amber-Allen Publishing. https://www.amazon.com/Creating-Affluence-Z-Steps-Richer/dp/1878424343

Collier, J., & Esteban, R. (2000). Systemic leadership: Ethical and effective. *Leadership & Organization Development Journal, 21*(4), 207–215. https://doi.org/10.1108/ 01437730010335454

Collins, J. (2001). *Good to great*. New York: HarperCollins. https://www.harpercollins.com/ 9780066620992/good-to-great/

Collins, J. C., & Porras, J. I. (1996, September–October). Building your company's vision. *Harvard Business Review*. Retrieved from https://hbr.org/1996/09/building-your-companys-vision

Cullen, K. L., Edwards, B. D., Casper, W. C., & Gue, K. R. (2014). Employees' adaptability and perceptions of change-related uncertainty: Implications for perceived organizational support, job satisfaction and performance. *Journal of Business Psychology, 29*(2), 269–280. https://doi. org/10.1007/s10869-013-9312-y

Dani, R. (2008). Understanding South Africa's economic puzzles. *The Economics of Transition, 16* (4), 769–797. https://doi.org/https://doi.org/10.1111/j.1468-0351.2008.00343.x. Retrieved from http://onlinelibrary.wiley.com/doi/10.1111/j.1468-0351.2008.00343.x/full

Datar, S. M., Garvin, D. A., & Cullen, P. G. (2010). *Rethinking the MBA: Business education at a crossroads*. Boston, MA: Harvard University Press. https://www.hbs.edu/faculty/Pages/item. aspx?num=37295

Denis, J.-L., Lamothe, L., & Langley, A. (2001). The dynamics of collective leadership and strategic change in pluralistic organizations. *Academy of Management Journal, 44*(4), 809–837. https://doi.org/10.2307/3069417

Denton, M., & Vloeberghs, D. (2003). Leadership challenges for organisations in the New South Africa. *Leadership & Organization Development Journal, 24*(2), 84–95. https://doi.org/ https://doi.org/10.1108/01437730310463279. Retrieved from http://www.emeraldinsight.com/ doi/abs/10.1108/01437730310463279

Discovery (n.d.). Discovery about our business, Accessed 26 August 2019. https://www.discovery. co.za/corporate/our-business

Eagly, A. H., & Johannesen-Schmidt, M. C. (2001). The leadership style of women and men. *Journal of Social Studies, 57*(4), 781–798. https://spssi.onlinelibrary.wiley.com/doi/abs/10. 1111/0022-4537.00241

Feldstein, S. (2017, November 16). After coup, will Zimbabwe see democracy or dictatorship? *News24*. Retrieved from https://www.news24.com/Africa/Zimbabwe/after-coup-will-zimbabwe-see-democracy-or-dictatorship-20171116

Freeman, R. E. (2010a). *Strategic management: A stakeholder approach*. Boston, MA: Pitman. https://books.google.co.za/books?id=NpmA_qEiOpkC&printsec=frontcover#v=onepage&q& f=false

Freeman, R. E. (2010b). Managing for stakeholders: Trade-offs or value creation. *Journal of Business Ethics, 96*(1), 7–9. https://doi.org/10.1007/s10551-011-0935-5

Freud, S. (1924). *A general introduction to psychoanalysis.* Project Gutenberg, E-books for free, Originally published by Horace, Liveright. Retrieved July 27, 2019, from http://www.gutenberg.org/ebooks/38219?msg=welcome_stranger

Fryer, B. (2007, March). The ethical mind. *Harvard Business Review.* Retrieved July 27, 2019, from https://hbr.org/2007/03/the-ethical-mind

Garret, N., Lazzaro, S. C., Ariely, D., & Sharot, T. (2016). The brain adapts to dishonesty. *Nature Neuroscience, 19,* 1727–1732. https://doi.org/10.1038/nn.4426

Garvare, R., & Johansson, P. (2010). Management for sustainability—A stakeholder theory. *Total Quality Management, 21*(7), 737–744. https://doi.org/https://doi.org/10.1080/14783363.2010.483095. Retrieved from http://www.tandfonline.com/doi/abs/10.1080/14783363.2010.483095?src=recsys&journalCode=ctqm20

Ginwala, F. (2002). Charlotte Maxeke, the mother of freedom. *ANC Today, 2*(31), 2–8. Retrieved from www.sahistory.org.za/sites/default/files/Thozama_April_paper.pdf

Greenleaf, R. K. (1977). *Servant leadership.* New York: Paulist Press. https://books.google.co.za/books?id=AfjUgMJlDK4C&printsec=frontcover&dq=Greenleaf,+R.+K.+(1977).+Servant+leadership.+New+York:+Paulist+Press.&hl=en&sa=X&ved=0ahUKEwi2h6D_5vTpAhXNfMAKHXJWB9IQ6AEIKDAA#v=onepage&q&f=false

Harman, O. (2015). The evolution of altruism. *The Chronicle of Higher Education.* Retrieved July 26, 2019, from https://www.chronicle.com/article/The-Evolution-of-Altruism-/151625

Heifetz, R. A., & Linsky, M. (2002). *Leadership on the line: Staying alive through the dangers of leading* (Vol. 465). Cambridge, MA: Harvard Business Press. https://www.amazon.com/Leadership-Line-Staying-through-Dangers/dp/1578514371

Hofstede, G. (2001). *Cultures' consequences. comparing values, behaviours, institutions and organisations across nations* (2nd ed.). Thousand Oaks, CA: Sage. https://digitalcommons.usu.edu/unf_research/53/

Hofstede, G., Hofstede, G. J., & Minkov, M. (2010). *Cultures and organisations: Software of the mind* (3rd rev. ed.). New York: McGraw Hill. https://www.amazon.com/Cultures-Organizations-Software-Mind-Third/dp/0071664181

HSBC. (2016). *What are emerging markets?* Retrieved March 3, 2016, from https://investorfunds.us.hsbc.com/investing-in-emerging-markets/content/what-are-em.fs

Institute of Directors in Southern Africa. (2016). *The King IV report on corporate governance for South Africa, 2016.* Retrieved from https://c.ymcdn.com/sites/iodsa.site-ym.com/resource/collection/684B68A7-B768-465C-8214-E3A007F15A5A/IoDSA_King_IV_Report_-_WebVersion.pdf

Kuhn, T. S. (1962). *The structure of scientific revolutions.* Chicago: University of Chicago Press. https://www.researchgate.net/publication/305296586_The_structure_of_scientific_revolutions_Thomas_S_Kuhn_1970_2nd_ed_Chicago_London_University_of_Chicago_Press_Ltd_210_pages

Kutz, M. R. (2008, Winter). Toward a conceptual model of contextual intelligence: A transferable leadership construct. *Kravis Leadership Institute, Leadership Review, 8,* 18–31. Retrieved from https://www.researchgate.net/publication/228464894_Toward_a_conceptual_model_of_contextual_intelligence_A_transferable_leadership_construct

Lewis, L., Schmisseur, A., Stephens, K., & Weir, K. (2006). Advice on communicating during organizational change: The content of popular press books. *Journal of Business Communication, 43*(2), 113–137. https://doi.org/https://doi.org/10.1177/0021943605285355. Retrieved from http://media.kemsos.go.id/images/49820066022.pdf

Liberman, V., Samuels, S. M., & Ross, L. (2004). The name of the game: Predictive power of reputations versus situational labels in determining prisoner's dilemma game moves. *Personality and Social Psychology Bulletin, 30*(9), 1175–1185. Retrieved from https://journals.sagepub.com/doi/10.1177/0146167204264004

Littau, P., Jujagiri, N. J., & Adlbrecht, G. (2010). 25 Years of stakeholders theory in project management literature (1984–2009). *Project Management Journal, 41*(4), 17–29. https://doi.org/10.1002/pmj.20195

Lord, R. G., Brown, D. J., Harvey, J. L., & Hall, R. J. (2001). Contextual constraints on prototype generation and their multilevel consequences for leadership perceptions. *Leadership Quarterly, 12*, 311–338. https://www.semanticscholar.org/paper/Contextual-constraints-on-prototype-gen eration-and-Lord-Brown/f308a81a394ec1c30b1386a9c6655038315edb9f

MacKay, H. (n.d.). https://www.brainyquote.com/quotes/harvey_mackay_528767. Retrieved July 26, 2019.

MacKinnon, A. (2014). The founders: The origins of the ANC and the struggle for democracy in South Africa. *The International Journal of African Historical Studies, 47*(3), 507. https://onlinelibrary.wiley.com/doi/abs/10.1111/hisn.12249

Marketline. (2017, February). Unilever Company Profile. Reference code: 4FBBC2583F7F. London. https://store.marketline.com/report/4fbbc2583f7f–unilever-strategy-swot-and-corpo rate-finance-report-2/

McLeod, S. A. (2015). *Unconscious mind*. Retrieved April 22, 2018, from www.simplypsychology. org/unconscious-mind.html

Meintjes, S. (2012). *Rebuilding Peace: The case of South Africa*. Cape Town: Pambazuka Press. http://www.fahamu.org/resources/3_meintjes_v2.pdf

Miller, T., & Kim, A. B. (2015). The Heritage Foundation in partnership with The Wall Street Journal. *Index of Economic Freedom*. Retrieved from https://www.heritage.org/index/pdf/2015/book/index_2015.pdf

Moletsane, R., & Reddy, V. (2010). *Gender and poverty reduction: Voice dialogue and targeting. Policy analysis and capacity enhancement (PACE)*. In *Human Sciences Research Council (HSRC)*. Pretoria. Retrieved from www.hsrc.ac.za/en/research-data/ktree-doc/5932

Nkomo, S. M., & Kriek, D. (2011). Leading organizational change in the 'new' South Africa. *Journal of Occupational and Organizational Psychology, 84*(1), 453–470. https://doi.org/https://doi.org/10.1111/j.2044-8325.2011.02020.x. Retrieved from https://onlinelibrary.wiley.com/doi/pdf/10.1111/j.2044-8325.2011.02020.x

O'Neill, J. (2001, November 30). *Building better global economic BRICs*. Global Economics, Paper No: 66. New York: Goldman Sachs Economic Research Group. Retrieved from http://www.goldmansachs.com/our-thinking/archive/archive-pdfs/build-better-brics.pdf

Osborn, R. N., Hunt, J. G., & Jauch, L. R. (2002). Towards a contextual theory of leadership. *The Leadership Quarterly, 13*, 797–837. https://doi.org/10.1016/j.leaqua.2009.01.010

Palese, E. (2013). *Zygmunt Bauman. Individual and society in the liquid modernity*. Cham: Springer. https://springerplus.springeropen.com/articles/10.1186/2193-1801-2-191

Pfaff, D. W. (2015). *The altruistic brain: How we are naturally good*. Oxford: Oxford University Press. https://www.amazon.com/Altruistic-Brain-How-Naturally-Good/dp/0199377464

Philips. (2016). *About Royal Philips*. Retrieved from https://www.philips.com/a-w/about/news/archive/standard/news/press/2016/20160920-koninklijke-philips-nv-announces-tender-offer-for-certain-out standing-notes.html

Philips. (2018). *Philips launches new sustainability program 2016–2020 'healthy people, sustainable planet'*. Retrieved from https://www.philips.com/content/corporate/en_AA/about/news/archive/standard/news/press/2016/20160620-philips-launches-new-sustainability-program-2016-2020-healthy-people-sustainable-planet.html

Pihlak, Ü., & Alas, R. (2012). Resistance to change in Indian, Chinese and Estonian organizations. *Journal of Indian Business Research, 4*(4), 224–243. https://doi.org/10.1108/17554191211274767

Principles for Responsible Management Education (PRME). (2018). *2017 Annual report and 2018 outlook*. Retrieved from http://www.unprme.org/resource-docs/2017AnnualReportand2018Outlook.pdf

Pujol, J., Batalla, I., Contreras-Rodríguez, O., Harrison, B. J., Pera, V., Hernández-Ribas, R., et al. (2012). Breakdown in the brain network subserving moral judgment in criminal psychopathy. *Social Cognitive and Affective Neuroscience, 7*(8), 917–923. https://doi.org/10.1093/scan/nsr075

Scheepers, C. B., Maphalala, J., & Van der Westhuizen, C. (2014). *Nedbank: Transformational leadership in sustainable turnaround*. Ivey Publishing, 9B14C027. https://store.hbr.org/product/nedbank-transformational-leadership-in-sustainable-turnaround/W14219

Scheepers, C. B., White, L., & Kitimbo, A. (2017). *Political economy of Malawi: Contextual leadership in expanding entrepreneurial businesses*. Emerald Emerging Markets Case Studies, EEMCS-03-2017-0039. https://www.emerald.com/insight/content/doi/10.1108/EEMCS-03-2017-0039/full/html

Scheepers, C. B., & Swart, S. (2015). *Momentum and metropolitan merger: Authentic transformational leadership*. Ivey Publishing, 9B15C004. https://www.iveycases.com/ProductView.aspx?id=70560

Scheepers, C. B., & Van der Veen, N. (2018). Unilever South Africa: Contextual intelligence in leading culture of inclusive growth. *Ivey Publishing*, 9B18C015. https://store.hbr.org/product/unilever-south-africa-contextual-leadership-of-culture-for-inclusive-growth/W18333

Schein, E. H. (1996). *Organizational culture and leadership*. San Francisco, CA: Jossey-Bass Publishers. https://www.amazon.com/Organizational-Culture-Leadership-Edgar-Schein/dp/0470190604

Seitanidi, M., & Crane, A. (2009). Implementing CSR through partnerships: Understanding the selection, design and institutionalization of non-profit-business partnerships. *Journal of Business Ethics, 85*(Suppl 2), 413–429. https://link.springer.com/article/10.1007/s10551-008-9743-y

Shermer, M. (2011a). *The believing brain: From ghosts and gods to politics and conspiracies—How we construct beliefs and reinforce them as truths*. New York, NY: St Martin's Press. Retrieved from https://books.google.co.za/books/about/The_Believing_Brain.html?id=i_ihCeNpcaQC&redir_esc=y

Shermer, M. (2011b). *The science of right and wrong can data determine moral values?* Retrieved from https://www.scientificamerican.com/article/the-science-of-right-and-wrong/

Sinek, S. (2009). *Start with why, TED talk on YouTube*. Retrieved July 27, 2019, from https://www.youtube.com/watch?v=IPYeCltXpxw

South African History Online. (2011). *White women achieve suffrage in South Africa*. Retrieved May 19, 2015, from www.sahistory.org.za/dated-event/whitewomen-achieve-suffrage-south-africa

South African Government. (2014). *Medium-term strategic framework 2014–2019*. Part of the National Development Plan of the South African Government. https://www.gov.za/sites/default/files/gcis_document/201409/mtsf2014-2019.pdf

Svetlova, M., Nichols, S. R., & Brownell, C. A. (2010). Toddlers' prosocial behavior: From instrumental to empathic to altruistic helping. *Child Development, 81*(6), 1814–1827. https://doi.org/10.1111/j.1467-8624.2010.01512.x

Swaab, D. F. (2014). *We are our brains: A neurobiography of the brain, from the womb to Alzheimer's* (J. Hedley-Prôle, Trans.). Spiegel & Grau/Random House. https://www.amazon.com/Are-Our-Brains-Neurobiography-Alzheimers/dp/0812992962

Swart, T., Chisholm, K., & Brown, P. (2015). *Neuroscience for leadership: Harnessing the brain gain advantage*. London: Palgrave Macmillan. https://www.palgrave.com/gp/book/9781137466853

Taylor, A. (2014, March 24). The Exxon Valdez oil spill: 25 years ago today. *The Atlantic*. Retrieved March 4, 2018, from https://www.theatlantic.com/photo/2014/03/the-exxon-valdez-oil-spill-25-years-ago-today/100703/

The Ease of Doing Business Survey. (2014). Retrieved from http://www.doingbusiness.org/rankings

The Economist. (2013). When giants slow down. Retrieved May 27, 2015, from http://www.economist.com/news/briefing/21582257-most-dramatic-and-disruptive-period-emerging-market-growth-world-has-ever-seen

The Global Innovation Index. (2014). Retrieved from https://www.globalinnovationindex.org/content.aspx?page=data-analysis

The Human Development Index. (2014). Retrieved from http://www.undp.org/content/undp/en/home/presscenter/events/2014/july/HDR2014.html

Van Tulder, R., Seitanidi, M., Crane, A., & Brammer, S. (2016). Enhancing the impact of cross-sector partnerships: Four impact loops for channelling partnership studies. *Journal of Business Ethics, 135*(1), 1–17. https://link.springer.com/article/10.1007%2Fs10551-015-2756-4

Vermeulen, S. (1999). *EQ: Emotional intelligence for everyone*. Rivonia: Zebra Press. https://www. amazon.com/gp/product/1868723313/qid=1139993909/sr=1-1/ref=sr_1_1/104-2402283- 9559900?s=books&v=glance&n=283155

Von Humboldt, W. (1792/1851). *Ideen zu einem Versuch, die Gränzen der Wirksamkeit des Staats zu bestimmen* [On the limits of state action]. Breslau: Verlag von Eduard Trewendt. (Original work published 1792). https://oll.libertyfund.org/titles/humboldt-the-sphere-and-duties-of-gov ernment-1792-1854

Walsh, R. (1999). *Essential spirituality: The 7 central practices to awaken heart and mind*. New York: Wiley. https://www.amazon.com/Essential-Spirituality-Central-Practices-Awaken/ dp/0471392162

Wells, J. (1993). *We now demand! The history of women's resistance to pass laws in South Africa*. Johannesburg: Witwatersrand University Press. https://www.worldcat.org/title/we-now- demand-the-history-of-womens-resistance-to-pass-laws-in-south-africa/oclc/30557721

Wenger, E. (1998). *Communities of practice: Learning, meaning, and identity*. Cambridge University Press. Retrieved from http://wenger-trayner.com/wp-content/uploads/2012/01/09-10-27- CoPs-and-systems-v2.01.pdf

Wilson, D. S. (2015). *Does altruism exist? Culture, genes and the welfare of others*. New Haven, CT: Yale University Press. https://www.tandfonline.com/doi/abs/10.1080/00332747.2017. 1383127

World Economic Forum. (2014). *Global competitiveness report*. Retrieved from http://reports. weforum.org/global-competitiveness-report-2014-2015/

Zinn, S. (2016). *Swimming upstream*. Randburg: Knowres Publishing. http://www.kr.co.za/ knowres-publishing-1/swimming-upstream-a-story-of-grit-and-determination-to-succeed-1

Reference List for Quotes

Retrieved July 26, 2019, from https://www.brainyquote.com/quotes/albert_camus_118026

Second Enabler

Ego Mastery

Progress is impossible without change, and those who cannot change their minds cannot change anything.
(George Bernard Shaw, n.d.)
Everyone thinks of changing the world, but no one thinks of changing himself.
(Leo Tolstoy, n.d.)

Electronic supplementary material The online version of this chapter (https://doi.org/10.1007/978-3-030-40846-6_6) contains supplementary material, which is available to authorized users.

C. B. Scheepers, S. Swart, *Change Leadership in Emerging Markets*, Future of Business and Finance, https://doi.org/10.1007/978-3-030-40846-6_6

Learning Outcomes
At the end of this chapter change leaders will be able to:

- Understand how the past has influenced the self
- Know own strengths and weaknesses
- Find a trusted change partner to obtain feedback
- Identify own personal values, passions and desired learnings, motivators and sources of energy
- Develop own personal vision and change plan
- Identify potential burnout and depression signals

6.1   Orientation to Ego Mastery

While the First Enabler considered contextual ethos; the Second Enabler endeavours to examine the internal contextual ethos and to adapt this internal context towards Ego Mastery. In this leadership role, leaders are required to transcend context and act from their personal convictions. To this end, this enabler needs leaders to reflect on their motives and intentions, prior to embarking on change processes.

6.2   Importance of Ego Mastery for Change Leadership

For change management initiatives to be a success, the leader should act as a role model by demonstrating a commitment to change and must demonstrate a positive attitude towards the strategic initiatives (Al-Ali, Singh, Al-Nahyan, & Sohal, 2017). Therefore leaders have to sort themselves out, through being self-aware and realise when they do not truly support the changes. Their lack of commitment would cause employees to lose faith in the change process. As an example, the country manager of a pharmaceutical company in South Africa had to be clear about the reasons for a certain acquisition, before he could sell the idea to his employees.

In times of change, employees often feel insecure and seeing that the attachments to the familiar are strong, the uncertainty creates a need for trust in leadership. Trust is thus a prerequisite for dealing with the insecurities associated with organisational change. Psychological climate dimensions of "trust, participation and support are preconditions for an environment conducive of change" (Bouckenooghe, Devos, & van den Broeck, 2009, p. 562). To trust leadership, employees have to be convinced of their good intentions. In cases where leadership is perceived as being egocentric and egotistical, they will not be trusted. For leaders to overcome their egotistical needs and to transcend them for the common good, ego mastery is required.

The Second Enabler implies that it is essential who leaders are, not what they do. Through the Second Enabler, we advise leaders to become internally directed, by clarifying their core values to increase their integrity, confidence and ultimately their authenticity. Authentic leadership has been receiving scholarly attention over the last decades, and several organisational outcomes have been reported. For example, Scheepers and Elstob (2016) reported a positive relationship with employees' work engagement. Authenticity is dependent on an internal moral compass and as a result, this Second Enabler has exercises as a practical application to assist leaders in clarifying their non-negotiables or boundaries as to how far they would go to adhere to others' requirements and pressure.

In seminal works such as *The Leadership Mystique* scholars like Kets de Vries (2006) have been explicit about the importance of emotional stability in leadership effectiveness. To maintain emotional stability, leaders have to manage their energy levels, and in this chapter, several exercises will be offered to assist in this quest. Classical works, like Stephen Covey (2003) in *Seven habits of highly effective people* and *Putting first things first* (Covey, Merrill, & Merrill, 1994), emphasise that private victory precedes public victory. These principles are relevant to the discussion of the Second Enabler. Gandhi is known to have said, "Be the change that you want in the world".

In situations where leaders collaborate, their values and ideals could differ, Kets de Vries (1996) warns that this reciprocal interaction will involve constructive conflict. We argue that especially under these circumstances, this Second Enabler: Ego-Mastery would be essential. In cases where there is a lack of ego mastery, people tend to become defensive and insist on their own way. Collaboration thus depends on whether leaders are willing to engage in constructive conflict towards a common goal. True leadership is about raising issues that challenge the status quo. This requires the courage of personal conviction.

Walsh (1999, p. 52) advises that "at the summit of higher motives is the pull to self-transcendence. That is the desire to transcend our usual false, constricted identity to awaken to the fullness of our being, and to recognise our true nature and our true relationship with the sacred". Ethical leadership entails that leaders would consider, "What are the right things to do?"; "What are the right ways to do them?" and "Are we doing them for the right reasons?" (Ciulla, 1998). Walsh (1999, p. 59) concurs, that "while changing what we do is essential changing the underlying motives may be even more vital. The same act can be done with dramatically different motives and results". Sometimes leaders change things for the sake of changing them. They are also under pressure to show that they are introducing improvements. Building in this self-check and questioning of own motives could assist leaders in taking the right decisions for the right reasons. Like one of our interviewees, reflected "In some instances, one's ego could get in the way of taking a good decision for the good of the company. I had to question myself and discuss intended actions with my trusted colleagues, prior to embarking on them".

Leaders are under tremendous pressure to ensure profitability; while at the same time they are required to refine their strategy regularly to be competitive (Franken, Edwards, & Lambert, 2009). Strategic interventions looking to implement strategic actions need strong leadership to combat complacency and address resistance to change (Kotter, 1996). This declaration of Kotter (1996) is a typical principle that is regularly taught at business schools and published in books as well as in the business press. It represents the pressure to perform and could, however, pose a trap for leadership to introduce strategic change to protect their reputation and thus for their own ego's sake. In this regard the article, "Once an outsider, always an outsider? CEO origin, strategic change, and firm performance", Zhang and Rajagopalan (2010) examine the relationship between the appointment of a CEO, the execution of strategic change and the effect on organisational performance and identified an inverted U-shape (Zhang & Rajagopalan, 2010).

In addition, leaders' life stories played significant roles in how they responded to the change situation (Nkomo & Kriek, 2011, p. 453). Concerning the Second Enabler, leaders would need to be self-aware and realise the influence of their own life stories or narrative on their specific reactions towards change situations. For example, how might your life story influence the role that you choose to play in the change process? Many leaders might not realise that their egos could get in the way of making good decisions. For instance, it might serve them to reflect on the following pertinent question: How would you know it is time to make an exit and step aside so that others may lead? Contracting the services of a business coach might assist leaders to create a space to reflect on these issues around change leadership (Scheepers, 2012, 2013).

A study by Toscano, Price, and Scheepers (2018) found that arrogant CEO's had an adverse effect on the engagement, collaboration and cohesion of board members. For these reasons, participating in a coaching programme could assist change leaders, since they would receive feedback through the coaching on characteristics like arrogance.

6.3   Ego Mastery in Practice

As a change leader, one can often be led to believe that you have the power to change others, organisations or systems. One of our most profound and most difficult personal insights was, that although we have the power to influence others, the only real power we have, is the power to change ourselves.

6.3.1   Road to Ego Mastery

We developed the model below to map out the practical steps on *the road towards personal mastery*. It is based on the Sigmoid curve discussed in Chap. 4 and consists of three S-curves. The first curve indicates your past, the second is the current phase you are in, and the third, is your future journey (Fig. 6.1).

The process starts with an ongoing practice of mindfulness as the road towards personal mastery continues. The authors believe mindfulness to be a prerequisite for the five steps on this road to personal mastery.

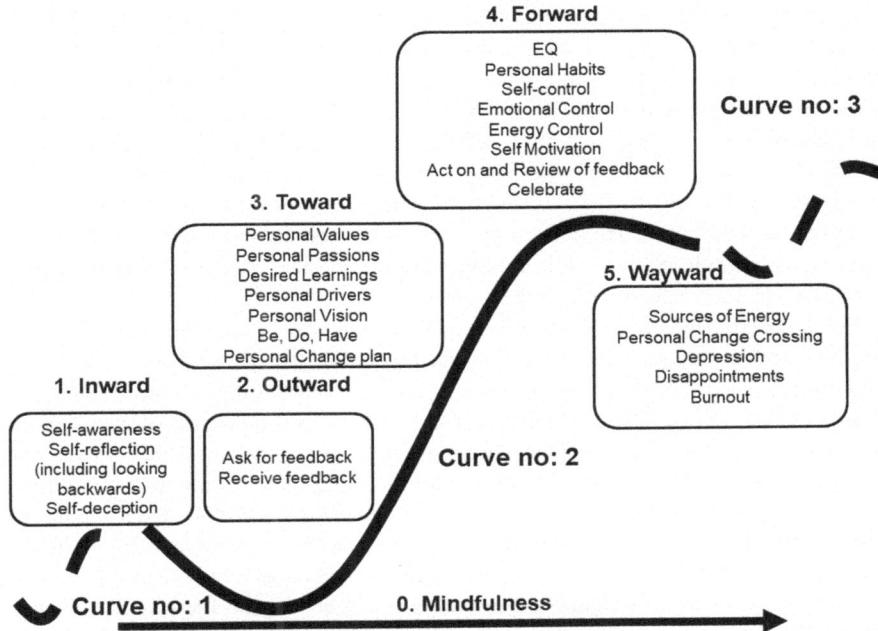

Fig. 6.1 The road to ego mastery (Authors' own)

The process consists of 5 steps: looking **inward, outward, toward, forward** and finally looking out for when things could potentially go **wayward**. Very few of us take regular time out to reflect and work on mastering our egos. To do this, one requires quality time to reflect deeply on where you have come from, where you are and where you are going. One can think of it as servicing your car. It seems like a luxury to spend time thinking about oneself, but without it, we run the risk of "running out of fuel or oil" (energy) or "causing an accident because of brake failure" (burnout). Your own inner work is essential for functioning effectively as a change leader.

6.3.1.1 Step 0: Mindfulness
Although there is no one universally accepted definition of mindfulness (Van Dam et al., 2017), mindfulness has been defined as a state of mind where one focusses one's attention on the present situation or experience—be it an awareness of one's surroundings, emotions or breath. It can be developed through the practice of meditation or other forms of training (Kabat-Zinn, 2013; Stetka, 2017). Siegel defines mindfulness as paying attention in the present moment on purpose without making any judgments (Siegel, 2007). Stahl and Goldstein (2010) define mindfulness as the practice of cultivating non-judgmental awareness in day-to-day life. The concept has been part of the Buddhist philosophy for over 2000 years and is

currently in vogue in popular literature and business after MIT professor Jon Kabat-Zinn popularised the concept and made it relevant to the world of work. Kabat Zinn adds to the definition that mindfulness is paying attention in a particular way: on purpose, in the present moment, and non-judgmentally. Daniel Siegel notes that mindfulness is the ability to pause before we act and Tang, Hölzel, and Posner (2015) define mindfulness as the non-judgmental attention to experiences in the present moment. Latham (2016) differentiates between concentration meditation and mindfulness meditation. He defines concentration meditation as keeping the mind focused on a single object, while mindfulness meditation notices whatever mental states occupy the focus of one's consciousness.

We suggest dedicating at least ten minutes per day to practice mindfulness. During mindfulness practice, sit in a quiet place where nothing will disturb you. Chopra and Tanzi (2012) suggest closing your eyes and going inward to give the brain a chance to reset itself. Chopra further encourages the process of checking in on ourselves (Chopra, n.d.). This allows us the opportunity to check in on our moods, emotions, physical sensations and all the things that fill the mind. Mindfulness is a way of checking how self-aware one is. Kabat-Zinn (1994) states one has to allow the body to pause long enough to let the present moment sink in—without judging. One should notice the thoughts, but do not get attached to the thoughts. It is useful to anchor one's thoughts on a sound or one's breath and focus on the anchor for the duration of the mindfulness session. When thoughts start wandering, it should be noted, but not judged. The attention should then compassionately be brought back to the anchor—again without any judgment. Being mindful is self-monitoring without judgment. It is also of great benefit if one can become aware of the signals coming from inside you. This is called interoception. Yoga exercises, breathing deeply and consciously, increase one's interoceptive awareness. Research has shown that people who meditate have greater interoceptive awareness. Also, see the benefits of mindfulness in the "Insights into neuroscience of ego mastery" below.

Mindfulness differs from concentration. The difference is that concentration involves keeping the mind focused on a single object, while mindfulness requires noticing whatever mental states occupy the focus of one's consciousness.

Learning to tune into our bodies also has beneficial consequences. Here the mindfulness practice of body scanning helps us to become aware of where we are experiencing stress in our bodies. Then we can practise stress release techniques to deal with these strains on the body. In a body scan practice, we sit quietly in a place where we will not be disturbed. We use deep breaths to relax and then start with the top of the skull and systematically work our way down the body, focusing on each part of the body and tune into where our sources of stress might originate from. For some, it might be in the shoulders, for others the gut and others in the lower back. When we become aware of the stress centre, we can visualise the stress being released and being replaced by a soft, gentle area of light.

In our everyday rush to get things done, we often direct our attention outward and we rarely really experience life. Research suggests that our greatest moments of pleasure are times we spend fully involved and engaged in a situation: be it physical activity, a sensory experience or intimacy with another person. When we are distracted, we are depriving ourselves of some of the most significant sources of happiness. Through learning to focus on the current moment, we become more effective in the moment and more aware of the nuances we might be missing than when not aware. We also begin the journey towards leading a more conscious life.

Cellphone apps are useful methods of starting with mindfulness practice. These apps allow users to set reminders and set time limits. As a starting tool, these guided sessions found on apps are instrumental in entrenching the habit. It has been said that mindfulness is a simple process but it is not easy and takes practice and discipline to be consistently mindful (Van Hecke, Callahan, Kolar, & Paller, 2010).

Benefits of Mindfulness
The practice of mindfulness is highly beneficial if one wants to grow one's own Emotional Quotient (EQ). When confronted with an emotionally charged situation, a few deep breaths could clear the mind to give you the time needed to respond appropriately. Farb et al.'s (2007) research suggest that we have an inbuilt ability to calm ourselves down.

Despite criticism from the scientific community that many mindfulness studies had been poorly designed (Van Dam et al. 2017), numerous benefits of mindfulness have been reported. Benefits include stress reduction, lowered blood pressure, improved outcomes for heart disease, better quality sleep, and improved pain management and gastrointestinal health (Hölzel, Lazar, et al., 2011). Organisations such as Aetna, Google, Apple, Goldman Sachs Group, Nike and General Mills have now started offering mindfulness leadership training and are providing relaxation rooms for meditation (Kim, 2018; Levin, 2017; Schaufenbuel, 2015).

Nataraja (2012) lists the following positive benefits of mindfulness meditation:

- Reduced anxiety
- Reduced risk of relapse in depression
- Reduced anxiety and depression in bipolar disorder
- Improved sleep time and efficiency in chronic insomnia
- Improved decision-making in substance abuse
- Improved well-being
- Quality of life
- Improved coping strategies in cancer patients
- Reduced anxiety and stress in schizophrenia

Chopra (n.d.) refers to studies that prove that meditators have larger volumes of grey matter in their prefrontal cortices than non-meditators. Tibetan Buddhist monks who meditated regularly showed activity in areas of the brain associated with compassion.

Mograbi (2011) asserts that meditation is an important form of self-control and a healthy practice. He believes it augments focus and attention and could be used to enhance empathy and all attentional capacities. He also claims that meditation is worthy of practice and could lead to a better quality of life.

6.3.1.2 Step 1: Inward

The teacher is within, so you have to learn to be still. You have to live your life so that you are listening within. No matter what you are doing (Bartholomew, n.d.).

The first step in the **INWARD** process consists of taking time out to look backwards to consider the journey your life has taken so far. The *My Life Line* tool (Tool 2.1) below is an excellent method to review your past successes, crises and disappointments. Considering the regrets you have in life, *Regrets* (Tool 2.2), is another way of taking stock and being honest with yourself, about what you feel you could have done better, or what you should have done, or not have done. Tools 2.3 and 2.4 consider your current reality and highlight your current strengths and weaknesses, opportunities, fears and motivators.

The idea is not to rush through the process or to just jump through hoops to get this part of the process over and done with. It is really critical for you to look inward and to spend enough time to discover your current reality. This will ensure you become self-aware and understand your motivators during the difficult phases of the change project.

Tool 2.1 My Lifeline

The lifeline template (Tool 2.1) provides an opportunity to map your life. Change leaders should follow these instructions: Start on the last line with your birthdate in the first column. Next, write today's date in the first row. Now work your way up from the bottom of the page to the top of the page recalling pivotal moments in your life. Complete the lifeline. Now return with a number of highlighter pens and highlight the highs and the lows of your life in different colours. You can use the third column to reflect on whether the event was a high, low or medium point in your life.

For everything you have missed you have gained something. For everything you gain, you lose something else. It is about your outlook towards life. You can either regret or rejoice (Ralph Waldo Emerson, n.d.).

Tool 2.2 Regrets

The regrets' tool provide an opportunity for leaders to look back at their lives so far and reflect on:
What you did or did not do, what you should or should not have done, in order to identify what you still want to do in your life or what you should avoid in future? It is also an opportunity to make peace with past decisions and let go of the regrets. "If only's" only slow us down and are a waste of energy.

Self-Awareness

Our most significant source of suffering is when we take things personally or seek approval. Taking yourself too seriously and identifying yourself too strongly with something (such as your work, your career, your change process) or when we try and possess something ("it is my project, my idea"), makes life difficult. On the other hand, when you relax and go with the flow, life becomes a lot easier (Hanson & Menius, 2009). To master our ego, we need to attempt to understand ourselves and why we behave the way we do. This calls for self-awareness.

The road to ego mastery is impossible without self-awareness. Without being aware of the impact of one's actions, as well as how one is perceived by others, ego mastery remains impossible. Although self-awareness is a complex concept (Parry, 2012), we believe it can be taught and should remain an ongoing quest.

Ochsner and Gross (2005) define self-awareness as the capacity to step outside your own skin and look at yourself with an objective eye. Rock (2009, p. 89) describes it as "having a third-person perspective on one's self".

Self-Reflection

Lieberman (2007) defines self-reflection as becoming aware of and reflecting on one's current and past experiences and one's self-concept, including the self-relevance of trait words. Self-reflection has also been defined as cognitively reflecting on one's sense of self, thus focusing on a collection of paradigms regarding one's abilities and traits (Johnson et al., 2002). The following self-reflection tools have been developed to allow change leaders to do thorough self-reflection.

We do not learn from experience. . . We learn from reflecting on experience (John Dewey, n.d.).

Tool 2.3 My Current Reality. (The Good, the Bad and the Ugly)

This tool helps us to take stock of our current reality. What is going well, what is not going well and what is really making our lives hell at the moment? Take time here to think deeply about your life. We seldom take decent stock of where we are and seem to drift along week after week without ever being honest with ourselves about how our life is panning out. This is the time to do so.

Another step in the self-awareness journey is completing a personalised SWOT analysis. The next tool offers an opportunity for leaders to reflect on their strengths, opportunities, threats and weaknesses.

Tool 2.4 Personal SWOT (Strengths, Opportunities, Threats and Weaknesses)

Take quality time out to reflect and honestly identify your own strengths, weaknesses, opportunities for improvement or new ventures, as well as potential threats in the workplace or in your personal life. This is an excellent dipstick to assess where you are regarding self-awareness. It could also be beneficial to use the tool in a conversation with a trusted partner. Ask them if they agree or if they would like to add to your personal assessment. This enables you to accurately identify the areas of strength that could be celebrated and tapped into, as well as the areas of "weakness". These red flags might be

(continued)

Tool 2.4 (continued)
an opportunity to consider who you need to surround yourself with to complement your weaknesses or it could serve as a way of identifying personal
opportunities for growth and development. Once opportunities have been
developed, these can be transferred to the Personal Change Plan (Tool 2.11)
to address particular gaps.

Self-Deception

Another classic and influential international bestselling book by the Arbinger Institute called *Leadership and Self-deception: Getting out of the Box* (2010), contributed
significantly to our understanding of the concept of self-deception. The idea is
compelling because it appeals to a global leadership audience—from Beijing to
Brazil and has been translated into 20 languages. Understanding self-deception is
essential as it determines your experience in every aspect of life.

The notion of being "in the box" refers to the issue of having a biased view of
your own problems, seeing others as objects and the cause of your problems,
thinking your problems are more important than others' problems and being blind
to the role you play in creating the problem. When you get "out of the box", you stop
blaming others and see them as real people with hopes, fears, cares and needs.
People have an uncanny ability to pick up subconsciously when they are just being
tolerated, manipulated or outsmarted and this leads to resentment. The trick, however, is not to now focus on instances where everybody else is in the box, but to
focus instead on yourself staying out of the box.

The impact of the concept of self-deception on the road to ego mastery is that we
often know what we should do, but then choose not to do it. Arbinger calls this self-
betrayal and believes self-betrayal is the germ that creates the disease of self-
deception. Although we know what the right thing is to do, we justify our actions
or lack of actions to ourselves, inflate our own virtue and start blaming others.
Unfortunately, this blame game is contagious, and soon everybody around you
follows suit. They too start blaming others. And so, the finger-pointing continues.

Being in the box can become engrained in our being and can be a tough habit to
break. To get out of the box, we need to become aware of the moments in our
everyday lives when we practice self-betrayal and resist doing what we intuitively
know is right. Once we become aware, we can start the process of acting on what we
know is right. The following reflection tool was developed based on the work of the
Arbinger Institute and can assist change leaders with starting to move out of the box.

The Tool 2.5a, 2.5b will take change leaders through the process of reflecting on
their day and their choices and actions about what is right, and to reflect on other
people whom they might perceive as the cause of their problems.

Tool 2.5a Me Getting in the Box

Reflect on your day. Was there a situation when you knew what the right thing was to do and still chose not to do what was right?

Tool 2.5b Me Getting OUT of the Box

I can correct my actions by doing the following. . . .
We also need to reflect daily on people we see as being the source of our problems. We need to choose to see these people as real people whom we want to help succeed and achieve results at home and at work.

6.3.1.3 Step 2: Outward

The second step in the Ego Mastery journey is checking one's own perceptions of yourself with others, ensuring that you are not out of touch with reality. We all have a sense of who we think we are. However, research has shown that our views tend to be unrealistically positive (Berkman, 2012). That is why we need to consult trusted guides who can hold up the mirror, and provide us with a more realistic view. In this step, we seek and graciously accept feedback.

Seeking Feedback

The next tool (Tool 2.6) offers leaders an opportunity to decide who they can approach to be a trusted change partner. It allows for an opportunity to clarify expectations with the change partner and to have a discussion on how and when feedback will be obtained.

Tool 2.6 Trusted Change Partner

The Trusted Personal Change Partners tool helps us to reflect who we can identify as a possible "coach" to hold up the mirror and reveal the truth to us on our road to Ego Mastery. You will have to make sure you select the right partner—someone who will take your success seriously, will not be afraid to call a spade a spade and who will be prepared to devote time to giving you open and honest feedback. You will need to agree with them what this will entail and how much time will be required from them to assist you in this role.

Once change partners have been identified, leaders could use the next tool (Tool 2.7) as a template to obtain feedback.

Tool 2.7 Personal Feedback from Trusted Change Partners

Tool 2.7 provides a template for a frank discussion of strengths and weaknesses as well as reaching an agreement on how the feedback will be dealt with.

Once you have discussed the feedback given to you by your change partner, you should now continue to Tool 2.11 Change Plan to decide if and how this feedback will be addressed. We recommend you do this with your change partner and agree when the next feedback session will be.

Feedback could also be elicited from multiple stakeholders: supervisors, followers, colleagues and any other stakeholders. This form of feedback will be discussed in detail under Enabler 9: Evaluate.

6.3.1.4 Step 3: Toward

The next step in the process is to start the process of identifying what you want to change. Change leaders could use the next worksheet (Tool 2.8) to reflect on their personal values, and determine how congruent these values are to the life they are living. Plans could be devised to make desired changes.

Tool 2.8 Living My Top Ten Values

In Enabler 1: Ethos, we discussed your personal values in detail. You will recall that we said that identifying your values in the values worksheet will help you to prioritise what you value and therefore what you should be aiming at in your personal life (Tool 1.1). Tool 2.8 is similar to Tool 1.1, but here we encouraged you to use the tool to reflect on the extent to which you are living your values and whether there might be a conflict between what you want your values to be and the values you are actually living up to.

The process of Ego Mastery needs to include an opportunity to reflect what leaders want to achieve during their lifetime. The next tool (Tool 2.9) offers this opportunity to take stock of leaders' passions.

Tool 2.9 My Personal Passions and Desired Learnings

This worksheet provides a chance for you to take time to find out what it is that you really love doing, because that would generally also be what you will excel in. Identifying what you would like to know more of, or what you want to learn to do is another way of pointing yourself in the right direction.

The next tool (Tool 2.10) offers an opportunity to consider a personal vision and in the worksheet provided a vision can be formulated, taking into account desires and what is important to achieve and become in the next five years.

Tool 2.10 Personal Vision

In this tool, we encourage you to identify the dream for your life. We ask questions such as "If you won the lotto and had total carte blanche, what would you do with your life?"

The next tool (Tool 2.11) will offer an opportunity for leaders to now create a personal change plan in the template provided.

Tool 2.11 Personal Change Plan

Now that you have completed all the tools above and spent quality time reflecting on what you love and what you desire for your future, you now need to develop an action plan to get to the life you desire. Complete the template by writing down what you want, how you will achieve this goal, by when and what resources are required to achieve this goal.

6.3.1.5 Step 4: Forward

Emotional Intelligence

The work of Joseph E. LeDoux inspired Daniel Goleman to popularise the concept of emotional intelligence (EQ) in his 1996 book, *Emotional Intelligence: Why it can matter more than IQ*. EQ remains a challenge most change leaders still struggle with. Although the concept of EQ has been the topic of a plethora of books and courses, it is still something most of us need to work on practically from moment to moment, especially during stressful change processes.

Although many different definitions and schools of thought exist in the EQ realm, the mixed model of Goleman (2004) will be used here to define the construct. Goleman outlines the following five dimensions of EQ: being self-aware, regulating one's own emotions (self-control), motivating one's self, having empathy and social skills (or managing relationships to move people in the desired direction).

Self-awareness was discussed in Step 1 of the Road to Personal Mastery. Self- and emotional-regulation and self-motivation will be discussed in more detail below, and empathy and social skills will be dealt with in Enabler 6: Engage.

Emotional Control

Two emotional control tools are discussed in the Neuroscience Insights section below. Daniel Siegel's hand model has been found to be a useful tool to explain how emotional control is lost ("flipping your lid") and Daniel Goleman's concept of emotional hijacking. The next tool (Tool 2.12) is designed to assist leaders in identifying what motivates them and what they consider to be rewards.

Tool 2.12 Personal Drivers

This tool has been designed to help you identify what motivates you and what rewards you prefer that will be meaningful to you. During a change process, personal motivation levels can often reach rock bottom. This is the time to ask yourself why you are doing this and, what is the personal reward for you to complete this process.

6.3.1.6 Step 5: Wayward

Leading and participating in change could potentially be an exhausting endeavour. Your internal resources could easily be depleted with disastrous effects taking its toll on personal, mental and physical health and relationships at home and at work. The Wayward step addresses the issue of managing one's own internal resources to prevent such derailment. It serves as a warning mechanism and a guide to ensure those leading and participating in change are equipped to deal with such issues within themselves and others.

Sources of Energy

The next tool (Tool 2.13) offers an opportunity to reflect on your sources of energy.

Tool 2.13 Sources of Energy

Energy is considered a scarce resource that needs to be managed. Part of ego mastery is the ability to control one's own sources of energy. This tool will help you identify who or what drains your energy and who or what gives you energy. By identifying these sources, you can decide what you need to stop, start and continue doing to manage your own energy effectively (Figs. 6.2 and 6.3).

By identifying the sources that drain and supply you with energy you can start the process of managing your energy levels. Ensure that you avoid the sources that drain your energy and consciously create opportunities for your energy levels to be boosted.

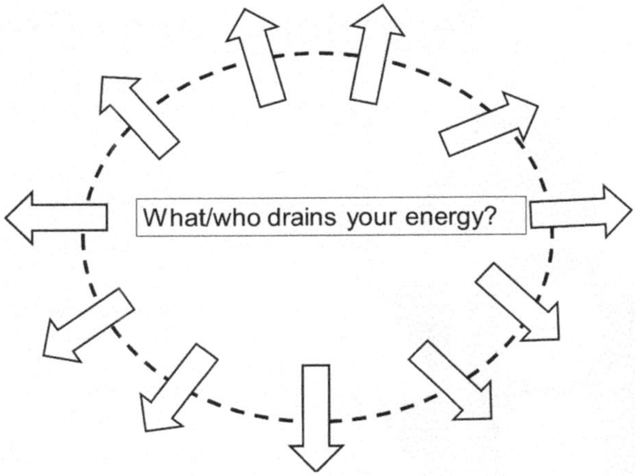

Fig. 6.2 Who/what drains my energy? (Authors' own)

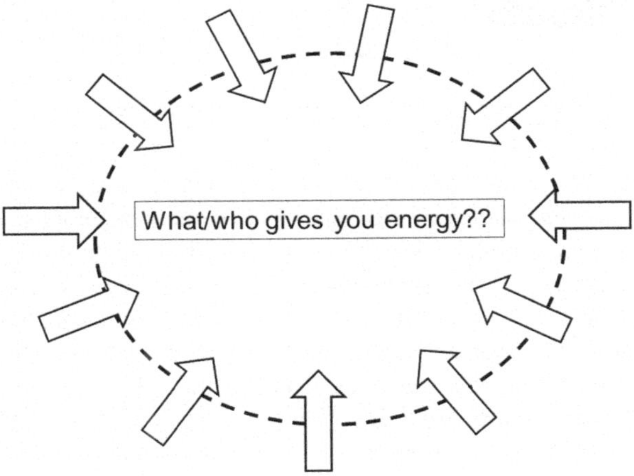

Fig. 6.3 Who/what gives me energy? (Authors' own)

Personal Change Crossing

Through the years, we have found Brock and Salerno's Change Cycle to be highly beneficial to many clients during change processes, and we highly recommend reading the book, *The Change Cycle: How People Can Survive and Thrive in Organizational Change* (2008). We have adopted the model somewhat and called it the Personal Change Crossing. It has proven to be very useful for those going through change—whether it is to explain their own feelings, thoughts and behaviour, or helping others go through the change process. Figure 6.4 maps the human experience of change and illustrates how the process works.

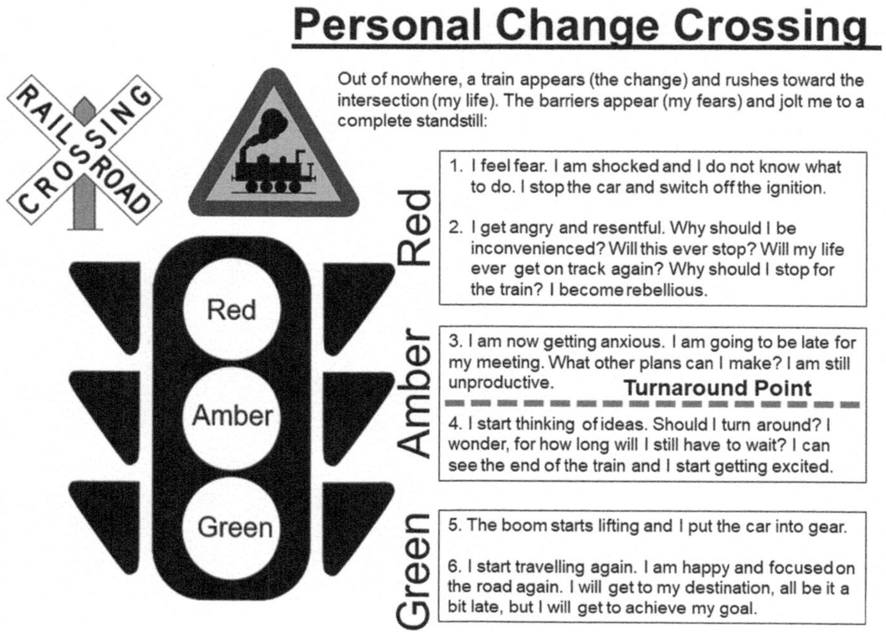

Personal Change Crossing

Out of nowhere, a train appears (the change) and rushes toward the intersection (my life). The barriers appear (my fears) and jolt me to a complete standstill:

Red

1. I feel fear. I am shocked and I do not know what to do. I stop the car and switch off the ignition.

2. I get angry and resentful. Why should I be inconvenienced? Will this ever stop? Will my life ever get on track again? Why should I stop for the train? I become rebellious.

Amber

3. I am now getting anxious. I am going to be late for my meeting. What other plans can I make? I am still unproductive. **Turnaround Point**

4. I start thinking of ideas. Should I turn around? I wonder, for how long will I still have to wait? I can see the end of the train and I start getting excited.

Green

5. The boom starts lifting and I put the car into gear.

6. I start travelling again. I am happy and focused on the road again. I will get to my destination, all be it a bit late, but I will get to achieve my goal.

Fig. 6.4 Personal Change Crossing. Authors' own, adapted from Brock and Salerno (2008)

The Personal Change Crossing model equates the change to a fast-moving train that appears unexpected and startles us and forces us to come to a complete standstill. The barriers (our fears) appear, and we cannot move. The traffic light displays a bright red colour, and we have to stop. We are totally paralysed and have no energy to make any decisions, let alone display a positive attitude towards the change. We start getting angry and resentful. This was not supposed to happen. Why does it always happen to me? We become rebellious and want to sabotage the train. This is entirely normal, and we can expect these feelings from any change—even if it is a seemingly positive change or a change we chose for ourselves (such as a new job or a new baby).

In stage three, we start becoming anxious and worried. How long will this change last? We are still unproductive and negative about the change. At the turnaround point, we are given the option to stay negative or move towards the positive. This is the point in the change process when individuals either decide to adapt to the change or stay negative, not moving forward. We teach people undergoing change to use this turnaround point as a pivotal moment, where a decision is made. For example, they would say, "I want to make this change work. I am moving from being against the change to being for the change". We might not yet feel like it, but we do have a choice. If we start making plans, look up and see what is going on in the environment, the mind shifts, and the amber light starts flashing indicating that something is about to happen. When the green light appears, the boom lifts, and we can switch the car on and put it into gear. Finally, the car starts moving again, and we are back on track travelling towards our goal.

Considering that we want people in our organisations to be productive most of the time, we as change leaders need to aim to get them through the red and amber lights as soon as possible. We want people to be satisfied, focused and generous. This is when the value is created and organisations start to thrive.

Although it is ultimately up to the individual to choose in which light he wants to spend most of the time at work, this tool is beneficial in assisting change leaders to help followers identify where they are and therefore help them reach the green light as soon as possible. In addition, the change leader should also use the tool for personal insights. They could ask themselves, "where am I and where do I want to be?"

Practical Application of Personal Change Crossing

We often use the Personal Change Crossing model to coach individuals through personal changes and to normalise the emotions of those going through change. Through the years we have exposed many individuals to this tool, and they found this model easy to understand and given a safe environment and the right opportunity, they can identify without much effort where they are and where they want to be.

The model was used extensively when three IT departments had to be consolidated as a result of a merger between three fast-moving consumer goods companies in South Africa. Employees chose to use the model as a screen saver on their laptops to serve as a daily reminder of where they wanted to get to and as a discussion tool indicating where they personally were in the process at any given moment during the day and where they wanted to be. They also used the tool to encourage each other not to be cynical, resentful, sceptical or unproductive, despite huge threats of retrenchments and layoffs.

Depression

According to the World Health Organization, depression is highly prevalent in emerging market countries. Out of the top 10 depressed countries in the world, seven are emerging market countries. India is number one, China number two followed by the United States, Indonesia, Brazil, Russia, Pakistan, Bangladesh, Nigeria and Iran. Depression is clearly an issue we need to consider when dealing with personal mastery. The aim of this section is not to provide an exhaustive guide to dealing with depression but to highlight what the symptoms might be and what to do in case you detect a condition (McPhillips, 2016).

It is normal to feel sad and despondent during a period of change—it is a typical reaction to loss and uncertainty. However, when these feelings become overwhelming, cause physical symptoms, last for long periods of time, or when it affects your ability to lead a healthy, active life, assistance should be sought.

We developed a depression checklist with a list of possible symptoms of depression, based on information from WebMD (https://www.webmd.com/depression/guide/detecting-depression#1) to enable the reader to assess the potential occurrence of depression in themselves during the change process. The tool can also be given to others to allow them to test themselves. If the symptoms persist, it is best to see a medical practitioner who can prescribe a treatment process, which might include medication or therapy. It is always advisable to seek professional help if you suspect you or someone in your team might be depressed.

The next tool (Tool 2.14) gives an opportunity for leaders to assess whether they have experienced depressive symptoms.

Tool 2.14 Depression Checklist

Have you experienced any of the following symptoms continuously during the last eight weeks? For example, trouble concentrating, remembering details and making decisions. Use this tool to identify whether you or others might be depressed.

It is important to note that many people at work might be reluctant to consider or admit depression as a cause of these symptoms. Depression is often seen as a weakness and to admit to such a weakness might cause discrimination or being labelled as inferior and not fit for the job at hand. Change leaders should look out for these symptoms in themselves and others and create an environment where these issues are openly discussed and addressed.

Also see neuroscience of depression below for the causes of depression, an explanation of what happens in the brain during depression and further tips on how to deal with depression.

Disappointments

The road towards the achievement of the change vision is filled with many ups and downs. Note that the big grey arrow in the change enabler model is filled with lots of S-curves scattered all over—not neatly following one other. So too, is it within the change process. It is messy and unpredictable. A student once remarked that the road towards the vision is a lot more like a dirt road in Africa—lots of potholes, lots of bumps and unexpected turns, cattle and goats crossing in unexpected places and never a moment to relax and cruise the way we do on a tarred highway. During a change process, disappointments will invariably be part of the journey. Disappointments can be important opportunities for growth.

The best way to deal with disappointments is to reflect on what one can learn from the disappointment. Here journaling is a beneficial practice. Journaling involves clearing your mind by writing down the feelings and frustrations you keep on repeating to yourself, within your own mind. It should be done without holding back and without judgement. It is a good idea to obtain a journal for this purpose and to write as if no-one will be reading it. It is also essential to ensure that your journal cannot land in the wrong hands, where what you are thinking can be held against you. Therefore, you need to keep your journal in a safe place and ensure it is for your eyes only. Many of our clients benefit from using their electronic devices to do their journaling. Ensure these documents are password protected—that will give you the courage to be totally open and honest during the process.

During the journaling process, you will need to take particular notice of the emotional impact of the disappointment you are working through. At first, you might feel numb, as if you do not care, but continue with the practice, and soon you will see significant benefits. As a change leader, it is also important to watch out for disappointments in others. These disappointments might be masked as denial, rationalisation and minimalisation others.

Burnout

A lot of research has been done about burnout, and in this volume, we will not be covering the topic in detail. Gunderman (2014) describes the incremental onset of burnout as the accumulation of hundreds or thousands of tiny disappointments, each one hardly noticeable on its own.

We have experienced that during stressful change processes, change leaders often display behaviour that indicates they are approaching burnout. We have learnt that it is better to get change leaders to identify the potential risks before their health is compromised and total burnout is experienced. We, therefore, provide the following tool based on the work of Demerouti, Mostert, and Bakker (2010). The tool is based on the Oldenburg Burnout Inventory to help you determine the extent to which you are likely to be approaching burnout. It is meant to be a guideline to hold the mirror up to change leaders and to help them put corrective action in place before the behaviour impacts the project.

The next tool (Tool 2.15) offers an opportunity to reflect on burnout symptoms.

Tool 2.15 Burnout Check List

Have you experienced any of the following symptoms continuously during the last eight weeks? For example, loss of compassion for others, feeling disengaged from your job or being cynical about everything and everybody. Use this tool to identify whether you might be suffering from burnout. If the leader ticked ten or more of these symptoms, then there is a likelihood of potential burnout syndrome being present.

The next worksheet (Tool 2.16) offers actions that could be taken to address the symptoms and perhaps contact a coach or psychologist to conduct a professional assessment.

Tool 2.16 Dealing with Burnout/Potential Burnout

Ideas for dealing with potential burnout include: Getting physically active—even 15 min per day of stretching, walking or yoga; Getting a change partner/some assistance; Practice mindfulness—10 min per day.

Practical Application of Burnout Behaviour

As change consultants, we often work with change leaders under immense pressure, displaying the behaviours mentioned in the Burnout Checklist (Tool 2.16) above. It remains a challenge to get strongheaded leaders to see the need to address the issue of burnout. We have used the above-mentioned tool to encourage leaders to discover for themselves how close they are to burnout and to get them to choose their own remedies.
We both have also been through experiences where we have come very close to burnout. While working very hard to remain professional and competent during stressful projects, we have had instances where we would burst out in tears at the most inopportune time (very embarrassing and frustrating to say the least!). Knowing that it is normal and common, we could support each other, understanding that it is a symptom of being close to burnout and then help each other put in place strategies to restore balance and return to a more energized place.

6.4   Neuroscience Insights into Ego Mastery

It has been said that the only real power we have, is the power to change ourselves by changing our own way of thinking. Knowing the complexity of the brain and the power of habits, changing the brain remains a considerable challenge. The exciting insight neuroscience brings, is the fact that the brain can change itself.

The road to ego mastery model above (Fig. 6.1) provides a framework that will now be used to discuss the insights neuroscience offer to help us understand the process better.

6.4.1 Step 0: Mindfulness

Although there has been a lot of hype and popular psychology around the topic of mindfulness, there has also been a lot of reliable scientific studies conducted by reputable neuroscientists in this regard. According to Tang (2017), more than 500 works of mindfulness meditation are published every year.

Neuroimaging studies show that the following brain areas are involved in mindfulness: For attention control, the anterior cingulate cortex (ACC), the medial prefrontal cortex (mPFC) and the striatum/basal ganglia (including the nucleus accumbens (NAc)) are involved. Multiple prefrontal and limbic regions, as well as the striatum, are involved in emotional regulation. The insula, medial prefrontal cortex, posterior cingulate cortex and the precuneus are all involved in self-awareness.

Harvard neuroscientists conducted research involving 16 participants who agreed to participate in a study where they had to complete guided meditation sessions of 45 minutes per day for eight weeks. They were also exposed to mindful yoga, body scans and sitting meditations. FMRIs scans were taken pre and post the study. Apart from the fact that brain activity produced an increase in the activation of alpha waves, it also showed more permanent, denser, grey matter in areas such as the hippocampus, which is crucial for learning and memory and areas associated with self-awareness, the temporoparietal junction, responsible for compassion and empathy and the amygdala, responsible for the fight or flight response reaction to threat (Chopra & Tanzi, 2012; Hölzel, Lazar, et al., 2011; Zapletal, 2017). In another study, long-term meditators were compared to a control group, larger volumes of grey matter were found in meditators than in non-meditators (Chopra & Tanzi, 2012).

Lazar et al. (2005) researched individuals with extensive meditation experience, showing that meditation slows down or prevents age-related thinning of the frontal cortex and that 40–50-year-old meditators had the same amount of grey matter in their cortex as the 20- to 30-year-old ones. Nataraja (2012) found that mindful meditation results in changes in the frontal and the parietal lobes. The frontal lobes display an increase in attentional networks, and a decrease in the surrounding areas, while in the parietal lobes there is a decrease in the orientation area and in the networks involving relaying experiences through language.

Mindfulness can result in profound improvements in a range of physiological, mental and interpersonal spheres. Physically it can improve the cardiac, endocrine and immune functions and interpersonally empathy, compassion and interpersonal sensitivity can be enhanced. It can further lead to a more profound sense of well-being and better mental coherence. It also leads to enhanced growth in middle prefrontal regions and preserves neural tissue in these regions with ageing. (Siegel, 2006).

6.4.1.1 During Meditation

Meditation helps to show the brain a place of rest, where no aspect of yourself is fighting with another aspect. It is immensely helpful. It gives your brain a foundation for change (Chopra & Tanzi, 2012).

The most highly evolved part of the brain, the frontal lobe, responsible for reasoning, planning, emotions and self-conscious awareness, tends to go offline during meditation. The area responsible for processing sensory information about the surrounding world and orientating one in time and space, the parietal lobe, also slows down. The thalamus, fulfilling the role of gatekeeper for the senses reduces the flow of incoming information and the reticular formation, the brain's sentry, quietens the arousal signal.

In the video clip below, Sarah Lazar shares her research showing that changes in brain structure underlie reported improvements and that people are not just feeling better because they are spending time relaxing.

YouTube Clip: Presentation by Neuroscientist Sara Lazar About How Meditation Affects Your Brain

http://www.collective-evolution.com/2014/06/15/a-neuroscientist-explains-what-happens-to-your-brain-when-you-meditate/

6.4.2   Step 1: Inward (Self-Awareness, Self-Reflection, Self-Deception)

We always have an image of ourselves in our brain (Pfaff, 2015, p. 58).

Self-awareness is a complex concept, and there is still a debate amongst neuroscientists whether it arises in the brain (Parry, 2012). Hanson and Menius

(2009) believe the self exists as a pattern in the mind and in the brain. It involves many different structures and processes throughout the brain and the nervous system. The way we view ourselves is based on numerous neural networks and can be categorised in a variety of ways, inter alia the reflective self, the emotional self, the autobiographical self and the core self. When you actively think of yourself, the self-as-object construct arises. We string together parts of ourselves to create a story of who we are. This happens in the midline-cortical structures (Farb et al., 2007) as well as at the back end of the temporal lobe and where the temporal and parietal lobes come together. These areas are not explicitly dedicated to thinking about self only, as many other functions are performed here. Neurologically the "I" is just a paradigm built from many subsystems with no fixed centre. You as a person exists as a human body-mind, an autonomous and dynamic system interacting in the world today (Hanson & Menius, 2009). Seppala (2012) believes the insula and posterior cingulate cortex plays a part in observing our internal worlds.

6.4.2.1 Self-Deception

One of the most common types of self-deception is self-enhancement (Hutson, 2017).

At the University of Queensland, Smith, Trivers, and Von Hippel (2017), conducted research to determine why we deceive ourselves. It seems that we process information in a biased fashion to convince ourselves so that we can persuade others. They further state that if we see ourselves as better than we really are, others will start believing us and this might lead to better opportunities for cooperation and mating. This was supported in a study by Anderson, Brion, Moore, and Kennedy (2012) showing that overconfident people are perceived as being more competent and having higher social status. Self-deception evolved for the purpose of other deception.

When longitudinal studies were conducted with 1000 overconfident schoolboys in Australia, overconfidence did not have any effect on academic or athletic performance. However, overconfidence in athletic ability predicted popularity over time.

6.4.3   Step 2: Outward (Ask for and Receive Feedback)

Receiving feedback starts with understanding and managing the feelings we experience when we receive feedback. Stone and Heen (2014) note that there are three ways in which your emotional buttons can be pushed: If you think the feedback is untrue (the truth trigger), if you have a problem with the person giving you the feedback (the relationship trigger) and when your sense of self becomes undone through the feedback (the identity trigger). These feelings are normal, and one should not try and avoid feeling this way, but instead seek ways of learning how to deal with the emotions. Throughout our lives, we have received many forms of feedback, and through the years we have adopted our own personal "standard operating procedure" on how we deal with feedback. We should become aware of how we receive feedback, notice trends and learn from these. We might also need to separate the message from the messenger. Another tip is to explore in more depth and to seek to understand what has been said by asking probing (not defensive) questions and digging into general statements without seeming to attack.

When you put yourself out there asking for feedback, you have to understand that you will experience a sense of fear. You will feel under attack, the thinking brain will shutdown, and you will become emotional, entering into a fight or flight response. Your self-esteem might also feel under threat (Resker, 2012).

The video clip below discusses the neuroscience of feedback.

YouTube Clip: Feedback and Neuroscience

https://www.youtube.com/watch?v=NhjSecFOEfY

Three parts of the brain are involved in receiving feedback. The first is the PFC. Our logical brain tells us that feedback is useful and needed, and will benefit us greatly. The second is our basal ganglia responsible for motor functions, learning and reward. The basal ganglia want us to get positive feedback because it will make us feel good. If the feedback is terrible, we will feel bad. The third area is the amygdala—our emotional centre. The amygdala is looking out for threats, and its primary objective is to keep us safe. These are conflicting systems. For feedback to be useful, it should thus be given logically, positively and safely. If any of these systems are triggered, we can stand back, reflect on what is happening and choose our response.

6.4.4   Step 3: Toward (Personal Values, Passions, Learnings, Drivers, Vision, Goals)

Berkman (2012) believes the brain contains a lot of information on how goals can be delivered successfully. By setting concrete personal goals and breaking these goals down into milestones, we can move towards a better future. When achievable steps are reached, dopamine is released, motivating us to take another step towards our future. A series of small successes keeps the dopamine flowing, resulting in the achievement of the overall vision.

6.4.4.1 Neuroplasticity

The concept of Neuroplasticity was discussed in Chap. 3, Sect. 3.3, Brain Basics. Neuroplasticity is defined as the change in neural connectivity induced by experience (Siegel, 2006). Now, as we move towards achieving our goals, the concept contributes significantly to our understanding of how the brain functions when change needs to be implemented. As Rock (2009) mentions, our attention has the tendency to be distracted and if you want to achieve a goal the only way to do that, is to focus your attention. By focussing and forcing our attention on the goal, we facilitate self-directed neuroplasticity and start the rewiring process in our brain (Rock & Schwartz, 2006).

Neuroscience teaches us that repetition, focus, and attention can result in hard wiring our actions. We need to shift our conscious intention to automatic processing to enable us to act without too much effort and to form a new habit. It is useless to try and erase a habit. We have to decide what we want to replace the old pattern with and then take considerable effort to consciously redirect our attention—especially in the face of danger. When we repeat actions, they become hard-wired, and that then becomes the basis for future actions. This has enormous importance in change management (Rock & Page, 2009).

The video clip below contains an interview with Jeffery Schwartz dealing with neuroplasticity.

YouTube Clip: by Jeffery Schwartz

https://www.youtube.com/watch?v=1KuZeVc9sfE
https://www.youtube.com/watch?v=kuABDAAns7w

6.4.5   Step 4: Forward (EQ, Personal Habits, Self-Control, Emotional Regulation, Personal Work, Energy and Emotions, Act on and Review Feedback, Celebrate)

6.4.5.1 Emotional Intelligence

Neuroscience proposes excellent insights that can assist with the development of EQ. As a rule, positive emotions generally work in another way than negative emotions. While emotions like fear, anxiety, stress and anger narrow our focus, inhibit our concentration and decrease our cognitive abilities—positive emotions can do the opposite. When we are feeling content, positive and cheerful, we will be more inclined to include others and be less self-centred, resulting in better cognitive performance (Parsons, 2014).

6.4.5.2 Personal Habits

For change to take place in the brain, learning should take place over short periods, throughout the day, with full focus. Enabler 8: Execute, contains useful information on how habits can be changed, and how new habits can be entrenched.

6.4.5.3 Self-Control/Regulation

The capacity to self-regulate enables human beings to become good group members allowing them to change or inhibit behaviours that will lead to group exclusion. To self-regulate we need to be self-aware, know how others will perceive our actions, recognise threatening situations and understand how to balance self and social expectations (Heatherton, 2011).

Self-control is also something that can be strengthened using the brain's natural plasticity (see section on Neuroplasticity above). Healthy self-regulation comes through relationships, and self-reflective observation can depend on integration of circuits in prefrontal regions (Siegel, 2006).

6.4.5.4 Emotional Control/Regulation

Emotional regulation is an ongoing internal process and often a challenge (Herwig, Kaffenberger, Schell, Jäncke, & Brühl, 2010), especially during times of change. Goleman (1996) coined the term *emotional hijacking* to describe emotional responses that are immediate, overwhelming and out of control, such as road rage, a fist fight on a school ground or an emotional outburst when service in a bank or restaurant is unacceptable. He explained that when we perceive danger or threat, whether or not it is real, a stimulus received from the thalamus is sent to amygdala, while another part is sent to the neocortex. The amygdala responds 80–100 times faster than the neocortex, scans our experience, compares what is happening now with what happened in the past and then reacts. We feel before we think and respond, without being immediately aware of why. Our perception of the current event may be distorted, and it may be only vaguely similar to a past event, but the amygdala can trigger the same emotional reaction. The amygdala also releases stress hormones to the body that take 3-4 hours to clear out. In an emotional hi-jacking situation, we can act in ways we do not understand or like because established patterns of behaviour from previous, similar emotional situations are conjured up. This can lead to disastrous consequences (Fig. 6.5).

The middle PFC is the region that calms the emotionally reactive lower limbic and brainstem layers. When this part of our brain stops being able to regulate all the energy being stirred up, our brain goes out of balance (Siegel, 2006).

The good news though is that the PFC can be taught to "manage" the reaction of the amygdala. Awareness of the fact that the amygdala is operating from a position of threat and fear is already a step in the right direction (Herwig et al., 2010). The next step is to practice dealing with hijackings, by pausing when you are about to react irrationally, take deep breaths to allow the oxygen to flow freely to the PFC and

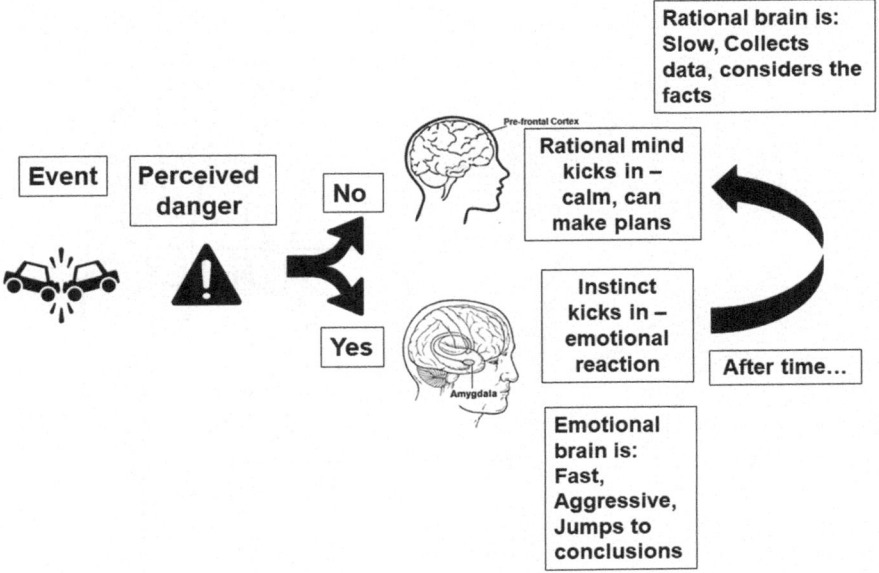

Fig. 6.5 Emotional hi-jacking process (Authors' own)

then engage it with rational thoughts such as reciting a poem or recalling a cell phone number or the date of birth of your best friend. This will allow the PFC to catch up and give you time to calm down and think before you react. Another technique is to try and step out of your own body and view yourself from a distance. This will offer you perspective and time to think before you act.

6.4.5.5 Daniel Siegel's Hand Model
Daniel Siegel (2006) uses the hand to provide an easy-to-understand model of what happens in the brain when we experience a lack of emotional control (Fig. 6.6). Understanding how the brain works is the first step in the process of understanding how to control our emotions. Siegel explains that the hand represents the triune brain described in Chap. 3, Introduction to Neuroscience and Change. The spinal cord is represented by the wrist, while the palm of the hand is the brain stem. If the thumb is locked into the palm of the hand, it describes the limbic system. Folding the other four fingers over the thumb and forming a fist represents the cortex (thinking brain). Siegel suggests that when we lose emotional control, it is as if we "flip our lid" by exposing the limbic brain. The challenge is to become aware that it is happening when we lose control, and then apply our cortex to return to being rational as soon as possible.

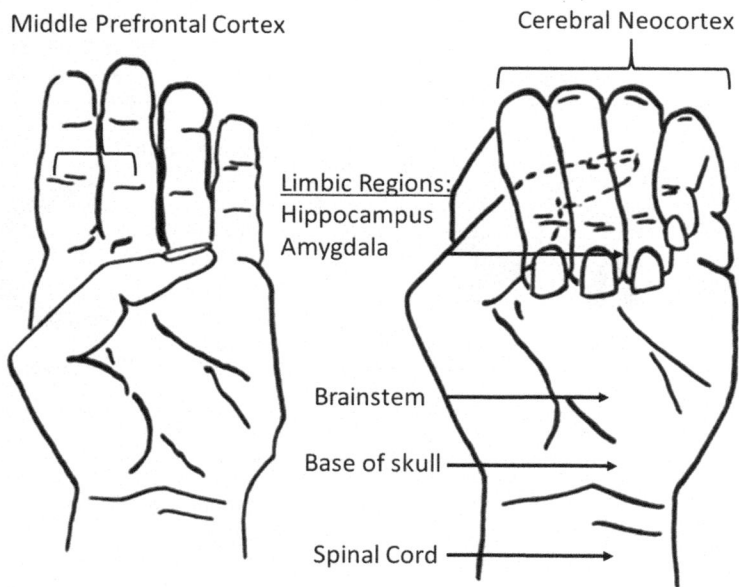

Fig. 6.6 Daniel Siegel's hand model (Authors' own)

6.4.5.6 Energy Control

The brain is the body's most energy-intensive organ. It is powered by glucose and oxygen in the blood. Neurons use a lot of energy while firing. Glucose produces adenosine triphosphate (ATP), the primary currency of chemical energy within cells. When neurons in a specific area of the brain fire, capillaries dilate to deliver more blood and thus more glucose and oxygen. This process is what makes fMRI scans possible.

6.4.5.7 Celebrate

When we succeed at something, our brain releases dopamine. The Ventral Tegmental Area (VTA) found in the midbrain is activated when we receive praise or when we celebrate success. The VTA produces dopamine and forwards the information to other parts of the brain (nucleus accumbens, septum, amygdala and PFC) via dopamine, leading to the sensation of pleasure. We repeat behaviours that release dopamine (Simpkins & Simpkins, 2010).

When you taste a good cup of coffee or bite into your favourite chocolate, your brain releases dopamine. It is a natural part of how the brain functions, producing the sensation of pleasure whenever you do something enjoyable. It is also released when we achieve our goals. It is important to note that the dopamine response is not just a once-off occurrence. The brain remembers the feeling and the association. Dopamine is firmly connected to motivation, driving us to repeat the behaviours that create the release of it in the first place. Unfortunately, after a while, the initial dopamine release is no longer sufficient, and the reward wears off.

Change leaders can use this knowledge to create new opportunities for dopamine release. The challenge is to find new successes, building on previous achievements, using newly acquired skills and experiences. But the initial success is necessary to build on. One could say that the expression "Success breeds success" is genuinely based on what happens in the brain (Lukens, 2015).

6.4.6   Step 5: Wayward (Disappointments, Depression, Burnout)

6.4.6.1 Disappointments

The emotion of disappointment was studied by a team of neurobiologists led by Dr. Malinow. During the study, it was found that two neurotransmitters—glutamate and gamma-aminobutyric acid (GABA) were released simultaneously by neurons in a small region of the brain called the lateral habenula. The more glutamate in relation to GABA, the stronger the feeling of disappointment. In another study with monkeys, they were led to believe they were going to receive a sip of fruit juice or another reward. When they did not receive the treat, the lateral habenula was activated (Wanjek, 2014).

6.4.6.2 Depression

Three parts of the brain appear to play a role in depression: the hippocampus, amygdala and PFC.

The hippocampus, located near the centre of the brain, stores memories and regulates the production of cortisol released during times of depression and physical and mental stress. When excessive amounts of cortisol are released due to stressful events or chemical imbalances, complications occur. The long-term exposure to these increased cortisol levels can slow down the production of new neurons or can cause the neurons in the hippocampus to shrink, leading to memory problems. The amygdala is the part of the brain that regulates emotional responses and is our centre of pleasure and fear. Continued exposure to cortisol can cause the amygdala to enlarge and become hyperactive. This can lead to sleep disturbances and the release of variable amounts of hormones and other chemicals in the body. The PFC located in the front of the brain is responsible for regulating our emotions and other higher-order functions such as making decisions. Excess amounts of cortisol can lead the PFC to shrink (Cirino, 2016).

6.4.6.3 Burnout

Burnout is indeed not just a matter of malingering. Not only does it affect personal and social functioning, but it can also put massive pressure on cognitive abilities as well as the functioning of the body's neuroendocrine systems. It could even lead to notable anatomical and functional changes in the brain. Using state-of-the-art technology and integrated research, studies proved that burnout sufferers had greater difficulty controlling strong negative emotional responses. They also reacted more strongly to sudden loud sounds than the control group. Research also showed that burnout sufferers had relatively enlarged amygdalae and appeared to have significantly weaker connections between the amygdala and other brain areas such as the medial prefrontal cortex (mPFC), involved in executive functions. These weaker connections between the brain structures explain why participants in the burnout group had more difficulty controlling their negative emotions (Michel, 2016).

Burnout also affects the body's neuroendocrine system that controls the release of the stress hormone cortisol. Cortisol is released when we experience a threat. The release triggers a range of bodily reactions such as an increased heart rate, affecting the immune system or the ability to remember things. After the perceived threat has subsided these functions return to normal. If, however, chronic stress is experienced these normal states are not achieved and can result in serious health problems. A study of 9000 working adults proved that burnout could significantly increase the risk of coronary heart disease (Michel, 2016).

6.5 Ego Mastery in Emerging Markets

6.5.1 Case Examples in the Emerging Markets Contexts

Admittedly, the influential publications mentioned under the importance of ego mastery for change leadership had been from a Western mindset for mainly a Western audience. The question might be asked whether these principles are truly universal and thus applicable in an emerging markets' context. Interestingly, several of specifically Covey's principles are similar to Eastern philosophy and in current Western personal mastery self-help books and courses. Meditation for instance, as well as principles of mindfulness and centeredness, relate to ancient Eastern practices. For example, Hinson and Osborn (2014) advise change leaders, who need to bring calm in times of turmoil and uncertainty to regularly practice meditation, "by maintaining a calm presence, leaders can transform the anxiety of the organisation" (Hinson & Osborne, 2014, p. 327). They also recommended mindfulness in their article "Leading in complex times", in *Practicing Social Change* (Osborne & Hinson, 2011).

Several of the ego mastery principles are indeed universal. For example, in the well-known book on Shaka Zulu (Madi, 2000), one of the leadership lessons is "never to believe your own praise singer". Applied to our modern organisational context, that would mean never to believe your own public relations officer. These are thus universal principles in terms of seeking feedback and objective opinions on your effectiveness as a leader.

In some of the emerging markets, with high power distance, leaders might find it challenging to gather feedback and would need to find a way of eliciting honest, direct feedback. For example, in the GLOBE study, intercultural differences across countries had an influence on feedback to leaders.

In South Africa, a great example of humbleness and ability to forgive his prosecutors and build relationships across races is, of course, the former President, Nelson Mandela.

Walsh (1999, p. 266) advises that "an enormous advantage of awakening the motive of service is that it transforms daily activities into spiritual practices. With its help, we need not change what we are doing so much as how and why we are doing it". Regular reflection and evaluation of the true service motive would serve leaders.

The Second enabler: Ego Mastery could be enhanced through regular feedback on leadership effectiveness. On one of our courses on change leadership, a group of leaders was asked to obtain feedback from their subordinates. Thirty respondents rated their leaders by answering the following questions:

- My leader inspires and motivates me
- My leader demonstrates the values of my organisation
- Leaders in my department ensure I understand what the organisation needs to achieve
- My leaders/managers gives me individual attention when I need it

Based on the results, 76% of the participants agreed that leadership within the organisation's departments ensures that the staff understand what the organisation needs to achieve. Seventy-one percent of the participants agreed that they receive individual attention from their leaders and 65% agreed that leaders demonstrate the values of the organisation. Only 47% of the participants agreed that they were inspired and motivated by their leaders.

6.5.1.1 Featuring Gandhi as Change Leader with Ego-Mastery in India as Emerging Market

Gandhi was a prominent change leader with his passive resistance to the colonising of his home country, India. He demonstrated ego-mastery with his hunger strikes and giving his life to the cause of liberating India. As such, he is an outstanding example in this volume of a change leader with ego-mastery. For this reason, India was chosen by the authors to be the emerging market to focus on in the discussion of this enabler.

Casanova and Miroux (2017) report on the E20 grouping or the top 20 emerging markets, namely Argentina, Brazil, Chile, China, Colombia, Egypt, Indonesia, India, Iran, Malaysia, Mexico, Nigeria, Philippines, Poland, Republic of Korea, Russia, Saudi Arabia, South Africa, Thailand and Turkey. In 2017 these countries accounted for more than 50% of the world's population. They also account for almost half of the global GDP. Around 30% of the Fortune Global 500 organisations were from the E20 in 2017; whereas in 2007, they were less than 10%. Since this chapter features a specific E20 country, the next sections will focus on India as one of them.

Ülle Pihlak and Ruth Alas' study (2012) showed that in India, the cause of resistance was mainly fear. Stress during change processes was primarily caused by leadership problems, and thus communication was essential in this country to combat resistance. Since India was colonised by the British, it would be important to adhere to Brazzel's (2007) encouragement to OD practitioners to track, name and address the legacy of colonialism and oppression. This volume is an answer to the call of Brazzel (2007) to consider the impact of colonialism since the focus of our research is on the emerging market countries, where most of them were colonised during certain phases of their respective histories.

Hema Parbhoo, one of our interviewees for this book, conducted an extensive study on India, during her research towards the *Women leadership in emerging markets*' (Chengadu & Scheepers, 2017). Only a short summary of her research could be incorporated in that volume, due to word count constraints. Her accounts and some of her findings are discussed here. Hema Parbhoo laments that India is known to be the land of many contradictions. Despite being one of the fastest growing economies in the world, the struggle and plight of women continue to be a key challenge within the society. India is a patriarchal society, which, by definition, is a culture in which males as fathers or husbands are assumed to be in charge and are seen as the official heads of households. To highlight aspects of the Indian history and develop insight into realities when doing business in India, the pre-independence period, independence and post-independence eras are discussed below.

6.5.1.2 Pre-independence
European colonists in the eighteenth century denounced the social evils of local Indian rituals, such as the practice of Sati. Gangoli (2007) explains that Sati refers to a funeral ritual within some Indian communities. A recently widowed woman was forced to commit suicide by fire, typically on the husband's funeral pyre. Between 1772 and 1947, the British introduced several laws, which aimed to liberate women in India. In 1891, the Age of Consent Act was introduced that raised the legal age of marriage from 10 to 12 years for girls. Many laws that were introduced during this phase further enhanced both human and women rights (Basu, 2009).

6.5.1.3 Independence
Essential learning for change leadership is to take note that in the Indian society, the laws had not lessened the resistance of Indian men, due to their power being threatened and their fear of losing their dominance. Despite basic rights and democracy for all, the strong patriarchal social and cultural ideologies failed to support and honour these changes. The colonialists were also met with resistance when they tried to modernise the Hindu family (Kumar, 1998). Mahatma Gandhi who was the key voice in India at the time, legitimised and expanded Indian women's public activities by initiating them into the non-violent civil disobedience movement against the British. He praised their feminine roles of caring, sacrifice and tolerance.

6.5.1.4 Post-independence
Nationalist agendas on nation building took precedence over women issues right after India's 1947 independence (Gangoli, 2007). Indira Gandhi became the first female Prime Minister of India, which was a key milestone in the history of India (1966–1977). India's patriarchal culture has made the process of gaining land-ownership rights and access to education challenging.

Change leaders in India have to be sensitive about the traditional customs and nuances around class-castes in Indian society and workplaces. The different approaches to and treatment of people from different class–castes create a diversity dimension that is not well known in other countries. Change leaders have to be sensitive to these nuances in the Indian society and workplaces.

6.5.2 Case Examples of Ego Mastery in Emerging Market Organisations

One of our interviewees reflected on how she had to grow and discover hidden aspects of herself, for example that she could interact with the media to promote her magazine or talk to potential advertisers when she was convinced of the merits of her product. She had to allow herself to develop confidence and belief in herself, the same way her mentor believed in her. "I had to overcome my own limitations before I could be successful in my work." During our interviews, we observed that several of the South African multinationals followed the same strategy.

A case study was published on the performance of South African Airways (SAA) over many decades and the corresponding CEO's leadership during that time. The SAA case was published by Harvard Business School Press by Joshua Margolis, Laura Margan Roberts and Laura Winig in 2007. This case is in the public domain, and the following analyses have been conducted on this case study. For example, in this SAA case study, various leaders provide examples of poor, good and great leadership: Myburg, SAA CEO, between 1993 and 1998, had the courage to discontinue unprofitable routes. Andrews, CEO between 1998 and 2000, on his part, took shortcuts by selling fleet and initially showing a profit of $40 million, but eventually a loss of $75 million, when taking sold assets into account. This shortcut attracted a customer "Swiss Air", but the global aviation environment made the deal difficult. He received a severance package of $34 million.

During Viljoen's (2001–2004) tenure, he took the risk of hedging fuel prices by signing a contract for 10 years, which caused the airline to lose $ 968 million. In his turn, Ngqula had a good track record at the IDC but lacked aviation experience. The fact that he acknowledged it and recruited a COO with experience assisted the organisation. Although downsizing was probably his only option to show a profit, it increased staff's frustration. However, while the organisation was on a cost-cutting mission, there were reports of the CEO's excessive spending. When Ngqula had to decide between attending a party on a client's invitation or attending wage negotiations when the union warned that they would strike, he opted for the party. As a result, the strike went ahead, and the airline's operations seized, resulting in an R7.5 million daily loss for the airline. Ngqula and Andrews are examples of how leaders who do not behave in alignment with the values of the organisation lose credibility.

In the discussion of the Eighth Enabler: Execute, the training of managers as part of an Organisational Development (OD) intervention at an Indian state-owned entity (SOE) will be highlighted. Refer to that chapter for an example of change at an Indian company.

For example, in our published case study of MMI (Scheepers & Swart, 2015), the Second Enabler: Ego Mastery was illustrated by the Momentum CEO, Nicolaas Kruger, who realised that his own career was not the point. There was a superordinate goal that would transcend both organisations during the merger and that he had to let go of his own insecurities and career aspirations and instead focus on building something that would transcend his own career at Momentum.

In the Metropolitan case, Wilhelm van Zyl also had to put aside his own career aspirations. There was uncertainty for a prolonged period of seven months about who would be promoted to the group CEO position before it was announced in 2011, and thus they were uncertain for a prolonged period of seven months. Since they had both experienced the change cycle in their own lives, they realised that they had to reach agreement on these issues as soon as possible on the lower levels.

6.6   Measuring Ego Mastery

Reflection Questions Enabler 2: Ego Mastery

Reflection Questions Enabler 2: Ego Mastery, contains a short questionnaire to help you assess the extent to which you are practicing this enabler. You can also ask others to assess your change leadership using this instrument.

6.7   Conclusion and Outcome of the Second Enabler, Ego Mastery

As mentioned in the orientation section of this chapter, private victory precedes public victory. We offered examples from our interviewees of where the cases illustrated this principle. The outcome of excelling at this Second enabler: Ego-mastery is Authentic leadership. Where leaders are able to master their egos, they demonstrate self-directed leadership that make independent decisions built on their own convictions.

References

Al-Ali, A. A., Singh, S. K., Al-Nahyan, M., & Sohal, A. S. (2017). Change management through leadership: The mediating role of organizational culture. *International Journal of Organizational Analysis, 25*(4), 723–739. https://doi.org/10.1108/IJOA-01-2017-1117

Anderson, C., Brion, S., Moore, D. A., & Kennedy, J. A. (2012). A status-enhancement account of overconfidence. *Journal of Personality and Social Psychology, 103*(4), 718–735. https://doi.org/10.1037/a0029395

Arbinger Institute. (2010). *Leadership and self-deception: Getting out of the box.* San Francisco, CA: Brett-Koehler Publishers. https://www.amazon.com/Leadership-Self-Deception-Getting-Out-Box/dp/1576759776

Basu, S. (2009). *Gender stereotypes in corporate India.* Kolkata: Sage. https://www.amazon.com/Gender-Stereotypes-Corporate-India-Response/dp/8178298511

Berkman, E. T. (2012, November 12). Goals, motivation and the brain. What can neuroscience tell us about how to succeed at our goals? *Psychology Today.* Retrieved from https://www.psychologytoday.com/blog/the-motivated-brain/201211/goals-motivation-and-the-brain

Bouckenooghe, D., Devos, G., & van den Broeck, H. (2009). Organizational change questionnaire-climate of change, processes, and readiness: Development of a new instrument. *Journal of Psychology, 143*(6), 559–599. https://doi.org/https://doi.org/10.1080/00223980903218216. Retrieved from https://www.ncbi.nlm.nih.gov/pubmed/19957876

Brazzel, M. (2007). Diversity and social justice practices for OD practitioners. *OD Practitioner, 39*(3), 15–21. http://michaelbrazzel.com/wp-content/uploads/2012/07/Brazzel2007ODParticledivSjPractices.pdf

Brock, A., & Salerno, L. (2008). *The change cycle: How people can survive and thrive in organizational change.* San Francisco, CA: Berrett-Koehler Publishers. https://www.amazon.com/Change-Cycle-People-Survive-Organizational/dp/1576754987

Casanova, L., & Miroux, A. (2017). *The emerging market multinationals report (EMR).* Emerging Markets Institute (EMI), S.C. Johnson Graduate School of Management, Cornell University. Retrieved from http://www.iberglobal.com/files/2017/Emerging_EMNs_Casanova_Miroux.pdf

Chengadu, S., & Scheepers, C. B. (Ed.). (2017). *Women leadership in emerging markets.* New York: Routledge, Taylor and Francis. Retrieved from https://www.routledge.com/Women-Leadership-in-Emerging-Markets-Featuring-46-Women-Leaders/Chengadu-Scheepers/p/book/9781138188969

Chopra, D., & Tanzi, R. E. (2012). *Superbrain unleash the explosive power of your mind.* London: Rider. https://www.amazon.com/Super-Brain-Unleashing-Explosive-Well-Being/dp/0307956830

Chopra. (n.d.). *What happens to the brain during meditation?* Retrieved April 22, 2018, from https://chopra.com/articles/what-happens-to-the-brain-during-meditation

Cirino, E. (2016, February 29). The effects of depression on the brain: What is depression? *Healthline.* Retrieved July 26, 2019, from https://www.healthline.com/health/depression/effects-brain#1

Ciulla, J. B. (1998). Theorising the ethical organization. *Business Ethics Quarterly, 8*(4), 621–654. https://www.cambridge.org/core/journals/business-ethics-quarterly/article/theorising-the-ethical-organization/2D5342F4040EC09689B38409BA5936E3

Covey, S. (2003). *The 7 habits of highly effective people.* New York: Touchstone, Simon & Shuster. https://www.amazon.com/s?k=Covey%2C+S.+%282003%29.+The+7+habits+of+highly+effective+people.+New+York%3A+Touchstone%2C+Simon+%26+Shuster.&i=stripbooks-intl-ship&ref=nb_sb_noss

Covey, S., Merrill, A. R., & Merrill, R. R. (1994). *First things first: To live, to love, to learn, to leave a legacy.* New York: Simon & Schuster. https://www.amazon.com/First-Things-Learn-Leave-Legacy/dp/B00005VX87

Demerouti, E., Mostert, K., & Bakker, A. B. (2010). Burnout and work engagement: A thorough investigation of the independency of both constructs. *Journal of Occupational Health*

Psychology, 15(3), 209–222. https://www.semanticscholar.org/paper/Burnout-and-work-engagement%3A-a-thorough-of-the-of-Demerouti-Mostert/119989bafadcb75a9b3f85acff0611b3e429ee9f

Farb, N. A., Segal, Z. V., Mayberg, H., Bean, J., McKeon, D., Fatima, Z., & Anderson. A. F. (2007). Attending to the present: Mindfulness meditation reveals distinct neural modes of self-reference. *Social Cognitive and Affective Neuroscience, 2*(4), 313–322. https://doi.org/https://doi.org/10.1093/scan/nsm030. Retrieved April 22, 2018, from https://www.ncbi.nlm.nih.gov/pubmed/18985137

Franken, A., Edwards, C., & Lambert, R. (2009). Executing strategic change: Understanding the critical management elements that lead to success. *California Management Review, 51*(3), 49–73. Retrieved from http://algu.weebly.com/uploads/1/9/2/4/1924527/stra.mgtcase2.pdf

Gangoli, G. (2007). *Indian feminisms: Law patriarchies and violence in India.* Farnham: Ashgate Publishing Company. https://www.amazon.com/Indian-Feminisms-Patriarchies-Violence-India/dp/0754646041

Goleman, D. (1996). *Emotional intelligence: Why it can matter more than IQ.* New York, NY: Bantam Books. https://www.amazon.com/Emotional-Intelligence-Matter-More-Than/dp/055338371X

Goleman, D. (2004, January). What makes a leader. *Harvard Business Review.* http://athena.ecs.csus.edu/~buckley/CSc233/What-makes-a-Leader-HBR.pdf

Gunderman, R. (2014, February 21). For the young doctor about to burn out. *The Atlantic.* Retrieved from http://www.theatlantic.com/health/archive/2014/02/for-th0e-young-doctor-about-to-burn-out/284005

Hanson, R., & Menius, R. (2009). *Buddha's brain: The practical neuroscience of happiness, love & wisdom.* Oakland: New Harbinger Publications. https://www.amazon.com/Buddhas-Brain-Practical-Neuroscience-Happiness/dp/1491518669

Heatherton, T. F. (2011). Neuroscience of self and self-regulation. *Annual Review of Psychology, 62,* 363–390. https://doi.org/10.1146/annurev.psych.121208.131616

Herwig, U., Kaffenberger, T., Schell, C., Jäncke, L., & Brühl, A. B. (2010). Self-related awareness and emotion regulation. *NeuroImage, 50,* 734–741. https://pubmed.ncbi.nlm.nih.gov/20045475/

Hinson, J., & Osborne, D. (2014). Chapter 15. Tapping the power of emergent change. In B. B. J. M. Brazzel (Ed.), *The NTL handbook of organization development and change. Principles, practices and perspectives* (2nd ed., pp. 305–328). San Francisco, CA: Wiley. https://www.wiley.com/en-us/The+NTL+Handbook+of+Organization+Development+and+Change%3A+Principles%2C+Practices%2C+and+Perspectives%2C+2nd+Edition-p-9781118836163

Hölzel, B. K., Lazar, S. W., Gard, T., Schuman-Olivier, Z., Vago, D. R., & Ott, U. (2011). How does mindfulness meditation work? Proposing mechanisms of action from a conceptual and neural perspective. *Perspectives on Psychological Science, 6,* 537–559. https://doi.org/10.1177/1745691611419671

Hutson, M. (2017, April 4). Living a lie: We deceive ourselves to better deceive others. *Scientific American.* Retrieved from https://www.scientificamerican.com/article/living-a-lie-we-deceive-ourselves-to-better-deceive-others/

Johnson, S. C., Baxter, L. C., Wilder, L. S., Pipe, J. G., Heiserman, J. E., & Prigatano, G. P. (2002). Neural correlates of self-reflection. *Brain, 125*(Pt 8), 1808–1814. https://pubmed.ncbi.nlm.nih.gov/12135971/

Kabat Zinn, J. (1994). *Wherever you go there you are.* New York: Hyperion. https://www.amazon.com/Wherever-You-There-Are-Mindfulness/dp/1401307787/ref=sr_1_1?dchild=1&keywords=Wherever+you+go+there+you+are.&qid=1591719874&s=books&sr=1-1

Kabat-Zinn, J. (2013). *Full catastrophe living (revised edition): Using the wisdom of your body and mind to face stress, pain, and illness.* New York, NY: Bantam Books. https://www.amazon.com/Full-Catastrophe-Living-Revised-Illness/dp/0345536932

Kets de Vries, M. F. R. (1996). *Leadership or creativity: Generating peak experiences*. INSEAD Working Paper, 1996/62. http://www.opengrey.eu/item/display/10068/7932

Kets de Vries, M. F. R. (2006). *The leadership mystique: Leading behavior in the human enterprise* (2nd ed.). Harlow: Prentice Hall/Financial Times. https://www.bookdepository.com/Leader ship-Mystique-Manfred-F-R-Kets-de-Vries/9781405840194

Kim, H. H. (2018, January 29). *The meditation industry*. Sage Business Researcher. Retrieved April 22, 2018, from http://businessresearcher.sagepub.com/sbr-1946-105603-2878495/20180129/the-meditation-industry?type=hitlist&num=5

Kotter, J. P. (1996). *Leading change*. Boston, MA: Harvard Business Press. Retrieved from http://www.hbs.edu/faculty/Pages/item.aspx?num=137

Kumar, R. (1998). *The history of doing*. New Delhi: Kali for Women. http://www.spinifexpress.com.au/fasiapub/india/kali.htm#histofdo

Latham, N. (2016). Meditation and self-control. *Philosophical Studies: An International Journal for Philosophy in the Analytic Tradition, 173*(7), 1779–1798. https://link.springer.com/article/10.1007/s11098-015-0578-y

Lazar, S. W., Kerr, C. E., Wasserman, R. H., Gray, J. R., Greve, D. N., Treadway, M. T., et al. (2005). Meditation experience is associated with increased cortical thickness. *Neuroreport, 16* (17), 1893–1897. https://pubmed.ncbi.nlm.nih.gov/16272874/

Levin, M. (2017). *Why Google, Nike, and Apple love mindfulness training, and how you can easily love it too*. Retrieved April 22, 2018, from https://www.inc.com/marissa-levin/why-google-nike-and-apple-love-mindfulness-training-and-how-you-can-easily-love-.html

Lieberman, M. D. (2007). Social cognitive neuroscience: A review of core processes. *Annual Review of Psychology, 58*(1), 259–289. https://www.scn.ucla.edu/pdf/Lieberman%20(2006)%20Ann%20Review.pdf

Lukens, M. (2015, October 29). How to tap into the neuroscience of winning. *Fast Company*. Retrieved from https://www.fastcompany.com/3052754/how-to-tap-into-the-neuroscience-of-winning

Madi, P. M. (2000). *Leadership lessons from Emperor Shaka Zulu the great*. Randburg: Knowres. https://www.worldcat.org/title/leadership-lessons-from-emperor-shaka-zulu-the-great/oclc/47068553

Margolis, J., Roberts, L. M., & Winig, L. (2007a). *South African Airways, A and B (SAA). Case study: 9-407-014 (A), 9-407-024 (B)*. Harvard Business School Publishing, Feb 26, 2007, pp. 1–21 (A); 9-407-024, Feb 26, 2007, pp. 1–4. https://store.hbr.org/product/south-african-airways-a/407014?sku=407014-PDF-ENG

McPhillips, D. (2016). *The ten most depressed countries*. Retrieved April 22, 2018, from https://www.usnews.com/news/best-countries/articles/2016-09-14/the-10-most-depressed-countries

Michel, A. (2016, January 29). Burnout and the brain. Association for Psychological Science. *The Observer*. Retrieved July 26, 2019, from https://www.psychologicalscience.org/observer/burn out-and-the-brain

Mograbi, G. J. C. (2011). Meditation and the brain: Attention, control and emotion. In A. R. Singh & S. A. Singh (Eds.), *Brain, mind and consciousness: An international, interdisciplinary perspective. MSM, 9*(1), 276–283. https://www.ncbi.nlm.nih.gov/pmc/articles/PMC3115297/

Nataraja, S. (2012). *The blissful brain: Neuroscience and the proof of the power of meditation*. Utah: Jensen Books. https://www.amazon.com/Blissful-Brain-Neuroscience-Meditation-Thinking/dp/1856752917

Nkomo, S. M., & Kriek, D. (2011). Leading organizational change in the 'new' South Africa. *Journal of Occupational and Organizational Psychology, 84*(1), 453–470. https://doi.org/https://doi.org/10.1111/j.2044-8325.2011.02020.x. Retrieved from https://onlinelibrary.wiley.com/doi/pdf/10.1111/j.2044-8325.2011.02020.x

Ochsner, K. N., & Gross, J. J. (2005). The cognitive control of emotion. *Trends in Cognitive Sciences, 9*(5), 242–249. https://pubmed.ncbi.nlm.nih.gov/15866151/

Osborne, D., & Hinson, J. (2011). Leading in complex times. *Practicing Social Change, NLT's Practitioner's Journal, 1*(4), 26–30. http://www.ntl-psc.org/archive/leading-in-complex-times/

Parry, W. (2012, August 22). *Brain damaged 'Patient R' challenges theories of self awareness.* Retrieved from https://www.livescience.com/22614-self-awareness-brahin.html

Parsons, J. (2014). *How the brain responds to feedback.* IEDP. Retrieved from https://www.iedp.com/articles/how-the-brain-responds-to-feedback/

Pfaff, D. W. (2015). *The altruistic brain: How we are naturally good.* Oxford: Oxford University Press. https://www.amazon.com/Altruistic-Brain-How-Naturally-Good/dp/0199377464

Pihlak, Ü., & Alas, R. (2012). Resistance to change in Indian, Chinese and Estonian organizations. *Journal of Indian Business Research, 4*(4), 224–243. https://doi.org/10.1108/17554191211274767

Resker. (2012). Retrieved from https://www.slideshare.net/NonprofitWebinars/the-top-ten-reactions-to-performance-feedback-and-how-to-respond

Rock, D. (2009). *Your brain at work: Strategies for overcoming distraction, regaining focus, and working smarter all day.* New York: HarperCollins. https://www.harpercollins.com/9780061771293/your-brain-at-work/

Rock, D., & Page, L. J. (2009). *Coaching with the brain in mind: Foundations for practice.* Upper Saddle River, NJ: Wiley. https://www.wiley.com/en-us/Coaching+with+the+Brain+in+Mind%3A+Foundations+for+Practice-p-9780470405680

Rock, D., & Schwartz, J. (2006). The neuroscience of leadership. *Strategy Business, 43*, 72–82. https://www.strategy-business.com/article/06207?gko=f1af3

Schaufenbuel, K. (2015, December 28). Why Google, Target, and General Mills are investing in mindfulness. *Harvard Business Review.* https://hbr.org/2015/12/why-google-target-and-general-mills-are-investing-in-mindfulness

Scheepers, C. B. (2012). *Coaching leaders: The 7 P tools to propel change.* Randburg: Knowres. http://www.kr.co.za/mentoring-coaching/coaching-leaders-7-p-tools-to-propel-change

Scheepers, C. B. (2013). *The coaching leaders programme and DVD.* Randburg: Knowres. http://knowledgeresources.businesscatalyst.com/knowres-publishing-1/the-coaching-leaders-programme

Scheepers, C. B., & Elstob, S. L. (2016). Beneficiary contact moderates the relationship between authentic leadership and engagement. *South African Journal of Human Resources Management, 14*(1), a758, 1–10. https://doi.org/10.4102/sajhrm.v14i1.758

Scheepers, C. B., & Swart, S. (2015). *Momentum and metropolitan merger: Authentic transformational leadership.* Ivey Publishing, 9B15C004. https://www.iveycases.com/ProductView.aspx?id=70560

Seppala, E. (2012). *The brain's ability to look within: A secret to self-mastery.* Retrieved from https://www.psychologytoday.com/blog/feeling-it

Siegel, D. J. (2006). An interpersonal neurobiology approach to psychotherapy. *Psychiatric Annals, 36*(4), 248–252. https://www.healio.com/journals/psycann/2006-4-36-4/%7B231a1eb0-7230-4ff8-b173-c7f31c6b823f%7D/an-interpersonal-neurobiology-approach-to-

Siegel, D. J. (2007). *The mindful brain. Reflection and attunement in the cultivation of well-being.* New York: W&W Norton & Company. https://www.amazon.com/Mindful-Brain-Reflection-Attunement-Cultivation/dp/039370470X

Simpkins, C. A., & Simpkins, A. M. (2010). *The Dao of neuroscience: Combining Eastern and Western principles for optimal therapeutic change.* New York, NY: W.W. Norton & Company. https://www.amazon.com/Dao-Neuroscience-Principles-Therapeutic-Professional/dp/0393705978

Smith, M. K., Trivers, R., & Von Hippel, W. (2017). Self-deception facilitates interpersonal persuasion. *Journal of Economic Psychology, 63*, 93–101. https://psycnet.apa.org/record/2017-10854-001

Stahl, B., & Goldstein, E. (2010). *A mindfulness-based stress reduction workbook* (A New Harbinger Self-Help Workbook). Oakland, CA: New Harbinger Publications. https://www.amazon.com/Mindfulness-Based-Stress-Reduction-Workbook/dp/1572247088

Stetka, B. (2017, October 11). Where is the proof that mindfulness meditation works? *Scientific American.* Retrieved April 22, 2018, from https://www.scientificamerican.com/article/wheres-the-proof-that-mindfulness-meditation-works1/

Stone, D., & Heen, S. (2014). *Thanks for the feedback: The science and art of receiving feedback well*. New York, NY: Penguin Random House. https://www.amazon.com/Thanks-Feedback-Science-Receiving-Well/dp/0670014664

Tang, Y. Y. (2017). *The neuroscience of mindfulness meditation: How the body and mind work together to change*. Cham: Palgrave Macmillan. https://doi.org/10.1007/978-3-319-46322-3_2

Tang, Y., Hölzel, B. K., & Posner, M. I. (2015). The neuroscience of mindfulness meditation. *Nature Reviews Neuroscience, 16*(4), 213–225. https://doi.org/10.1038/nrn3916

Toscano, R., Price, G., & Scheepers, C. B. (2018). The impact of CEO arrogance on top management team attitudes. *European Business Review, 30*(6), 1–15. https://doi.org/10.1108/EBR-12-2016-0156

Van Dam, N. T., van Vugt, M. K., Vago, D. R., Schmalzl, L., Saron, C. D., Olendzki, A., et al. (2017). Mind the hype: A critical evaluation and prescriptive agenda for research on mindfulness and meditation. *Perspectives on Psychological Science, 13*(1), 36–61. https://doi.org/10.1177/1745691617709589

Van Hecke, M. L., Callahan, L. P., Kolar, B., & Paller, K. A. (2010). *The brain advantage: Become a more effective business leader using the latest brain research*. Amherst, NY: Prometheus Books. https://www.amazon.com/Brain-Advantage-Effective-Business-Research/dp/1591027640

Walsh, R. (1999). *Essential spirituality: The 7 central practices to awaken heart and mind*. New York: Wiley. https://www.amazon.com/Essential-Spirituality-Central-Practices-Awaken/dp/0471392162

Wanjek, C. (2014, September 25). Feeling bummed? How disappointment works in the brain. *Livescience*. https://www.livescience.com/48022-disappointment-brain.html

Zapletal, K. (2017). *Neuroscioence of mindfulness: What happens to your brain when you meditate*. Retrieved February 5, 2018, from http://observer.com/2017/06/neuroscience-mindfulness-brain-when-you-meditate-development/

Zhang, Y., & Rajagopalan, N. (2010). Once an outsider, always an outsider? CEO origin, strategic change, and firm performance. *Strategic Management Journal, 31*, 334–346. https://doi.org/10.1002/smj.812. Retrieved from http://onlinelibrary.wiley.com/doi/10.1002/smj.812/full

Reference List for Quotes

Retrieved July 26, 2019, from http://skdesigns.com/internet/articles/quotes/bartholomew/

Retrieved July 26, 2019, from https://www.brainyquote.com/quotes/george_bernard_shaw_386923

Retrieved July 26, 2019, from https://www.brainyquote.com/quotes/ralph_waldo_emerson_390833

Retrieved July 26, 2019, from https://www.goodreads.com/quotes/664197-we-do-not-learn-from-experience-we-learn-from-reflecting

Retrieved July 26, 2019, from https://www.goodreads.com/quotes/tag/change

Third Enabler: Explore

Exploration is really the essence of the human spirit.
(Frank Borman, n.d.)

Learning Outcomes
At the end of this chapter, change leaders will be able to:

- Create a conducive environment for others to explore the environment
- Use analytical methods to assess the environment

Electronic supplementary material The online version of this chapter (https://doi.org/10.1007/978-3-030-40846-6_7) contains supplementary material, which is available to authorized users.

7.1   Orientation to Exploring

While the Second Enabler focused on the ego mastery of the individual leader and
others whose egos might get in the way of change leadership, the next enabler is
focused on the bigger picture. This role encourages leaders to investigate and then be
acutely aware of environmental factors that might influence the organisation so that
proactive plans can be put in place to either capitalise on opportunities or mitigate
risks. It involves thus more than awareness and includes the response based on this
awareness. Generally, when responding, it is a calculated action, which differs from
a mere reaction. China is particularly effective in seizing opportunities in other
emerging markets as well as developed markets to expand their footprint (Casanova
& Miroux, 2017) and is thus featured in this chapter.

7.2   Importance of Exploring

To survive and thrive in today's fast-paced world, a leader must monitor world
events. We can no longer afford to refrain from gathering contextual intelligence and
not be vigilant about what is happening around us. The translation of the impact of
these environmental changes on our organisations, is as important as being aware of
them. In this regard, change leaders must identify relevant environmental factors as
they provide unique predictions regarding a strategic fit of the organisation with
these factors (Grant, 2003). Reeves and Deimler (2011) identify the ability to read
and act on signals as an important organisational capability that assists in attaining an
adaptive advantage in times of change. A firm must have its antennae tuned to
signals of change from the external environment, then decode the signals and
quickly act to refine or reinvent its business model. Scholars like Sujova and Rajnoha
(2012) warn that long-term and sustainable competitiveness can only be achieved if
changes in the enterprise are ahead of the changes in the environment.

Strategic change can be defined as a difference in the form, quality or state over
time in an organisation's alignment with its external environment (Van de Ven &
Poole, 1995). MacKay and Chia (2013) too refer to strategic change as a process that
is determined by a dynamic external environment. The external environment
presents factors that cannot be controlled by the organisation, but that could influence it (Pop & Maier, 2012). Zajac, Kraatz, and Bresser (2000) state that "the
appropriateness of a firm's strategy can be defined in terms of its congruence with
the environmental contingencies facing the firm" (p. 429). However, increased
volatility of the business environment makes systematic strategic planning more
difficult.

At this point, we would like to emphasise that although we are referring to
leadership roles, it does not imply that the leaders have to collate the business
intelligence themselves. Instead, they must ensure that the organisation is vigilant
and enable monitoring and sense making. In this regard, Osborn, Hunt, and Jauch
(2002) advise that leadership in organisations allow patterning of attention, by, for
example, ensuring contact with external networks, which then feed new information

into the organisation about the external environment. Osborn and Marion (2009) on their part, offer examples of network leadership, where leaders enable interaction of people across silos in the organisation, such as cross-functional communication and purposefully promote diversity of thinking. It is valuable to note that scholars like Osborn, Uhl-Bien, and Milosevic (2014), in turn, emphasise that there are three approaches when considering the context of leadership, and they include leadership that fits hierarchically or as a social system or both. We concur that organisations should realise this aspect and as a result enable opportunities for people to lead outside of the formal hierarchy.

While Osborn et al. (2002) advocate that leadership is socially constructed and entrenched in the context, we would like to add to what these researchers declare. We are adamant that actually, leadership not only is, but should be, entrenched in the context. Leaders must make it their business to understand their organisational and larger environmental context.

This Third Enabler includes exploring opportunities provided by the environment to increase competitiveness (Pop & Maier, 2012). Competitiveness involves the combination of assets and processes, where processes transform assets to achieve economic gains from customer sales which are superior to those offered by their competition. Porter's Five Forces shape the competitive interaction within an industry, and an organisation should be positioned where these forces are the weakest for sustainable growth, including supplier power, customer power, the threat of substitute products or services, threats of entry and rivalry among competitors (Porter, 2008).

The question is how an organisation could achieve an advantage in the changing environment, through its configuration of resources and competencies with the aim of fulfilling stakeholder expectations (Johnson, Scholes, & Whittington, 2008). Vithessonthi and Thoumrungroje (2011) warn that a change in the environment does have the potential to make an organisation's product or capability obsolete, even in a stable industry. The business environment must thus be continuously scanned to develop an understanding of the opportunities and challenges that present themselves in the environment (Fleming, 2012). In some instances, leaders become so focused on internal politics that they take their eye off the ball and it drains their energy.

7.3 Exploring in Practice

Vigilance is required in today's volatile business environment. Going through a systematic process of analysing environmental factors ensures rigorous diagnosis and assessment of the impact on the organisation. In addition, virtual contexts mark today's workplace (McCallum & O'Connell, 2009). Leaders could thus benefit from considering not only the physical but certainly virtual contexts. In this regard, the leadership of organisations could purposefully examine virtual contexts that could influence their organisation or that they could capitalise on as an opportunity. The several ways in which organisations use social media in their marketing and advertising campaigns are examples of capitalising on these prospects. On the other hand, the reputational risks to the organisation, with leaders' social media "Tweets" are also relevant to this discussion.

The Third Enabler represents a critical phase in the strategic change process, during which the business case for change is being formulated. The reason for change flows logically from external market opportunities and or threats, and as a result, a systematic process of identifying relevant environmental variables is important. Building a compelling business case for change requires thus an investigation into relevant contextual variables. The adage "Never let a good crisis go to waste" has been attributed to Winston Churchill in reference to the conditions post the Second World War that allowed for the formation of the United Nations (https:// bestquotes.com, n/a). This is also true for this Third Enabler.

7.3.1 The Exploration Process

In this section, models, processes, worksheets and tools will be provided to assist the change leader in analysing the organisation's external environment. We developed the Exploration Process framework to explain how the process works. The Exploration Process in Fig. 7.1 starts with the change leader ensuring that a conducive environment for seeking opportunities is created. Without a conducive environment, all new ideas will be rejected, and the hard work of seeking these new opportunities will be a waste of time. Once a conducive environment has been

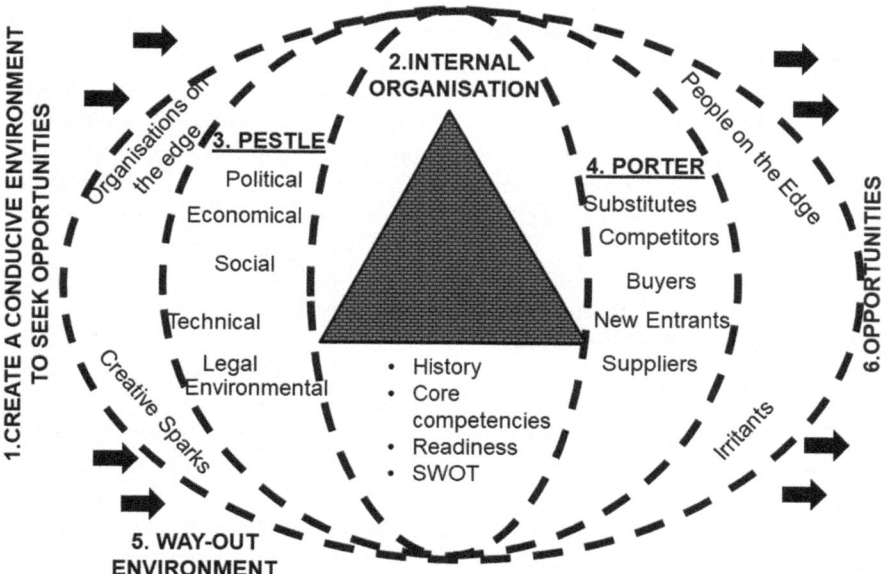

Fig. 7.1 Exploration process (Authors' own)

created, the process moves to 2, the internal organisation represented here as the grey triangle in the middle of the picture. The organisation in which the change leader operates is surrounded by the immediate internal environment indicated as the first oval in which the organisation is embedded. Change leaders need to be acutely aware of this internal organisational environment as it is in this context that they will be expected to implement the change once it has been identified. The organisation and change history, core competencies or lack of competence, the organisation's strengths, weaknesses and opportunities and threats and the extent to which the organisation is ready for the change, all need to be considered.

The second bigger oval represents the larger environment, and here the change leader needs to understand PESTLE and Porter's Five Forces which will be discussed in detail below. On the outer edges, change leaders should be engaging with thought leaders outside of the apparent environment, people who think differently from the way people think within the context in which the change leader operates. This may include people or technologies who might be experienced as irritants, mavericks or weird creative sparks. Input from these sources should be sought as they will not be encountered regularly by the change leader. By interacting with these sources of input, which could be people, the media, articles, books or personal reflections and observations, the change leader will identify opportunities that could be potential ideas for Eureka moments (Enabler 4).

7.3.1.1 Creating a Conducive Environment to Explore Opportunities

In the next tool (Tool 3.1), we encourage change leaders to ensure a conducive environment exists in which opportunities are sought. When such an environment is created, people are unafraid to make suggestions for improvements and become eager to embrace change.

Tool 3.1 Create a Conducive Environment to Explore Opportunities

Consider the internal organisation environment and answer the following questions:
For example: How are people in the organisation treated when they criticise current ways of being and doing?

7.3.1.2 Considering the Organisation's Change History and Core Competencies

In the next tool (Tool 3.2) we offer the opportunity for leaders to consider their internal organisational environment to identify their core competence.

Tool 3.2 Organisational Change History and Core Competencies

What are the organisation-wide change processes of the past that people in the organisation talk about? Do they consider it to have been a success or a failure? What worked, what did not work in their opinion?

7.3.1.3 SWOT Analysis

In the next worksheet (Tool 3.3) the application of the SWOT analysis can be applied to your own organisation. Take note that even a current strength could pose a risk in future and has to be sustained. In other instances, an opportunity for the organisation might also pose a risk, especially as the competition catches up on the opportunity.

Tool 3.3 Organisational SWOT

Identify the strengths, weaknesses, opportunities and threats of the organisation and complete the template by identifying ways in which the strengths can be capitalised upon and how to mitigate risks.

Practical Application of SWOT

The most well-known systematic environmental analysis is undoubtedly the SWOT analysis. The practical application below features a short-term insurance company, originally from South Africa, a company listed on the Johannesburg Security Exchange (JSE) under the insurance (non-life or short-term insurance) financial services sector. The company had been profitable amidst enormous challenges in the short-term insurance industry for over 100 years. In addition to

(continued)

trading in South Africa, it had business interests in Asia and Sub-Saharan Africa. Its head office was in Cape Town. As per their financial reports of year-end December 2013, the company attributes its success to its ability to adapt to a dynamic systemic risk landscape. Their core value proposition includes their ability to continually reposition and improve themselves in the changing business environment, to employ the best people, to provide a relevant offering to clients, and to optimise systems to drive efficiency. The disappointing performance of the South Africa economy has led to lower household incomes and has had a negative impact on the insurance sector. In addition, there has been an increase in the number of weather-related claims, fraud and losses as a result of devaluation in the rand.

The following SWOT analysis is based on the Business Monitor International (BMI 2014, pp. 9–13, 41–44 and 59) report on the South African Insurance Industry.

Strengths: The financial services sector in South Africa is well regulated, with a highly regarded Financial Services Board. There is a unique competitive landscape, dominated by a couple of large corporates. Compared to other developing countries, South Africa's insurance companies have scale and have sophisticated insurance markets. In South Africa it is relatively easy to access finance through the matured financial markets, as well as institutional investors.

Weaknesses: There is a lower disposable income available. South Africa's short-term insurance companies are vulnerable to exposure to natural disasters, such as drought, hail and floods that put pressure on premium rates. For example, natural disasters like massive fires in the coastal areas, like Knysna, caused 20 000 households to be affected. In the insurance industry, profitability levels had been falling. There are barriers to entry for foreign countries in place causing lower market share for these firms, apart from Zurich Insurance.

Opportunities: There is a reduction in claim costs, for example with regards to motor insurance. Tremendous opportunities regarding legislation requirements for lower income groups exist in the emerging markets. Other opportunities are expansions into other continents, such as Australasia and Asia.

Threats: The most critical threat is the volatility and vulnerability of the South African economy, which in turn causes lower household incomes. Margins are under pressure, due to demands from clients and distribution channels. With the delays that the sector is experiencing in legislation as well as regulation, there is duplication of efforts and higher expenditure. These regulations also increase the cost to comply, monitor and report. Huge threats exist in the volatility and lower interest rates of global markets.

7.3.1.4 PESTLE Framework

The PESTLE framework, which includes political, economic, social, technological, legal and environmental factors, is a useful way to analyse the environment (Johnson & Scholes, 2002). Tool 3.4 offers change leaders the opportunity to systematically consider the political, economic, social, technological, legal and environmental factors that concern them.

Tool 3.4 PESTLE Framework

For each of the environmental variables, the opportunities and challenges are identified and captured in the template.

Challenges, as well as opportunities, are essential. In Fig. 7.2 we illustrate how an organisation's strategy is a buffer and a means to deal with the environment. In this sense, the Third Enabler, where systematic environmental awareness is obtained, takes notice of the changes in the environment with regards to all PESTLE aspects. PESTLE could also be used to identify opportunities and challenges and then devise ways to mitigate risks.

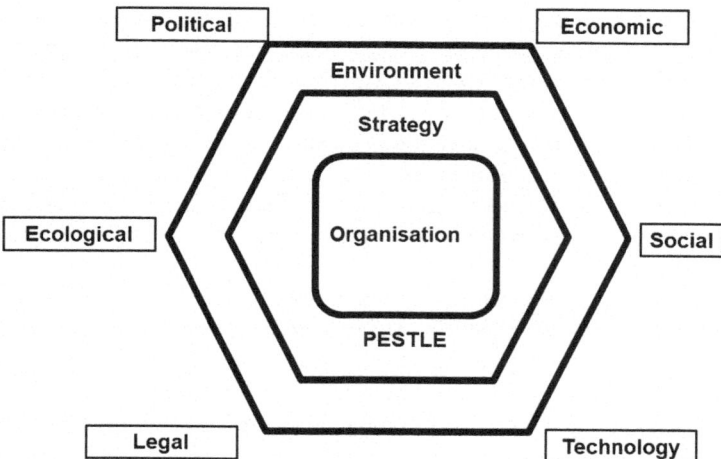

Fig. 7.2 PESTLE framework (Authors' own adapted from Johnson & Scholes, 2002)

Practical Application of PESTLE

Margolis et al., (2007) (See the reference list for the full reference of the published case study on SAA that these PESTLE and Industry analyses were based upon)

As an example of how to apply the PESTLE analysis practically, the South African Airways (SAA) company will be used. SAA is a state-owned airline organisation operating from South Africa, has around 12 000 employees, runs from its hubs in Johannesburg, Durban and Cape Town, is a member of International Star Alliance and has a reach of approximately 800 destinations around the world. It was founded in 1936 and went through the Apartheid system during the 1970s and 1980s.

Political aspects: South Africa was affected by the legacy of apartheid injustices, racial discrimination and decades of political infighting. Although post-apartheid South Africa was more stable, political influences still included probable privatisation and Broad-Based Black Empowerment Enterprises (BBBEE) initiatives. Through Employment Equity legislation, SAA's workforce had to be diversified to such an extent that 70% would be Black and 30% White by 2000. In 2004, the government announced that SAA would remain state owned.

Economical aspects: The airline industry has high input costs and low-profit margins in a highly competitive industry. The African continent offered a 7% annual growth in air traffic. SAA had vital resource dependency on jet fuel, and it thus was one of the significant influences on SAA's profitability. The volatility of the Rand had a considerable impact on the profitability of the airline, as a significant portion of its operational expenses or OPEX, like fuel, maintenance and leasing of planes were billed in US dollars. Oil prices had a direct bearing on fuel costs and were largely outside of SAA's control.

Social aspects: Social transformation was required in the airline industry. SAA had to ensure that the country's image was upheld while carrying out its duties. Being a parastatal organisation, SAA had an authoritarian approach. SAA was also closely watched by political and social commentators. SAA was highly unionised. Rising income levels with the development of a stronger middle class would increase business and tourism travel. South Africa suffered from allegations of corruption, high levels of HIV/Aids as well as high poverty levels.

Technological aspects: New planes were more energy efficient and could assist in lowering fuel costs. Technology such as the Internet and mobile

(continued)

phones cut out travel agents and brought new channels to market directly to passengers. Since air safety was paramount, airlines had to invest to a large extent in new technologies that contributed to high safety standards.

Legal aspects: Various laws had to be taken into account around the hiring of employees to fill quota requirements for economic and social transformation to address previous injustices. Aviation laws that prescribed safety standards and labour laws, like basic conditions of employment acts around working hours all affected SAA. SAA also had to adhere to tax laws. The competition tribunal found SAA guilty of transgressions regarding commission paid to travel agents and was fined SAA $6–8 million, a huge blow to their bottom line.

Environmental aspects: Airlines' carbon footprint had come under scrutiny during the last couple of years, and SAA was under pressure from environmental groups.

7.3.1.5 Porter's Five Forces

Porter's (1980) Five Forces is a systemic framework to ascertain the industry forces that could influence an organisation's competitiveness. The next tool, Tool 3.5 offers an opportunity for leaders to use the five forces to identify opportunities and to mitigate risks. Figure 7.3 illustrates an example of Porter's Five Forces applied to the SAA case study.

We could again utilize the SAA case study (Margolis et al., 2007) to analyse the external environment according to this systematic model. The bargaining power of SAA's suppliers was huge. The industry was held to ransom by the fuel price and the uncertainty of the oil price. Airport Company South Africa (ACSA) dominated the airport ownership and therefore, airport taxes were described as excessive. Labour forces were important with unions wielding high power. Due to the scarcity of skills and training required, the bargaining power of pilots was strong.

The power of the customer was also high, with many international carriers to choose from and locally low-price airlines competing for limited routes. At the height of Apartheid, customers demonstrated their power by boycotting the airline. The entry of 9 domestic and 70 international carriers increased the choice for travellers and created price competition. RSA had seen a lot of new entrants, such as Kulula, 1Time, etc. causing prices to decrease. The industry was very capital intensive and made it difficult for new entrants. For business travellers, alternatives included videoconferencing, phone calls, skype or webinars.

New no-frills airlines had different pricing models, which stifled the growth for SAA. Rivalry was very high in the aviation sector due to high oil prices, older jets needing heavy fuel and restrictive aviation policies that left very little space to manoeuvre. Price wars were high and uncompetitive practices were used by airlines, such as SAA, via increasing commissions to travel agents, so they could sell more seats, ultimately incurring heavy fines from the Competition Commission.

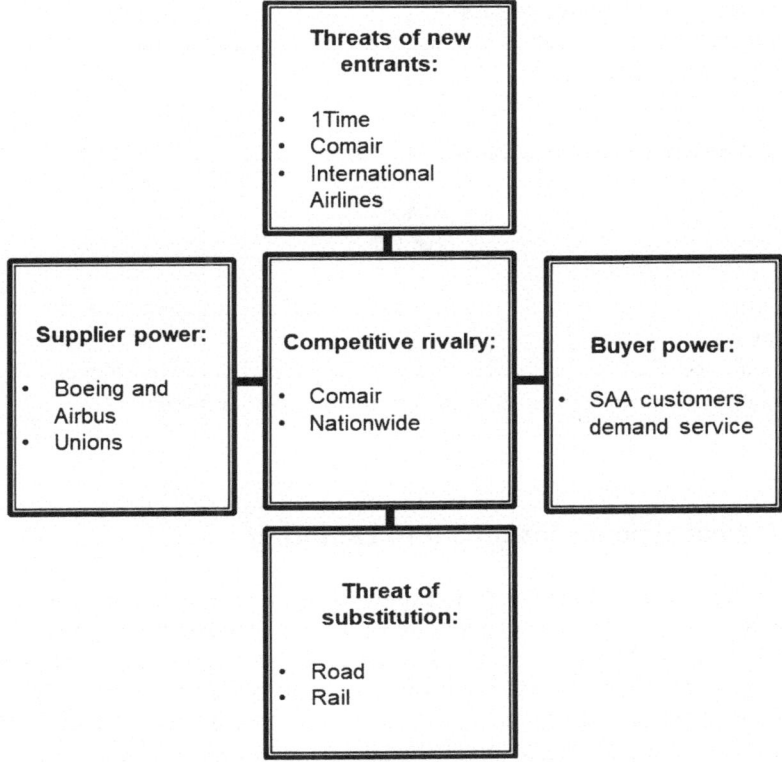

Fig. 7.3 SAA case study applied to Porter's (1980) Five Forces (Authors' own)

SAA was highly dependent on resources, such as fuel and they had high information uncertainty, with regards to price and currency fluctuations, SAA's environment could thus be described as having maximal environmental constraints.

Tool 3.5 Porter's Five Forces

Use the worksheet to consider the five forces to identify opportunities and to mitigate risks.

7.3.1.6 Way-Out Environments

The next tool (Tool 3.6) will offer leaders the opportunity to consider way-out or maverick types of environmental factors.

Tool 3.6 Way-Out Environment

Looking way out towards the edges of your environment consider the following:
Who are the creative sparks/mavericks on the edge of your environment, that can help you identify opportunities you might not be aware of?

7.4   Neuroscience Insights into Exploring

It seems that our brains were made to explore! It is fascinating to note that just our eyes alone receive and send ten million signals every second of the day (Van Hecke, Callahan, Kolar, & Paller, 2010). Not only are we wired to explore, we also have the ability to use the information we gather to seek opportunities to improve. No other species on earth has the ability to manipulate the environment to make life easier as much as humans do. To enable information in our environment to be utilised to our advantage, we need to make sense of these inputs and create an environment where we explore new opportunities without fear. In this section, we will discuss how our brains manage to stay in touch with the environment and how we should create spaces in which the brain is unafraid to explore new opportunities.

We are hard-wired to appreciate and seek novelty. If it is new, different or unusual, it will catch our eye. The substantia nigra/ventral tegmental area (SN/VTA) in our mid-brain is believed to be our novelty centre responding to novelty stimuli. It is closely linked to the hippocampus and the amygdala both involved in memory and learning. The hippocampus also plays a part in comparing stimuli against existing memories, and the amygdala responds to emotional stimuli and strengthens associated long-term memories (Cooper, 2013).

Researchers, Bunzeck and Düzel, devised the "oddball" experiment in which they used fMRI imaging to test how the brain reacts to novelty. They showed the subjects images such as indoor and outdoor scenes and faces with random novel images (oddballs) thrown inbetween (Bunzeck & Düzel, 2006). The study found that seeing new "odd" images, never been seen before, activated the SN/VTA. When there was only a slight difference in the images, the SN/VTA would not be activated. When the subjects were exposed to novelty, dopamine was released. The dopamine pathways, which are activated when we are exposed to something new, are indicated by the dark grey areas in the illustration of the brain below (Cell Press, 2006; Fig. 7.4).

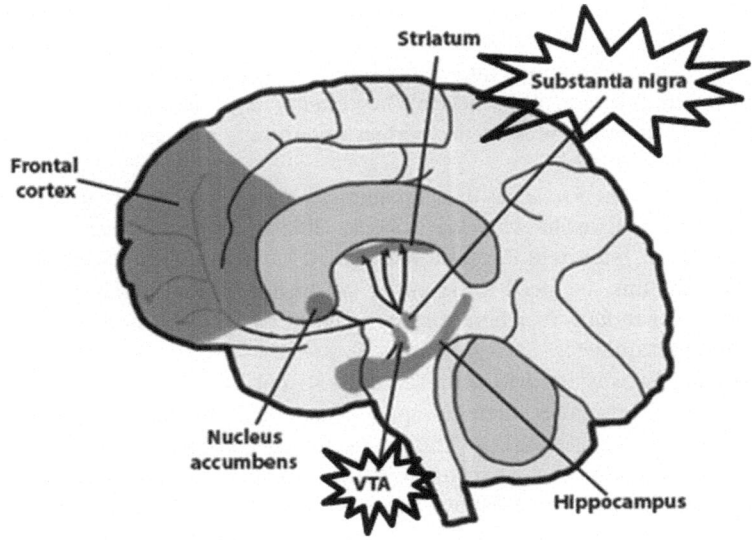

Fig. 7.4 Parts of the brain activated when experiencing novelty (Authors' own)

As humans we are wired to seek rewards in our environment. When we see something new, we investigate the potential for it to present us with a reward. When the brain then learns that the now familiar item has no reward associated with it, it loses its potential. For this reason, only completely new objects activate the midbrain area and increase our levels of dopamine (Wittmann, Bunzeck, Dolan, & Düzel, 2007). When students were introduced to novel items during learning sessions combined with the more familiar material, they fared 19% better than when they were not given novel facts in between (Cooper, 2013).

As a mechanism for survival, the brain developed a highly effective capacity to scan the environment to detect what neuroscientists call "errors" (perceived differences between expectation and actuality) (Rock & Schwartz, 2006). Once "abnormalities" have been detected, plans are then devised to react to changes in the environment. Humans are generally particularly well developed to react to these "dangers" and to put corrective action into place.

The orbital cortex (located right above the eyesockets, or orbits) is an effective error detection "device" programmed to detect changes in the environment and to alert us if there is something unusual or extraordinary (Rock & Page, 2009). The orbital cortex is closely linked to the amygdala (the brain's fear circuitry). The orbital cortex and the amygdala redirect brain resources away from the PFC the centre of higher intellectual thoughts. It is this capacity that is engaged when change leaders scan the environment. When we understand that our PFC is no longer active, and the amygdala is activated, we can manage our resistance to new ideas and extend our capacity to not only detect errors but also to seek opportunities.

Change leaders can purposefully attempt to identify and consciously seek opportunities in every danger they detect (for example, when identifying a threat in the SWOT, it can be turned into an opportunity). Errors made by others could be used as opportunities to fulfil a need. When clients' expectations in the market are not being met, it might present the perfect opportunity to step in with improved services or new products.

The limbic system also scans data streaming into the brain, telling us what to pay attention to as well as in what way (Rock, 2009a, 2009b). When we scan the environment, our brain will tag stimuli as "good" and engage or "bad" and disengage. Knowing this, we need to be aware not to reject ideas based on the limbic system's fear of failure. It is here that we need to be "open-minded" and actively search for opportunities.

Neuroimaging was used to discover the two cortical systems responsible for conscious awareness: the external input system and the internal input system (Vanhaudenhuyse et al., 2011). This is useful to consider when we view the environment. In the process of scanning the environment, we should be aware that we view the world using our existing "lenses". From a very early age, we form lenses through which we view the world and judge what is acceptable and unacceptable (We refer to these lenses as paradigms and discuss this in detail in Enabler 4, Eureka). Because we are so attached to our paradigms and see anything different as either a threat or irrelevant, we need to take heed that our paradigm might be outdated and not resist gaining input from diverse others or experiencing activities that might expose us to different paradigms.

7.5   Exploring in Emerging Markets

7.5.1   Case Examples of Exploring in the Emerging Markets Contexts

We suggest that in the emerging markets, there is even more volatility and dynamism than in the developed countries and as a result, this Third Enabler is even more relevant to the emerging markets. Due to globalisation, emerging markets experience global competition on their doorstep and should not forget that we are part of the global village and cannot operate as an island.

Environmental dynamism describes the rate of change and the unpredictability of change in an organisation's external environment (Dess & Beard, 1984). Dynamic environments are characterised by changes in technologies, variations in customer preferences and fluctuations in product demand or supply of materials (Jansen, Van Den Bosch, & Volberda, 2006).

In the *South Asian Journal of Management*, scholars emphasised that technology was an important force of the current dynamic business environment (Shahzad, Bajwa, Ali, & Zia, 2012).

They also advised that international competition as a threat to an organisation should be analysed (Shahzad et al., 2012). For example, global events leading to increased costs, lower demand and volatility of the financial markets and cause environmental changes and uncertainties within organisations. Uzkurt, Kumar, Kimzan, and Sert (2012) recommend that further research must be conducted on external environmental factors, as well as considering other cultures of developing nations.

Further to the theme of contacts being important in emerging markets' contexts, Bonaglia, Goldstein and Mathews' study (2007) found that emerging markets' multinational enterprises (MNEs) built alliances with already established MNEs to grow their businesses and accelerate internationalisation. They also did not wait to become large before they expanded internationally. This study quoted Haier in China, Mabe in Mexico and Arçelik in Turkey as examples of emerging multinationals following this strategy.

This Third Enabler would thus include exploring the landscape of new alliance formation and how that might influence the prospects of your organisation. It also entails being proactive and ensuring that networks are updated and include important role players in the market.

Another important contextual variable is culture. In emerging markets, there regularly are multiple cultures to consider. Cultural competence is thus important for leadership in emerging markets. Linked to the previous discussion on emerging multinationals, leading multinational teams is relevant in this context. The study of Hajro and Pudelko (2010) investigated competencies required of leading in the context of the multi-nationality of the workforce. They discovered that these leaders had to be cross-culturally competent as well as multilingual to fully explore, exploit and transfer valuable knowledge in these teams.

Linked to the discussion of cross-cultural competence in the previous paragraph, Ahlstrom and Burton (2002) declared that Chinese culture remains strongly influenced by Confucianism. Accordingly, there are strict hierarchical relationships, and business relationships are directed to where there are established relationships or "guanxi". However, in an interesting study on innovation in China, of Tjosvold and Yu (2007), they found that within the collectivist Chinese culture that frowns upon conflict and criticism of authority, the high pressure for innovation caused the teams to have more open-minded discussions and take more risks toward innovation. Innovation is indeed a vital driver to achieve and retain competitive advantage, and leadership would thus benefit from increased attention to enable innovation in the emerging markets. Where alliances are formed with Chinese companies or in other business relationships, it would serve leadership to realise that Chinese people tend to act in strong accordance with others' expectations, as the research of Farmer, Tierney, and Kung-McIntyre (2003) highlighted.

Veldsman (2013) points out that there are, for example, companies in China that are homegrown and aspiring to develop and distribute their products and services to the developed countries as well as offer consumer products that are cheaper and with less functionality to the emerging markets.

Schumpeter (2011) in his "Khaki Capitalism" column in *The Economist*, points out that in emerging markets the state controls a significant portion of the available natural resources, through state-owned enterprises (SOEs). In this column, Schumpeter refers particularly to the military's role in the economy. For example, he quotes from the film "Catch-22" and likenes the Egyptian military to the character in the film, he notes

> Milo Minderbinder's spirit is still alive in the land. . . .The Egyptian army . . . runs about 10% of the economy. Military-backed companies produce cement, olive oil and household appliances as well as arms. They also provide pest control, catering and even childcare. The army owns . . . .land, particularly on the Red Sea coast. In China the People's Liberation Army . . . in the late 1980s was running nearly 20,000 firms. Zimbabwe's army has recently formed joint ventures with Chinese partners in farming and mining. Even in democratic India, the army runs about a hundred commercial golf courses.

Casanova and Miroux (2017) from Cornell University found that emerging markets are vulnerable to external shocks and currency volatility. In 2015, China and Korea were among the top 15 investors in the world, with China in the third position. These researchers reported that while in 2000, China virtually had no outbound merger and acquisitions (M&As) outside of China, the value of its announced outbound M&As, reached 138 billion dollars in 2015. They describe China's financial performance as a remarkable surge as a global investor, especially after the global financial crisis. China expanded in both emerging and developed markets and emerged as a global acquirer. Chinese multinationals are making progress in the global corporate world. Casanova and Miroux (2017) report several economic and political implications, which they called the new international order, which is worthy of further exploration. China is expected to grow at 6–7 percent during the next few years (Rayner, 2015).

Pihlak and Alas (2012) report on their research comparing resistance to change in Indian, Chinese and Estonian organisations and found that the cause of resistance in Chinese organisations was the inertia that increased stress. Communication was essential in this country to combat resistance as well as educating the employees on the change.

Guanxi, which means relationship in Chinese as described above, is typically developed through social occasions and gift giving. In the Chinese business world, it refers to the network of relationships amongst people who cooperate and support each other. Personal guanxi is used to exchange promises for doing favours for each other, such as finding a job. Chen and Tjosvold (2007) research revealed that personal guanxi promoted open-minded dialogue with employees and these employees shared more of the local knowledge that was crucial for multinationals in host countries.

As the discussions in the previous two chapters on Enabler One and Two, the discussion of the Third Enabler refers to a specific emerging market, namely China. We chose China as an example of capitalising on opportunities, since China had proven through the performance of their multinationals that originated in China, that an emerging market can become a globally recognised influential country, through their own transformation from an agricultural to an industrialised economy. We hope that the historical background offered here will assist change leaders in the developed and emerging markets in gaining insight into the nuances and dynamics that they need to take into account in leading change in their organisations. Organisations might conduct business with Chinese companies and could explore opportunities to access the huge consumer markets in China.

Since the emancipation of women offered a point of comparison between the emerging markets, we refer to a high-level chronological account of the evolution of women's status in Chinese society and refer to particularly interesting current research on women in business environments. Women's liberation in China is closely linked to its civil rights movements and therefore reveals important elements of Chinese society.

The waves of change that were experienced in China's life cycle illustrate the rich history of the fabric in their society and how change leaders like Deng Ziaoping's reforms in the seventies assisted China in becoming the industrial giant and global influence that it is today. The waves will be framed in the phase up to 1911 of Confucianism, then the Republic and Market Economy periods and finally current dynamics.

7.5.1.1 Confucianism (up to 1911)

Zhou (2003) observed that the basic characteristic of pre-communist society was a highly centralised political system. Ming-Hsuan (2011) emphasises that over thousands of years of Chinese history, Confucianism has served as an officially supported patriarchal ideology that has deemed women inferior to men and limited the role of women to their households. Zhou (2003, p. 68) declared that "For more than 2000 years, the double chains—foot binding and inhuman ethical codes confined Chinese women to the domestic sphere", as illustrated in a Chinese saying, "if you marry a chicken, you must stay with the chicken; if you marry a dog, you must obey the dog". In ancient times, women's feet were bound to restrict the growth of their feet to enable their feet to stay small, since it was perceived as feminine to have small feet.

Korabik (1993, p. 52) declares that women's self-confidence is often undermined by their acceptance of the Confucian adage that "it is a virtue if a woman has no ability". During that time, women were understood to belong to their fathers or elder brothers; after marriage, a woman belonged to the family of her husband and was expected to be obedient to her husband and later to her sons (Ming-Hsuan, 2011). This ideology, together with China's non-farm workforce being completely dominated by males, convinced parents that investing in daughters was a waste of money. As a result, parents usually placed a higher value on the nutritional intake and education of sons than on that of daughters.

7.5.1.2 Republic Period (1911–1949)

Zhou (2003) explains that the Chinese Revolution of 1911 had overthrown the last Chinese emperor—the symbol of the Chinese feudal system and indicated that China had entered into the era of the republic. However, the revolution only changed the top leader of China but did not touch the grassroots of Chinese society. Korabik (1993) states that until 1949, China was still a feudal society, isolated from the outside world and characterised by poverty, illiteracy and premature mortality.

Furthermore, Zhou (2003) summarises this phase as follows: The May Fourth Movement of 1919 was the first great cultural movement of modern China. Thousands of Chinese students for the first time in modern Chinese history marched to the Square to protest, and it turned to violence against the corrupt Chinese government. In the 1930s, the new government established legislation to grant women property and marriage rights. Korabik (1993) explains that in 1949, the All-China Women's Federation was founded to oversee policies that improve conditions for women.

7.5.1.3 Market-Driven Economy (1949–1978)

Between 1934 and 1935, Mao Zedong and his communist army marched 10 000km to establish a new basis point in north-west China, while being attacked by the National government's army. Zhou (2003) emphasises that the Communist Revolution of 1949 brought Chinese women to a new stage of liberation as the new government paid particular attention to the women's movement. Ming-Hsuan (2011) contends that the 1970s market-orientated economic reform transformed China's economy from an agricultural economy to a manufacturing and service-based economy, creating a large number of employment opportunities. Zhou's (2003) investigation reveals that 90% of Chinese women were illiterate before 1949 and by 1958, 16 million women had became literate.

7.5.1.4 Cultural Revolution

Unfortunately, during the Mao Cultural Revolution, social science research fell into disfavour, and China closed its doors to foreigners (Korabik, 1993). Korabik (1993) contends that the Cultural Revolution represented a shift towards scepticism around intellectual achievement and foreign ideas. After the death of Mao Zedong in 1976, Deng Xiaoping instituted a program of reforms designed to quickly bring about modernisation so that China could compete in the world economy. Keith (1997, p. 39) states that "paradoxically, rights and interests gained greater status after the Tiananmen Square 'massacre' in a fresh round of debate over the legal dimensions of economic reform". The focus on protection of women's lawful rights and interests was integral to the post-Tiananmen human rights debates. Korabik (1993) observes that the winds of change have slowed due to the government's response to the demonstrations in Tiananmen Square in June 1989.

Ming-Hsuan (2011) emphasises that the one-child policy was implemented in China in 1979 to slow down the country's explosive population growth and has allegedly decreased the total population by 400 million people compared to the population that the country was predicted to reach without the policy. An opposing view on the one-child policy is that it "led to increased violence against women,...to increased female infanticide and abuse and divorce of women who bear daughters" (Korabik, 1993, p. 50). And yet, the policy has reduced the amount of time women had to spend on activities relating to mothering and freed them to take on other roles in society. Nonetheless, China's orphanages in the nineties were still disproportionately filled with girls (Johnson, 1993).

Hussain, Scott, Harrison, and Millman (2010) warn that care should be taken before making generalisations in Western situations and in assuming that practices are equally applicable across all locations, without factoring in sociocultural contexts, including the traditions of Chinese familial collectivism into the analysis. Hussain et al. (2010, p. 141) defend the guanxi system:

> although some authors have questioned whether guanxi is ethical, it is used extensively in the business world in China. In the Chinese context of the primacy of the family and the indivisibility of society and culture, contrary to the more individualistic and culturally diverse West. The concept of guanxi can be perceived as socio-cultural capital.

They found that whilst a majority of participants in their study used guanxi to access finance, it was more significantly used by men than by women, supporting European and American research that suggests that men would more readily have access to social networks than women.

Change leadership will benefit from taking note of the discussion above, especially around the guanxi and existing relationships of their potential Chinese business partners that might influence their prospects. These realities in the Chinese context point to the importance of having local partners and joint ventures as an appropriate organisational structure to enter these emerging markets.

With regards to our case study (Scheepers & Swart, 2015) on the MMI merger, the Third Enabler, Explore, indicates that as individual companies, they each had to look for a partner, and they found each other. Their business models at the time would not take them into the future. They had to make a change. With Momentum having battled at the lower end of the market segment and Metropolitan battling at the higher end of the market segment, they needed each other. Their individual visions of their organisations were therefore complementary.

7.6   Measuring the Third Enabler, Explore

Reflection Questions Enabler 3: Explore

Reflection Questions Enabler 3: Explore, contains a short questionnaire to help you assess the extent to which you are practicing this enabler. You can also ask others to assess you using this instrument.

7.7   Conclusion and Outcome of the Third Enabler, Explore

In-depth understanding of the external environment is the outcome of this enabler. Schilling, Werr, Gand, and Sardas (2012) contend that strategic change comprises changes in a way the organisation relates to its environment, which may originate both from inside the firm and from its environment. This Third Enabler endeavours to position the organisation, given the external environmental variables that influence it currently and or will influence the organisation in the future, in either providing an opportunity or posing a significant threat. Gaining the contextual intelligence is, however, not adequate, the eureka or moment of profound insight is also required, and the next enabler pays attention to this aspect.

References

Ahlstrom, D., & Bruton, G. D. (2002). An institutional perspective on the role of culture in shaping strategic actions by technology-focused entrepreneurial firms in China. *Entrepreneurship: Theory and Practice, 26*(4), 53–70. https://doi.org/10.1177/104225870202600404

Bonaglia, F., Goldstein, A., & Mathews, J. A. (2007). Accelerated internationalization by emerging markets' multinationals. *Journal of World Business, 42*(4), 369–383. https://www.oecd.org/dev/36317032.pdf

Bunzeck, N., & Düzel, E. (2006). Absolute coding of stimulus novelty in the human substantia nigra/VTA. *Neuron, 51*(3), 369–379. https://doi.org/10.1016/j.neuron.2006.06.021

Business Monitor International (2014). BMI Report on the South African Insurance Industry. pp. 9–13, 41–44 and 59. https://www.marketresearch.com/Timetric-v3917/Governance-Risk-Compliance-South-African-10155010/

Casanova, L., & Miroux, A. (2017). *The emerging market multinationals report (EMR)*. Emerging Markets Institute (EMI), S.C. Johnson Graduate School of Management, Cornell University. Retrieved from http://www.iberglobal.com/files/2017/Emerging_EMNs_Casanova_Miroux.pdf

Cell Press. (2006, August 27). Pure novelty spurs the brain. *ScienceDaily*. Retrieved April 24, 2018 from www.sciencedaily.com/releases/2006/08/060826180547.htm

Chen, N. Y., & Tjosvold, D. (2007). Guanxi and leader member relationships between American managers and Chinese employees: Open-minded dialogue as mediator. *Asia Pacific Journal of Management, 24*(2), 171–189. https://doi.org/10.1007/s10490-006-9029-9

Cooper, B. B. (2013, May 21). Novelty and the brain: Why new things make us feel so good. *Lifehacker*. Retrieved July 26, 2019, from https://lifehacker.com/novelty-and-the-brain-why-new-things-make-us-feel-so-g-508983802

Dess, G. G., & Beard, D. W. (1984). Dimensions of organizational task environments. *Administrative Science Quarterly, 29*(1), 52–73. Retrieved from http://www.jstor.org/stable/2393080

Farmer, S. M., Tierney, P., & Kung-McIntyre, K. (2003). Employee creativity in Taiwan: An application of role identity theory. *Academy of Management Journal, 46*(5), 618–630. Retrieved from http://citeseerx.ist.psu.edu/viewdoc/download?doi=10.1.1.572.7165&rep=rep1&type=pdf

Fleming, S. R. (2012). Ensuring organizational resilience in times of crisis. *Journal of Global Business Issues, 6*(1), 31–34. https://web.b.ebscohost.com/abstract?direct=true&profile=ehost&scope=site&authtype=crawler&jrnl=1931311X&AN=91851400&h=To9vN5asfMbRIplloDSP4BkEvP8HdK98%2bkI0YaubZLeWKNYgyOab5U%2fnOS%2bkjpqFHqbxfAGIy2Er%2bMmi2jvNlw%3d%3d&crl=c&resultNs=AdminWebAuth&

resultLocal=ErrCrlNotAuth&crlhashurl=login.aspx%3fdirect%3dtrue%26profile%3dehost%
26scope%3dsite%26authtype%3dcrawler%26jrnl%3d1931311X%26AN%3d91851400

Grant, R. M. (2003). Strategic planning in a turbulent environment: Evidence from the oil majors. *Strategic Management Journal, 24*(6), 491–517. https://doi.org/10.1002/smj.314

Hajro, A., & Pudelko, M. (2010). An analysis of core-competences of successful multinational team leaders. *International Journal of Cross-Cultural Management, 10*(2), 175–194. https://doi.org/10.1177/1470595810370910

Hussain, J. G., Scott, J. M., Harrison, R. T., & Millman, C. (2010). "Enter the dragoness": Firm growth, finance, guanxi, and gender in China. *Gender in Management: An International Journal, 25*(2), 137–156. Retrieved from www.emeraldinsight.com/doi/full/10.1108/17542411011026302?fullSc=1

Jansen, J. J. P., Van Den Bosch, F. A. J., & Volberda, H. W. (2006). Exploratory innovation, exploitative innovation, and performance: Effects of organizational antecedents and environmental moderators. *Management Science, 52*(11), 1661–1674. ERS-2006-038-STR. Retrieved from https://www.researchgate.net/publication/220534832_Exploratory_Innovation_Exploitative_Innovation_and_Performance_Effects_of_Organizational_Antecedents_and_Environmental_Moderators

Johnson, K. (1993). Chinese orphanages; saving China's abandoned girls. *Australian Journal of Chinese Affairs, 30*, 61–88. https://doi.org/10.2307/2949992

Johnson, G., & Scholes, K. (2002). *Exploring corporate strategy: Text and cases.* London: Financial Times/Prentice Hall. https://trove.nla.gov.au/work/19305020?q&versionId=41367079

Johnson, G., Scholes, K., & Whittington, R. (2008). *Exploring corporate strategy.* New York: Prentice Hall. https://www.amazon.com/Exploring-Corporate-Strategy-Gerry-Johnson/dp/0273711911

Keith, R. C. (1997). Legislating women's and children's "rights and interests" in the People's Republic of China. *The China Quarterly, 149*, 29–55. https://www.cambridge.org/core/journals/china-quarterly/article/legislating-womens-and-childrens-rights-and-interests-in-the-prca/136C6A10ED234AD31C9123CD1C57A75A

Korabik, K. (1993). Managerial women in the People's Republic of China: The long march continues. *International Studies of Management and Organisation, 23*(4), 47–64. https://iaap-journals.onlinelibrary.wiley.com/doi/abs/10.1111/j.1464-0597.1993.tb00750.x

MacKay, B., & Chia, R. (2013). Choice, chance, and unintended consequences in strategic change: A process understanding of the rise and fall of NorthCo Automotive. *Academy of Management Journal, 56*(1), 208–230. https://doi.org/10.5465/amj.2010.0734

Margolis, J., Roberts, L. M., & Winig, L. (2007). South African Airways, A and B (SAA). Case study: 9-407-014 (A), 9-407-024 (B). Harvard Business School Publishing, Feb 26, 2007, pp. 1–21 (A); 9-407-024, Feb 26, 2007, pp. 1–4. https://store.hbr.org/product/south-african-airways-a/407014?sku=407014-PDF-ENG

McCallum, S., & O'Connell, D. (2009). Social capital and leadership development: Building stronger leadership through enhanced relational skills. *Leadership and Organizational Development Journal, 30*(2), 152–166. https://doi.org/10.1108/01437730910935756

Ming-Hsuan, L. (2011). The one-child policy and gender equality in education in China: Evidence from household data. *Journal of Family Economic Issues, 33*, 41–52. https://www.cpc.unc.edu/projects/china/publications/705

Osborn, R. N., Hunt, J. G., & Jauch, L. R. (2002). Towards a contextual theory of leadership. *The Leadership Quarterly, 13*, 797–837. https://doi.org/10.1016/j.leaqua.2009.01.010

Osborn, R. N., & Marion, R. (2009). Contextual leadership, transformational leadership and the performance of international innovation seeking alliances. *The Leadership Quarterly, 20*, 191–206. https://isiarticles.com/bundles/Article/pre/pdf/19488.pdf

Osborn, R. N., Uhl-Bien, M., & Milosevic, I. (2014). The context and leadership. In D. Day (Ed.), *The Oxford handbook of leadership and organizations* (pp. 589–612). Oxford: Oxford University Press. https://books.google.co.za/books?hl=en&lr=&id=lDiTAwAAQBAJ&oi=fnd&pg=

PP1&dq=The+Oxford+handbook+of+leadership+and+organizations+(pp.+589%E2%80% 93612).+Oxford:+Oxford+University+Press.&ots=Y5qBRf3jE-&sig= iuTvm8sqNLrwlnTRien4xIla1Qw#v=onepage&q&f=false

Pihlak, Ü., & Alas, R. (2012). Resistance to change in Indian, Chinese and Estonian organizations. *Journal of Indian Business Research, 4*(4), 224–243. https://doi.org/10.1108/ 17554191211274767

Pop, Z. C., & Maier, V. (2012). The impact of internal and external environment upon the competitiveness of firms. *Managerial Challenges of the Contemporary Society, 4*(2012), 20–23. https://econ.ubbcluj.ro/jmccs/Volume_no_4_2012.pdf

Porter, M. E. (1980). *Competitive strategy: Techniques for analyzing industries and competitors.* New York: Simon & Schuster. https://www.amazon.com/Competitive-Strategy-Techniques-Industries-Competitors-ebook/dp/B001CB34J0

Porter, M. E. (2008). The five competitive forces that shape strategy. *Harvard Business Review, 86*(1), 25–40. https://www.ibbusinessandmanagement.com/uploads/1/1/7/5/11758934/porters_ five_forces_analysis_and_strategy.pdf

Rayner, L. (2015, March 19). Examining prospects in global emerging markets. *Professional Adviser,* 22–23. https://www.professionaladviser.com/feature/2399223/sector-report-examin ing-prospects-global-emerging-markets

Reeves, M., & Deimler, M. (2011, July–August). Adaptability: The new competitive advantage. *Harvard Business Review.* Retrieved from https://hbr.org/2011/07/adaptability-the-new-compet itive-advantage

Rock, D. (2009a). *Your brain at work: Strategies for overcoming distraction, regaining focus, and working smarter all day.* New York: HarperCollins. https://www.harpercollins.com/ 9780061771293/your-brain-at-work/

Rock, D. (2009b, October 4). *Easily distracted: Why it's hard to focus and what to do about it.* Psychology Today. https://www.psychologytoday.com/za/blog/your-brain-work/200910/eas ily-distracted

Rock, D., & Page, L. J. (2009). *Coaching with the brain in mind: Foundations for practice.* Upper Saddle River, NJ: Wiley. https://www.wiley.com/en-us/Coaching+with+the+Brain+in+Mind% 3A+Foundations+for+Practice-p-9780470405680

Rock, D., & Schwartz, J. (2006). The neuroscience of leadership. *Strategy Business, 43,* 72–82. https://www.strategy-business.com/article/06207?gko=f1af3

Scheepers, C. B., & Swart, S. (2015). *Momentum and metropolitan merger: Authentic transforma-tional leadership.* Ivey Publishing, 9B15C004. https://www.iveycases.com/ProductView.aspx? id=70560

Schilling, A., Werr, A., Gand, S., & Sardas, J.-C. (2012). Understanding professionals' reactions to strategic change: The role of threatened professional identities. *The Service Industries Journal, 32*(8), 1229–1245. https://doi.org/10.1080/02642069.2010.531269

Schumpeter Column. (2011, December 3). Khaki Capitalism. In some countries the "military-industrial complex" is more than a metaphor. *The Economist,* 67. Retrieved from http://www. economist.com/node/21540985

Shahzad, K., Bajwa, S. U., Ali, Q., & Zia, S. A. (2012). Role of incubation in women entrepreneur-ship development in Pakistan. *South Asian Journal of Management.* https://doi.org/10.2139/ ssrn.2048316

Sujova, A., & Rajnoha, R. (2012). The management model of strategic change based on process principles. *Procedia: Social and Behavioural Science, 62,* 1286–1291. https://doi.org/10.1016/ j.sbspro.2012.09.220

Tjosvold, D., & Yu, Z. (2007). Group risk taking: The constructive role of controversy in China. *Group & Organization Management, 32*(6), 653–674. https://doi.org/10.1177/ 1059601106287110

Uzkurt, C., Kumar, R., Kimzan, H. S., & Sert, H. (2012). The impact of environmental uncertainty dimensions on organisational innovativeness: An empirical study on SMEs. *International Journal of Innovation Management, 16*(2), 1–23. ZDB-ID 13395828. https://doi.org/10.1142/

S1363919611003647. Retrieved from http://www.worldscientific.com/doi/abs/10.1142/S1363919611003647

Van de Ven, A. H., & Poole, M. S. (1995). Explaining development and change in organizations. *Academy of Management Review, 20*(3), 510–540. Retrieved from https://pdfs.semanticscholar.org/0335/f47eb46c5a936da304b2d44e9328ee392442.pdf

Vanhaudenhuyse, A., Demertzi, A., Schabus, M., Noirhomme, Q., Bredart, S., Boly, M., et al. (2011). Two distinct neural networks mediate the awareness of environment and of self. *Journal of Cognitive Neuroscience, 23*(3), 570–578. https://pubmed.ncbi.nlm.nih.gov/20515407/

Van Hecke, M. L., Callahan, L. P., Kolar, B., & Paller, K. A. (2010). *The brain advantage: Become a more effective business leader using the latest brain research.* Amherst, NY: Prometheus Books. https://www.amazon.com/Brain-Advantage-Effective-Business-Research/dp/1591027640

Veldsman, T. (2013). Chapter 8. People professionals fit for emerging markets. In S. Bluen (Ed.), *Talent management in emerging markets* (pp. 179–203). Randburg: Knowres. http://www.kr.co.za/knowres-publishing-1/talent-management-in-emerging-markets-mobi

Vithessonthi, C., & Thoumrungroje, A. (2011). Strategic change and firm performance: The moderating effect of organisational learning. *Journal of Asia Business Studies, 5*(2), 194–210. https://doi.org/10.1108/15587891111152348

Wittmann, B. C., Bunzeck, N., Dolan, R. J., & Düzel, E. (2007). Anticipation of novelty recruits reward system and hippocampus while promoting recollection. *Neuroimage, 38*(1–9), 194–202. https://doi.org/10.1016/j.neuroimage.2007.06.038

Zajac, E. J., Kraatz, M. S., & Bresser, R. K. F. (2000). Modeling the dynamics of strategic fit: A normative approach to strategic change. *Strategic Management Journal, 21*(4), 429–453. https://doi.org/10.1002/(SICI)1097-0266(200004)21:4<429::AID-SMJ81>3.0.CO;2-#

Zhou, J. (2003). Keys to women's liberation in communist China: An historical overview. *Journal of International Women's Studies, 5*(1), 67–77. Retrieved from http://vc.bridgew.edu/jiws/vol5/iss1/4

Reference List for Quotes

Retrieved July 26, 2019, from https://www.brainyquote.com/quotes/frank_borman_162112
Retrieved July 26, 2019, from https://best-quotations.com/authquotes.php?auth=15

Fourth Enabler

Eureka Moments

Creativity takes courage

(Henri Matisse, n.d.)

Learning Outcomes
At the end of this chapter, change leaders will be able to:

- Identify opportunities in the environment
- Find moments of insights that can lead to opportunities
- Verbalise with clarity the move from—to

Electronic supplementary material The online version of this chapter (https://doi.org/10.1007/978-3-030-40846-6_8) contains supplementary material, which is available to authorized users.

C. B. Scheepers, S. Swart, *Change Leadership in Emerging Markets*, Future of
Business and Finance, https://doi.org/10.1007/978-3-030-40846-6_8

8.1   Orientation to Eureka Moments

While the previous enabler featured the Third Enabler: Exploring the environment, this Fourth Enabler endeavours to bring a critical change leadership role to the forefront, namely Eureka Moments. This awakening to a new idea or insight, and its resultant heightened emotional response is an under-researched area, and limited attention has been given in the leadership literature to this aspect. We argue that it will contribute to an understanding of how to actually elicit emotional commitment and support for change.

The idea of a eureka or light bulb moment has been around for a very long time. Psychologists have studied these moments of insight using behavioural methods for nearly a century. We chose to use the term Eureka Moments for the Fourth Enabler because the word "*eureka*", means "*I found it*". It is commonly attributed to the ancient Greek scholar, Archimedes. According to legend, he shouted "eureka" after getting into a bath and realising that the buoyant force on a submerged object is equal to the weight of the fluid displaced by it. Being so elated by his discovery, he ran out into the streets shouting, "I found it" (eureka in Greek), and so the Archimedes principle was born (Van Hecke, Callahan, Kolar, & Paller, 2010). In this Fourth Enabler, we want change leaders to "find" the change they will need to lead.

We believe a crucial building block to understanding how people, organisations and societies change is contained in the concept of *paradigms*. A paradigm is defined as a pattern or a problem-solving model. Paradigms are also defined as a set of rules and regulations that set boundaries in which we solve problems. It was first used by Thomas Kuhn (1962) in his book, *The Structure of Scientific Revolutions* to explore why scientists often overlook information that does not suit their expectations. Joel Barker popularised the term in business in the 1980s through his video, *Discovering the Future: The Business of Paradigms.* The video had a significant impact on business thinking and is fundamental to the understanding of change. When we change the way we look at something from one way to another, our paradigm shifts and we form new neural networks that replace the old way of looking at something.

We believe that even today many people still do not understand the importance of paradigms and participants are always fascinated by the concept when first introduced to it. Paradigms can also be considered to be neural networks that fire together and then wire together in a set way of seeing the world. This will be explored in more detail in the section, Neuroscience Insights into Eureka Moments.

For change to occur, it is essential for a paradigm shift to take place. That is when the way of seeing something changes fundamentally to a new way of seeing the same thing. The moment when a paradigm shifts, is called a *eureka* moment. A *eureka* moment then refers to a cry of joy or satisfaction when something is discovered. It is a response or a solution to what was perceived as a challenge in the environment. Eureka moments are also called "a-ha" moments (a moment of sudden insight or discovery) or a paradigm shift. An "a-ha" moment arrives when a person, team or society "sees" the "world" in a different light or finds a solution or realises an opportunity that might not have been there before.

Fig. 8.1 White Vase or Two Black faces? (Rubin, 1915)

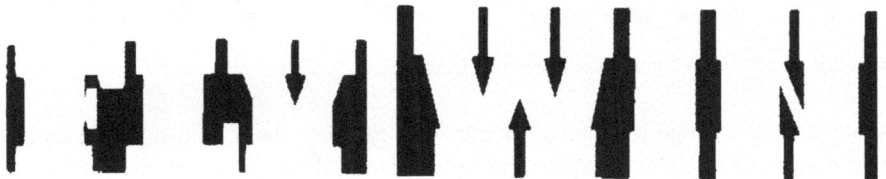

Fig. 8.2 Black and White Arrows or WINFLY?

A paradigm shift can also be defined as a sudden comprehension that solves a problem, reinterprets a situation, explains a joke or resolves an ambiguous perception and is also called a moment of insight (MOI). There is something magical about experiencing an a-ha moment as well as seeing it in others. It is the actual split second when an individual reaches a significant new insight or realisation, by unlocking the very issue, which just seconds before they had viewed as insurmountable. In the blink of an eye, they have moved from a position of being stuck to finding an answer or a way forward.

In our training sessions, we often use the illustration above (Figs. 8.1–8.3) to illustrate examples of paradigm shifts and to highlight the moment of insight. When we first look at Fig. 8.1, we observe either a white vase or two black faces facing each other. Depending on our perspective, we might at first only see one of the pictures. In change processes, the same phenomenon might occur where we miss information if we believe the way we see something is the only *correct* perspective (Fig. 8.1).

Figure 8.2 illustrates how two paradigms can exist simultaneously. Some observers will notice black up and down arrows, while others will see black exhaust pipes, automatic teller machines, slot machines and half a house. Some might observe the two words FLY and WIN.

In some cases in the same team, one person might observe black arrows, while another team member is seeing the two words. A debate might even ensue about who is wrong and who is right. But in fact, both parties are right. Each has their own perspective. When we communicate a paradigm shift, we face the exact same

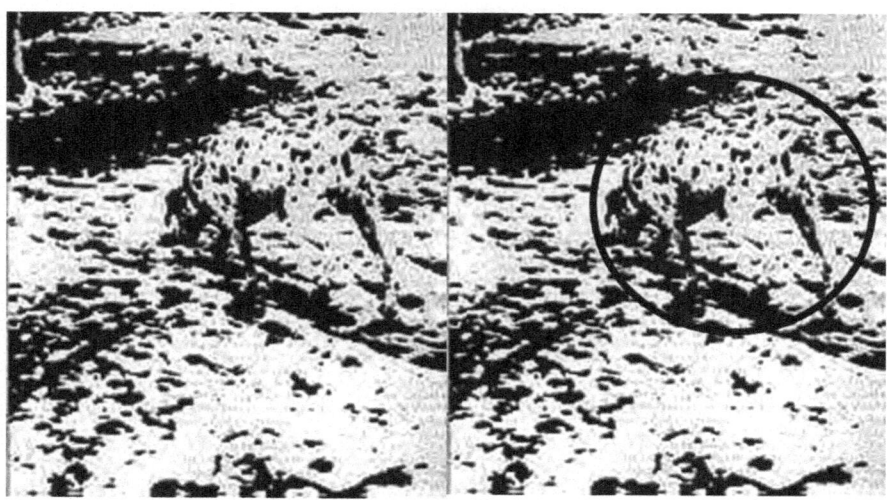

Fig. 8.3 Black and White Dots or Dalmatian Dog? (Gregory, 1970)

challenge. As change leaders, we might want to bring about a change that others might not yet see. Helping the other person understand what it is you see, while they perceive themselves to be correct and you being wrong, is at the heart of the challenge of leading change.

Of course, bringing about change might be a lot more complex than seeing different images on a page. The pictures are powerful analogies to understanding how difficult communication can be and how critical understanding each other's perspectives can be.

The final picture (Fig. 8.3) is, at first glance, just a messy collection of black and white dots, utterly confusing with no meaning to the reader. When we discover the dog in the outlined circle on the right, the picture suddenly has meaning. So it is often with change. When we cannot see the picture of the future (vision), it remains a useless, senseless and confusing mess. Sometimes the change leader might see the dog, but the followers are still in the dark, seeing only black and white dots. It is the responsibility of change leaders to help others see the dog. The danger is that we lose our patience when others do not seem to see things the way we do. We encourage change leaders to take care in their communication and to be patient with others.

The importance of eureka moments will now be explored followed by a discussion regarding eureka moments in practice and case studies illustrating eureka moments.

8.2   Importance of Eureka Moments

The reason why the concept of a paradigm is so important is that unless, as change agents, we are able to communicate the new, desired paradigm clearly, we have no hope of ever achieving the desired change. We have to be able to make others "see" the picture of the future, sell the benefits of the new paradigm, and continually inspire them to "fight" for the achievement of the future paradigm. We also have to understand others' paradigms and be prepared to change ours. Without understanding how our minds function, leading change is impossible.

We sense that there is an energy feature to prompt movement in the required direction. Often, it is those problematic starting points that inhibit change processes. Without these eureka moments, it is very difficult to master sufficient momentum to get change projects and initiatives off the ground. There is a saying that a rocket uses the most energy in the first few minutes of the launch to overcome gravity. This is where eureka moments have the most value. We have all experienced how someone's enthusiasm can be contagious. There is something about their heightened emotional state that touches others in such a way, that the spirit of the moment or conviction of this person spreads through to others.

Please note that we are speaking here about eureka moments and not only one moment of insight. Our experience indicates that leadership entails multiple eureka moments along the way. This leadership role indeed relates to the literature on intuition. However, we would like to emphasise that it does not mean that knowledge or experience is not required. Instead, we argue that you require extensive knowledge and experience and need to apply adequate effort, prior to having these moments of true insight. Eureka moments are the impetus to get moving and acting on insight. We call it "awakening" as it is similar to the Zulu word, "Vuka", meaning waking up.

There is something about the energy of the interviewees that we observed in our research towards this volume. We found it difficult to name it or place our finger on it, but it was undeniably there! We thought it was mere enthusiasm; dedication or like some of them mentioned, "I think I am a little bit mad to dedicate so many hours"; "I get carried away"; "My intensity is sometimes too much for others"; "My passion is sometimes interpreted as aggression" or "Others often mention to me that I come across as very passionate".

These quotes illustrate the effort and sheer determination and dedication that these interviewees put into their work and then a bonus is awarded in that sometimes a cathartic moment happens and "eureka!", the breakthrough occurs. It is as much a surprise to them as to others. First prize is always of course, in terms of leadership that the eureka moment is shared with others so that there could be support for the action that has to be taken, based on the insight. Typically, leadership is on the one hand about self-mastery. However, it cannot stop there, and the influencing of others to ultimately share the leadership role is even more critical.

The question thus remains, how could leadership ensure that eureka moments are happening throughout the organisation? How could leaders create the environment for eureka moments to take place regularly? This Fourth enabler relates to the work on creativity and innovation, where the idea generation is an essential first phase. In cases where people have come up with ideas, they feel committed and invested in making the idea work and ultimately implementing it.

An example from our interviewees was when the CEO of a manganese mine, explained the productivity improvement projects, through the facilitation of consultants from Australia. "They made a huge effort in managing an ideas pipeline, where people would brainstorm which were the low hanging fruit, that would make the most impact on the business processes. Subsequently, they would create what they called "wiring" where these ideas were loaded onto a system and performance and revenue from the idea closely tracked". From these quotes, it is clear that initially, creative ideas are important and later on it is pure discipline to ensure implementation of these ideas and to derive value from them.

Having explored the environment, as the Third Enabler illustrates, the leader needs to move on to find solutions to the issues in the environment. Organisations require appropriate responses to the challenges in the environment. This will mean that they would need to think out of the box and use creative thinking and the creative thinking of others to come up with something new.

An organisation is more likely to adapt and survive if the change is embraced with an open and positive attitude (Tan & Tiong, 2005). With a change in management, the higher a CEO's openness to change, the greater the likelihood of the choice of strategic over status-quo-preserving business actions (Decker & Mellewigt, 2012).

Organisations also require paradigm shifts. The change process requires organisational unlearning which is defined as a process of "organisational memory eliminating" where there is a significant change in beliefs and routines (Akgün, Byrne, Lynn, & Keskin, 2007). Akgün et al. (2007) indicate that the change and pressures in macroeconomic and micro-economic landscapes require adaptable organisations to unlearn old "competency traps" (Akgün et al., 2007, p. 795) that inhibit the organisation to move forward.

Strategic changes, such as mergers and acquisitions, require organisations to unlearn some of the highly vested ways of doing things, and embrace new cultures and learning new routines. Unlike organisational change that is an end state, organisational unlearning "is a collective cognition that coordinate organisational change process" (Akgün et al., 2007, p. 800), involving the process of unfreezing, transition and refreezing. Lewin's model (1947) also illustrates this organisational process of unlearning, as described by Akgün et al. (2007), which may result in disequilibrium, symmetry breaking, experimentation and reformulation in an organisational unlearning process.

Johnson (1992) in "*Managing strategic change - strategy, culture and action*" notes that while individual managers may hold varying sets of beliefs about many different aspects of their organisational world, there is likely to exist to some degree a core set of beliefs and assumptions commonly held by most managers. These core beliefs and assumptions are what Johnson (1992) refers to as *paradigms*. These paradigms are often so entrenched in the organisation's way of thinking that they are often more readily perceived by outsiders than those immersed in the organisation. Therefore, a paradigm is a cognitive structure likely to be found to a greater or lesser extent in most companies.

Since paradigms are incrementally changed over time, these can be seen as a feedback mechanism that not only defines an action plan but also takes the responses of these actions into consideration and changes the actions accordingly. It is primarily made up of unique organisational competencies and skills, therefore can articulate the organisation's real competitive advantage. On the other hand, it can also lead to significant strategic problems. Thus, the paradigm is a filter for environmental forces and changes within the organisation, which will undoubtedly affect organisational performance, but Johnson (1992) argues that these factors should not impinge upon the organisational strategy, as the strategies that managers' advocate and those that emerge through the social and political processes are typically configured within the boundaries of these paradigms. Change leaders must therefore have a "mental model" or picture in their own minds about the changes that they want to propel or instigate. Barsh, Mogelof, and Webb (2010) identify dimensions of centred leadership, amongst others as those that can manage energy and conduct positive reframing.

Hamel (2000) emphasises that companies that are incapable of changing either themselves or their industry are acquisition fodder for more imaginative companies that will redeploy their skills and assets. Business competitiveness thus requires speed, flexibility and continuous self-renewal. Change leaders cannot wait for clarity and for all the answers to emerge before they act. Instead, they need to get things done with limited information, all the while assessing and adapting their policies as new data emerge.

We observed that the eureka moment creates an effective commitment, for example one of our interviewees posited, "You know, we have conducted the organising for the learnerships/internships and it is a lot of work and at times feels like a sausage machine. Then one day, I heard the founder of this process, speaking about the reason for starting it and the bigger picture made so much sense to me, that it was an AHA-moment! It motivated me to understand what it was actually all about!" We noticed that while she was talking about this, her eyes were shining and she looked excited. Her enthusiasm was palpable, and it was clear that she was committed to give extra energy and focus on this project.

We realise that, although the leadership literature does not focus on this maybe metaphysical phenomenon of eliciting energy, it is not to say that it does not exist. We would like to emphasise that there is something here that must not be underestimated.

8.3   Eureka Moments in Practice

8.3.1   Paradigm Shifts

The concept of a paradigm was discussed in detail above in Orientation to Eureka Moments. We see the idea of a paradigm shift as the essence of any change process and the primary objective of the change leader. Now change leaders need to understand how to bring about a change from one paradigm to another—thus

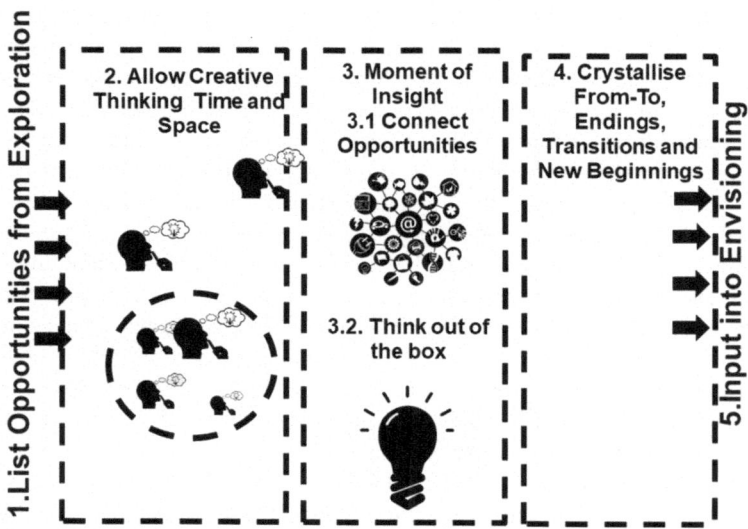

Fig. 8.4 Eureka moments process (Authors' own)

shifting the paradigm to a new way of thinking and doing. This happens first in the change leader's own mind and next in the mind of others.

Manfred Ketz De Vries (2006), in his classic book *The Leadership Mystique*, defines leaders as merchants of hope. Extending this definition, we consider change leaders to be merchants of paradigm shifts. Like marketers and salespeople, we believe change leaders trade in the business of paradigm shifts. Therefore, it is essential for change leaders to have an in-depth understanding of the concept and mechanics of paradigms shifts.

Eureka moments of insight are critical in the establishment of creative ideas. Most organisations today experience constant pressure to increase their creativity and innovation. Change leaders have to be able to not only create conducive conditions for moments of insight to unleash organisational creativity, but also to ensure these creative ideas are brought to life.

The authors developed the Eureka Moments Process to illustrate how to attain these moments of insight that will lead to the start of paradigms being shifted. This process is captured in Fig. 8.4.

8.3.2   Eureka Moments Process

8.3.2.1 List the Opportunities
The process starts with listing all the possible opportunities obtained during the exploration process. This might be a once off or an ongoing process of finding opportunities.

Practical Application of Listing Opportunities

The CEO of a large short-term insurance company in South Africa has a Notes section on his cell phone where he captures novel ideas, opportunities or moments of insight when traveling or just when an idea pops up. Because moments of insight happen when we are not consciously thinking about them (see Neuroscience Insights below), we believe this is a brilliant way of capturing an idea to prevent these gems from slipping away in the everyday rush of operations.

The next tool (Tool 4.1), offers leaders an opportunity to list their opportunities from the exploration phase.

Tool 4.1 List of Opportunities from Exploration

Consider the opportunities that were identified during the exploration phase.

8.3.2.2 Allow Creative Thinking Time and Space

Following the opportunities that were identified in Enabler 3: Explore and listed in Tool 4.1, it is now time to ensure a creative space is provided for ideas to germinate. Completing the worksheet provided in Tool 4.2 will facilitate the process of allowing time and space to come up with the eureka moment.

Tool 4.2 Creative Thinking Time and Space

Complete questions on creative thinking: time and space, for example: When and how will I allow myself time off to *not* think of new opportunities or about work at all?

8.3.2.3 Moment of Insight

The next tool will help you think creatively about how the opportunities you have listed can lead to a paradigm shift in your organisation.

Tool 4.3 Moment of Insight, Endings, Transitions and New Beginnings

In Tool 4.3, you can complete questions, for example: How can the opportunities identified in Tool 4.1 be connected or used to take the organisation to the next level?
What are the creative ideas I would like to bring to the organisation?

8.3.2.4 Crystallise the Paradigm Shift

The next worksheet, in Tool 4.4 offers an opportunity to create a very clear picture of the paradigm we want to shift to. A basic yet potent tool we use when consulting with clients is the "From-To" tool. It is easy to use, yet it is often just what is needed to crystallise precisely what the change is about.

Tool 4.4 Paradigm Shift From–To

Complete the template, by articulating the paradigm shift from . . . to . . .?

8.3.2.5 The Compact Disc (CD) Model

The Compact Disc (CD) model was introduced in Enabler 1: Ethos to explain how values are formed. In this chapter, it is discussed again to describe the process of changing paradigms. It is based on the work of Edgar Schein (1996) but evolved to take on a life of its own. It is a conceptual model used to explain how to change one's own and others' paradigms.

In the field of change, having eureka moments is of critical importance. Changing old paradigms and getting others to change their paradigms form the essence of what change is all about, and is not an easy task. This is where understanding the CD Model adds value.

Paradigms are formed from our birth. Over time our parents, family, friends, schools, church and society at large extend our paradigms by giving constant input to the way we view the world.

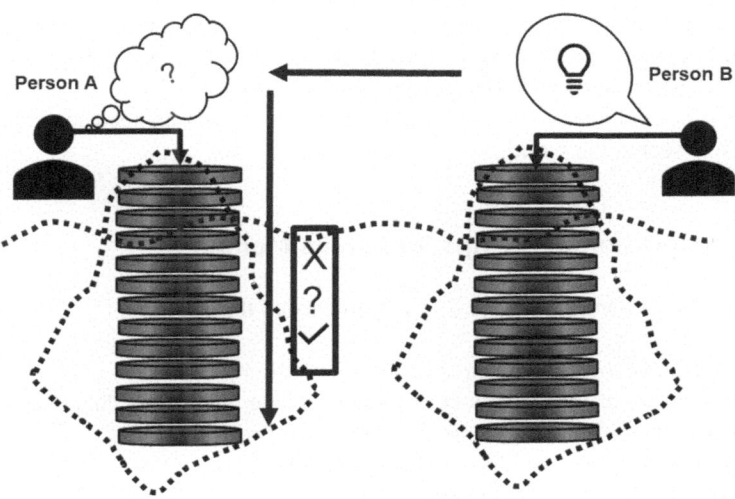

Fig. 8.5 Person B sharing his eureka CD with Person A (Authors' own)

We like to think of paradigms as CDs stacked one upon another in a CD shuttle. Every time a stimulus is received through our senses, we access the CD and "music" starts playing in our heads. We have an immediate opinion, and as a rule, we automatically judge the stimulus as either good or bad. This causes us to either accept the paradigm, which in turn confirms that our paradigm is correct, or reject the paradigm altogether and switch off completely. We need to understand this dynamic if we are to successfully "sell" our eureka moments.

In this model (Fig. 8.5), CDs are stacked according to their level of consciousness and emotive value. Deep-seated emotional paradigms are very difficult to challenge as they are often assumed to be so accurate that they are never even questioned and are perceived as the absolute truth. They, therefore, remain at an unconscious level. An example of a deep-seated CD could be one's own sexual orientation or religious beliefs. Higher-level CDs are easier to change. They could include physical choices such as fashion preferences or a favourite type of car.

Of course, this is entirely dependent on the individual in question and what might be deep-seated for one person could be shallow for the next person. When there is substantial emotive resistance to change we can be pretty sure the issue is of great value to the person and is therefore at a deep level.

This explains why some changes are easier for some people to implement than others.

Driving the CD shuttle is our sense of self. When anyone dares to challenge or change one of our deep-seated CDs (those we hold onto very dearly) or if something of value to someone is discarded, it will lead to protecting it with one's "life".

CDs are intricately linked together and wanting to change one CD can trigger many other CDs. Not wanting to change one's CD or not understanding others' CDs is the root of all resistance to change, all conflict, all divorces and even all wars.

We know from the complex network of neurons in our brain that this model is an oversimplification, but the model succeeds in making it easy for change leaders to understand how to lead and manage change (Fig. 8.5).

Change leaders need to be clear which existing paradigms need to change to a new way of seeing the world.

8.3.3   Implementation Tips for Eureka Moments

We share the following practical tips as summary to this section:

- Play devil's advocate, but take care not to overdo it.
- Become aware of your own mental models and be unafraid to challenge them.
- It takes years to disassemble these mental models or paradigms.
- Experiment constantly with new mental models or paradigms.
- Fail early and often, through experimentation.
- Learn as much as possible.
- Ask the type of powerful, stretching, thought-provoking questions that cause individuals to pause and reflect.
- Provide and create plenty of space for self-reflection and time for the individual to ponder. This requires leaving room for silence and being comfortable with this.
- Be prepared to move on from an issue when the individual appears to be stuck and revisit it later.
- Ask reframing questions and use lateral thinking techniques to help the individual look at a problem from a different angle and see alternative perspectives.
- Give encouragement and positive reinforcement when people shift their paradigms.

8.4   Neuroscience Insights into Eureka Moments

The real voyage of discovery consists not of seeking new lands but seeing with new eyes. (Marcel Proust, n.d.)

8.4.1   Eurekas Really Exist!

Evidence from brain science helps explain how these moments of insight are reached (Jung-Beeman, Collier, & Kounios, 2013). Although the idea of a light bulb or eureka moment has been around for many years, it is only now with the advent of advanced cognitive neuroscience equipment that we can be sure it exists. Using innovative, cost-effective technologies such as functional magnetic resonance imaging (fMRI) and electroencephalography (EEG) scans, these light bulb moments can now be proven. When we observe a new idea, it chemically causes changes in the brain. New ideas have enormous power to change how the mind works and how we do things (Jacobs, 2009).

8.4.2 Where in the Brain Does the Eureka Moment Happen?

Leading cognitive neuroscientist, Jung-Beeman and his fellow researchers conducted the Remote Associates Test (RAT) by presenting three-word problems to participants and using fMRI scans and EEG to test brain activity at the moment a solution was found—the moment of insight (Jung-Beeman et al., 2013). In the RAT, three words are presented to participants, and they are then requested to find one noun that could be used with all three words. Examples include storm, wave and drain with the solution being brain: brain-wave, brain-storm and brain-drain. Another example might be cottage, Swiss, cake. With the answer being cheese: cottage cheese, Swiss cheese and cheesecake. While monitoring the research subjects during these a-ha moments, the area most active was the *anterior temporal lobe of the right hemisphere* (Jung-Beeman et al., 2004; Jung-Beeman et al., 2013). This part of the brain is thus involved in integrating information that is distantly related. At the exact moment of insight, a complex set of new connections is created. These connections have, "the potential to enhance mental resources and overcome the brain's resistance to change" (Rock & Schwartz, 2006, p. 8). At the moment of insight, the anterior superior temporal gyrus is activated. Eureka moments occur on the right side of the brain, towards the front.

About 1.5 seconds before the moment of insight, there is an increase in lower frequency brain waves in this area of the brain. The activity levels within the brain are in an alpha state—quiet, relaxed and internalised. Then, a second smaller wave of electrical activity is seen on EEG. Weak solution-related activity gains momentum and then bursts into consciousness as insight. It is almost like closing your eyes to concentrate when you are trying to solve a difficult problem. Your brain blocks out the visual inputs to your right hemisphere. The visual cortex shuts down. Then a couple of moments (300 milliseconds) before the eureka moment occurs, there is a sudden and confident recognition of the solution. The right temporal activity experiences a high-frequency gamma spike in the wave activity when new neural pathways are created, and the insight is born (Jung-Beeman et al., 2013).

Rock and Davis (2016) believe silence and solitude are crucial conditions for cultivating moments of insight. They suggest setting aside reflection and alone time during the pressurised working day to enable moments of insight. Spending time in a place of peaceful relaxation could be just what is needed to spark a creative idea. This should encourage change leaders to induce alpha states as fertile ground for the emergence of insights (Jung-Beeman et al., 2013).

Another tip for generating moments of insight is to practice mindfulness (see Enabler 2, Ego Mastery for more information on mindfulness). When you focus your thoughts inwards on an anchor such as the breath and block out external stimuli, alpha brain waves are produced in the visual cortex indicating the reduction of external information. This provides a fertile breeding ground for a-ha moments.

Allowing the mind to wander aimlessly also proves to be more effective when wanting to elicit moments of insight. Baird et al. (2012) conducted a research study in which they showed that respondents who engaged in an undemanding task during an idea incubation period, performed better than those who were given a demanding task. This suggests mind wandering facilitates creative problem solving. Rock and Davis (2016) encourage social media fasting and switching off devices leaving the mind free to wander.

Being pressurised and stressed out to come up with a paradigm shift is a massive inhibitor to creating moments of insight. Subramaniam, Kounios, Parrish, and Jung-Beeman (2009) found that participants experiencing a positive mood had more insight and solved more problems, compared to those in a more negative mood. Research studies proved that a positive mood boosts activity in the ACC and "opens the mind" to alternative solutions.

Innovation is at the intersection of previously unrelated patterns. The brain loves patterns and predictability, but the downside of patterns is that we want to stay as we are and our thinking becomes outdated.

One way of getting a moment of insight is to pose a thought-provoking question that will cause you to pause and reflect, then perform an easy, undemanding, nonrelated activity and allow the brain to simmer and work on the creation of a solution.

The neurons in the left hemisphere have shorter dendrites, and they pull together related information while neurons in the right hemisphere branch out much wider and access distant, unrelated ideas in the brain causing unrelated connections to be made. While doing something unrelated to the issue at hand, we allow the right superior gyrus reaction to gather a wide range of ideas found in different parts of the brain. This results in a moment of insight.

It is interesting to note that sleep can boost creativity. Sleep is essential for memory consolidation and when we sleep memories are transformed from "soft" to more durable, and memories are then easier to retrieve. As sleep at work is somewhat impractical (except for Google's nap pods!), daydreaming is an option. In daily functioning, the PFC plays a gatekeeper role making thinking creatively difficult. Daydreaming makes the PFC go to" sleep" so ideas can flow more freely from the subconscious mind.

YouTube Clip: John Kounios: The Neuroscience Behind Epiphanies

https://www.youtube.com/watch?v=7uyw5y_tHEM
https://www.youtube.com/watch?v=J1IWm8tJroo
https://www.youtube.com/watch?v=F7t9i0sWGy8&t=63s

Thus far, we have only addressed eureka moments with respect to individuals. It is important though to remember that large-scale organisational change will require a large-scale change in paradigms. This means many eureka moments will be required throughout the organisation (Rock, 2009; Rock & Schwartz, 2006).

Your best ideas, the eureka moments that turn the world upside down, seldom come when you are juggling e-mails or straining to make your voice heard in a high-stress meeting. They happen when you are walking the dog, soaking in the bath or swinging in the hammock (Carl Honore, n.d.).

8.5   Eureka Moments in Emerging Markets

8.5.1   Case Examples of Eureka Moments in the Emerging Markets Contexts

The unfolding political and socioeconomic changes in South Africa over recent years, coupled with the re-entry of the country into the international business arena, have created new challenges for local businesses. As the new political dispensation unfolds, organisations have to make profound adjustments to negotiate the tide of change and remain competitive in an economy that is global, information based, knowledge driven and service intensive.

There are many paradigms about emerging markets. For example, when developed countries refer to emerging markets, they often actually refer to the developing countries that would include the frontier markets. The emerging markets in itself could become a paradigm in that the diversity within the emerging markets are not recognised. Casanova and Miroux (2017) from Cornell University found that while the Global Fortune 500 companies overall are from a diverse group of industries, those from the emerging markets top 20 countries (E20) are concentrated around seven specific industries, namely petroleum refining, mining, crude oil products, commercial and savings banks, metals, motor vehicle parts, energy and engineering as well as construction. They represent more than 60% of all the E20 emerging market multinationals (MNCs).

Unfortunately, many emerging markets are still dependent on foreign investments. With regards to Ernst and Young (EY's) Attractiveness Programme on Africa of May 2017: The key hub economies (South Africa, Nigeria, Kenya, Egypt and Morocco) remain Africa's top recipients for Foreign Development Investment (FDI) projects. Asia-Pacific has become a more visible FDI investor, and China emerges as the largest job creator. External factors, particularly oil prices, primarily drove the low growth. Nigeria also had lower production levels as a result of domestic insurgency. EY also reports that more countries will grow at 3% or more per annum, and a record number of high-growth economies more than 5% per annum. Between 2001 and 2015, there were 14 such countries. This number is expected to rise to 19 by 2030. Foreign investors tend to gravitate towards the larger, more diverse economies in Africa, such as South Africa in the south, Morocco and Egypt in the north, Nigeria in the west and Kenya in the east. Collectively, these markets attracted 58% of the continent's total FDI projects in 2016.

The emerging market that we focus on in the discussion below is Russia (the word Russia in Russian is Россия). We chose Russia to describe a paradigm shift since Russia is most known for the Communist regime during the Cold War and the end of the Cold War with the Soviet Union that dissolved in 1991.

8.5.1.1 Russia as an Emerging Market

The change leader who we pay attention to in this section is President Mikhail Gorbachev who became a leader of the Soviet Union in 1985. The reforms that he brought had been unexpected, which can be perceived as paradigm shifts. He initiated, for example glasnost or openness, in terms of a greater willingness to Western ideas and products. See more information on his reforms at The Independence Hall Association (2018) at *US History* (http://www.ushistory.org/us/59e.asp), 2018, 59e, "The End of the Cold War" with a chart on the transition from the single USSR Communist nation to the confederation of smaller independent nations. See also images of the collapse of the Soviet Union by The Guardian (2014), which described President Mikhail Gorbachev, head of the Communist Party from 1985 to 1991, as a reforming politician who introduced policies of perestroika and glasnost (restructuring and openness) at the 27th party congress in 1986.

For Aaltio and Peltonen (2009) the historical trends in Russia remain relevant today due to the slow pace of change with regard to culture. Russia's issues create difficulties for Europe, not necessarily in a military sense, but more the impact of the severe economic slowdown and currency devaluation occurring in Russia. "Economic sanctions are hitting Russia hard, and it is possible that at some stage Vladimir Putin may try to retaliate if only to boost internal solidarity over his policies" (Rayner, 2015, p. 23).

We will discuss Russia's history through the lens of the emancipation of women, similar to the previous chapter's discussions on specific BRICS countries. The rise of the socialist movement occurred and led to a shift from an authoritarian ruler to the implementation of the Duma (parliament)—and the associated democratic practices. This was followed by the revolution of 1917, and institution of an authoritarian socialist state—the so-called dictatorship of the proletariat. Finally, a state capitalist model replaced the proletariat in 1991, with the disbanding of the Soviet Union.

Russia Until 1917

The family structures and role of women in maintaining them were of great importance in Russian society in the late 1800s and early 1900s. The classic work of Edmonson (1977) reveals that the paradigm of associating feminism with an industrialising society does not hold true in Russia, "Nowhere is the inadequacy of a theory which sees feminism as a product of an industrializing society more evident than in the case of Russia, where industrial power began to have a notable effect on the economy a full twenty years after the 'woman question' first became a burning topic" (p. 19).

She also highlights that, "...by 1880, the women's movement, ... could quite reasonably claim to be in the vanguard of feminism throughout Europe. Hundreds of women could now study a wide range of subjects to an advanced level, with opportunities for professional employment on graduation" (Edmonson, 1977, p. 37). With the overthrowing of the Tsar, the League of Equal rights engaged on a campaign to ensure that gender equity was upheld in the new dispensation, culminating in a 40,000 strong march after just 2 weeks of campaigning to ensure that women had the right to vote (Edmonson, 1977).

From 1917: Revolution

Under Soviet rule, very little was able to flourish in terms of an environment that favoured freedom and creativity. Gulags or forced labour camps were used in order to suppress dissent and provide a large supply of labour to implement various state-directed projects (Skiles, 2012). Rhein (1998) states that the Soviet system was one of duality, wherein the formal dictates of the law prescribed equality for all yet, in reality, it was "vastly unequal and openly discriminatory ... [and relegated] women to an economic and social second class" (1998, p. 352).

White (2005, p. 431) indicates that during the period of Soviet Rule, "...the constraints on sociological research made it hard to assess how Russians 'really' thought during the Soviet period. It is therefore hard to map how much has changed, and in what directions change has occurred".

The Soviet period thus appears to be marked by a lack of information—which may indicate that the feminist movement was dormant, or that it operated effectively underground. Only when President Gorbachev introduced Perestroika in 1985, were private businesses allowed to operate and entrepreneurship was thus a new occurrence (Aaltio & Peltonen, 2009).

After Soviet Era: From 1991

The prejudicial attitude towards women in the workplace is also evident in the state sector, which is, understandably, still a significant employer in the country. In the 1990s, women represented two-thirds of all unemployed persons in Russia (Rhein, 1998). The Russian historical events are remarkable cases on large-scale societal change, for example in managing the major transition away from the Soviet state to a managed democracy. It is interesting to note that often the state is still seen as central in the provision of rights and remains relevant due to the historical provision of labour to the state, and perceptions around what is deemed a fair exchange (Turbine, 2012).

Lidia and Feng (2014) discuss how culture and nationality affect the leadership style and the way in which companies operate. An example of this could be Hofstede's concept of "individualism versus collectivism" (Robbins & Judge, 2015, p. 173). Here society—in the instance of Russia being predominantly collectivist, but in transition—has an impact on the nature and style of leadership that is expected to occur. With the abolition of quotas mandating women's representation in the Soviet system, their proportion declined drastically.

It would appear that in the years shortly after the dissolution of the Soviet State, there was a reversion to more traditional gender roles and a shift away from forced equality. Country Watch (2010) reports that Russia ranks sixteenth out of 80 countries with regards to the Gender Empowerment Measure.

The relevance for this discussion to the Eureka enabler is illustrated in the prevailing paradigm about women, "The conservative patriarchal stereotype of attitudes toward women, which exists in the mass consciousness, makes it difficult to accept women's ability to be political leaders and make independent state decisions, persists and has even been revived" (Kanap'ianova, 2008, p. 68).

In concluding this discussion, it is important to note some of the present-day issues in Russia. There are high levels of corruption with an estimated cost to the economy of $300–$500 billion each year. Russia ranks 6.75 on a corruption scale of 7. Another trend, similar to other former Soviet Union countries, is the high levels of youth emigration. Between 2012 and 2013 more than 300,000 Russians left the country, and there are a high mortality and a low fertility rate, according to Smith (2016).

The Kremlin owns the news since 90% of all Russians get their news from Kremlin-approved news stations, according to Bremmer (2015). In Russia, the middle-class earns an income of more than $1000 per capita, a car and an apartment. However, international standards indicate a different picture, where the global average, for 2015, is an income of $7200 per capita, considered to be middle-class. Stierli, Shorrocks, Davies, Lluberas, and Koutsoukis (2015) indicate that by international standards, Russia has very rich and very poor people with a limited middle-class. Russia, the largest country in the world, is a geopolitical force at the forefront of the events that will play out across the world in the coming years, mainly as a major supplier of energy to Western Europe. Bacon (2012) states, "Russia's richness in natural resources has a key role to play in its future development" (Bacon, 2012, p. 1165).

Dr. Charlene Lew, who has been leading global elective educational trips to Russia with the GIBS MBA students over the last couple of years, observed that students' thinking or paradigm about Russia usually change once they visit the country. They realise that often the Russian culture resembles Eastern rather than Western characteristics such as collectivism and high power distance, referring to Hofstede's dimensions. Authoritarian leadership personifies the current era. Given their long-term orientation, another interesting observation is that many Russians believe that their historical development and change spirals through eras and does not in the mind of people, resemble the straight line which is a more Western perspective on time. New waves and spirals of ideologies repeat over time. Viewpoints and ways of being grow and at some point disband, to start a new wave or cycle of change that unites the country and starts reforms, which later on dissolves, which in turn would start a new cycle. For a general perspective of cyclical change, see the definitions of Form and Wilterdink (2018) in Encyclopaedia Britannica.

It is important to note these trends, especially when seeking business opportunities in Russia, as well as taking note of close relations between Russia, China and progressively with Southeast Asian countries such as Thailand and Laos, and the Philippines (ASEAN countries) and Vietnam.

Reading more about Russia and with any luck visiting the country, would hopefully lead to eureka moments. Featuring Russia in this section was appropriate since the country has experienced significant change through embarking on a programme of reform by the process of glasnost and perestroika, as discussed above.

In closing, regarding the MMI merger case study (Scheepers & Swart, 2015), their two leading thinkers, Nicolaas Kruger of Momentum and Wilhelm van Zyl of Metropolitan, independently had a eureka moment to compete with large life insurers like Sanlam and Old Mutual. They realised that they had to pool their resources and expertise. One evening in 2009, at dinner, they decided to merge their organisations into one.

8.6   Measuring Fourth Enabler, Eureka Moments

Reflection Questions Enabler 4: Eureka Moments

Reflection Questions Enabler 4: Eureka Moments, contains a short questionnaire to help you assess the extent to which you are practicing this enabler. You can also ask others to assess you using this instrument.

8.7   Conclusion and Outcome of the Fourth Enabler, Eureka Moments

In this chapter, the fourth Enabler, Eureka moments were highlighted. The outcome of this enabler is a changed paradigm or mind shift, which prepares the change leader for the next enabler, envisioning of a preferred future.

References

Aaltio, I., & Peltonen, H. (2009). Portraits of Russian women entrepreneurs: Identification and ways of leadership. *Journal of Enterprising Culture, 17*(4), 443–471. https://doi.org/10.1142/S0218495809000424

Akgün, A. E., Byrne, J. C., Lynn, G. S., & Keskin, H. (2007). Organizational unlearning as changes in beliefs and routines in organizations. *Journal of Organizational Change Management, 20*(6), 794–812. https://doi.org/10.1108/09534810710831028

Bacon, E. (2012). Writing Russia's future: Paradigms, drivers and scenarios. *Europe-Asia Studies, 64*(7), 1165–1189. https://www.tandfonline.com/doi/abs/10.1080/09668136.2012.698046

Baird, B., Smallwood, J., Mrazek, M. D., Kam, J. W. Y., Franklin, M. S., & Schooler, J. W. (2012). Inspired by distraction: Mind wandering facilitates creative incubation. *Psychological Science, 23*, 1117. https://doi.org/10.1177/0956797612446024

Barker, J. (1980). *Discovering the future: The business of paradigms.* Video of Joel Barker. Star Thrower. http://www.formavision.com/dlgs/dlgsenglish/ParadigmPrincinciples.pdf

Barsh, J., Mogelof, J., & Webb, C. (2010, October). How centered leaders achieve extraordinary results. *McKinsey Quarterly.* Retrieved from https://www.mckinsey.com/global-themes/leadership/how-centered-leaders-achieve-extraordinary-results

Bremmer, I. (2015, April 14). These 5 facts explain Russia's economic decline. *Time.* Retrieved from http://time.com/3998248/these-5-facts-explain-russias-economic-decline/

Casanova, L., & Miroux, A. (2017). *The emerging market multinationals report (EMR).* Emerging Markets Institute (EMI), S.C. Johnson Graduate School of Management, Cornell University. Retrieved from http://www.iberglobal.com/files/2017/Emerging_EMNs_Casanova_Miroux.pdf

Country Watch. (2010). Status of women: Social overview. *Russia Review*, 249–251. Retrieved from http://www.countrywatch.com/Content/pdfs/reviews/B43M5Z4L.01c.pdf

Decker, C., & Mellewigt, T. (2012). Business exit and strategic change: Sticking to the knitting or striking a new path? *British Journal of Management, 23*(2), 165–178. https://doi.org/10.1111/j.1467-8551.2010.00706.x

Edmonson, L. H. (1977). *Feminism in Russia 1900–1917.* London: University of London. https://discovery.ucl.ac.uk/id/eprint/1317593/

Ernst & Young. (2017, May). *EY's attractiveness program Africa.* http://www.ey.com/za/en/issues/business-environment/ey-attractiveness-program-africa-2017

Form, W., & Wilterdink, N. (2018). Social change, sociology. *Encyclopedia Britannica.* Retrieved from https://www.britannica.com/topic/social-change#ref748360

Gregory, R. (1970). *The intelligent eye.* New York: McGraw-Hill. https://openresearch-repository.anu.edu.au/bitstream/1885/108976/1/Paula%20Ozola.pdf

Hamel, G. (2000). *Leading the revolution.* Boston, MA: Harvard Business School Press. https://www.amazon.com/Leading-Revolution-Thrive-Turbulent-Innovation/dp/0452283248

Jacobs, C. (2009). *Management rewired: Why feedback doesn't work and other surprising lessons from the latest brain science.* New York, NY: Penguin Books. https://www.amazon.com/Management-Rewired-Feedback-Surprising-Lessons/dp/B002WTC8UW

Johnson, G. (1992). Managing strategic change—Strategy, culture and action. *Long Range Planning, 25*(1), 28–36. Retrieved from https://www.ncbi.nlm.nih.gov/pubmed/10118379

Jung-Beeman, M., Bowden, E. M., Haberman, J., Frymiare, J. L., Arambel-Liu, S., Greenblatt, R., et al. (2004). Neural activity when people solve verbal problems with insight. *PLoS Biology, 2*, 500–510. https://journals.plos.org/plosbiology/article?id=10.1371/journal.pbio.0020097

Jung-Beeman, M., Collier, A., & Kounios, J. (2013). How insight happens: Learning from the brain. *Neuro Leadership Journal, 1*, 20–25. https://neuroleadership.com/portfolio-items/how-insight-happens-learning-from-the-brain/

Kanap'ianova, R. M. (2008). Women in structures of authority. *Sociological Research, 47*(4), 61–73. https://doi.org/10.2753/SOR1061-0154470403

Kets de Vries, M. F. R. (2006). *The leadership mystique: Leading behavior in the human enterprise* (2nd ed.). Harlow: Prentice Hall/Financial Times. https://www.bookdepository.com/Leadership-Mystique-Manfred-F-R-Kets-de-Vries/9781405840194

Lewin, K. (1947). Frontiers in group dynamics: Concept, method, and reality in social science; social equilibria and social change. *Human Relations, 1*, 5–41. https://doi.org/10.1177/001872674700100103

Lidia, R., & Feng, L.G. (2014). *Cultural profile of Russian leadership: A female leader in Russian business*. School of Management Science, Harbin Institute of Technology. V69(15). https://doi.org/10.7763/IPEDR.

Rayner, L. (2015, March 19). Examining prospects in global emerging markets. *Professional Adviser,* 22–23. https://www.professionaladviser.com/feature/2399223/sector-report-examining-prospects-global-emerging-markets

Rhein, W. (1998, Fall). The feminisation of poverty: Unemployment in Russia. *Journal of International Affairs, 52*(1), 351. Retrieved from http://www.jstor.org/stable/i24356848

Robbins, S. P., & Judge, T. A. (2015). *Organizational behaviour* (16th ed.). Boston, MA: Pearson. https://www.amazon.com/Organizational-Behavior-16th-Stephen-Robbins/dp/0133507645

Rock, D. (2009). *Your brain at work: Strategies for overcoming distraction, regaining focus, and working smarter all day*. New York: HarperCollins. https://www.harpercollins.com/9780061771293/your-brain-at-work/

Rock, D., & Davis, J. (2016, October 12). 4 Steps to having more "Aha" moments. *Harvard Business Review*. Retrieved April 22, 2018, from https://hbr.org/2016/10/4-steps-to-having-more-aha-moments

Rock, D., & Schwartz, J. (2006). The neuroscience of leadership. *Strategy Business, 43*, 72–82. https://www.strategy-business.com/article/06207?gko=f1af3

Rubin, E. (1915). *Synsoplevede Figurer*. København og Kristiania, Gyldendal: Nordisk forlag. Retrieved from https://www.worldcat.org/title/synsoplevede-figurer-studier-i-psykologisk-analyse/oclc/20647963

Scheepers, C. B., & Swart, S. (2015). *Momentum and metropolitan merger: Authentic transformational leadership*. Ivey Publishing, 9B15C004. https://www.iveycases.com/ProductView.aspx?id=70560

Schein, E. H. (1996). *Organizational culture and leadership*. San Francisco, CA: Jossey-Bass Publishers. https://www.amazon.com/Organizational-Culture-Leadership-Edgar-Schein/dp/0470190604

Skiles, C. M. (2012). Gender-specific prison reform: Addressing human rights violations against women in Russia's prisons. *Pacific Rim Law and Policy Journal, 21*(3), 655–689. Retrieved from https://digital.law.washington.edu/dspace-law/bitstream/handle/1773.1/1167/21PRPLJ655.pdf?sequence=1

Smith, S. (2016, January 6). Russia's biggest challenges for 2016 are domestic. *Real Clear World*. Retrieved from http://www.realclearworld.com/articles/2016/01/06/russias_biggest_challenges_for_2016_are_domestic_111645.html

Stierli, M., Shorrocks, A., Davies, J. B., Lluberas, R., & Koutsoukis, A. (2015). *World wealth report 2015* (Vol. 46). Credit Suisse Research Institute. Retrieved from http://pbwm.ru/library/global-wealth-report-2015/download

Subramaniam, K., Kounios, J., Parrish, T. B., & Jung-Beeman, M. (2009). A brain mechanism for facilitation of insight by positive affect. *Journal of Cognitive Neuroscience, 21*(3), 415–432. https://pubmed.ncbi.nlm.nih.gov/18578603/

Tan, V., & Tiong, T. N. (2005). Change management in times of economic uncertainty. *Singapore Management Review, 27*, 49–68. Retrieved from http://www.scirp.org/(S(351jmbntvnsjt1aadkposzje))/reference/ReferencesPapers.aspx?ReferenceID=768138

The Guardian. (2014, July 14). Collapse of the USSR in pictures. *Bridget Coaker*. Retrieved from https://www.theguardian.com/world/gallery/2014/jul/14/soviet-union-collapse-in-pictures

The Independence Hall Association. (2018). The end of the cold war (59e). *US History*. Retrieved March 12, 2018, from http://www.ushistory.org/us/59e.asp

Turbine, V. (2012). Locating women's human rights in post-soviet provincial Russia. *Europe-Asia Studies, 64*(10), 1844–1869. Retrieved from https://www.tandfonline.com/doi/abs/10.1080/09668136.2012.681245

Van Hecke, M. L., Callahan, L. P., Kolar, B., & Paller, K. A. (2010). *The brain advantage: Become a more effective business leader using the latest brain research*. Amherst, NY: Prometheus Books. https://www.amazon.com/Brain-Advantage-Effective-Business-Research/dp/1591027640

White, A. (2005). Gender roles in contemporary Russia: Attitudes and expectations among women students. *Europe-Asia Studies, 57*(3), 429–455. https://doi.org/10.1080/09668130500073449

Reference List for Quotes

Retrieved July 26, 2019, from http://www.wothquotes.com/2017/12/vision-quotes.html
Retrieved July 26, 2019, from https://www.brainyquote.com/quotes/carl_honore_633757
Retrieved July 26, 2019, from https://www.brainyquote.com/quotes/henri_matisse_380058

Fifth Enabler

Envision

Vision is the culmination of thought

(Utkarsh Sharma, n.d.)

Learning Outcomes
At the end of this chapter, change leaders will be able to:

- Identify dissatisfaction with status quo/reason for the change
- Develop a compelling and measurable picture of the future
- Identify the root cause of the need for the change
- Determine the costs and risks of the change
- Verbalise the doom scenario/burning platform

Electronic supplementary material The online version of this chapter (https://doi.org/10.1007/978-3-030-40846-6_9) contains supplementary material, which is available to authorized users.

9.1   Orientation to Envisioning

While the previous enabler focused on the eureka moments and offered the impetus for action, this Fifth Enabler pays attention to the cognitive exercise of envisioning the future. Once the change leader has seen the opportunity, he needs to move closer to concretising the idea. It is not necessarily an individual going through the process of imagining a detailed picture of what the future would look like yet, in most instances, it starts with an individual leader. Often, this leader would then enrol others and group brainstorming might follow, where the one idea feeds into another and the reciprocal stimulation creates an even more vivid picture of the ideal future. Again, this is an opportunity to create hype and energy that are required to get the change off the ground.

We were first introduced to the concept of visioning through the 1989 *Power of Vision* video of Joel Barker, one of the best-known futurists in the world. We believe it to be a classic. Barker popularised the concept of envisioning the future and illustrated the value and importance of the concept. He also suggested ways of holding corporate discussions about the organisation's future and emphasised the following four principles of envisioning:

- The vision should be led by leaders
- The vision should be positive and inspiring
- The vision should be shared and understood by all
- The vision should be comprehensive and detailed

Visioning is defined as "[a] mental process in which images of the desired future (goals, objectives, outcomes) are made intensely real and compelling to act as motivators for the present action" (Jack, Boyatzis, Khawaja, Passarelli, & Leckie, 2013).

The emerging market featured in this chapter is Brazil, the final BRICS country that we will discuss, since "The Dilma Effect" of their first female president offered hope and even vision to the women in their country who created entrepreneurship opportunities for them.

9.2   Importance of Envisioning

In times of change, employees want to know where the organisation is going and what the business case or reason for the change is. To this end, leadership entails being able to paint a picture of what will make all the effort worth it. The more descriptive the picture, the easier it is for people to see the future and get excited about it.

Reeves, Love, and Tillmanns (2012) declare that an organisation's strategy is dependent on predictability around how far into the future and how accurately we can confidently forecast demand, corporate performance, competitive dynamics and market expectations, as well as malleability of these factors. Obviously, we will not have all this information at hand in this envisioning process. However, leadership needs to make it their business to find out about the future and gathering information about what the trends are that could influence the organisation. This Fifth Enabler is thus closely related to the Third Enabler on environmental awareness.

During the interviews, an interviewee reported that she believed,

As ordinary people, we can accomplish extraordinary things together. In 2007, when I became Acting MD; we were no-where near being a top ICT player, and I shared my dream with the executive team and later on the whole organisation. We pulled together and envisioned how we would be number 1 in the market.

It is thus not just about having a dream but sharing it. Another CEO, in his turn, noted,

... whatever we do, that we build the nation through investing in initiatives that will offer a return on investment that is higher than the input cost. We are developing a metrics around it. The more I talked about it as the MD, with our people as well as our customers, the more we were getting like-minded people together to collaborate on how to implement the vision.

This Fifth Enabler is essential, because without being able to describe what the end state would look like, it will merely stay a dream. Without a target date, procrastination would withhold progress towards the achievement of the vision. Without measures, we would never know whether we achieved our dream. In cases where the vision could be made vivid, it will create tension between the "Now" and the "Future picture". This is the tension that will be the impetus for action towards change.

Rosenberg (2003) investigated the characteristics of organisations that were able to successfully effect change and identified eight characteristics, at the heart of which is vision. Again, as we discussed in the introduction, the leadership team has to take accountability for envisioning, and not only an individual change leader. Franken, Edwards, and Lambert (2009) emphasise harmonising of the leadership team to support the change portfolio. Therefore, the whole team should be involved and singing from the same hymn sheet.

For example, change leaders identified an opportunity for outsourcing, as a result of their environmental awareness. They then gained the insight or experienced a eureka moment about the solution. The vision around outsourcing was thus about painting a rich picture about what it would look like. The benefits of being able to focus on core business activities, while the non-core elements are outsourced, would be part and parcel of this envisioning process. As Craumer (2002) points out, outsourcing of non-core activities could provide higher profit margins. An outsourcing decision should thus be perceived as a long-term decision that will bring value rather than an opportunistic change, where the provider is seen as an outsourced partner (Scott, 2008). Outsourcing could also be used to fill important expertise that cannot be found internally in the organisation. Kraatz and Zajac (2001) in this regard emphasise that this strategy is usually aimed at creating efficiency.

The accounts on the benefits of outsourcing from the scholars mentioned above, sound rather bland and plain vanilla; whereas, what is required to get energy around the change would be to envision the benefits in a vivid manner. Envisioning could, therefore, entail that we imagine, "A day in the life of. . . .", for instance, one day when we have successfully outsourced, how would that day look like for us, when we no longer must contend with the difficulties of our non-core processes? In this sense, the relief of having fewer issues to deal with is then the motivation to keep going with the process of getting the outsourcing contracts in place.

Using the five senses is an excellent way of creating a vivid picture, for example on that day in the future that is imagined, what are you feeling, seeing and hearing? Invernizzi, Romenti, and Fumagalli (2012) found that visioning encompasses the definition and circulation of corporate vision, mission, strategies and organisation values within the organisational context. It channels the collective energies of employees with a common goal for the business (Invernizzi et al., 2012).

This Fifth Enabler, Envision the future, goes further than the formal printed version of the vision, or perhaps hanging on the walls of the organisation, instead, it refers more to the process of coming up with the vision and a non-tangible picture or image of the future.

Merrell (2012) suggests a balanced set of measures to define success and secure continuous improvement of change activities. It is important for the organisation to set clear goals upfront and manage the change against these performance metrics. It would be too late to start measuring activities halfway through the change process and thus it is important from the outset. The measurements must be fully integrated into the change plan.

Interestingly, while we are emphasising in this Fifth enabler, the vision around the change, we would simultaneously also want to discuss how certain conditions might stay the same. Change leadership would thus balance the attention on change, with a focus on maintaining the psychological safety of the employees, through for example, emphasising the organisation's identity and mission that would remain constant. By (2005) declares that there has been a lack of empirical evidence to support or refute change models over the last 60 years. We hope that our data gathered through the interviews would contribute to the validation of some of these change models.

In some cases, the vision is born out of necessity, for example, the big five professional accounting firms traditionally mainly provided a standard set of service offerings in the accounting and consulting sphere (Brock & Powell, 2005). Seeing that some of them expanded to include legal services, the others had to follow. This trend towards multidisciplinary practice created the need to have a vision around including these legal services (Brock & Powell, 2005).

If people like the way things are, there will be no perceived need for change. If a group has tolerated a poor situation for a long time, they often accept it, and there is no active dissatisfaction. In most cases, real pain is necessary to cause change. Dissatisfaction is an initial source of energy.

9.3   Envisioning in Practice

9.3.1   The Envisioning Process

The Envisioning Process was developed to give structure to how the envisioning process unfolds. Figure 9.1 explains the process and the tools that follow help the change leader complete the process. The graphic resembles the picture we used in Chap. 4 to describe the Ten Enablers Model, but it focuses only on the essence of the model: the future, the now, the past and the doom scenario (What will happen if we do not change?).

The envisioning starts with identifying the reasons for the change (the dissatisfaction with the status quo). It continues by creating a vivid picture of the future and defining the end goal through quantifying the Big Hairy Audacious Goal (BHAG) and balanced SMART vision. It further considers the past by identifying the causes and effects of the problem, the costs and the risks of changing and not changing, and ends with creating a clear picture of what would happen if the problem is not addressed (the Doom Scenario). All this information will be used in the engagement, embarking and execution processes.

The best way to develop a vision is to get stakeholders to list their problems, their pain and their unmet objectives, then to jointly develop the vision for them to address their needs. They will not buy into your vision. They will buy into a vision that will benefit them.

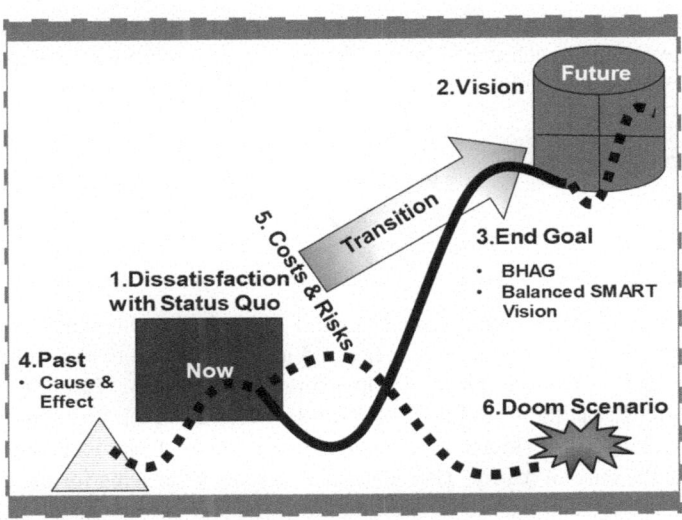

Fig. 9.1 The envisioning process (Authors' own)

9.3.1.1 Dissatisfaction with Current Reality/Status Quo (SQ)

Bringing about change requires considerable effort. If there is not enough dissatisfaction with the status quo, there might not be enough energy to sustain the process of achieving the vision—no matter how attractive the vision might be. We therefore need to make sure there is significant dissatisfaction with the status quo. Tool 5.1 starts the process of building the case for the change. Change leaders can use this tool to consider the pain and dissatisfaction with the status quo.

Tool 5.1 Dissatisfaction with Current Reality/Status Quo (SQ)

In this exercise consider questions like: Describe the hassles you have at the moment (the "pain"); Why do we need to change?

9.3.1.2 Creating a Vision

Vision Board

The next step to achieve buy-in to the vision is to get the stakeholders to start the envisioning process by illustrating the direction the change wants to move towards. The idea is to pull out the "From-To" tool (Tool 4.4, Enabler 4, Eureka Moments) which started the identification of the current reality and the vision of the future and to obtain more detailed information about the vision by developing a vision board. The vision board exercise uses pictures as powerful symbols and metaphors of what we want the change to achieve—the end destination. It is a fun way of capturing the essence of what needs to be achieved. Tool 5.2 explains this exercise.

Tool 5.2 Vision Board

Obtain a big piece of white paper (4 m × 1 m) and stick the paper on a wall long enough to enable a team of between 5 and 9 members to sketch pictures on the paper. Divide the piece of paper into three sections: Now, Transition and Future. Break the team into 2 or 3 sub-teams and ask the first sub-team to draw symbols or stickmen or even cut out pictures from magazines that resemble the current reality. The other sub-team does the same for the desired future. The third sub-team observes and then brainstorms ways to get from the now to the future.

Video Clip: Draw Your Future by Patti Dobrowolski

https://singjupost.com/draw-your-future-take-control-of-your-life-by-patti-dobrowolski-transcript/

Vision Worksheet

We find the definitive work of Collis and Porras (1997) in their book *Built to Last* to be an excellent tool to propel change forward. We use their principles and the framework (or derivatives of it) in most of the change processes we have consulted on, and it never fails to bring clarity to the end goal. It also remains a robust method to get conversations between stakeholders going and ensure the vision is shared amongst stakeholders.

The next tool, Tool 5.3 offers an opportunity to formulate big hairy audacious goals that could motivate the team.

Tool 5.3 Vision Worksheet: Big Hairy Audacious Goal (BHAG)

Consider the following questions: What would we like to have achieved by... (completion date); If you could wave a magic wand... how would you want things to be?

Dream Worksheet

The next template (Tool 5.4) is called "Our Dream Worksheet". In this tool, the team is given the opportunity to formulate their dream, as well as answer questions on how measurable it is, etc.

Tool 5.4 Our Dream Worksheet

Our Dream for our team is...
Is this measurable? Is it a real challenge? Is it positive and inspiring?

Practical Application of Visioning Worksheet and Purpose

During 2017, we consulted an African University that decided to change from an agricultural college to a world-class university. They developed the following purpose and high-level dream vision statement.

Our Dream for our Team

Our Vision:

By 31 Dec 2023, we the senior management team, would have led OUR UNIVERSITY towards being:
- The No. 2 university in OUR COUNTRY
- Listed under the 50 top agricultural and natural resources universities in the world

Our Purpose

We exist to.....
- Advise the Board
- Give direction, support and guidance to our staff
- Deliver outputs to our fellow team members
- Live our team values
- Produce industry ready students
- Support our communities

We feed the nation

They also created a vision board (picture below). The "poster" portrays the idea that they had a dream to:

- Be a proudly African University
- Working together to build a world-class university
- By imparting wisdom to their students
- Producing students who are able to feed the nation

(continued)

(Photos courtesy of Ray Topp)

Balanced SMART Vision

Based on the work of Kaplan and Norton's Balanced Scorecard Framework (1996), we have found that it really helps to encourage teams to formulate their vision in a "balanced" and measurable way. We developed the 2×2 framework found in Tool 5.5 and then ask teams to describe their vision in terms of the financial end state, an end state as defined by clients and markets, a process end state and a people and innovation end state. We found that most teams find this a very useful and easy to use framework and most teams latch onto this approach without any difficulty. We also insist that teams check each of the four blocks to ensure the end state descriptions in each block are specific, measurable, attainable, realistic and has a target date for implementation (SMART). Although we use this tool relatively early on in the change process, it will need to be expanded upon in a lot more detail later in the change process during Enabler 7, Embark and Enabler 8, when we start setting and delivering goals.

The next worksheet, Tool 5.5, offers leaders an opportunity to complete a template to balance their SMART vision, for example the instructions include: Use all four quadrants below to find SMART goals that will ensure you achieve your vision. SMART = Specific, Measurable, Attainable, Realistic and Time bound.

Tool 5.5 Balanced SMART Vision

Use the 4 quadrants to set SMART goals that will ensure you achieve your vision. SMART = **S**pecific, **M**easurable, **A**ttainable, **R**ealistic and **T**ime bound.

9.3.1.3 The Past

Cause and Effect Analysis

A useful technique for defining the origin of the change problem is the cause and effect analysis. Problems/concerns/dissatisfiers are usually identified as unacceptable effects. With complex problems, many effects have multiple causes. In addition, a single cause can sometimes give rise to more than one effect. The cause/effect analysis is therefore, not a single string but rather a network of causes and effects. Tool 5.6 offers leaders the opportunity to map out the causes and effects.

Tool 5.6 Cause and Effect Diagram

In Tool 5.6, we start with stating the problem (or the dissatisfaction with the status quo) in the middle of the page. We next work up the page asking the question "Why, Why, Why?" Record the causes in the blocks as the answers are given. By asking the question: "Why did this problem occur?" or "What is the cause of this problem?", a number of causes may be extracted. By asking the same question of the extracted causes, a network of causes is compiled. Now do the same for the "effects" part of the diagram by asking, "What is the result/effect of this?". Connect the interactions. Once completed, consider the total problem and decide if the perceived problem is the real problem. Then proceed to define what things would look/be/feel like if there was no problem (preferred future). This will allow you the opportunity to go back to Tools 5.1 to 5.4 and add to your initial thinking.

9.3.1.4 Costs and Risks

Cost of Change

Before we can continue with the change process, it is critical to consider the "pain" involved in the change. This may include considering the costs: financially, emotionally, physically and in terms of time. When we have had the eureka moment, and we can "see" the vision we want to achieve, we can sometimes run ahead with the idea, without considering the cost. This can result in running out of steam and giving up on the change before the vision is achieved. The following tools will help the change leader to consider the cost before starting with Enabler 6, Engagement. Tool 5.7 offers the opportunity for leaders to consider the cost for change.

Tool 5.7 Cost of Change

Consider the cost of change by completing the following:
What will we have to give up/sacrifice?
What will it cost to bring about this change? (This could be financial, physical, emotional, time, etc.)

Risk Analysis

In the Risk Analysis tool, Tool 5.8, we further explore the risks of not changing and weigh up these risks against the risks of changing.

Tool 5.8 Risk Analysis

In this tool, we consider the following questions: What are the risks of *not* changing? What are the risks of changing?

9.3.1.5 Doom Scenario

In the Doom Scenario tool, Tool 5.9, we demonstrate what will happen if we continue on the current trajectory. This starts the process of building a case for the change, which will be explored further in Enabler 6, Engage.

Tool 5.9 Doom Scenario

Here you need to answer the following questions: What would happen if we do not change/What is the worst that can happen? What will the cost be if we do not change?
How can we create "pain" to ensure the change takes place (Burning platform)?

Stabilisers

When people are bombarded with change, it is sometimes also a good idea to clarify to stakeholders the things that will not change. This tool, Tool 5.10, can be used throughout the change project to communicate the stabilisers (those things that will remain stable amidst continuous, unsettling change). Here we need to take care not to make promises we might not be able to keep. Think deeply before committing to not changing something that might need to change later on in the change project.

Tool 5.10 Stabilisers

Consider what will change and make a list, then next to it, consider what will not change and list those things.

9.3.2   Implementation Tips for Envisioning

We would like to share the following tips in applying Envisioning:

- Envision all potential phases of the change project, up to the moment the project is dissolved.
- Envision who will form the coalition to lead the change.
- Envision where money would come from to finance your vision.

Useful tests exist to assess whether the chosen vision and roadmap would provide the desired outcomes: For example, *the market advantage test* implies an evaluation whether the intended intervention would support the organisation's main sources of competitive advantage and does it direct attention to its market segment? Another one is the *people test* that implies that the interventions should assist people in clarifying their roles and responsibilities and prevent duplication of effort, which could demotivate people in the organisations. Finally, the *feasibility test* implies that interventions have to take into account constraints like culture in the organisation and whether information systems are supported. These three are examples of tests that we adapted from Goold and Campbell (2002).

Practical Application of Not Needing to Change

It is important to note that it is not always necessary to lead with large-scale disruptive change. For example, at SASOL, during the financial year 2012, the new Chief Executive Officer (CEO), David Constable, appointed from outside of the organisation stated in the Integrated Annual Report (2012),

> When I started at Sasol, many people expected me to introduce wide-reaching changes at the outset. However, based on my initial assessment that the organisation was, for the most part, heading in the right direction, a more measured approach was appropriate (p. 15).

9.4 Neuroscience Insights into Envisioning

Although there are still debates raging about whether animals have the ability to envision the future (Balter, 2013), it seems that most researchers today agree that humans are uniquely designed to imagine a future that does not exist today and can coordinate activities to realise dreams of the future (Popova, n.d.). As far as we know, humans plan further into the future than any other beings, and we are the most adept at simulations, imaginations and planning our futures. We have our brain to thank for these incredible abilities (Eagleman, 2015).

The brain accesses memories and uses information from the present and the past to create scenarios about the future and predict possible outcomes of the future. Memories are not just about the past but are also used to simulate the future (Schacter et al., 2012).

This remarkable evolutionarily human characteristic is called *mental time travel (MTT)* by psychologists and cognitive scientists (Balter, 2013). *MTT* is a potent bidirectional projection that combines episodic memory, which allows us to draw on our autobiographical experience and recall events, experiences and emotions that occurred in the past, with the ability to imagine and anticipate future events (Falk, 2008; Popova, n.d.). The ability to perform mental time travel enabled early humans to have the edge in the struggle for survival. MTT gives us the ability to act wisely in the present to improve our chances for success in future. The lessons learned in the past enables us to avoid future disastrous scenarios. Modern neuroscience can now confirm that from the brain's perspective the act of imagining the future seems to be very similar to the act of remembering (Falk, 2008).

9.4.1 Visualisation

Visualisation is the process of focusing your brain on an image or an event that might occur in future and can be a useful tool for change. Using images to rewire old patterns can change behaviour significantly (Graham, 2008). By closing your eyes and imagining a future object, scene or occurrence you are participating in the practice of visualisation. Brain research has discovered the neurology behind its effects. The occipital lobe located at the back of the head is responsible for vision and occupies approximately 20% of the brain's overall capacity. It also has the capacity to imagine future scenes or those never seen before.

We remember things better when they are attached to a picture—65% better to be exact (Dobrowolski, 2015).

Electromyography has been used to prove that the brain does not understand the difference between the thought of an action and a real action. When we imagine something, be it an object, scene or an occurrence, the same physiological chemicals are released, and neural pathways are stimulated similarly to when the actual object or scene is observed or experienced. If one wants to develop new neurological pathways, you can visualise the event as if you are performing the action. Research has proven that many of the same parts of the brain are activated whether we are imagining or actually participating in an event (Pillay, 2011). Visualisation affects the brain plasticity nearly as much as actual activity. Professional athletes and Olympic champions have long been using the practice of visualising their desired actions or states during their preparation for major events (Loehr & Schwartz, 2001).

Pillay (2011) uses the example of patients who have suffered from a stroke to explain the power of visualisation. During a stroke, a blood clot enters a brain artery and prevents blood from reaching the tissue. Due to lack of oxygen and nutrients, the tissue then dies. The surrounding area is also affected as it no longer receives blood leading to loss of functionality of a particular limb. However, if a person who had a stroke visualises using the affected arm or leg, blood will flow to the affected area and increase blood flow enough to diminish the amount of tissue death. This clearly shows the value of visualisation. Because the brain does not differentiate between real and imagined events, serotonin is released when we reflect on past achievements. This provides an opportunity for us to use visualisation of past successes as a morale booster.

9.4.2 Warning!

It should be noted that even though imagining the future can be beneficial, too much dreaming and not enough action can have disastrous effects and prevent you from achieving your goals (Ciotti, 2012). The challenge in the brain is that too much dreaming can make us believe that we have already achieved our goal. It takes the attention away from working on the current problems and leaves us with less motivation. In a way, it is a paradox, but here too the sweet spot needs to be found to ensure we have just the right amount of visualisation and the right amount of hard work and attention devoted to action in the current reality (Dean, 2011). Visualisation without action will remain a dream. You need to Envision (Enabler 5), but also Execute (Enabler 8).

9.4.3 Resisting Change and the Cost of the Change

Visualisation is all good and well. However, the brain is programmed to want to stay in its comfort zone—living in the status quo. When we are uncertain about what to do, we would rather revert to what we know than to uncertainty. With numerous options available, the energy needed to make a decision is just too intense and the brain might well decide to opt for inertia (Fleming, Thomas, & Dolan, 2010). Even in life-threatening situations, habits could persist despite rational knowledge clearly spelling out the consequences of persisting with the habit. Only 9% of heart disease patients altered their behaviour after undergoing bypass surgery (Deutschman, 2007). This is because changing habits are very difficult (see Enabler 8 Entrench for a detailed discussion on changing habits).

We agree with Goldberg's (2009) remarks in his book, *The New Executive Brain*, that "the status quo has to be really terrible for us to embark on a change" (p.122). Goldberg continues to explain that the seat of novelty and dissatisfaction are logically linked together in the brain in a shared neural territory in the right hemisphere and that dissatisfaction drives novelty seeking.

Another reason we prefer the status quo is because the brain dislikes surprises. When we are confronted with change—be it as an individual, a team or as an organisation, the brain perceives the change as potentially dangerous. Anything unfamiliar will be perceived as a threat, and the brain's error detection system will kick in. When a threat is detected, the amygdala draws energy away from the PFC, activating energy to deal with the threat. Once the threat has been eliminated, we want to return to our comfort zone again.

Threats can be treated by fighting or attacking the threat, but another way of dealing with a threat is by avoiding the issue altogether. When we are uncertain, negativity kicks in, and one way of coping might be to disengage entirely. This explains why in organisations, we get those who resist change (fighting), and those who just avoid the change completely (withdrawing).

Now that we know that the brain dislikes surprises and seeks certainty, we need to explain the reason for the change in great detail. That will address the need for the PFC to understand the rational reasons behind the change. The limbic system's fears and emotions still need to be addressed. This needs to be done by understanding the fears and emotions of stakeholders by engaging at an emotional level too. Understanding the potential debilitating habits that are entrenched in the organisation also need to be unpacked.

Stakeholders will support the change if their brains perceive the change to be beneficial to their survival. The change, therefore, needs to be positioned as something specific that the individual will benefit from. This has been called a WIIFM—what is in it for me. Even if the change benefits the organisation, individuals will always translate it back to what it means for their survival and how it will be of benefit to themselves.

9.5   Envisioning in Emerging Markets

9.5.1   Case Examples of Envisioning in the Emerging Markets Context

One of the threats in the emerging markets is the competition of developed countries' multinational companies on their own turf, or in other instances, when emerging market companies internationalise, they compete head-on with these organisations. Seeing that one of the emerging markets is Thailand, we would like to mention the study of Pinprayong and Wongsurawat (2012) on the Siam Commercial Bank (SCB) in July 2001. They identified in this case that foreign investment in the Thai banking sector created serious challenges. Economic fluctuation too gave rise to a need to evolve or change the way they were doing business in order to survive the crisis. The Asian financial crisis, which had already occurred in 1997, was, of course, a major disruption. SCB reported that they had learned a number of lessons from the Asian financial crisis. The main lesson was that SCB had to diversify its customer base, through a portfolio diversification strategy. They subsequently created a vision to reach out to multiple market segments. We now turn to the discussion on Brazil.

9.5.1.1 Brazil as an Emerging Market

For the purposes of this chapter, the discussion below highlights historical events and women emancipation, featuring the first female president Dilma Rousseff as an important change leader, since her impact was referred to as "The Dilma Effect". Brazil is the largest country in South America, the fifth largest in the world and the largest Catholic country in the world. *Pau Brasil* (brazilwood) was the reddish wood that the Portuguese colonisers exploited and gave Brazil its name. See the history of Brazil and Brazilian culture at *Countries and their Cultures*, "Brazilian" on the *everyculture* and at *BBC News* a timeline of the Brazilian history at "Brazil Profile—Timeline".

Colonial Era to Independence in 1822

During the colonial period, starting in the fifteenth century, people born in Brazil were subject to rules and taxes from distant Portugal. A small white elite of Portuguese were the owners of sugar plantations, whereas the Indian and African slaves laboured on the plantations, since slavery was only abolished in 1888. The colonialists of Spain and Portugal brought with them strong patriarchal traditions that all had a significant influence on the way women in Brazil were treated through history and even how they perceive themselves and are perceived by others (Metcalf, 1990).

The Portuguese colonisers brought with them the concept of *machismo*, which identifies men with authority and strength and women with weakness and subservience. This worldview, combined with the patriarchy of the Catholic Church, laid the foundation for male dominance.

Racial inter-breeding makes Brazil one of the most racially diverse nations on earth (see information on this at the every culture website).

The feminist movement in Brazil was started in the mid-nineteenth century. Women were not given the vote until 1932 and, until the 1960s, women were the equivalent of children under Brazilian law. Bertha Lutz was a biologist and a lawyer who created the Brazilian Federation for Women's Progress in 1922 (Lôbo, 2010). In 1933, she was part of the delegation who drafted the first page of the new Constitution, promoting equal rights for men and women.

Military Dictatorship from 1964

The Military rule was associated with repression, but also with rapid economic growth based on state-ownership of key sectors (BBC News, 2017). Brazil experienced repressive regimes and massive impoverishment. Divorce was only made legal in 1977, due to the strong opposition of the Catholic Church (BBC News, 2017).

Democracy from 1989

Brazil's constitution of 1988 prohibited all forms of discrimination (Van Klaveren, Tijdens, Hughie-Williams, & Martin, 2009). In 1989, Fernando Collor de Mello introduced radical economic reform. However, the promised economic improvements failed to materialise, and inflation remained out of control. According to the World Economic Forum's Global Gender Gap Report (2013), Brazil ranks 62nd out of 136 countries measured, but women still lag behind in salaries and political influence and are paid 30% less than men.

In 2010, Dilma Rousseff was elected the first female president of Brazil and she had no family ties to power (Jalalzai & Dos Santos, 2013). Her emphasis on entrepreneurship has inspired a new generation of start-ups. Rousseff was ranked fourth in Forbes 2014 list of the most powerful women in the world and seventh in the 2015 report (Forbes, 2014). Unfortunately, on 15 March 2015, nearly one million

Brazilians protested against rising prices and corruption and instigated a call for the impeachment of President Dilma Rousseff. In December 2015, Congress agreed to launch impeachment proceedings against President Rousseff (BBC News, 2017).

9.5.2   Case Examples of Envisioning in Emerging Markets Organisations

To illustrate the envisioning process, we could refer to the SAA case study (Margolis et al., 2007) that we had mentioned. To successfully drive the necessary strategic changes for SAA's turnaround, Ngqula had to be geared for it. He had a clear strategic vision for SAA articulated around ambition to become a "world–class airline". He created a sense of urgency by setting tight deadlines for senior management to deliver on a plan. A well-defined plan was also put in place to give effect to governance, control and efficiency objectives. Ngqula attempted to create enthusiasm for the strategy by publicising SAA's objectives internally and in the media.

In 2004, SAA formally launched a "turnaround strategy" consisting of three key points as their strategy to transform the airline: Control costs by reducing waste and improve efficiency and get more from talented employees; stimulate growth by expanding routes, attracting international customers and improve network with star alliance; and deliver exemplary service.

In terms of this case example, at SAA Ngqula rushed in and got his initial visioning exercise done in less than 10 days. He struggled to get buy-in though. This illustrates that it is important to take the organisation's history into account. For instance, between 1993 and 2005 SAA changed CEO's four times, each new CEO brought his own vision and did not build on what others before him accomplished.

In closing of this section, we refer to the MMI Case Study (Scheepers & Swart, 2015). Envisioning the future at MMI revolved around being a leader in meeting financial services' needs. The vision included that they would meet clients' needs by providing a range of appropriate, value-for-money financial solutions in our market segments. To do this, they would use their insight into the needs of their clients, through their strong client-facing brands, product innovation and service excellence.

MMI's vision included that they would operate in South Africa, other African countries and selected international markets. Their game-changing strategy would establish MMI as a leader and enable them to deliver superior shareholder returns on a sustainable basis.

The merger assisted MMI to form the third largest insurer in South Africa. They would be one of the big players, and they realised that they could create a giant. The two companies would help each other, through the economies of scale and their purchasing power as a large player. The merger process went fast, given that on 01 April 2010 they announced the merger and on 1 December of the same year, they listed on the Johannesburg stock exchange.

9.6   Measuring Fifth Enabler, Envision

Reflection Questions Enabler 5: Envision

Reflection Questions Enabler 5: Envision, contains a short questionnaire to help you assess the extent to which you are practicing this enabler. You can also ask others to assess you using this instrument.

9.7   Conclusion and Outcome of the Fifth Enabler, Envision

The outcome of this Fifth Enabler is an articulated coherent picture of the future, which is inspiring. It leads to the understanding and buy-in of followers into the vision. This vision and mission must be translated into the organisation's strategy. Change leaders must formulate, implement and communicate the vision and mission to the employees, shareholders and other stakeholders. The next enabler pays attention to engagement with these stakeholders.

References

Balter, M. (2013). Can animals envision the future? Scientists spar over new data. *Science, 340* (6135), 909. https://doi.org/10.1126/science.340.6135.909

Barker, J. (1989). *The power of vision*. A 21st century look. Video of Joel Barker. Star Thrower. https://starthrower.com/products/power-of-vision-joel-barker

BBC News. (2017, July 4). *Brazil profile timeline*. Retrieved March 12, 2018, from http://www.bbc.com/news/world-latin-america-19359111

Brock, D. M., & Powell, M. J. (2005). Radical strategic change in the global professional network: The "big five" 1999–2001. *Journal of Organizational Change Management, 18*(5), 451–468. https://doi.org/10.1108/09534810510614940

By, R. T. (2005). Organisational change management: A critical review. *Journal of Change Management, 5*(4), 369–380. https://doi.org/10.1080/14697010500359250

Ciotti, G. (2012, July 11). How our brains stop us achieving our goals and how to fight back. *Buffer*. Retrieved July 26, 2019, from https://blog.bufferapp.com/how-our-brains-stop-us-achieving-our-goals-and-how-to-fight-back

Collins, J. C., & Porras, J. I. (1997). *Built to last: Successful habits of successful companies*. London: Random House. https://www.amazon.com/Built-to-Last-Jim-Collins-audiobook/dp/B0813QCVN9/ref=sr_1_fkmr0_1?dchild=1&keywords=Collins%2C+J.+C.%2C+%26+Porras%2C+J.+I.+%281997%29.+Built+to+last%3A+Successful+habits+of+successful+companies.+574+London%3A+Random+House.&qid=1591712769&s=books&sr=1-1-fkmr0

Craumer, M. (2002, May). *How to think strategically about outsourcing*. Harvard Management Update, Working Knowledge. Retrieved from https://hbswk.hbs.edu/archive/how-to-think-strategically-about-outsourcing

Dean, J. (2011). The right kind of visualisation. *Psyblog*. Retrieved from https://www.spring.org. uk/2011/03/the-right-kind-of-visualisation.php

Deutschman, A. (2007). *Change or die: The three keys to change at work and in life.* New York: HarperCollins Publishers. https://www.amazon.com/Change-or-Die-Alan-Deutschman-audio book/dp/B000MV8X3I/ref=sr_1_fkmr0_1?dchild=1&keywords=Deutschman%2C+A.+% 282007%29.+Change+or+die%3A+The+three+keys+to+change+at+work+and+in+life.+New +York%2C+655+NY%3A+HarperCollins+Publishers.&qid=1591698512&s=books&sr=1-1- fkmr0

Eagleman, D. (2015). *The brain: The story of you.* Edinburgh: Canongate Books. https://www. amazon.com/Brain-Story-You-David-Eagleman/dp/0525433449

Falk, D. (2008). *In search of time: The history, physics, and philosophy of time.* New York, NY: St Martin's Press. https://www.amazon.com/Search-Time-History-Physics-Philosophy/dp/ 0312603517

Fleming, S. M., Thomas, C. L., & Dolan, R. J. (2010). Overcoming status quo bias in the human brain. *Proceedings of the National Academy of Sciences of the United States of America, 107* (13), 6005–6009. https://doi.org/10.1073/pnas.0910380107

Forbes. (2014). The world's 100 most powerful women. *Forbes.* Retrieved from https://www. forbes.com/sites/carolinehoward/2014/05/28/ranking-the-worlds-100-most-powerful-women- 2014/#2c703deb6d3e

Franken, A., Edwards, C., & Lambert, R. (2009). Executing strategic change: Understanding the critical management elements that lead to success. *California Management Review, 51*(3), 49–73. Retrieved from http://algu.weebly.com/uploads/1/9/2/4/1924527/stra.mgtcase2.pdf

Goldberg, E. (2009). *The new executive brain: Frontal lobes and a complex world.* New York: Oxford University Press. https://www.amazon.com/New-Executive-Brain-Frontal-Complex/ dp/0195329406/ref=sr_1_1?dchild=1&keywords=The+new+executive+brain%3A+Frontal +lobes+and+a+complex+world.&qid=1591712892&s=books&sr=1-1

Goold, M., & Campbell, A. (2002, March). Do you have a well-designed organization? *Harvard Business Review*, 117–124. Retrieved from https://hbr.org/2002/03/do-you-have-a-well- designed-organization

Graham, L. (2008). The neuroscience of attachment. *Linda Graham.* Retrieved July 26, 2019, from https://lindagraham-mft.net/the-neuroscience-of-attachment/

Invernizzi, E., Romenti, S., & Fumagalli, M. (2012). Identity, communication and change manage- ment in Ferrari. *Corporate Communications: An International Journal, 17*(4), 483–497. https:// doi.org/10.1108/13563281211274194

Jack, A. I., Boyatzis, R. E., Khawaja, M. S., Passarelli, A. M., & Leckie, R. L. (2013). Visioning in the brain: An fMRI study of inspirational coaching and mentoring. *Social Neuroscience, 8*(4). https://doi.org/10.1080/17470919.2013.808259

Jalalzai, F., & Dos Santos, P. G. (2013). *The Dilma effect-symbolic, descriptive, and substantive representation of women under Rousseff's presidency.* American Political Science Association (APSA) 2013. Annual Meeting Paper. https://papers.ssrn.com/sol3/papers.cfm?abstract_id= 2303147

Kaplan, R. S., & Norton, D. P. (1996, January–February). Using the balanced scorecard as a strategic management system. *Harvard Business Review.* Retrieved from https://hbr.org/2007/ 07/using-the-balanced-scorecard-as-a-strategic-management-system

Kraatz, M. S., & Zajac, E. J. (2001). How organizational resources affect strategic change and performance in turbulent environments: Theory and evidence. *Organization Science, 12*(5), 632–657. https://doi.org/10.1287/orsc.12.5.632.10088

Loehr, J., & Schwarz, T. (2001, January). The making of a corporate athlete. *Harvard Business Review, 79*(1), 120–128. https://hbr.org/2001/01/the-making-of-a-corporate-athlete

Lôbo, Y. L. (2010). *Bertha Lutz.* Recife, PE: Fundação Joaquim Nabuco. http://www. dominiopublico.gov.br/download/texto/me4693.pdf

Margolis, J., Roberts, L. M., & Winig, L. (2007). South African Airways, A and B (SAA). Case study: 9-407-014 (A), 9-407-024 (B). Harvard Business School Publishing, Feb 26, 2007, pp.

1–21 (A); 9-407-024, Feb 26, 2007, pp. 1–4. https://store.hbr.org/product/south-african-airways-a/407014?sku=407014-PDF-ENG

Merrell, P. (2012). Effective change management: The simple truth. *Management Services, 56*(2), 20–23. Retrieved from http://connection.ebscohost.com/c/articles/77508042/effective-change-management-simple-truth

Metcalf, A. C. (1990). Women and means: Women and family property in colonial Brazil. *Journal of Social History, 24*(2), 277–298. https://www.jstor.org/stable/3787499?seq=1

Pillay, S. (2011). The science of visualization: Maximizing your brain's potential during the recession. *The Blog.* Retrieved July 26, 2019, from https://www.huffpost.com/entry/the-science-of-visualizat_b_171340

Pinprayong, B., & Wongsurawat, W. (2012). Strategic change for sustainability in Thai Commercial Bank. *Emerald Emerging Markets Case Studies, 2*(8), 1–10. https://www.emerald.com/insight/content/doi/10.1108/20450621211291824/full/html?queryID=

Popova, M. (n.d.). *The science of mental time travel and why our ability to imagine the future is essential to our humanity.* Retrieved July 26, 2019, from https://www.brainpickings.org/2014/07/01/mental-time-travel-dan-falk/

Reeves, M., Love, C., & Tillmanns, P. (2012, September). Your strategy needs a strategy. *Harvard Business Review*, 76–83. Retrieved from https://hbr.org/2012/09/your-strategy-needs-a-strategy

Rosenberg, R. (2003, Summer). The eight rings of organisational influence: How to structure your organisation for successful change. *The Journal for Quality & Participation, 26*(2), 30–34. Retrieved from http://asq.org/qic/display-item/?item=19162

SASOL. (2012). SASOL Integrated Annual Report 2012. Retrieved August 20, 2019, from https://www.sasol.com/sites/default/files/financial_reports/Annual%20integrated%20report%2C%2030%20June%202012.pdf

Schacter, D. L., Addis, D. R., Hassabis, D., Martin, V. C., Spreng, R. N., & Szpunar, K. K. (2012). The future of memory: Remembering, imagining, and the brain. *Neuron, 76*(4). https://doi.org/10.1016/j.neuron.2012.11.001

Scheepers, C. B., & Swart, S. (2015). *Momentum and metropolitan merger: Authentic transformational leadership.* Ivey Publishing, 9B15C004. https://www.iveycases.com/ProductView.aspx?id=70560

Scott, D. (2008). Outsourcing's evolution from commodity to partner. *Applied Clinical Trials*, 60–68. https://search.proquest.com/openview/15951be835002bce46753dfba138683e/1?pq-origsite=gscholar&cbl=44052

Van Klaveren, M., Tijdens, K., Hughie-Williams, M., & Martin, N. R. (2009). *Work and employment in Brazil.* Amsterdam Institute for Advanced Labour Studies (AIAS), University of Amsterdam. https://www.ituc-csi.org/IMG/pdf/Country_Report_No12-Brazil_EN.pdf

World Economic Forum Gender Gap (WEF). (2013). *Gender Gap Index: Brazil* (p. 155). Retrieved from http://www3.weforum.org/docs/WEF_GenderGap_Report_2013.pdf

Reference List for Quotes

Dobrowolski, P. (2015). *Draw your future, take control of your life by Patti Dobrowolski* (Transcript). Retrieved July 26, 2019, from https://singjupost.com/draw-your-future-take-control-of-your-life-by-patti-dobrowolski-transcript/3/?print=print

Retrieved July 26, 2019, from http://www.wothquotes.com/2017/12/vision-quotes.html

Sixth Enabler

10

Engage

> *Anytime you use your influence to affect the thoughts and actions of others, you are engaging in leadership.*
> (Ken Blanchard, 2007)
> *To change other people's thinking is one of the hardest tasks in the world.*
> (David Rock, 2009, p. 218)
> *If you want to make peace with your enemy, you have to work with your enemy. Then he becomes your partner.*
> (Nelson Mandela, 1994)

Electronic supplementary material The online version of this chapter (https://doi.org/10.1007/978-3-030-40846-6_10) contains supplementary material, which is available to authorized users.

Learning Outcomes

At the end of this chapter, Change Leaders will be able to:

- Identify stakeholders, their desires and fears and plan how to get their buy-in
- Obtain sign-off on the project from decision makers
- Obtain buy-in from stakeholders
- Appoint a competent change agent team
- Set goals for change agent team

10.1   Orientation to Engaging

Leadership plays a strategic role in managing resistance to change by motivating employee participation in the change process (Al-Ali, Singh, Al-Nahyan, & Sohal, 2017). Quinn (2004) states that leadership is responsible for communicating to the organisation the risks in clinging to the status quo. In the discussion of this Sixth Enabler, we would like to emphasise that leadership is responsible for communication, not only to stakeholders within the organisation, as Quinn (2004) suggests, but also external to the organisation. Nonetheless, we concur with Quinn (2004) that the potential rewards of embracing a radically different future must also be communicated. This Sixth Enabler and the previous enablers are interdependent. Envisioning entails that the interventions to achieve the vision, had also been thought through. Then the gap in terms of whether the current organisation's philosophy, structure and culture comply with the intended vision and strategy, must be considered. Specifically, in situations where these elements would need to be addressed, engagement of relevant stakeholders is crucial prior to embarking on the change, which is the Seventh Enabler.

We support perspectives on stakeholders of scholars, such as Freeman (2010a, 2010b) with his seminal work on this subject in his articles, including, "Managing for Stakeholders: Trade-offs or Value Creation" on the compatibility of stakeholder interests, as well as others like Freeman, Wicks, and Parmar (2004). For example, in cases where the organisation is unionised, negotiations with the unions, as important stakeholders, earlier rather than later, are essential. During our interviews, an interviewee reflected, "when we realised that the restructuring of the mining processes, would require fewer teams at the face and as a result would mean fewer employees, we purposefully engaged with the unions upfront and ensured that they understood the implications from the start".

Because of this proactive engagement with the unions and several collective agreements, the mine was able to conduct a Section 189A (the statement to initiate a retrenchment process, in line with South African labour laws) twice in 6 months in 2015, entailing retrenchments, without a labour strike. This was quite remarkable, especially considering the labour relations climate in mining at the time.

Identifying the relevant stakeholders to engage with, is part of this important Sixth Enabler. For example, on their website, the Johnson and Johnson's Credo (https://www.jnj.com/about-jnj/jnj-credo), identify their responsibilities towards particular stakeholders, "our first responsibility is to the doctors, nurses and patients, to mothers and fathers and all others who use our products and services; We are responsible to our employees, the men and women who work with us throughout the world; We are responsible to the communities in which we live and work and to the world community as well; Our final responsibility is to our stockholders. Business must make a sound profit".

This Sixth Enabler requires effective one-on-one relationships, with trust and adequate bonding; as well as effective small team operations with team bonding. An important stakeholder in this process is the change team. Again, as mentioned in the previous enablers, the authors of this volume do not assign the enablers to an individual leader. Instead, we advocate for collective leadership, where multiple individual leaders and teams throughout the organisation are involved in leading change (Yammarino, Salas, Serban, Shirreffs, & Shuffler, 2012). Other scholars called for leadership that is distributed throughout an organisation and especially in the management of education, it is known as distributed leadership. Spillane (2005) explains this in the article called "Distributed Leadership" in *The Educational Forum*. In this regard, leadership at the top of the organisation must regularly appoint change teams, consisting of representatives throughout the organisation as the steering committee, which focuses on the strategic decisions around the change, as well as an operational change team that pays attention to the day-to-day operations of the change process.

10.2 Importance of Engaging

The change team must identify relevant role players that should be engaged to implement the change process successfully. In the practical application section of this Sixth Enabler, tools and methodologies include stakeholder mapping, with corresponding stakeholder strategies. This enabler also entails setting up the measurement tool towards measuring the effectiveness of the change in the organisation; which includes the measurement of engagement throughout the organisation. In cases where this Sixth Enabler had not been implemented, people sabotaged the change, by resisting implementation overtly or even covertly by finding excuses. On the other hand, when people are engaged, they show commitment and buy-in and make the change happen. Leaders battle to bring about change on their own and need others with the power to lead the change. Implementation occurs when people do the work, but will they do it and why would they? In this regard, we advise to communicate the rationale for change and only to implement changes with a clear basis for improvement. Franken, Edwards, and Lambert (2009) emphasise too that leaders must continuously motivate people in order to avoid resistance to change.

Leadership is required to perceive the interconnectedness of reality, in order to reach out to stakeholders. In this regard, Uhl-Bien and Arena (2017, p. 9) referred to

IBM's survey of CEO's in 2010, which highlights that the biggest problem that organisational leaders worldwide must cope with, is the increase in complexity of situations, accompanied with even more "volatility, uncertainty and interconnectedness". In the discussion below, we highlight two aspects of the Sixth Enabler, namely political acumen, as well as emotional acumen required for this enabler.

10.2.1 Political Acumen

A prerequisite for leadership of stakeholders is political acumen. For example, Kutz (2008) emphasises the importance of the political reality as part of considering the context, in reflecting that contextually intelligent leaders know that context is not merely a fixed GPS co-ordinate, but a social construct. Cummings and Worley (2015) include building political support as one of the five steps to implement change in organisations. Boeker (1997) contends that political resistance is a difficult issue in change leadership. In a study by Van Eeden, Sutherland, and Scheepers (2016), they identify senior management as the stakeholder with the most power during change processes. Subsequently, these senior managers need to have a clear understanding and be totally committed to the process, once decisions have been made to ensure successful change implementation. In this regard, Todd (1999) describes the politics within change processes as a combination of power, influence and authority. Politics during a time of change indefinitely increases. Consideration has thus to be given to the emotional consequences of individuals that are impacted by change processes, as it might prompt them to revert to political manoeuvring.

Franken et al. (2009) state that leaders must agree as a collective and support and defend the decisions they make. We would like to contribute in this regard, that, it is indeed important that leaders have consensus, and we would like to add that actually it forms part of political acumen. We contend that alignment at the top is especially essential when required to negotiate with influential stakeholders. Behaviour should be reinforced through reward and recognition of performance. Leadership with political acumen would realise when they could use their power to offer rewards and recognition to important stakeholders or withhold it, to ensure engagement.

Engagement might not be the right word to use, as it implies commitment. We would like to state that engagement and true emotional commitment to change is always the ideal or first prize. However, we are also realistic and have observed that in some instances, with powerful stakeholders who do not want to support change, a "harder" stance was required, where they had been given an ultimatum and had to show their support or would not be rewarded and in some instances, had to leave the organisation. These ultimatums would of course, unfortunately not breed commitment. However, compliance was sufficient to make progress and get the change off the ground. In this regard, Schilling, Werr, Gand, and Sardas (2012) advise that one of the explanations for resistance to change is the belief that the organisation should be moving in a different direction. In these cases, it is better for the organisation when these executives leave the organisation. We observed that it was also the best for the relevant executive, who could not authentically support the direction that the organisation was taking.

We encountered several of these examples during our interviews, where especially on the executive level, an ultimatum had been given to some members, and they ultimately left the organisation as they did not support the change process. For the sake of confidentiality and sensitivity around these matters, we would not share these specific examples here. One of the interviewees, who offered permission for us to report the story, made a point of going back to Head Office, where radical decisions had been taken, to ascertain the reasons and the rationale behind these decisions. Only after he realised that he could buy-in to the decisions, could he sell the new direction to his employees. He shared, "I made a trip to London to get more background information, as I knew that if I were not convinced, I would not be able to authentically discuss the vision around the acquisition".

The discussion above might come across as a transactional style of leadership, which focuses on the reward and recognition system to influence others, whereas a transformational leadership style is mostly preferred, which aims to be inspirational to others, so that they would want to accept changes. As authors of this volume, we agree: this illustrates our main thesis that leadership must be contextualised. In some instances, like here with dealing with resistant, powerful stakeholders, a transactional style is actually required, and leaders have to be able to adopt to this style to be effective in this Sixth Enabler.

10.2.2 Emotional Acumen

Some scholars, such as Hazy and Uhl-Bien (2015) advise leaders to include stakeholders to build a sense of community and form a shared identity. Harris and Sohal (2002) suggest appealing to both intellect and emotions of individuals to ensure success with strategic change. It might take longer initially and be time-consuming, but would save time later and achieve the necessary results. As such, leaders' emotional intelligence, as described by Doe, Ndinguri, and Phipps (2015) is crucial in gauging the feelings of stakeholders. Engagement requires leadership's understanding of the underlying reasons for resistance to change. On their part, Cunningham et al. (2002) contribute that readiness to change is influenced by an individual's perception of the risk and or benefit of the change. Already in 1980s, Buller (1988) declared that ensuring readiness for change is the first step to getting acceptance of the change process.

Schilling et al. (2012) warn that resistance is innate to human nature and stems from a fear of loss of control. This fear can cause emotional stress or depression, which can lead to rejection of the change. They will thus resist change if there is a potential negative consequence or threat to them on a personal level. John Kotter (1996) from Harvard, agrees that people by their very nature are resistant to change. The general hesitation to implement any new change is usually an apprehension that can hinder the progression of organisational growth and potentially derail the change processes.

Sonenshein (2010) states that unfortunately managers and employees create meaning during change, based on the positive or negative perceptions of the change. This limited focus results in employees resisting change and managers attempting to overcome this resistance through positive meanings. They do not internalise management's ideas about change, but rather enlarge them, which can influence others negatively. Gagnon, Jansen, and Michael (2008) too declare that strategic change failure lies with the individual due to resistance to commit and adopt new behaviour to accomplish strategic objectives. Open communication and involvement of employees during strategic change are likely to develop trust and reduce organisational resistance (Lines, 2004). Wellman (2007) agrees that open communication even increases in significance during change processes. Doz and Kosonen (2007) in this regard, contrast traditional ritualised meetings and public consent, but private dissent, with the new open, informal communications and collective responsibility.

An important competence as part of this Sixth Enabler is the ability to engage with different stakeholders. In this regard, Yukl and Mahsud (2010) advise leadership to behave flexibly, where leaders are able to demonstrate different leadership capabilities in different situations (Yukl & Mahsud, 2010). In a way, they need to be able to switch between contexts, and it relates to Kutz's (2008) notion of Contextual leadership.

10.2.3   Opposing Views in Current Literature on Resistance

On the one hand, Balogun (2007) advises leadership to combat the resistance phenomenon with clear direction from the top, with a clear message that resistance will not be tolerated. He feels strongly about this since resistance to change is an indication of people trying to defend their turf and self-interest, which can derail the strategic change.

On the other hand, scholars like McClellan (2011) recommends opening dialogues for the effective communication of change in engagement and consultation processes. This researcher also emphasises that communication was traditionally seen as merely a tool for enabling change, whereas it is now regarded as one of the reasons why change potentially fails. Critically, leadership must address the differing opinions that are raised in the change dialogues and not suppress them to promote genuine interactions where all parties deem that their opinions matter. Invernizzi, Romenti, and Fumagalli (2012) too find that a "push" approach to information sharing from top management is not adequate. Change communication should create a sense of community and belonging, and follow a participative and relational approach, to energise employees through communication that reassures them. It is crucial to not only give adequate information on the change process but also to listen to ensure feedback is generated. This, in turn, will ensure further improvements in future communication.

Other scholars, like Barratt-Pugh, Bahn and Gakere's (2013) recommendations are in line with the second view. They advise to involve employees and allow them to participate at the beginning of the change process. Through involving employees, they gain a sense of ownership and become contributors to the change process. Eby, Adams, Russell, and Gaby (2000) too, identify the following elements as crucial in promoting organisational readiness, namely flexible organisational policies and procedures, as well as a positive organisational climate and good working relationships. Elving (2005) conceives change readiness as one end of a continuum, whereas resistance to change is the other end. The scholar contends that the change will be more effective if employees are ready to accept the change. Franken et al. (2009) likewise, declare that a common challenge is the low levels of involvement of a large number of managers across all functions at an early stage of strategy execution.

We noticed that there had been limited scholarly research on the impact of previous change processes on the current intended change. In this regard, Shin, Taylor, and Seo (2012, p. 728) find that change can be a "long, emotionally intense, stressful, and fatiguing process for most employees" that could lead them to become change averse. In our modern organisations, it is thus important to take cognisance of change fatigue. This change aversion would need to be addressed, prior to embarking on the next change wave.

The literature quoted above focuses on employees as an important stakeholder. We would like to emphasise customers as another stakeholder and would like to urge leadership to engage this stakeholder too, early in the process of introducing important changes.

10.3 Engaging in Practice

10.3.1 The Engagement Process

The engagement process is the first step towards taking the vision to the people. Figure 10.1 explains this process in detail.

10.3.1.1 Stakeholder Identification and Analysis

The Engagement process we developed starts with a stakeholder identification process using the stakeholder map. First stakeholders are identified, followed by getting buy-in and sign-off of decision makers. The next steps in the process involve appointing a steering committee and a change team. Next the needs, fears and desires of stakeholders are determined and finally these needs, fears and desires are confirmed with stakeholders through a process of engagement.

It is useful to realise that the change exists within an environment and is born out of the current reality. This environment consists of people or groups of people who are influencers, leaders, implementers or followers who will be involved in the change. The stakeholder map helps the change leader identify the key people or groups of people who will have an influence on the change process or on whom the change process will have an impact.

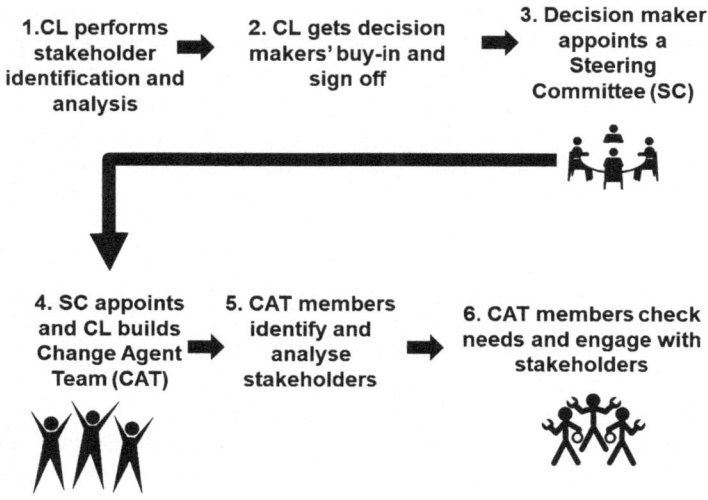

Fig. 10.1 Engagement process (Authors' own)

The stakeholder map is an essential tool, and we never start a change process without identifying the stakeholders. Considering all possible stakeholders is critical. Neglected stakeholders could become a real obstacle to change. It is always a good idea to show stakeholders the map and ask them whether they think all stakeholders have been considered.

Tool 6.1 Stakeholder Map

In the stakeholder map tool, the vision statement is placed in the centre of a flipchart. Next, all the people or groups of people who could possibly be relevant to the change process are mapped around the vision to form a spider diagram. It is essential to consider all possible stakeholders. Once this has been done, the half-dozen or so who are especially critical should be identified and marked on the map. Each of the stakeholder groups can be further expanded. See Toolkit for details.

Once the stakeholder map (that will look like a spider diagram) is completed, the next step in the process is to stand back and evaluate where the support for the change will come from, where the most resistance will come from and who the key decision makers and influencers will be. We like to highlight the resisters in red, the supporters in green and the decision makers and influencers in blue. This gives a good overview of where the focus of the engagement needs to be.

Role Players

Tool 6.2 Role Players

When considering the different role players, a checklist can be used to identify the types of stakeholders involved in the change process. This list may include the Chief Executive Officer (CEO), change leader, line managers, sponsor(s), opinion leaders, change agents, decision makers, informers, influencers, etc. See Toolkit for more details.

Rogers' Adopter Categories

We recommend using the Rogers Innovation Adoption Curve (Rogers, 2003) to categorise the stakeholders (Fig. 10.2). This will help us imagine how the stakeholders might react to the change and work on strategies how to engage and deal with the stakeholders. Everett Rogers established five adopter categories based on the way people tend to deal with change. *Innovators* are mavericks, always searching for innovative ideas to implement, but are often considered as outsiders and a bit weird by the rest of the organisation. *Early adopters* are the critical opinion

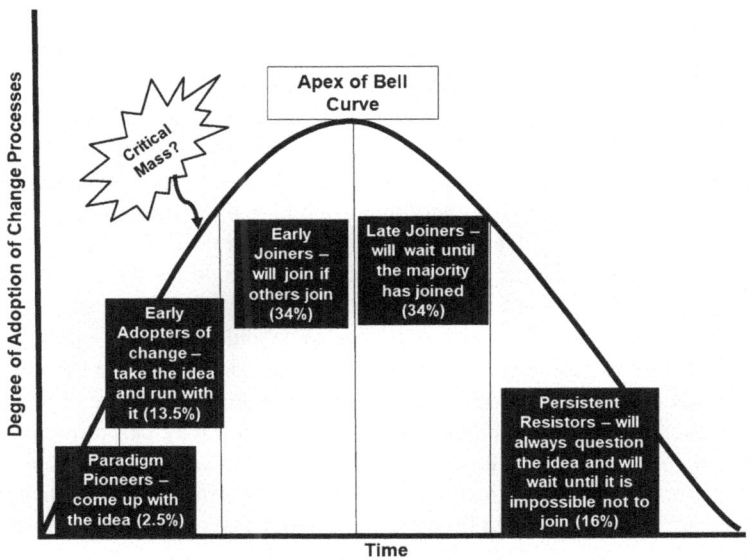

Fig. 10.2 Distribution of stakeholders joining the change process over time

leaders, respected and valued by the rest of the organisation and very valuable for the change process. During the initial stages of the project, the change leader will be spending a lot of time in these two categories. People in the *early majority* category are cautious and thoughtful and tend to be slow decision makers, but they adapt to the change earlier than the average person. The *late majority* category represents the sceptics, those who will only adopt the change when the majority has accepted it and often respond only to pressure from peers to change. Lastly, we find the *laggards* who tend to be the traditionalists. They tend to be suspicious, hang onto the past and will only adopt the change once the change has become mainstream. Rogers' categories were adapted to align with the paradigm discussion. Innovators are considered to be paradigm pioneers, the early and late majority are called early and late joiners and the laggards are termed persistent resisters.

Tool 6.3 Stakeholder Commitment Distribution

As a change leader, you can now try and anticipate which stakeholders will fit into which one of the Rogers Adopter Groups. Of course, this is only an estimated guess on your part, but it might provide valuable insight into how to deal with these stakeholders.
Tool 6.3 provides a template to identify which category the different stakeholders fit into.

Can Make It Happen: Want to Make It Happen Matrix

Mitchell, Agle, and Wood (1997) developed the Interest–Power stakeholder map to analyse stakeholders further and determine how to get their buy-in (Fig. 10.3). *Promoters* are the most important and most valuable stakeholders to change leaders as they have much power and are very interested in making the project work. They need to be fully engaged with as soon as possible; if their needs are not met, they can be highly disruptive to the process. Promoters will include the CEO and other key decision makers. The second category contains the *Latents*. They too have huge power but not much interest. Their needs need to be understood and met as they too can cause disruptions. Although they are critical, they do not require the same level of attention as the promoters. The *Defenders* are very interested in the project but do not have much power. Their input is very valuable and they can provide a lot of background information and insight on how best to deal with decision makers. Defenders can also ensure critical mass is obtained to bring about the change. The *Apathetics* have little power and little influence. They just need to be monitored. We adapted Mitchell et al.'s grid (1997) to contain two dimensions: *Can make it happen* due to having the power to make it happen and *Want to make it happen*, reflecting the interest to make it happen.

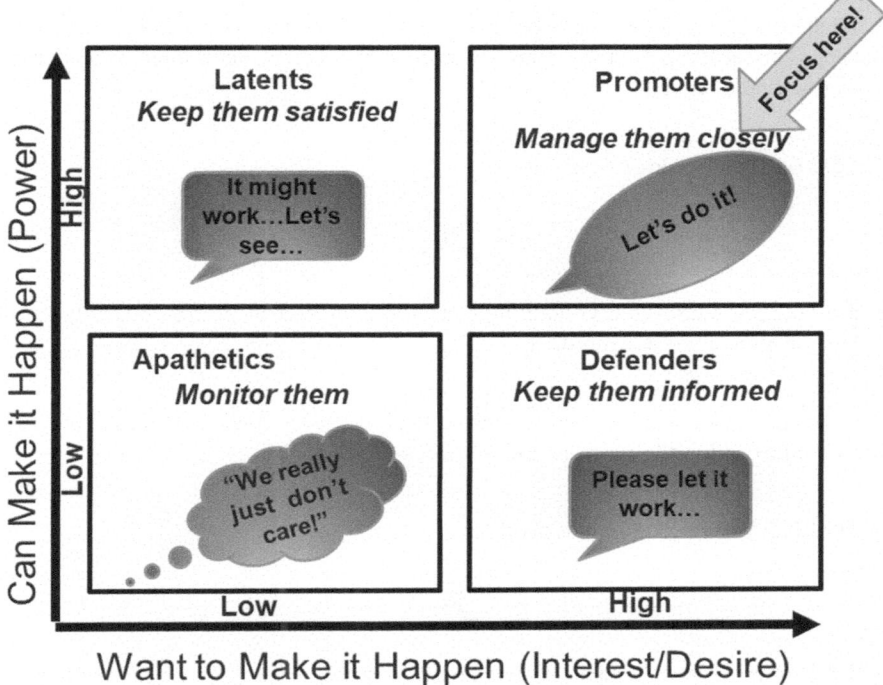

Fig. 10.3 Can make it happen—Want to make it happen matrix (Authors' own synthesis from the original concepts of Mitchell et al. (1997))

Never doubt that a small group of thoughtful, committed, citizens can change the world. Indeed, it is the only thing that ever has (Margaret Mead, n.d.).

Tool 6.4 Can Make It Happen: Want to Make It Happen Matrix

Tool 6.4 provides a matrix to plot which quadrant the different stakeholders belong to.

Stakeholder Analysis

A detailed analysis should now be done for the CEO, sponsors and key decision makers. This analysis will be done for each of the key players, after which their buy-in will be obtained.

Tool 6.5 Stakeholder Analysis I

Tool 6.5 provides a table containing questions to be used as prompts to analyse the stakeholders in greater depth.

Next, the fears and desires of stakeholders are identified, and strategies are developed to address these fears and desires.

Tool 6.6 Stakeholder Analysis II

Tool 6.6 provides a table listing the desired outcomes and fears for each of the stakeholder groups. It also provides an opportunity for the change leader to identify what strategies will be followed to deal with the desires and fears for each of the stakeholder groups.

10.3.1.2 Decision Makers Buy-In and Sign-Off

Tool 6.7 CEO, Sponsor, Decision Maker Buy-In and Sign-Off

Tool 6.7 offers the change leader a proforma document that can be presented to the CEO, decision makers or sponsors for sign-off.

10.3.1.3 Appoint Steering Committee

The next step in the process is to appoint a powerful, competent "guiding coalition" (Kotter, 1996). We suggest a Steering Committee (SC) be appointed with high-level decision makers sharing the vision and having a desire to make the project work.

10.3.1.4 Appoint Change Agent Team

Next, the Steering Committee should appoint change agents to form the Change Agent Team (CAT). Change agents should be representatives from the key stakeholder groups and should have the right competencies. In Tool 6.8, competencies for being a successful change agent have been listed. The change leader can now measure each potential candidate against the list of change agent requirements to ensure the right people are appointed to fulfil this crucial role.

Tool 6.8 Change Agent Competency Checklist

Tool 6.8 provides change leaders with a list of competencies change agents should possess. It can be used to assess potential candidates.

Change Agent Team

Following the competency assessment for each of the potential change agents, the change agent team is now finalised and appointed.

Tool 6.9 Change Agent Team

This tool allows change leaders the opportunity to list the change agents and identify the constituents the change agents will represent. See toolkit for template.

Change Agent Team Vision and Goals

Once the Change Agent Team has been appointed, they will go through a process of agreeing the vision, strategies and interventions and then develop their goals. Each Change Agent will develop personal goals aligned with the team goals. Tool 6.10 provides a template presenting a matrix listing the team outputs and the roles each agent will fulfil against each output. See the online toolkit for template. We define a goal as follows: A goal = an output + an accountable person assigned to the output + an agreed action plan + agreed dates for delivery of the output.

Goal = Output + Accountable Person + Action Plan + Delivery Date

Tool 6.10 Change Agent Team Goals

(Refer to Tools 7.3–7.6 in Enabler 7, Embark for more detail)

Practical Application: Afrika Transdisciplinary Research Network

The graphic below (Fig. 10.4) was created by the organisation Afrika Trans-disciplinary Research Network during a strategy workshop held in Cape Town, November 2017 and contains the goals they set to realise their vision. The network is dedicated to strengthening and mobilizing regional capacities for addressing complex global change challenges facing the African continent today. The artwork was done by graphic harvester Sonja Niederhumer (www. graphicharvest.co.za).

10.3.1.5 CAT Members Identify and Analyse Their Stakeholders
We suggest that Tools 6.5 and 6.6 (Stakeholder analysis I and II) now be repeated to reflect the rest of the stakeholder groups. Change agents are responsible for completing these worksheets for their constituents by engaging with them.

10.3.1.6 CAT Members Engage with Their Stakeholders
The last step in this process is for CAT members to engage with their stakeholders by confirming their needs, desires and fears. They could also ask them questions about solutions regarding the change process. This will help people arrive at their own insights. Then constant, specific, clear communication about the direction needs to be put in place.

Fig. 10.4 Graphical representation of organisational change goals (Sonja Niederhumer and Afrika Transdisciplinary Research Network)

Commitment, Readiness, Capability, Skill (CRCS) Matrix

The next tool assists in plotting the stakeholder groups' commitment, their readiness for the change, their actual capabilities and skills.

Tool 6.11 Stakeholder Commitment, Readiness, Capability, Skill (CRCS) Matrix

The CRCS tool determines the commitment, capability, readiness and skill of Stakeholder group members. Template 6.11 in the toolkit contains a matrix assessing each of the aspects by stakeholder group members.

10.3.2 Implementation Tips for Engaging

Here we share practical tips from our experience engaging with stakeholders:

- Consider conducting large-scale interventions and open space-type technology where you have a large number of your staff present at the same time or use Skype or Zoom type web-based technology to interact with them simultaneously.
- Remember the dark side of engagement is burnout (Puleo, 2011). The Burnout During Organizational Change (B-DOC) model graphically represented this lapse into and recovery from burnout during transformational change processes. Implications for positive social change include reasonable accommodation of the psychological and physiological dimensions of burnout under the Americans with Disabilities Act (ADA). ADA compliance would thus transform management practices by requiring incorporation of burnout mitigation policies into all aspects of organisational strategy and operations. The emergence and maintenance of burnout are due to a mutually reinforcing triumvirate of psychological pressure. Refer to Burn-out in Enabler 2, Ego Mastery (Tools 2.15 and 2.16).

10.4   Neuroscience Insights into Engaging

In Chap. 3, we learnt that the brain has an overarching organising principle to classify the world into things that will either hurt a person or help a person to stay alive. The motivation of people is mainly governed by this overarching organising principle of minimising threat and maximising reward. Introducing a change process will be perceived as either a threat or a reward by people experiencing or even just observing the change. Knowing about this principle can help us understand that those involved in the change will either support or resist the change process.

10.4.1 SCARF Model

The SCARF model, developed by David Rock (2009), captures the common factors that can activate a reward or threat and is an easy way to remember and act upon social triggers that can create the "*toward and away*" response. The goal of the model is to help minimise the threat response and maximise the reward response while collaborating and influencing others (Rock, 2009). It also assists in determining what stakeholders will require to buy into the vision and the implementation of the change process.

It proposes that the human brain seeks Status, Certainty, Autonomy, Relatedness and Fairness. (The first letter of each of these words spell SCARF, hence the SCARF model.) As a change leader, SCARF can be used to engage with stakeholders. Change processes often diminish the status of some stakeholders. We need to be aware of the potential dangers when that happens and build alternative sources of status into the process. Involvement in the process can often provide new status.

Change processes are by nature, times of severe *uncertainty* due to not having the necessary information or clarity to be able to communicate to the stakeholders. To mitigate this, we need to communicate regularly—even if there is nothing new to report. It is useful to emphasise what is certain or to repeat what has been said before.

Openness and honesty would be prerequisites for trust building amongst stakeholders, as well as between change leaders and followers. In the absence of communication, the grapevine will fill the void, often with inaccurate information. Stakeholders can also easily feel threatened when their *autonomy* is taken away from them. Here too, involvement in the change process can assist with feeling in control.

When stakeholders are left out of the loop with no participation, they can become resentful and join those who are resisting. Attending to the needs of stakeholders to feel *related* to the change process and change leaders, we can involve them in task teams and listen to, and act on their concerns.

Keep in mind that the brain is programmed to seek *fairness* and avoid unfairness. We can go as far as to say the brain is hardwired to perceive unfairness as disgusting. We must, therefore be as open minded as possible and communicate as soon as we know how the change will affect stakeholders. This will help with the perception that the change is dealt with in a fair manner.

10.4.2 Mirror Neurons

While researching the neural representation of motor movements in monkeys, the Italian neurophysiologist, Dr. Rizzolatti, discovered a set of neurons in the frontal and premotor cortex (Rizzolatti & Sinigaglia, 2016). These neurons were unique in that they not only fired when engaged in planning a motor movement but also while observing movement of another person or another monkey. These new cells were called "mirror neurons" because they seemed to map one person's actions into another's brain. This kind of imprinting explains why what we do is so important as it becomes a powerful influence on others. Leaders need to understand their potential impact as role models and mentors. Rizzolatti found that if you see someone doing something, for example eating a piece of fruit, the same neurons light up when you perform the task yourself. Random acts do not have this effect. It has to be an action with an intention behind it or a goal that needs to be reached.

Even though we as humans treasure our autonomy and love our independence, we also know we need each other for survival and are therefore first and foremost social animals. Mirror neurons seem to provide evidence of this interdependence as they form the connection between our thinking, feeling and actions—and other people. This is considered to be the neurological basis of human connectedness (Rizzolatti & Sinigaglia, 2016).

The following video clip contains an interview with the founder of mirror neurons, Dr. Rizzolatti.

Video Clip: Interview with Dr Giacomo Rizzolatti

http://gocognitive.net/interviews/discovery-mirror-neurons-1
http://gocognitive.net/interviews/mirror-neurons-monkeys-humans

10.4.3 The Brain Is a Social Organ, and Detests Rejection

It has been said that the brain is a social organ (Lieberman, 2013). Our minds are profoundly social (Siegel, 2006) and the brain's structure predisposes us to be socially orientated. Newborns experience a form of empathy. At the age of 6 months, well before babies can speak, they experience advanced socially orientated emotions like jealousy. We need connections to others to feel balanced and to develop well (Siegel, 2006). These new connections been critically tuned to social interactions, to understanding and communicate with other people and to live and work with them (Swart, Chisholm, & Brown, 2015). Our brains seek meaning in social interactions, to make sense of why we act the way we do, what affects our actions have on others and how they feel about us.

Most processes operating in the background when your brain is at rest are involved in thinking about people or yourself (Eisenberger & Matthew Lieberman, 2009).

This fact that we are socially connected, helps us understand why being excluded in decision making is often so painful. Hillebrandt, Sebastian, and Blakemore (2010) believe being socially excluded is intensely stressful. As part of their research, they used a virtual ball game, called Cyberball to explore what happens when individuals are excluded. Kip Williams and his colleagues at Purdue University developed an experimental technique called the "ball toss" paradigm, which has been used to study exclusion, rejection, discrimination and prejudice. It is a virtual ball-tossing game in which three people toss a virtual ball back and forth to each other. Two of the players then team up with the researcher and start excluding the third player (without him/her being aware of the conspiracy). Within a couple of minutes, the third player starts displaying negative emotions such as anger and sadness. This happens irrespective of self-esteem or personality differences (Williams & Sommer, 1997).

10.4.4 Getting Buy-In

When the brain is first exposed to a change, it will register the change as an "Error" as it does not conform to existing paradigms. Error detection will lead to a moving away response based on fear and anxiety. According to Ringleb and Rock (2008), the brain literally sees change as pain. A moment of insight is required in the brain of stakeholders to get them to buy into the change. We advise that change leaders should not just sell an idea. This could lead to buyers' remorse. The moment of insight needs to allow the individual to buy the change voluntarily. Only then will real buy-in be achieved.

10.4.5 The Brain and Resistance to Change

To a certain degree, the human neurology is built to resist change. To maintain the status quo, the brain creates discomfort when we try something new. Because we crave certainty, we oppose moving into new areas, but when we feel sufficiently secure, we are prepared to venture into unfamiliar territory.

Sometimes the human brain can behave like a 2-year-old child throwing a temper tantrum: if you tell it what to do, it will automatically push back. This is because the brain naturally moves towards equilibrium and away from change and likes to form patterns and innovative networks. People affected by the change prefer to decide for themselves how they will manage the change and want to solve their own problems. When they solve their own problems, a rush of adrenaline is released in the bloodstream. It is best during the engagement process to ask appropriate questions and support stakeholders in finding their own solutions (Rock & Schwartz, 2006).

While conducting the stakeholder analysis and engagement, change leaders can utilise the concept of moving Towards and Away discussed in Chap. 3. Having this insight can help identify who is for the change process and who is against the change process and why.

You might recall that in Chap. 3, we discussed the fact that the brain is programmed to perceive a change as either something it should go towards or run away from. The brain of the stakeholders will either regard the change as something that will hurt or help them. Based on their perception, they will then either go towards (support) the change or run away from (resist) the change. Stakeholders see the change brought to them by change leaders in the same way. If they perceive the change as something that might harm them or something they might not be able to do, or that it might be too difficult to cope with, they will metaphorically run away from the change and resist it in many ways. Change leaders need to get stakeholders to "run" towards the change, i.e. to understand how the change will benefit them and provide resources and skills development to get the stakeholder to want to support the change.

Even when someone tries to politely tell another person what they are doing is wrong and phrases the criticism as a question, the subconscious mind's alarm is triggered. People know when you are attempting to persuade them or when you are authentically trying to inquire and get them to find solutions on their own.

10.5   Engaging in Emerging Markets

10.5.1 Case Examples of Engaging in the Emerging Markets Context

In Africa, for example it is important to take note of scholars who write about African Leadership, such as Khoza (2012). He explains that the spirit of *Ubuntu* is about mutual dependency. It is the ethic of African humanism, namely that "a person is a person because of other people", which in the case of an organisation, can be described as the sum of all its parts. Ubuntu directly translated is "that my very being derives from yours and yours from all of ours". It is expressed in the Zulu proverb: Umuntu ngumuntu ngabantu—I am because you are; you are because we are (Khoza, 2012). Walumba, Avolio, and Aryee (2011) warn that sociocultural variables must not be dismissed or overlooked particularly in non-Western contexts, given the predisposition to promote Western leadership practices and thought where it may not be appropriate.

In the context of the Sixth Enabler, leadership in environments where there is a collectivist culture, such as in Africa, could refer to the Ubuntu concept to motivate for collaboration around a common goal. Stakeholders would be more prepared to be engaged if they could perceive the reciprocity in the Ubuntu concept. Western scholars, who researched cooperation stressed the importance of reciprocity, such as Christensen, Marx, and Stevenson (2009). There has to be some gain in it for stakeholders to cooperate. The relevant theory here is the Theory of Reciprocity of Blau (1964), who formulated the importance of a reciprocal relationship. In the emerging markets, this concept is even more critical, and stakeholders are even more sensitive to being exploited in these markets. The reason might be related to the fact that even basic human rights have only lately been protected in some emerging markets, such as in Malaysia (Abdullah, 2014). The history of colonialism might also have been sensitising emerging markets, like India, against being exploited (Scheepers, Swart, Alexander & Parbhoo, 2017).

Magner (2007) conducted research called, "Contextual leadership development: A South African perspective", which reveals that limited attention is given to leadership development in dealing with cultural diversity. She recommends real dialogue, where two people with different views, find something in common and be willing to stay in the dialogue long enough to make the change, which might mean your own views being challenged. Magner further explains that this process allows participants to suspend their own opinions and to respect the opinions of others. This process adds meaning by challenging one's own assumptions (Magner, 2007). As authors of this volume, we advocate following these processes as described by Magner (2007), and encourage leadership to participate in true dialogue, as this is the way towards true engagement of stakeholders.

Interestingly, a study on multinationals in dynamic, emerging markets, revealed an opposing view to the traditional view of dealing with or managing resistance, implying to suppress it, as described above. Vithessonthi (2010) found that resistance to change in these multinational organisations, was actually beneficial, especially resistance shown by those middle managers and operational managers who are close to customers, allowing them to have insights into these markets. In turn, their resistance served as a warning to top management about the implications of forging ahead with strategic change. In the long term, these warnings may save time and money as they make inroads into these markets.

While the previous five chapters offered background on the five BRICS countries, with a special focus on women's emancipation of the five countries, the remaining chapters comprise of more general discussions on other emerging market countries, with a limited emphasis on women issues. In this chapter on engagement, the emerging market of the United Arab Emirates (UAE) is relevant, since of the 9.2 million in 2013, only 1.4 million were Emirati citizens and 7.8 million were expatriate inhabitants, according to Freedom House. It is interesting that the UAE engages so many expatriates with the objective to grow their economy. A study on expatriates in UAE by Bozionelos and Singh (2017) revealed that those with the highest scores on Emotional Intelligence (EI), received the strongest job performance ratings. Those who were most disadvantaged in terms of job performance were not the lowest EI scorers, but rather those who found themselves near the middle of the EI scores continuum. The scholars explained their findings in terms of the trend of expatriates to have high EI and that those with high EI would probably also volunteer to take expatriate assignments in other countries. It would also point to the importance of choosing candidates for expatriate assignments with high scores on EI assessments.

The United Arab Emirates (UAE) is a country committed to change and has undertaken several projects and initiatives to significantly improve its economy over recent decades (Mimouni & Metcalfe, 2011). Research focused on understanding change management and its motivations, especially in the UAE is scarce, making the study of Al-Ali et al. (2017) on "Change management through leadership: the mediating role of organisational culture", published in the *International Journal of Organizational Analysis* all the more remarkable. They found that change-oriented leadership has a positive and significant direct effect on planned change. Busaibe, Singh, Ahmad, and Gaur (2017) also found that the literature on the UAE's industrial sector is limited with regards to organisational culture and innovation leadership. They also stated that leadership stereotypes affect the capacity of eligible women to achieve leadership positions despite studies showing that men and women can perform equally well. Their study took place in the petroleum and natural resources industry, and they found that even though it still plays a central role in the economy, the emirates have been very successful, especially Dubai which, of all the emirates, has the lowest reserves of oil.

Since 1971 three elections have been held in the UAE in 2006, 2011 and 2015. Flogging and stoning are legal judgments in UAE due to Sharia law, which is the personal status law that is applicable to Muslims and non-Muslim expatriates, who are subject to these Sharia rulings on marriage, divorce and child custody (Kirdar, 2010).

10.5.2 Case Examples of Engaging in Emerging Markets Organisations

Another interesting financial services case study was done on Standard Bank, which has a presence in 20 countries, including selected African countries as well as other emerging markets. Standard Bank is one of the largest African banks in the world, with nearly 50,000 employees. It was established in 1862, making it one of South Africa's oldest companies (Standard Bank Annual Report, 2014). Their strategy is, "To build the leading Africa-focused financial services organisation using all our competitive advantages to the full" (Standard Bank Annual Report, 2014).

Customers' evolving requirements are important to consider. For example, customers require simpler and easily accessible service from their financial services' organisations. Another important stakeholder is the Financial Services regulators, and they require compliance, which in turn results in complicated administration. An example of this juggling of the requirements of different stakeholders is the effort of a division, called Standard Bank Corporate and Investment Banking (CIB) to manage the complexities, regulations and risks associated with cross-border trade. This division realised that they need to proactively educate customers to ultimately comply with the regulations of government. To this end, they focus on risk management and advisory services, electronic channels, exchange control consulting as well as market knowledge and information sharing sessions with customers (Standard Bank, 2014). Standard Bank CIB recorded headline earnings of R6.5 billion in the 2013 financial year, which accounted for 38% of Group's headline earnings (Standard Bank, 2014). Another financial services company in South Africa is Nedbank. In a case study on this company, the authors illustrate that Nedbank includes government as a stakeholder in their vision (Scheepers, Maphalala, & Van der Westhuizen, 2014). Given the above discussion on Standard Bank and how important the alignment with regulations is, one can understand that for financial institutions government is an important stakeholder to consider.

Another example is Eskom, Africa's largest power utility, generating 45% of the electricity consumed in Africa. It was established in 1923, consisting of coal-fired power stations, nuclear, hydro and gas power. Eskom produces approximately 95% of South Africa's electricity, according to Scheepers and Marais (2012), who published a case study on the construction of the Medupi Power Station. Eskom buys electricity from and sells electricity to the countries of the Southern African Development Community (SADC). Eskom was converted from a statutory body into a public company in 2002. Eskom's purpose is to provide sustainable electricity solutions to grow the economy and improve the quality of life of the people in South Africa and the region. One of the values of Eskom is, "Sinobuntu", meaning "caring". They also have an employee volunteering programme with this name to encourage employees to participate in charity projects (ESKOM, 2017a).

Eskom initiated a programme, called Back2Basics to drive efficiencies and thus eliminate waste in Eskom. It was also important to them to integrate their silos and to make a "one Eskom" visible. Eskom created a well-structured change management programme, including leadership development, the establishment of a change network, change readiness assessment, impact assessment and communication (ESKOM, 2017b).

Relating to the Sixth enabler, Eskom initiated an extensive stakeholder relationship management programme. Their integrated reporting in their annual report illustrates the focus on multiple stakeholders. They report on the triple bottom line, matters such as Financial (revenue, growth in sales, profit, capital expenditure, debt, equity ratio); Safety (fatalities, employee lost-time incident rate); Socioeconomic (supplier development, BBBEE, Black Economic Empowerment, corporate governance, training and development, corporate social responsibility); Environmental (carbon dioxide, water consumption, etc.).

In terms of our SAA case, as mentioned in the Third enabler's chapter, Ngqula neglected to consult some of the very important role players in the industry (Margolis et al., 2007). His failure to consult labour representatives and internal players such as the pilots' association, and include them in the development of long-term plans, contributed to labour unrest. Ngqula's shortfalls were evident through three examples. He was regarded with suspicion due to a perception of corruption for receiving personal travel gifts, which called his integrity into question. In the middle of the difficult cost-cutting exercise, excessive expenditure on Ngqula's travel and accommodation sent signals that he was not leading by example. These inconsistent behaviours created ample opportunities for unions to claim hypocrisy. This demotivated the rest of the organisation (Margolis et al., 2007).

The extent of the support that Ngqula had in the senior management team was a concern. He sought to downsize from 600 to 300 managers, and only a few accepted the voluntary severance package. The best managers opted to leave, and this indicated that he had failed to establish cooperative relationships. Multiple lessons can be learnt from this SAA case study. Mechanisms should have been created to communicate bottom-up about the changes and not only top-down, for example by creating employee forums. It was particularly important to enlist unions and create opportunities to interact with them as well as employee groupings, so that leadership do not only use unions as a mechanism to talk to employees. We would also recommend leadership to be careful of representatives of certain stakeholder groups or groupings, as they do not always play their role and get a mandate from their groups, or offer feedback to their groups on what took place during project meetings.

In connection with the MMI Case Study (Scheepers & Swart, 2015), The Sixth Enabler: Engagement, is illustrated by the fact that even before the MMI merger, the respective CEOs had in-depth one-on-one discussions to explore the potential benefits of the merger and the prerequisites for its success. One of the former companies was not seen as a dominant player, both companies brought a lot of value to the table and wanted to perceive each other as equal partners.

Both CEOs had to convince their respective boards of the benefits and feasibility of the intended merger. A small group team, consisting of five from Metropolitan and five from Momentum was targeted. Confidentiality was essential as a leak would have caused havoc in the press and in the market, and this small group worked at thrashing out the details of the vision. Metropolitan said that if anything leaked out, then the deal would be off. They invested in building trust, and there was good cooperation within this small group as a merger team. It became evident that the integration between the two companies would be a merger and not an acquisition and that both parties would be equal partners to ensure success. They created a merger committee, consisting of two non-executive board members and two executive board members. Johan Burger was the chairman, who checked that there would be a balanced representation between the two organisations. The merger committee functioned as a governance forum.

Momentum had an informal culture, where titles were not important. The employees had a healthy disrespect for authority and were empowered to question their leadership on decisions.

On the other hand, the other company in the merger, namely Metropolitan had a hierarchical culture, which was more traditional and that had distinct power relationships. What strengthened the ties and overcame the cultural differences, were the values that luckily corresponded. They adhered to values of accountability, innovation, integrity, teamwork, excellence and diversity. A survey of 15,000 employees asked what the values should be and there were similar values across the two organisations.

There were formal communication sessions every week with all stakeholders between April and Nov of 2011. Leadership also conducted a communication road show every week. Even when they did not have anything new to communicate, they communicated anyway, stating that there was nothing new.

The communication included small groups, large forums, one-on-one communication and on the ground visible leadership to remove uncertainty. This assisted in the prevention of the grapevine and offered regular communication of facts and figures. During this time, the business case or reason for the change was communicated and used in decision-making. For example, there was a saying that was used by leadership, namely "the business case prevails", indicating that the common goal of the change process was important and this higher goal superseded the individual companies' goals. An external consulting company was contracted to assist in structuring communication messages to ensure they remained consistent in both the organisations.

10.6 Measuring Sixth Enabler, Engage

Reflection Questions Enabler 6: Engage

Reflection Questions Enabler 6: Engage contains a short questionnaire to help you assess the extent to which you are practicing this enabler. You can also ask others to assess you using this instrument.

10.7 Conclusion and Outcome of the Sixth Enabler, *Engage*

In this chapter, we discussed the sixth enabler, engaging others and demonstrated the importance and process of engaging various stakeholders to result in informed participants. Informing them then, in turn, contributes to committed stakeholders, which assistes in delivering results. The successful outcome of this enabler is therefore represented by employees participating in a change process who then ultimately also becoming change leaders.

In the next enabler, we pay attention to embarking on the change, since the engagement would enable stakeholders to support the change process and take the step of actually implementing the change which would be required next.

References

Abdullah, S. N. (2014). The causes of gender diversity in Malaysian large firms. *Journal of Management and Governance, 18*(4), 1137–1159. https://doi.org/10.1007/s10997-013-9279-0

Al-Ali, A. A., Singh, S. K., Al-Nahyan, M., & Sohal, A. S. (2017). Change management through leadership: The mediating role of organizational culture. *International Journal of Organizational Analysis, 25*(4), 723–739. https://doi.org/10.1108/IJOA-01-2017-1117

Balogun, J. (2007). The practice of organizational restructuring: From design to reality. *European Management Journal, 25*(2), 81–91. https://doi.org/10.1016/j.emj.2007.02.001

Barratt-Pugh, L., Bahn, S., & Gakere, E. (2013). Managers as change agents: Implications for human resource managers engaging with culture change. *Journal of Organizational Change Management, 26*(4), 748–764. https://doi.org/10.1108/JOCM

Blau, P. (1964). *Exchange and power in social life.* New York, NY: Wiley. https://books.google.co.za/books/about/Exchange_and_Power_in_Social_Life.html?id=qhOMLscX-ZYC&redir_esc=y

Boeker, W. (1997). Strategic change: The influence of managerial characteristics and organizational growth. *The Academy of Management Journal, 40*(1), 152–170. Retrieved from http://www.jstor.org/stable/257024

Bozionelos, N., & Singh, S. K. (2017). The relationship of emotional intelligence with task and contextual performance: More than it meets the linear eye. *Personality and Individual Differences, 1*(16), 206–211. https://doi.org/10.1016/j.paid.2016.08.036

Buller, P. F. (1988). For successful strategic change: Blend OD practices with strategic management. *Organisational Dynamics, 16*(3), 42–55. https://doi.org/10.1016/0090-2616(88)90035-6

Busaibe, L., Singh, S. K., Ahmad, S. Z., & Gaur, S. S. (2017). Determinants of organizational innovation: A framework. *Gender in Management: An International Journal, 32*(8), 578–589. https://doi.org/10.1108/GM-01-2017-0007

Christensen, C. M., Marx, M., & Stevenson, H. H. (2009). The tools of cooperation and change. In *Harvard business review collection. Collaborating across silos* (pp. 153–173). Boston, MA: Harvard Business School Publishing Corporation. https://hbr.org/2006/10/the-tools-of-coopera tion-and-change

Cummings, T. G., & Worley, C. G. (2015). *Organization development & change* (10th ed.). Cincinnati, OH: South-Western College Publishing. https://www.loot.co.za/product/thomas-cummings-organization-development-and-change/lszv-2176-g370?referrer=googlemerchant& gclid=CjwKCAjw5vz2BRAtEiwAbcVIL_ 49WYGXAaU1mrKBwWHl3ZZBiQ72sHG5Qwv5JACp9vKcDEEphNuZKhoCKWQQAv D_BwE&gclsrc=aw.ds

Cunningham, C. E., Woodward, C. A., Shannon, H. S., Macintosh, J., Lendrum, B., Rosenbloom, D., & Brown, J. (2002). Readiness for organizational change: A longitudinal study of workplace, psychological and behavioural correlates. *Journal of Occupational and Organizational Psychology, 75*, 377–392. Retrieved from https://pdfs.semanticscholar.org/784c/9c1db72642d882fbb348442dafb81dd71f47.pdf

Doe, R., Ndinguri, E., & Phipps, S. T. A. (2015). Emotional intelligence: The link to success and failure of leadership. *Academy of Educational Leadership Journal, 19*(3), 105–115. Retrieved from http://connection.ebscohost.com/c/articles/113050551/emotional-intelligence-link-suc cess-failure-leadership

Doz, Y. L., & Kosonen, M. (2007). The new deal at the top. *Harvard Business Review, 85*(6), 98–104. https://hbr.org/2007/06/the-new-deal-at-the-top

Eby, L. T., Adams, D. M., Russell, J. E., & Gaby, S. H. (2000). Perceptions of organizational readiness for change: Factors related to employees' reactions to the implementation of team-based selling. *Human Relations, 53*(3), 419–442. Retrieved from http://journals.sagepub.com/doi/10.1177/0018726700533006

Elving, W. J. L. (2005). The role of communication in organisational change. *Corporate Communications: An International Journal, 10*(2), 129–138. https://doi.org/10.1108/13563280510596943

ESKOM. (2017a, September 17). Eskom employees embrace spirit of sinobuntu. http://www.eskom.co.za/news/Pages/Sep17B.aspx

ESKOM. (2017b). Back2Basics programme, information on initiative, posted 26 January 2017. http://www.eskom.co.za/news/Pages/Jann26.aspx

Franken, A., Edwards, C., & Lambert, R. (2009). Executing strategic change: Understanding the critical management elements that lead to success. *California Management Review, 51*(3), 49–73. Retrieved from http://algu.weebly.com/uploads/1/9/2/4/1924527/stra.mgtcase2.pdf

Freeman, R. E. (2010a). *Strategic management: A stakeholder approach.* Boston, MA: Pitman. https://books.google.co.za/books?id=NpmA_qEiOpkC&printsec=frontcover#v=onepage&q& f=false

Freeman, R. E. (2010b). Managing for stakeholders: Trade-offs or value creation. *Journal of Business Ethics, 96*(1), 7–9. https://doi.org/10.1007/s10551-011-0935-5

Freeman, R. E., Wicks, A. C., & Parmar, B. (2004). Stakeholder theory and "the corporate objective revisited". *Organization Science, 15*(3), 364–369. https://doi.org/10.1287/orsc.1040.0066

Gagnon, M. A., Jansen, K. J., & Michael, J. H. (2008). Employee alignment with strategic change: A study of strategy-supportive behaviour among blue-collar employees. *Journal of Managerial Issues, 20*(4), 425–443. Retrieved from https://brainmass.com/file/226808/Article+-+A.pdf

Harris, A., & Sohal, A. S. (2002). Managing change in an aluminium can manufacturing plant: A case study. *Technovation, 22*, 615–623. https://doi.org/10.1016/S0166-4972(01)00063-3

Hazy, J. K., & Uhl-Bien, M. (2015). Towards operationalizing complexity leadership: How generative, administrative and community-building leadership practices enact organizational outcomes. *Leadership, 11*(1), 79–104. https://doi.org/10.1177/1742715013511483

Hillebrandt, H., Sebastian, C., & Blakemore, S. (2010). Experimentally induced social inclusion influences behaviour on trust games. *Cognitive Neuroscience, 2*(1), 27–33. https://doi.org/10.1080/17588928.2010.515020

Invernizzi, E., Romenti, S., & Fumagalli, M. (2012). Identity, communication and change management in Ferrari. *Corporate Communications: An International Journal, 17*(4), 483–497. https://doi.org/10.1108/13563281211274194

Khoza, R. (2012, September 15). *The Ubuntu philosophy as a conceptual framework for interpersonal relationships and leadership.* Retrieved from www.reuelkhoza.co.za: www.reuelkhoza.co.za

Kirdar, S. (2010). United Arab Emirates (UAE). In S. Kelly & J. Breslin (Eds.), *Women's rights in the Middle East and North Africa.* New York: Freedom House. https://www.amazon.com/Womens-Rights-Middle-North-Africa/dp/144220396X

Kotter, J. P. (1996). *Leading change.* Boston, MA: Harvard Business Press. Retrieved from http://www.hbs.edu/faculty/Pages/item.aspx?num=137

Kutz, M. R. (2008, Winter). Toward a conceptual model of contextual intelligence: A transferable leadership construct. *Kravis Leadership Institute, Leadership Review, 8,* 18–31. Retrieved from https://www.researchgate.net/publication/228464894_Toward_a_conceptual_model_of_con textual_intelligence_A_transferable_leadership_construct

Lieberman, M. (2013). *Social: Why our brains are wired to connect.* New York, NY: Oxford University Press. https://www.amazon.com/Social-Why-Brains-Wired-Connect/dp/0307889092

Lines, R. (2004). Influence of participation in strategic change: Resistance, organisational commitment and change goal achievement. *Journal of Change Management, 4*(3), 193–215. https://doi.org/10.1080/1469701042000221696

Magner, C. (2007). Contextual leadership development: A South African perspective. *European Business Review, 20*(2), 128–141. https://doi.org/10.1108/09555340810858270

Margolis, J., Roberts, L. M., & Winig, L. (2007). South African Airways, A and B (SAA). Case study: 9-407-014 (A), 9-407-024 (B). Harvard Business School Publishing, Feb 26, 2007, pp. 1–21 (A); 9-407-024, Feb 26, 2007, pp. 1–4. https://store.hbr.org/product/south-african-airways-a/407014?sku=407014-PDF-ENG

McClellan, J. G. (2011). Reconsidering communication and the discursive politics of organisational change. *Journal of Change Management, 11*(4), 465–480. https://doi.org/10.1080/14697017.2011.630508

Mimouni, F., & Metcalfe, B. (2011). *Leadership development in the Middle East.* Northampton, MA: Edward Elgar. https://www.amazon.com/Leadership-Development-Middle-Beverly-Metcalfe/dp/1847206158

Mitchell, R. K., Agle, B. R., & Wood, D. J. (1997). Toward a theory of stakeholder identification and salience: Defining the principle of who and what really counts. *Academy of Management Review, 22*(4), 853–888. Retrieved from http://www.jstor.org/stable/259247

Puleo, G. (2011). *Causes and maintenance factors of employee burnout during transformational organizational change.* Walden University, ProQuest Dissertations Publishing, 3475108. https://search.proquest.com/openview/02ba7bc8b55588891fb198f53fa3f759/1?pq-origsite=gscholar&cbl=18750&diss=y

Quinn, R. E. (2004). Building the bridge as you walk on it. *Leader to Leader, (34),* 21–26. https://doi.org/10.1002/ltl.97

Ringleb, A., & Rock, D. (2008). The emerging field of NeuroLeadership. *Neuroleadership Journal, 1,* 3–19. https://neuroleadership.com/portfolio-items/the-emerging-field-of-neuroleadership-2/

Rizzolatti, G., & Sinigaglia, C. (2016). The mirror mechanism: A basic principle of brain function. *Nature Reviews Neuroscience, 17*(12), 757. https://doi.org/https://doi.org/10.1038/nrn.2016.135. Retrieved from https://www.ncbi.nlm.nih.gov/pubmed/27761004

Rock, D. (2009). *Your brain at work: Strategies for overcoming distraction, regaining focus, and working smarter all day*. New York: HarperCollins. https://www.harpercollins.com/ 9780061771293/your-brain-at-work/

Rock, D., & Schwartz, J. (2006). The neuroscience of leadership. *Strategy Business, 43*, 72–82. https://www.strategy-business.com/article/06207?gko=f1af3

Rogers, E. M. (2003). *Diffusion of innovations* (5th ed.). New York, NY: Free Press. https://www. amazon.com/s?k=Rogers%2C+E.+M.+%282003%29.+Diffusion+of+innovations+%285th +ed.%29.+New+York%2C+NY%3A+Free+Press.&i=stripbooks-intl-ship&ref=nb_sb_noss

Scheepers, C. B., Maphalala, J., & Van der Westhuizen, C. (2014). *Nedbank: Transformational leadership in sustainable turnaround*. Ivey Publishing, 9B14C027. https://www.iveycases.com/ ProductView.aspx?id=63290

Scheepers, C. B., & Marais, S. (2012). *Constructing the Medupi power station*. Ivey Publishing, 9B12C015. https://www.iveycases.com/ProductView.aspx?id=54012

Scheepers, C. B., & Swart, S. (2015). *Momentum and metropolitan merger: Authentic transformational leadership*. Ivey Publishing, 9B15C004. https://www.iveycases.com/ProductView.aspx? id=70560

Scheepers, C. B., Swart, S., Alexander, K., & Parbhoo, H. (2017). Women's movements in emerging markets. In S. Chengadu & C. B. Scheepers (Eds.), *Women leadership in emerging markets* (pp. 65–104). New York, NY: Routledge, Taylor and Francis. Retrieved from https:// www.routledge.com/Women-Leadership-in-Emerging-Markets-Featuring-46-Women-Leaders/Chengadu-Scheepers/p/book/9781138188969

Schilling, A., Werr, A., Gand, S., & Sardas, J.-C. (2012). Understanding professionals' reactions to strategic change: The role of threatened professional identities. *The Service Industries Journal, 32*(8), 1229–1245. https://doi.org/10.1080/02642069.2010.531269

Shin, J., Taylor, M. S., & Seo, M.-G. (2012). Resources for change: The relationships of organizational inducements and psychological resilience to employees' attitudes and behaviors toward organizational change. *Academy of Management Journal, 55*(3), 727–748. Retrieved from https://journals.aom.org/doi/abs/10.5465/amj.2010.0325?journalCode=amj

Siegel, D. J. (2006). An interpersonal neurobiology approach to psychotherapy. *Psychiatric Annals, 36*(4), 248–252. https://www.healio.com/journals/psycann/2006-4-36-4/%7B231a1eb0-7230-4ff8-b173-c7f31c6b823f%7D/an-interpersonal-neurobiology-approach-to-

Sonenshein, S. (2010). We're changing—Or are we? Untangling the role of progressive, regressive, and stability narratives during strategic change implementation. *Academy of Management Journal, 53*(3), 477–512. http://www.jstor.org/stable/25684333

Spillane, J. P. (2005). Distributed leadership. *The Educational Forum, 69*(2), 143–150. https://doi. org/10.1080/00131720508984678

Standard Bank. (2014). Annual report of Standard Bank Ltd. https://reporting.standardbank.com/ results-reports/annual-reports/

Swart, T., Chisholm, K., & Brown, P. (2015). *Neuroscience for leadership: Harnessing the brain gain advantage*. London: Palgrave Macmillan. https://www.amazon.com/Neuroscience-Leader ship-Harnessing-Advantage-Business/dp/1137466855

Todd, A. (1999). Managing radical change. *Long Range Planning, 32*(2), 237–244. https://doi.org/ 10.1016/S0024-6301(99)00022-9

Uhl-Bien, M., & Arena, M. (2017). Complexity leadership: Enabling people and organizations for adaptability. *Organizational Dynamics, 46*, 9–20. https://doi.org/10.1016/j.orgdyn.2016.12.001

Van Eeden, A., Sutherland, M., & Scheepers, C. B. (2016). An exploration of the perceived relationship between the level of power of stakeholder groups and their resistance to organisational change. *South African Journal of Labour Relations, 40*(2), 99–117. Retrieved from https://repository.up.ac.za/bitstream/handle/2263/58439/VanEeden_Exploration_2016. pdf?sequence=1

Vithessonthi, C. (2010). Resistance to change as issue selling in multinational firms. *Journal of Organisational Transformation and Social Change, 7*(3), 265–284. https://doi.org/10.1386/jots. 7.3.265_1

Walumba, F. O., Avolio, B. J., & Aryee, S. (2011). Leadership and management research in Africa: A synthesis and suggestions for future research. *Journal of Occupational and Organizational Psychology, 84*(3). https://doi.org/10.1111/j.2044-8325.2011.02034.x

Wellman, J. (2007) Leadership behaviors in matrix environments. *Project Management Journal, 38* (2), 62–74. Retrieved from https://www.pmi.org/learning/library/leadership-behaviors-matrix-environments-2368

Williams, K. D., & Sommer, K. L. (1997). Social ostracism by one's coworkers: Does rejection lead to loafing or compensation? *Personality and Social Psychology Bulletin, 23*, 693–706. https://doi.org/10.1177/0146167237003.

Yammarino, F. J., Salas, E., Serban, A., Shirreffs, K., & Shuffler, M. L. (2012). Collectivistic leadership approaches. Putting the "we" in leadership science and practice. *Industrial & Organisational Psychology, 2*, 382–402. https://doi.org/10.1111/j.1754-9434.2012.01467.x

Yukl, G., & Mahsud, R. (2010). Why flexible and adaptive leadership is essential. *Consulting Psychology Journal: Practice and Research, 62*(2), 81–93. https://doi.org/https://doi.org/10.1037/a0019835. Retrieved from https://pdfs.semanticscholar.org/1fae/5d54bc194adce1d785c90a234f57034380f9.pdf

Reference List for Quotes

Blanchard, K. (2007). *The heart of a leader: Insights on the art of influence* (p. 3). Colorado Springs, CO: David C Cook Publishers. https://www.amazon.com/Heart-Leader-Insights-Art-Influence/dp/0781445434

Eisenberger, N., & Lieberman, M. (2009). The pains and pleasures of social life. *Science, 323* (5916), 890–891. https://pubmed.ncbi.nlm.nih.gov/19213907/

Mandela, N. R. (1994). *Long walk to freedom: The autobiography of Nelson Mandela*. London: Time Warner Books. https://www.amazon.com/Long-Walk-Freedom-Autobiography-Mandela/dp/0316548189

Seventh Enabler

Embark

You can never cross the ocean until you have the courage to lose sight of the shore.
(Christopher Columbus, n.d.)
Whatever you can do, or dream you can, begin it.
Boldness has genius, power and magic in it.
(Johann Wolfgang von Goethe, n.d.)
The brave man is not he who does not feel afraid, but he who conquers that fear.
(Nelson Mandela, 1994)

Electronic supplementary material The online version of this chapter (https://doi.org/10.1007/978-3-030-40846-6_11) contains supplementary material, which is available to authorized users.

© Springer Nature Switzerland AG 2020
C. B. Scheepers, S. Swart, *Change Leadership in Emerging Markets*, Future of Business and Finance, https://doi.org/10.1007/978-3-030-40846-6_11

Learning Outcomes

At the end of this chapter, change leaders will be able to:

- Identify forces for and against the change, pitfalls and barriers and design strategies to deal effectively with these
- Effectively deal with resistance to change
- Plan change interventions to support vision implementation
- Design a communication strategy to support vision implementation
- Jointly develop goals to deliver vision

11.1   Orientation to Embarking

While the Sixth Enabler paid attention to engaging stakeholders, the next enabler focuses on the actual embarking on the change, by paying attention to the finer detail of who needs to do what by when.

11.1.1 Change Process Mapping

Sometimes, strategic goals remain just that: goals. Without effective tactical and operational plans coherent with this change, strategy is not actually implemented. Fenton (2007) advises utilising process maps, which are traditionally applied to business process re-engineering. We concur; in our experience of being part of huge transformational change projects, the utilisation of detailed Gantt charts and/or Microsoft Project software with detailed plans on the rollout is critical, especially, regarding how the different streams interconnect and the phased rollout of certain parts of the project will influence the delivery of other sections. Isern, Meaney, and Wilson (2009) declare that successful strategic transformations share design themes, such as well-defined processes.

Fenton (2007), in this regard, recommends that these change process maps can be co-opted as a communication tool in diffusing strategic change. A change initiative is thus first mapped at a strategic level; tactical and operational plans are built by charting subsegments of this map in successively greater detail. Levin and Gottlieb (2009) too, advise building the right structure and environment to create commitment to organisational change. Manning (2012) also emphasises that having sufficient resources to implement change and developing an implementation plan (who, what and when) will lead to successful change.

11.1.2 Roles and Responsibilities

In this Seventh Enabler, change leadership must focus on creating a structure to embark on the change. We support Holbeche's (2007) explanation that structure governs and allocates responsibility and accountability to individuals and teams. It directs the distribution of power within the organisation, as well as encompasses outlining role descriptions, processes, remuneration and reward structures and boundaries. It is important to note here, that business as usual must be maintained, while change is being implemented. The current organisation must sustain service delivery to existing clients, while working on new realities for the future.

This phenomenon has recently been described in the literature as the importance for an organisation to be contextually ambidextrous (Havermans, Den Hartog, Keegan, & Uhl-Bien, 2015). To be contextually ambidextrous means to equally adapt the current strengths as well as the application of new possibilities within a subsystem, and it implies looking for new information, while at the "same time using the established information, and ultimately alternate between these abilities" (Havermans et al., 2015, p. 194). Dixon, Meyer, and Day (2010) too, emphasise that an organisation requires more than focussing on the current reality or operational capabilities. It is also crucial to focus on dynamic capabilities, where the resources must be modified to address the rapidly changing environments.

In our experience, it rarely happens that a large team is dedicated to the change project. There are regularly a couple of core team members, and the rest is seconded for a while during the project, and most of the people have a percentage of their time that they spend on the change project. These dual roles create an immense amount of stress, because it also creates a matrix-type structure, where the change project manager gives instructions as well as the line manager of the individual. The impact of this is frustration and must be managed with consideration. On the other hand, having people who are still functioning in the business, allocated to the project on a part-time basis, has the benefit of improving communication between the business and the change project. These change project team members are also in touch with the day-to-day functioning of the business and could offer input to the project on the implications of the changes.

Nonetheless, as Holbeche (2007) emphasises, when implementing these matrix structures, it is vital that leaders provide clear role descriptions. Having numerous managers requesting work from employees can result in a lack of focus and goal achievement, which can cause changes in the organisation to lose momentum and cause frustration (Holbeche, 2007). Salem (2008) also stresses that changes are messy, characterised by conflicting emotions among organisational members, as well as a lack of identification with the change and even a lack of trust (Salem, 2008).

We observed that the exposure that the seconded team members regularly have in these change projects accelerate their own career development, especially as these change projects often have consultants involved, who have experience of different organisations, often across different industries and this expertise and experience benefit the project team members. We will refer more to this phenomenon during the discussion of the final Tenth Enabler: Exit; however, it is sufficient to mention here that in cases where the seconded team members gained exposure and expertise in these change teams, it greatly benefited the organisation in sustaining the changes.

11.2   Importance of Embarking

This section pays attention to the importance of Embarking. We refer to how this enabler assists in mitigating risks and enables communication and participation in the change process.

11.2.1 Mitigating Risks

An essential element in the Seventh Enabler is to identify risks associated with the change implementation. One of the dangers is the disconnect between perception and reality of change. In this regard, Van de Ven and Sun (2011) suggest that leadership creates a framework to diagnose fixable weaknesses and to identify fatal breakdowns. One of the risks is being overloaded. Balogun (2007) warns that employees tend to buckle under the pressures of the change process, as well as the added responsibilities. Earlier in 2003, Balogun argued that the impact of having to help others through change and implement operational changes, while having to go through change yourself, creates a heavy workload for line managers, which can become unmanageable (Balogun, 2007).

Franken, Edwards, and Lambert (2009) identify the difficulty of securing the required resources to execute a strategy and emphasise that when an organisation gets to the point of executing a given strategy, it must attract, allocate and manage all the necessary resources to deliver the strategic change. During change processes, professional people might experience a risk to their professional identity and Schilling, Werr, Gand, and Sardas (2012) found that they either exit or voice their opposition. These researchers thus advise that attention has to be paid to the reactions of professionals to strategic change of either using the change process to promote and develop themselves (self-enhancement) or using the change process to differentiate themselves (self-distinctiveness).

Allen, Jimmieson, Bordia, and Irmer (2007) state that specific change-related uncertainties might be best addressed by different sources of communication. They recommend that direct supervisors are the preferred sources of implementation-related and job-relevant information during the change, while senior management typically should provide more strategic information. Trust was found to influence which sources employees would prefer, as well as how they appraise the information that they receive. It implies that effective communication between those responsible for formulating the strategy and those implementing it at the coalface, is critical.

11.2.2   Change Communication

Reissner, Pagan, and Smith (2011) recommend the use of stories and metaphors as a means of communicating an organisational change process. It may be interpreted differently by different stakeholders. Change leaders have to engage stakeholders on how they can assist in the organisational change. The story can demonstrate the need for all members of the organisation to play their role to implement the change successfully. They also warn that the story's ambiguity could lead to fragmentation.

Continuous information on the intention to change work practices contributes to significant improvements over time (Mortenius, Fridlund, Marklund, Palm, & Baigi, 2012). Lewis and Seibold (2009) emphasise formal as well as informal communication practices during the change. On the other hand, poorly managed change communication results in rumours and resistance to change, exaggerating the negative aspects of the change (DiFonzo, Bordia, & Rosnow, 1994). Communication should therefore largely be driven to alleviate the uncertainties around the aim, process and expected outcomes of the change and implications for the individual employees (Buono & Bowditch, 2003).

McGlone and Batchelor (2003) emphasise that people by nature are hesitant to deliver bad news and the deliverer often uses a euphemism to make the delivery of bad news easier. Dibble and Levine (2013) too, discovered people delay passing on negative feedback, distort information to appear less negative and seek less immediate channels to deliver bad news.

11.2.3   Participation

Encouragement to participate is critical in gaining buy-in to change. When ideas about the change are collected, they would need to be followed up by implementing suggestions where appropriate (Van Dijk & Van Dick, 2009). Participative decision-making has also been emphasised by Ferrin and Dirks (2002) as management practices through which trust may be increased.

We would like to encourage two-way communication. We have experienced during several change processes, that a feedback loop is important where a bottom-up interaction is required, in addition to the top-down communication. Gioia and Chittipeddi (1991) suggest, for example, that when the CEO communicates a planned strategic change to stakeholders, sense-giving by the CEO triggers sense-making by the stakeholders. This process can subsequently be reversed, leading to further sense-making by the CEO and to social construction that ultimately results in a jointly conceptualised view of the change. Rouleau (2005) also advises that this iterative sense-making and sense-giving continues at more operational levels as the strategic change is implemented, for example in the manner in which middle managers communicate with their stakeholders.

A radical shift in the role of senior managers from the traditional authoritarian, command and control style to a more open, participative management style is required.

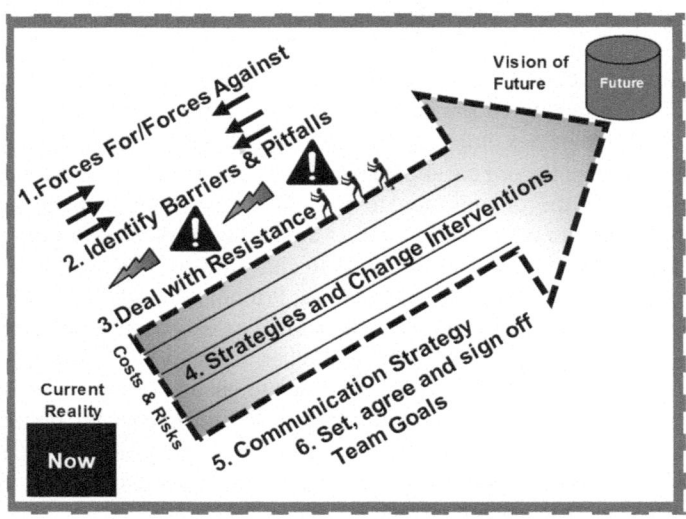

Fig. 11.1   The embarking process (Authors' own)

With the emphasis now on cooperation, collaboration and communication, managers need to hone a completely different range of leadership skills (Graetz, 2000).

11.3   Embarking in Practice

Once stakeholders have been identified, decision makers have signed off the initial project scope, change agents have been appointed and stakeholders' initial needs, fears and desires have been determined and confirmed, we can now start the embarking process. The illustration below demonstrates that the embarking process consists of the following steps: Determining the forces for and forces against the change and identifying the potential barriers and pitfalls during the change. The strategies for dealing with resistance are then determined, change interventions are planned, the communication strategy is formulated and team goals are set, agreed and signed off (Fig. 11.1).

11.3.1   Force Field Analysis

The force field analysis was developed in the nineteen forties by the father of Change Management, Kurt Lewin (1947) and is one of the oldest and most classic change tools available. Although it is really simple to use, it is very powerful and can provide many ideas on how to best manage the change to ensure successful implementation. It can be used in a team setting or as a stand-alone "desk tool" used by the change leader or the change agents. It only requires you to consider who will be your supporters (inside and outside the organisation) and how their support can be utilised to give the change a boost. It also asks you to consider who will be the resistors (inside and outside the organisation) to the change and what can be done to convince them otherwise. Other than just people it could also refer to non-human forces such as uncertainty, morale, legislation, lack of resources, timing, other changes in the environment, such as political volatility or leadership changes. The objective here is to compile as many positive and negative forces as possible to ensure all the bases are covered and strategies are in place to deal with the forces.

Tool 7.1 Force Field Analysis: Forces For and Against the Change

Tool 7.1 provides an opportunity for change leaders to identify the issues, things and/or people that will help the change and then devise strategies to capitalise on this positive force. It further helps with the identification of issues, things and/or people who will work against the change and identify what could be done to deal with the negative forces.

11.3.2 Potential Pitfalls/Barriers

In some instances, a simple analysis of which things or situations might pose pitfalls or barriers would suffice. The tool below considers potential pitfalls/barriers and offers an opportunity to conduct this analysis.

Tool 7.2 Potential Pitfalls/Barriers

In addition to the Force Field Analysis, the Pitfalls and Barriers tool can also be used to anticipate possible reasons for the failure of the change project and then develop action plans to address these. Once these strategies have been identified, they can be used to populate the action plans in Tool 7.9.

11.3.3 Dealing with Resistance

Change leaders must identify potential sources of resistance and deal with them proactively. The following tool offers an opportunity to conduct this analysis on resistance.

Tool 7.3 Dealing with Resistance

Tool 7.3 helps change teams anticipate sources of resistance and proactively strategise how they will deal with this resistance. It is also handy to use after an engagement meeting to analyse the objections that were offered in the meeting and to decide what to do about the objections. The checklist in Tool 7.3 also helps to point you in the right direction. Although the list is not definitive, it is a very good start.

11.3.4 Change Strategies

At this point in the change process, change leaders have to purposefully identify specific change strategies to move the organisation forward towards the vision. The next tool facilitates this identification process.

Tool 7.4 List of 5–8 Change Strategies

Once the vision has been defined using the Balanced SMART vision (see Tool 5.5, Enabler 5, Envision) by the decision makers, the next step in the process is to identify the 5–8 change strategies that need to be formulated to ensure the vision is realised. These strategies will be high-level drivers that will lead to the realisation of the vision. We advise that line managers of the organisation lead, own and drive these strategies. These strategies will thus also be communicated through line management to the rest of the organisation. Tool 7.4 in the Toolkit provides a template to list these strategies.

Practical Application: Change Strategies

In Tool 5.4, we shared the consulting work we conducted for an African university that decided to change from an agricultural college to a university. The following seven strategies were identified to take them from where they were to realising their vision.

Seven Strategies

Research
Graduates
Programmes
Employees
Staff
Outreach
Influence policy
Income

Once the Steering Committee (SC) has identified the 5–8 strategies, these strategies should then be communicated to and agreed with line management, who in turn will need to build these strategies into their daily goals. It remains the responsibility of line management to cascade the vision, strategies and goals to those reporting to them. The change agents are resources to support these efforts. Change agents also support by providing the change interventions that will be discussed in Tool 7.5.

Change agents will be tasked to meet with the decision makers in their respective stakeholder groups, engage with them regarding the vision and strategies, and then discuss how the vision could be translated into a vision for the particular stakeholder group. Once there is clarity on the vision and the measures of the vision for the stakeholder group, they can debate if the 5–8 strategies set by the SC are relevant to their area of responsibility and add or remove strategies. Change agents then move on to develop change interventions to support the change strategies.

11.3.5 Change Interventions

Once the "hard" strategies have been dealt with, the "softer" change interventions need to be put in place to support the change implementation. Change interventions are the groups of actions that need to be done over and above the abovementioned "hard" strategies to move the organisation towards realising the vision.

Tool 7.5 Change Interventions

This tool offers the opportunity to identify the "softer" change interventions. They will be led and supported by the steering committee, change leaders and change agents. It is specific to managing the change and ensures the "softer" side of change management is dealt with. Tool 7.5 lists the following "softer" strategies: Engagement, Awareness, Consultation, Education, Measurement and Reviews. It also encourages change leaders to develop action plans with target dates and accountabilities for each of these softer strategies.

11.3.6 Communication Strategy

It is essential to place emphasis on the communication strategy. The next tool offers the opportunity to systematically plan the when, what, how and who specific to each stakeholder group.

Tool 7.6 Communication Strategy

We believe the communication strategy is critical enough to justify its own strategy. A communication strategy template has thus been included in this volume to ensure it is dealt with in enough detail. Template 7.6 in the Toolkit provides an outline to develop a communication strategy for each of the stakeholder groups.

11.3.7 Team Goals

The next tool emphasises the formulation of specific achievable outputs with their respective responsibilities.

Tool 7.7 Team Outputs

For each of the 5–8 strategies, we suggest an output be formulated. An output consists of 2 to 3-word definitions, written in the end state, using nouns and

(continued)

Tool 7.7 (continued)
short descriptive adjectives. The outputs will be powerful responses to the challenges faced in the environment. Only actions will lead to achievement of the vision. The vision has to be broken into achievable outputs. Here the team spends time together to answer the question: What needs to be done to ensure the vision becomes a reality? Once outputs have been agreed upon, team members decide who will lead each output. Leading does not mean doing. Others might need to do the work, but the leader will be held accountable and needs to ensure the delivery of actions by others. Tool 7.7 outlines the outputs with the name of the change agent who will play the lead role.

Practical Application: Team Outputs

The African University mentioned in Tools 5.4 and 7.3, developed the following seven outputs:

Top Seven Outputs

Outputs	Lead Role
Impactful innovative research	FPJ
Industry ready graduates	RMP
Demand driven, quality academic programmes	BOL
Competitive conditions of service for employees	SK
Competent efficient productive staff	IMM
Effective knowledge dissemination and outreach	JB
Influence policy	ML
Income generating products and services	TN

As follow-up to the formulated outputs, the team must now specify the roles each team member will play.

Tool 7.8 Team Outputs and Role Matrix

For each output, a leader is now appointed by the team. The person fulfilling the leader role implies someone who engages with his fellow team members to

(continued)

Tool 7.8 (continued)
design an action plan, containing who will do what, how and when. He then holds these "supporters" accountable for delivering the actions as he is ultimately accountable for the delivery of the overall output. There might be team members who will not be required to do anything, but still need to be informed. They receive an "I" in the corresponding block. Those team members who need to be consulted, receive a "C", and if no role is required, these team members get a dash in their respective blocks. The Team Outputs and Role Matrix is then completed. Tool 7.8 enables the team to have a holistic view of who will be fulfilling which roles for each of the outputs.

Once the outputs and roles and responsibilities have been finalised, the next step is detailed action plans with delivery dates.

Tool 7.9 Team Action Plan

For each output, an action plan now needs to be developed. Each action needs to appoint an accountable person and agree on a target date for delivery with the accountable person. We have found this to be **the crux of execution**. When a person completes an action that is aligned to strategy and vision on a specific date, progress towards vision implementation is made. The dream is now becoming a reality! Tool 7.9 provides the Team Action Plan template.

11.3.8 Goal Pursuit

As mentioned in Enabler 6, Engage, we define a goal as follows: A goal = an output + an agreed action plan + an accountable person assigned to each action + agreed target dates for delivery of each action.

The SMART (specific, measurable, attainable, realistic and time bound) goal model was published first in the eighties. However, there is more to goal pursuit than goal setting, and many organisations often stop at goal setting. The AIM Model (Antecedents, Integration and Maintenance), developed by Berkman and Rock (2014) states that goal pursuit is a three-step process of setting goals, delivering goals and maintaining goals. In Enabler 7, we set goals and in Enabler 8, Execute, we focus on achieving and maintaining goals. Success requires setting, delivery, as well as maintenance of goals (Berkman & Rock, 2014).

Van Hecke et al., (2010, p. 183) confirms our belief that outputs must be "outcome-based and linked to the change vision". But goals must also be "sticky", meaning that they must remain front of mind and on the tip of the tongue, because people are busy and have limited attentional resources (Berkman & Rock, 2014).

11.4   Neuroscience Insights into Embarking

In Chap. 3, we explored what happens when the brain is exposed to a threat. The brain will either resist through fighting or avoid the issue by disengaging. If, however, we have completed the Envisioning (Enabler 5) and Engaging (Enabler 6) processes, we can now start the Embarking process by making it easy for the brain to get used to the idea of the change. Novel experiences positioned as positive contributors to survival can cause a dopamine rush. When we experience and learn something new, new neural connections are formed, and we become intrigued by the change. Although the vision is the ultimate destination, small goals will get us to our final destination.

As we learned in Chap. 3, our comfort zones and our existing routines are both pleasurable to the brain and when the brain experiences pleasure, the neurotransmitter dopamine is released. When we have to learn something new, the prefrontal cortex is utilised, a lot of energy is required, and the brain perceives this as something painful. Fortunately, if we perceive the new skill as something that will improve our chances of survival and if we manage to perform the new skills without too much disappointment, dopamine will also be released.

In the book *Change or Die*, Alan Deutschman (2007) researched what happens when people are told they will die for certain if they do not change their behaviour. Would they still resist the change? The odds are nine to one that they will not change their behaviour. Deutschman is very clear that Fear, Force and Facts are not effective strategies to deal with resistance to change and proposes the following effective strategies: Relate, Repeat and Reframe. When someone you admire coaches or guides you and relates to your resistance, when you repeat the healthy behaviour, until it becomes a habit, and when you reframe your future, by imagining what it could look like through a slow deliberate and disciplined process, it increases the probability of successful change (Deutschman, 2007).

Change leaders and agents are therefore required to position themselves as partners, mentors and role models. They need to allow those who have to change the opportunity to repeat the change often, until it becomes automatic, and they have to provide those involved in the change, hope and a belief that the future is going to be an improvement on the past. Paradigms are not changed by providing people with facts. Facts appeal to the PFC, but it does not address our survival instincts. If the centre of fear, our amygdala, perceives the change to be a threat to our existence, no facts can ever convince us to change our behaviour. Each step in the process needs to be designed to be non-threatening. That is, the cost of failure should not be high.

When successes are experienced, people get a dopamine rush and will support the change. However, this requires intensive repetition, and it requires a well-trained coach to regularly monitor and support the person going through the change. Over time, the new thinking and behaviour, will become new habits.

People don't resist change, they resist being changed (Peter Senge, n.d.).

11.4.1 Goal Setting

Goal setting is a surprisingly sophisticated psychological tool. When we set a goal, it has a profound effect on how we see ourselves. Even if we have not yet achieved the goal, it becomes part of who we think we are. This happens because the subconscious brain has trouble understanding the difference between what we want and what we have. When the conscious mind realises that the goal has not yet been reached, we are in a state of constant tension, because of this. The conscious brain then starts working towards the achievement of the goal (Kegler, 2014).

Once we consciously focus on a goal, the brain subconsciously evaluates goal-relevant information in our environment, which is consistent with achieving the goal (Kegler, 2014). Like radar, it selectively notices incoming data that may contribute to, or influence the goal. Simultaneously, the brain inhibits irrelevant information to protect us from information overload. Researchers found that subconscious goal-relevant factors contribute to conscious perceptions (Vorhauser-Smith, 2011).

We can use our senses to activate our brain into a state of high alert towards our goals. By using our imagination, we visualise what it would feel like, sound like, smell like, look like, when we have achieved our goal. This will activate the Reticular Activating System (RAS) of our brain. The RAS acts like a filter capturing anything related to the achievement of our goal and brings it to our conscious awareness. This will help our goals become "sticky" (Berkman & Rock, 2014).

As our brains reward us by releasing dopamine as every milestone is reached, it is useful to break the goal down into smaller action plans and ensure every step is measurable. This will provide a flow of constant morale boosters as milestones are being reached.

Our brain requires a large amount of energy. Although the brain accounts for less than 2% of a person's weight, it consumes 20% of the body's energy (Drubach, 2000). To conserve energy, our brain acts as a subconscious prediction machine and selectively limits the stimuli we notice and process. The brain is also attentive to noticing anomalies in our subconscious predictions.

YouTube Clip: Umar Hameed

7 Step Neuroscience-Based Goal Setting Process
https://www.youtube.com/watch?v=NdzqeePm5CY
Brain chemistry lifehacks: Steve Ilardi at TEDxKC
https://www.youtube.com/watch?v=8bnniNxqB4w

11.4.2 Decision-Making

In instances where people may display certain psychiatric disorders such as depression or hoarding, decision-making can become very difficult. For depressed individuals, nothing seems to be rewarding, and for the hoarder, nothing appears to be worthy of detachment. Here the cognitive control systems seem to be impaired.

When we have to choose between various options in differing situations, the neurons in the dorsolateral and ventromedial prefrontal cortex start interacting (Fig. 11.2). These areas are also active during flexible decision-making. Thus, the prefrontal cortex is not only active when self-control is required, but also when there are conflicting preferences during decision-making (Rudorf & Hare, 2014).

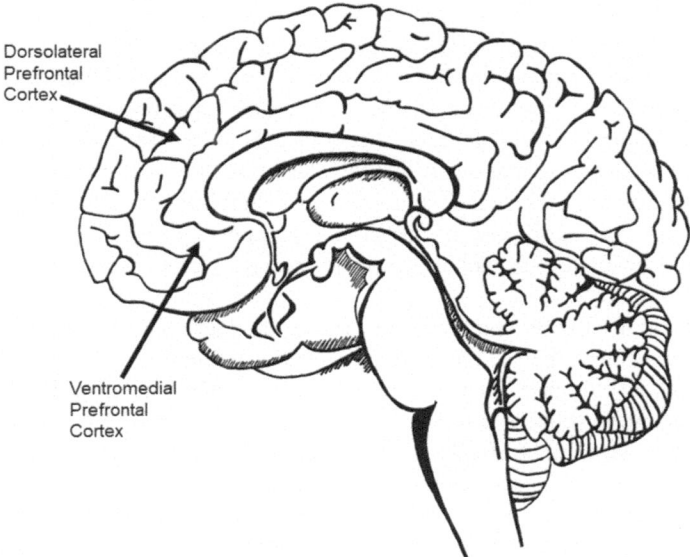

Fig. 11.2 Parts of the brain active in decision-making (Authors' own)

We cannot make effective decisions without the motivation and meaning provided by emotional input. The unusual case of Antonio Damasio's patient, "Elliott" proves this fact (Damasio, 2005). Elliot was a successful businessman, but after a brain tumour was removed, he lost his orbitofrontal cortex, the section of the brain that connects the frontal lobes with the emotions. Elliot could no longer show any emotions, and he could also no longer make any decisions. Damasio later hypothesised that emotion supports our decisions (Jarrett, 2014). However, emotions can also get in the way of rational decision-making. Commitment to a failing plan can be increased when employees become angry. If you as a change leader understand this, it could help you deal with these negative emotions by investigating and asking questions and trying to understand why employees are hanging onto the old way of doing things (Tsai & Young, 2009). There might be deeper reasons than the obvious ones, which have to be explored and evaluated. Engaging and asking pertinent questions to those who resist change are therefore essential.

11.5   Embarking in Emerging Markets

11.5.1   Case Examples of Embarking in the Emerging Markets Contexts

In emerging markets, informal relations are critical. For example, Gomes, Angwin, Peter, and Mellahi (2012) found that in the Nigerian banking sectors pre-merger Human Resource Management practices such as due diligence were influenced by existing social relationships between managers and owners of merged banks. Relating to this Seventh Enabler, their study also revealed that effective formal communication during pre-merger, during and postmerger processes, had a profound effect on the success of the transition and acceptance, thus assisting with alleviating fears of staff. Therefore, communication should be timely, appropriate and continuous, while using multiple media at region-specific levels to be effective. Another important feature of emerging markets is that there are generally multiple cultures to deal with. In this regard, these scholars advise that cultural differences on regional and national levels are significant. If the national cultures are too diverse, pre-existing banks could be trading separately to avoid cultural clashes, according to Gomes et al. (2012).

During the discussion above, we mentioned the lack of talented resources as a hindrance to change. This is particularly relevant for emerging markets. For example, in India, a study by Coad and Pawan (2012) revealed that although SMEs can translate technical skills to commercial success, they often do not have access to technical knowledge to be able to do this successfully. There are various options for increasing the resources required to execute change. For example, alliances and joint ventures can close this gap and offer SMEs more rapid growth opportunities than what internal growth strategies can offer. Alliances and joint ventures significantly involve large firms partnering with SMEs, thus sharing the risk, especially for projects with uncertainty around their outcome (Koryak et al., 2015).

We observed that it depends on the type of growth strategy that the organisation applies. For example, the majority of growth strategies are based on Ansoff's (1988) Product–Market Matrix, also known as Ansoff's growth matrix. Ansoff's growth matrix has four strategies: **market penetration** (selling more of the same product or market service to the same market) or **market development** (selling more of the same thing to different markets) or **product development** (selling different products or services to the same market) or **diversification** (selling completely different products or services to different markets). Depending on the strategy, the type of resources would need to be contracted.

The emerging markets are moreover, characterised by volatility. Companies that have been dealing more effectively with the economic recession, have been those that put great emphasis on transparent, swift and regular communication with customers, in addition to the usual focus on employees, particularly with regards to the possible business implications of the downturn (Kailasam, Johri, & Wongsurawat, 2013). Communication assists the affected parties in implementing better measures of dealing with the change.

In line with the issues around lack of resources, South Africa has a labour market paradox of an oversupply of unskilled labour and a shortage of skills required to enhance economic growth. Horwitz (2013) observes that there is growing mobility in the South African labour market and "churn" caused by professionals and skilled technical people job-hopping, which could be eased by more effective motivation and retention strategies regarding intellectual capital. This talent management research in South Africa and East Asia shows that professional workers at high skill levels in knowledge-intensive industries highly value work motivation, job satisfaction and effective skill utilisation.

The next section pays attention to change in several emerging markets and to Malaysia in particular. While the rest of Latin America's dependence on commodity-led growth has been negative, Mexico's economy was and will benefit from continued US growth (Rayner, 2015). Indonesia's new leader, Joko Widodo, has a different style to his predecessors and has a reform agenda of cutting wasteful fuel subsidies that rather benefitted the rich than the poor, for whom it was intended. With Indonesia's strong demographics and a low-cost labour force, it offers a tremendous opportunity to unlock manufacturing potential. Widodo realised that the subsidy system impaired the ability to develop infrastructure. It will eventually be stopped (Rayner, 2015).

The impact of globalisation has substantially increased government focus on economic development and industrialisation in Malaysia. As a newly industrialised market economy, which is relatively open and state-orientated, the economy of Malaysia is the third largest in Southeast Asia and 35th largest in the world (Boulton, Pecht, Tucker, & Wennberg, 1997). Malaysia is considered to be one of the most diverse and unique countries within Asia with three main racial groupings, namely ethnic Malays, Chinese and Indians. The ethnic Malays form the majority and are primarily Muslim, which the Malaysian Constitution recognises as the religion of the federation.

Malaysia has been strongly impacted by colonisation, for example first by the Portuguese in 1511, followed by the Dutch in 1641 and ultimately by the British. The Japanese invasion during World War II ended British domination in Malaysia and their occupation of Malaysia from 1942 to 1945 unleashed nationalism (Ryan, 1965).

At the fall of the British empire, all Malaysian citizens, both male and female, were granted the right to vote in 1957 (Ariffin, 1999). In Ufen's (2009) view, the ideological and religious shift in Malaysia meant that Muslims were expected to live under Sharia, a system of Islamic laws, which strongly supersedes the laws outlined in the Malaysian constitution.

It will thus benefit change leaders working with or collaborating in joint ventures with Malaysian organisations to take note of the influence of the Islamic religious requirements and public holidays associated with their customs.

Another example of an emerging market in which religion plays an important role is Columbia. Gonzalez (2000) notes that Columbia as a Catholic state, imposed a strict patriarchal social order on society. The fact that Columbia has been beset by conflict for over 50 years (Victor & White, 2015), is also important since many opportunities are present to assist the country in growing its potential. Change leadership has to thus take note of the social rules in these countries when conducting business with them, for example a male change leader would carry more weight and have more power than a female in these countries. Hofstede's (2001) framework is also relevant here, describing instances when large power distance causes employees to be reluctant to share when they do not agree with intended changes. Employees in this context are likely to exhibit compliance to what the change leadership implement but might lack true commitment (Oilivas-Luján et al., 2008).

11.5.2 Case Examples of Embarking in Emerging Markets Organisations

The case writer Killing (2003) published a case on the Nestlé's Global Business Excellence (GLOBE) program, which won the 2010 European Best Case Award of ECCH. It is a case in the public domain, and the following discussion will revolve around the authors' analysis of this case material against the background of the Seventh Enabler:

The case features Nestlé as the world's largest food and beverage company. Interestingly, less than 2% of the company's revenues (SFr80 billion in 2000) were generated in Switzerland, where their head office is located. Chris Johnson, at the age of 39 years, accepted the role of the head of the GLOBE project in 2000. He did not have an IT background, in spite of the project being an implementation of an ERP programme called SAP. Chris was the previous country manager in Taiwan and understood the challenges that business managers were facing. This allowed the project to be identified as an organisation wide strategic and ultimately transformational change rather than an IT roll-out.

Harvard University's John Kotter (1996), identifies a guiding coalition, meaning a group that leads the change, as one of the key steps in transforming an organisation. Unfortunately, Chris and the leadership of Nestlé did not create this guiding coalition adequately. Chris did not fully understand and engage his stakeholders and identify those with the power to impede or fast-track his progress. Nestlé had a structure of decentralisation, and this implied that country and zone managers had significant decision-making authority, and he needed their buy-in. Chris isolated his team in a separate building in Vevey, without regional representatives or owners of the project in the regions and this was a bad choice. It meant that decisions for the regions were taken at the centre. For a multinational corporation (MNC) like Nestlé, this was a suboptimal approach. As a result, the project failed to consider nuances of culture, failed to address regional issues or language barriers. Creating this elite, centralised team resulted in an entirely different environment with different reward systems and consisted at one point of 700 people. This sort of project team without regional ties to champion the initiative made transformation without regional participation difficult.

It was envisaged that GLOBE would be running as a business initiative rather than an IT project. However, through the minimum involvement of business managers, they understood little about the project and perceived it to be a centralised IT-driven project. At a conference of all country managers, Chris planned PowerPoint presentations, but on the third day of the conference, when it was time to share information on GLOBE, he realised that there would be no interest in sitting through more presentations. Instead, he facilitated an interactive session with these country managers. It was a brave choice and provided valuable insights into these stakeholders' mindset. Unfortunately, there were no board members present as there was another presentation on financial forecasting at the same time and the CEO and others opted to attend that one. The case related that Nestlé was committed to creating value for shareholders. However, Nestlé had not favoured short-term profit and shareholder value maximisation, at the expense of long-term successful business development. But Nestlé remained conscious of the need to generate a reasonable profit each year.

With regards to the MMI merger case study, that we discuss in each enabler (Scheepers & Swart, 2015), The Seventh Enabler: Embarking is illustrated through the complex negotiations that had to take place around the new branding of MMI. The complex decisions were made through consensus on board and executive levels. They used an assessment centre, a process called Evalex to assist with the selection process. The new management structure was announced. A big learning point for the executive team was to conduct these phases even faster to reduce the suspense in which it could keep people while the structure was being finalised.

11.6   Measuring Seventh Enabler, Embark

Reflection Questions Enabler 7: Embark

Reflection Questions Enabler 7: Embark, contains a short questionnaire to help you assess the extent to which you are practicing this enabler. You can also ask others to assess you using this instrument.

11.7   Conclusion and Outcome of the Seventh Enabler, Embark

This chapter revolved around the Seventh Enabler, namely Embarking on the change process. We illustrated the importance of a clear change plan and to get the actions started. The outcome of this enabler is, for example, the small wins that are achieved to show that the change process is on the right track and to build even more momentum. This enabler is a great step in the process to start showing business results and the next enabler, Execute, would take these results further to demonstrate progress towards the change goals.

References

Allen, J., Jimmieson, N., Bordia, P., & Irmer, B. E. (2007). Uncertainty during organizational change: Managing perceptions through communication. *Journal of Change Management, 7*(2), 187–210. https://doi.org/10.1080/14697010701563379

Ansoff, H. I. (1988). *New corporate strategy.* New York, NY: Wiley. https://www.worldcat.org/title/new-corporate-strategy/oclc/1019208071?referer=di&ht=edition

Ariffin, R. (1999). Feminism in Malaysia: A historical and present perspective of women's struggles in Malaysia. *International Journal of Women Studies, 22*(4), 417–423. Retrieved from https://www.researchgate.net/publication/257116130_Feminism_in_malaysia_A_historical_and_present_perspective_of_women's_struggles_in_malaysia

Balogun, J. (2007). The practice of organizational restructuring: From design to reality. *European Management Journal, 25*(2), 81–91. https://doi.org/10.1016/j.emj.2007.02.001

Berkman, E. T., & Rock, D. (2014, September 5). AIM: An integrative model of goal pursuit. *NeuroLeadership Journal.* https://cpb-us-e1.wpmucdn.com/blogs.uoregon.edu/dist/1/172/files/2014/09/Berkman-2014-AIM-An-integrative-model-of-goal-pursuit-2k2tp3c.pdf

Boulton, W., Pecht, M., Tucker, W., & Wennberg, S. (1997). *Electronics manufacturing in the Pacific Rim.* World Technology Evaluation Center, Chapter 4. Malaysia. Retrieved November 1, 2010, from Wtec.org

Buono, A. F., & Bowditch, J. L. (2003). *The human side of mergers and acquisitions.* Washington: Beard Books. https://www.amazon.com/Human-Side-Mergers-Acquisitions/dp/1587981769

Coad, A., & Pawan, J. (2012). Firm growth and barriers to growth among small firms in India. *Small Business Economics, 39,* 383–400. https://doi.org/10.1007/s11187-011-9318-7

Damasio, A. R. (2005). *Descartes' error: Emotion, reason and the human brain*. New York: Penguin Putman. https://www.amazon.com/Descartes-Error-Emotion-Reason-Human/dp/014303622X

Deutschman, A. (2007). *Change or die: The three keys to change at work and in life*. New York, NY: HarperCollins Publishers. https://www.amazon.com/Change-or-Die-Alan-Deutschman-audiobook/dp/B000MV8X3I/ref=sr_1_fkmr0_1?dchild=1&keywords=Deutschman%2C+A.+%282007%29.+Change+or+die%3A+The+three+keys+to+change+at+work+and+in+life.+New+York%2C+655+NY%3A+HarperCollins+Publishers.&qid=1591698512&s=books&sr=1-1-fkmr0

Dibble, J. L., & Levine, T. R. (2013). Sharing good and bad news with friends and strangers: Reasons for and communication behaviors associated with the MUM effect. *Communication Studies, 64*(4), 431–452. https://doi.org/10.1080/10510974.2013.770407

DiFonzo, N., Bordia, P., & Rosnow, R. L. (1994). Reining in rumors. *Organizational Dynamics, 23* (1), 47–62. https://doi.org/10.1016/0090-2616(94)90087-6

Dixon, S. E. A., Meyer, K. E., & Day, M. (2010). Stages of organizational transformation in transition economies: A dynamic capabilities approach. *Journal of Management Studies, 47*, 416–436. https://doi.org/https://doi.org/10.1111/j.1467-6486.2009.00856.x. Retrieved April 16, 2018, from https://www.researchgate.net/publication/46540356_Stages_of_Organizational_Transformation_in_Transition_Economies_A_Dynamic_Capabilities_Approach

Drubach, D. (2000). *The brain explained*. Upper Saddle River, NJ: Prentice-Hall. https://www.amazon.com/Brain-Explained-Daniel-Drubach/dp/0137961944

Fenton, E. (2007). Visualising strategic change: The role and impact of process maps as boundary objects in reorganisation. *European Management Journal, 25*(2), 104–117. https://doi.org/10.1016/j.emj.2007.02.003

Ferrin, D. L., & Dirks, K. T. (2002). Trust in leadership: Meta-analytic findings and implications for research and practice. *Journal of Applied Psychology, 87*(4), 611–628. Retrieved from http://ink.library.smu.edu.sg/lkcsb_research/675

Franken, A., Edwards, C., & Lambert, R. (2009). Executing strategic change: Understanding the critical management elements that lead to success. *California Management Review, 51*(3), 49–73. Retrieved from http://algu.weebly.com/uploads/1/9/2/4/1924527/stra.mgtcase2.pdf

Gioia, D. A., & Chittipeddi, K. (1991). Sensemaking and sensegiving in strategic change initiation. *Strategic Management Journal, 12*(6). https://doi.org/https://doi.org/10.1002/smj.4250120604. Retrieved April 16, 2018, from https://onlinelibrary.wiley.com/doi/pdf/10.1002/smj.4250120604

Gomes, E., Angwin, D., Peter, E., & Mellahi, K. (2012). HRM issues and outcomes in African mergers and acquisitions: A study of the Nigerian banking sector. *The International Journal of Human Resource Management, 23*(14), 2874–2900. https://doi.org/10.1080/09585192.2012.671509

Gonzalez, C. C. (2000). Agitating for their rights: The Columbian women's movement, 1930–1957. *Pacific Historical Review, 69*(4), 689–706. https://doi.org/https://doi.org/10.2307/3641230. Retrieved from http://www.jstor.org/stable/3641230

Graetz, F. (2000). Strategic change leadership. *Management Decision, 38*(8), 550–564. https://doi.org/10.1108/00251740010378282

Havermans, L. A., Den Hartog, D. N., Keegan, A., & Uhl-Bien, M. (2015). Exploring the role of leadership in enabling contextual ambidexterity. *Human Resource Management, 54*(S1), 179–200. https://doi.org/10.1002/hrm.21764

Hofstede, G. (2001). *Cultures' consequences. comparing values, behaviours, institutions and organisations across nations* (2nd ed.). Thousand Oaks, CA: Sage. https://digitalcommons.usu.edu/unf_research/53/

Holbeche, L. (2007). *Understanding change*. New York, NY: Routledge. https://www.routledge.com/Understanding-Change-1st-Edition/Holbeche/p/book/9780750663410

Horwitz, F. M. (2013). An analysis of skills development in a transitional economy: The case of the South African labour market. *International Journal of Human Resource Management, 24*(12), 2435–2451. https://doi.org/10.1080/09585192.2013.781438

Isern, J., Meaney, M. C., & Wilson, S. (2009, April 7–14). Corporate transformation under pressure. *McKinsey Quarterly, Voices on Transformation.* Retrieved from https://www.mckinsey.com/business-functions/organization/our-insights/corporate-transformation-under-pressure

Jarrett, C. (2014). *The neuroscience of decision making explained in 30 seconds.* Retrieved from https://www.wired.com/2014/03/neuroscience-decision-making-explained-30-seconds/

Kailasam, M., Johri, L. M., & Wongsurawat, W. (2013). Weathering the downturn: 11 lessons from Indian multinationals. *Strategic Direction, 29*(2), 34–37. https://doi.org/10.1108/02580541311298065

Kegler, A. (2014). *What happens in your brain when you set a goal.* Retrieved February 5, 2018, from https://blog.rjmetrics.com/2014/12/16/the-psychology-of-goal-setting/

Killing, P. (2003). *Nestle's GLOBE program A: The early months; B: July Executive Board Meeting; C: "GLOBE Day", IMD-3-1336 v. 06.03.2010,* won 2010 European Case Award by ECCH, International Institute for Management Development, IMD, Lausanne. https://www.thecasecentre.org/main/products/view?id=62961

Koryak, O., Mole, K. F., Lockett, A., Hayton, J. C., Ucbasaran, D., & Hodgkinson, G. P. (2015). Entrepreneurial leadership, capabilities and firm growth. *International Small Business Journal, 33*(1), 89–105. https://doi.org/10.1177/0266242614558315

Kotter, J. P. (1996). *Leading change.* Boston, MA: Harvard Business Press. Retrieved from http://www.hbs.edu/faculty/Pages/item.aspx?num=137

Levin, I., & Gottlieb, J. Z. (2009). Realigning organization culture for optimal performance: Six principles & eight practices. *Organization Development Journal, 27*(4), 31–46. https://www.semanticscholar.org/paper/Realigning-Organization-Culture-for-Optimal-Six-%26-Levin-Gottlieb/30eebf44a9e8f7dfcc13c4b130a63fb263a52c9a

Lewin, K. (1947). Frontiers in group dynamics: Concept, method, and reality in social science; social equilibria and social change. *Human Relations, 1,* 5–41. https://doi.org/10.1177/001872674700100103

Lewis, L. K., & Seibold, D. R. (2009). Reconceptualizing organizational change implementation as a communication problem: A review of literature and research agenda. *Annals of the International Communication Association, 21*(1), 93–152. https://doi.org/10.1080/23808985.1998.11678949

Manning, T. (2012). Managing change in hard times. *Industrial and Commercial Training, 44*(5), 259–267. https://doi.org/10.1108/00197851211244997

McGlone, M. S., & Batchelor, J. A. (2003). Looking out for number one: Euphemism and face. *Journal of Communication, 53*(2), 251–264. https://doi.org/10.1111/j.1460-2466.2003.tb02589.x

Morténius, H., Fridlund, B., Marklund, B., Palm, L., & Baigi, A. (2012). Utilisation of strategic communication to create willingness to change work practices among primary care staff: A long-term follow-up study. *Primary Health Care Research & Development, 13*(2), 130–141. https://doi.org/10.1017/S1463423611000624

Nauret, R. (2018). *Multitasking seems to serve emotional, not productivity, needs.* Retrieved July 25, 2019 from Psychcentral: https://psychcentral.com/news/2012/05/01/multitasking-seems-to-serve-emotional-not-productivity-needs/38057.html

Oilivas-Luján, M. R., Monserrat, S. I., Ruiz-Guiterrez, J. A., Greenwood, R. A., Gomez, S. M., Murphy, E. F., et al. (2008). Values and attitudes towards women in Argentina, Brazil, Colombia, and Mexico. *Employee Relations, 31*(3), 227–244. https://doi.org/10.1108/01425450910946442

Rayner, L. (2015, March 19). Examining prospects in global emerging markets. *Professional Adviser,* 22–23. https://www.professionaladviser.com/feature/2399223/sector-report-examining-prospects-global-emerging-markets

Reissner, S. C., Pagan, V., & Smith, C. (2011). 'Our iceberg is melting': Story, metaphor and the management of organisational change. *Culture and Organization, 17*(5), 417–433. https://doi.org/10.1080/14759551.2011.622908

Rouleau, L. (2005). Micro-practices of strategic sensemaking and sensegiving: How middle managers interpret and sell change every day. *Journal of Management Studies, 42*(7), 1413–1441. https://doi.org/10.1111/j.1467-6486.2005.00549.x

Rudorf, S., & Hare, T. A. (2014). Interactions between dorsolateral and ventromedial prefrontal cortex underlie context-dependent stimulus valuation in goal-directed choice. *Journal of Neuroscience, 34*(48), 15988–15996. https://doi.org/10.1523/JNEUROSCI.3192-14.2014

Ryan, N. J. (1965). *The making of modern Malaysia: A history from earliest times to independence.* Kuala Lumpur: Oxford University Press. https://www.amazon.com/Making-Modern-Malaysia-Singapore-Earliest/dp/0196381207

Salem, P. (2008). The seven communication reasons organizations do not change. *Corporate Communications: An International Journal, 13*(3), 333–348. https://doi.org/10.1108/13563280810893698

Scheepers, C. B., & Swart, S. (2015). *Momentum and metropolitan merger: Authentic transformational leadership.* Ivey Publishing, 9B15C004. https://www.iveycases.com/ProductView.aspx?id=70560

Schilling, A., Werr, A., Gand, S., & Sardas, J.-C. (2012). Understanding professionals' reactions to strategic change: The role of threatened professional identities. *The Service Industries Journal, 32*(8), 1229–1245. https://doi.org/10.1080/02642069.2010.531269

Tsai, M., & Young, M. J. (2009). Anger, fear, and escalation of commitment. *Cognition and Emotion, 24*(6), 962–973. https://doi.org/10.1080/02699930903050631

Ufen, A. (2009). Mobilising political Islam: Indonesia and Malaysia compared. *Commonwealth and Comparative Politics, 47*(3), 321–322. https://doi.org/10.1080/14662040903073761

Van de Ven, A. H., & Sun, K. (2011). Breakdowns in implementing models of organization change. *The Academy of Management Perspectives, 25*(3), 58–74. https://journals.aom.org/doi/abs/10.5465/amp.25.3.zol58

Van Dijk (Newton), R., & van Dick, R. (2009). Navigating organizational change: Change leaders, employee resistance and work-based identities. *Journal of Change Management, 9*(2), 143–163. https://doi.org/10.1080/14697010902879087

Van Hecke, M. L., Callahan, L. P., Kolar, B., & Paller, K. A. (2010). *The brain advantage: Become a more effective business leader using the latest brain research.* Amherst, NY: Prometheus Books. https://www.amazon.com/Brain-Advantage-Effective-Business-Research/dp/1591027640

Vietor, R. H. K., & White, H. (2015). *Colombia and the economic premium of peace.* Boston, MA: Harvard Business School Case Collection. https://www.hbs.edu/faculty/pages/item.aspx?num=48609

Vorhauser-Smith, S. (2011). The neuroscience of talent management. *Employment Relations Today, 28*, 17–22. https://onlinelibrary.wiley.com/doi/10.1002/ert.20327

Reference List for Quotes

Mandela, N. R. (1994). *Long walk to freedom: The autobiography of Nelson Mandela.* London: Time Warner Books. https://www.amazon.com/Long-Walk-Freedom-Autobiography-Mandela/dp/0316548189

Retrieved July 26, 2019, from https://quoteinvestigator.com/2016/02/09/boldness/

Retrieved July 26, 2019, from https://www.goodreads.com/quotes/125720-people-don-t-resist-change-they-resist-being-changed

Retrieved July 26, 2019, from https://www.goodreads.com/quotes/1318156-you-can-never-cross-the-ocean-unless-you-have-the

Eighth Enabler

Execute

12

It does not matter how slowly you go as long as you do not stop.

(Confucius, n.d.)

Motivation gets you going, and habit gets you there.

(Zig Ziglar, n.d.)

Learning Outcomes

At the end of this chapter change leaders will be able to:

- Ensure goals set and agreed are delivered
- Keep team motivated and engaged
- Celebrate milestones

Electronic supplementary material The online version of this chapter (https://doi.org/10.1007/978-3-030-40846-6_12) contains supplementary material, which is available to authorized users.

12.1 Orientation to Executing

Setting goals alone is not enough. We now need to drive action. We developed the execution process below to explain the steps in the implementation process (Fig. 12.1). In Enabler Seven, the change leader put a lot of effort into preparing plans to *Embark* on the Change Process. Once SMART goals have been set, agreed and signed off, resources need to be planned, provided for and monitored. Next, goal delivery needs to be reviewed and evaluated. Based on the outcomes of the review process, motivation, coaching and disciplining might be required. If goal delivery is repeatedly not achieved, a separation process might need to ensue. If goals are delivered successfully, these successes need to be celebrated and rewarded. The centre of the cycle contains the words: "DO THE WORK". This is because **work** is what is required to get things done, which will ultimately lead to the achievement of the vision.

12.2 Importance of Executing

Without this enabler in the change process, no value has been added yet. It is often easy to put plans on paper, but much more difficult to actually execute them. This enabler guarantees that action is indeed taken. It involves removing obstacles to ensure momentum is not lost. In this enabler, change leadership ensures that measurement is taken care of and problems are addressed. Motivation to sustain the change process is also part of this enabler.

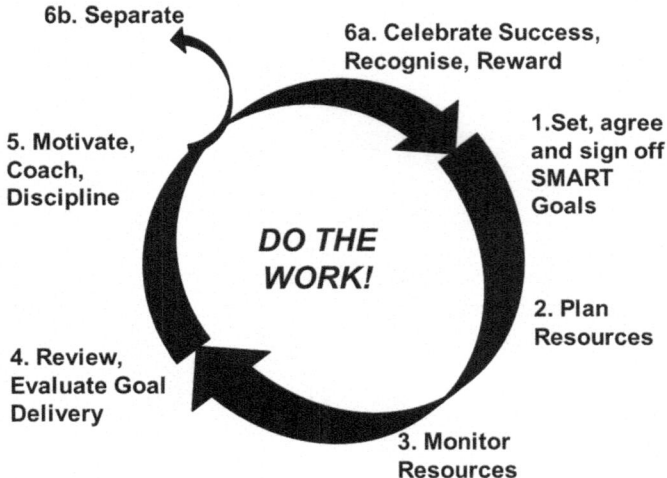

Fig. 12.1 Execution process (Authors' own)

We agree with Beer and Nohria (2000) who suggest that both "hard" and "soft" aspects within an organisation need to be combined during the change initiative in order to improve the success rate of the change. Sujova and Rajnoha (2012) also advise that the application of project management principles, which could be described as the hard aspect, allows for a systematic process of implementing change management, through identification, visualisation, measurement and evaluation. Following a rigorous process to implement interventions is even more important than the selection of appropriate interventions and assists in obtaining buy-in and commitment to move forward. Schmidt (2011) warns that when strategic plans change it affects operation planning, hence the importance of reviewing operational plans monthly. The frequency of operational planning can be affected by the change. If the change is frequent, operational planning must be aligned with changes, and this may occur daily or weekly.

Landrum, Howell and Paris (2000) declare that in dynamic environments, where organisations face rapid changes, multitalented teams of diverse individual teams are critical means of implementing strategic change. It gives some organisations a competitive advantage over others who remain focused on top management execution. The cascading of the change strategy in the form of real action lower down in the organisation is thus essential, since these diverse, sometimes cross-functional or within functional teams are required to execute and focus on relevant and wise actions.

It is one thing to set goals and start the delivery process as discussed in Enabler 7 Embarking. However, we have all experienced the frustration of a job started but not finished. Entrenching is part of this Eighth Enabler that deals with progressing with the goal until it has been successfully completed and the change is sustainable in the long term. For this goal maintenance is essential and forming new long-term habits can prevent falling back into the old way of doing things.

Organisations regularly embark upon implementing changes and then due to internal resistance or politics, external pressure or any number of reasons, they do not maintain the changes, and the organisation reverts to the way it was prior to the change being launched. In cases of culture change, the organisation might go back to the way things were done in the past. We would encourage organisations to focus their attention on this enabler, as it might be even more challenging to get another change off the ground after a failure of maintaining the previous change. Employees and customers alike could be more sceptical and make it difficult for the organisation's leadership to gain credibility.

The classic model provided by Prochaska, DiClemente, and Norcross (1992), a transtheoretical model, called the Prochaska and DiClemente model, is relevant for this Eighth Enabler, since it includes maintenance and the danger of relapsing. Although it is a model used for addictions, we feel it is useful because it emphasises the maintenance phase and what to do when there is a potential relapse. The authors of this volume adapted the Prochaska and DiClemente cycle somewhat to show how the enablers are aligned with the steps in Prochaska and DiClemente's cycle. The original cycle illustrates that the beginning of the cycle includes the initial resistance to start doing something about the addictive behaviour, then the contemplation, due

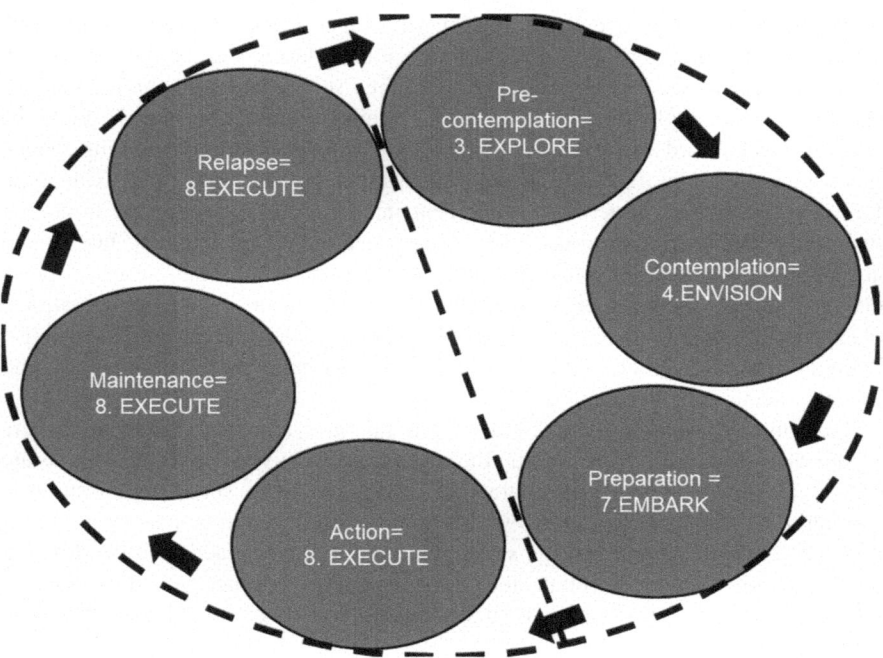

Fig. 12.2 How enablers integrate (Adapted from Prochaska and DiClemente's Cycle (1992))

to some awareness about the problem, next the preparation to take action and then the actual action is taken to actively modify the behaviour. With addiction, maintenance and relapse are two crucial steps in the process, and we believe this to be a valuable addition to be considered when leading change processes in organisations. In Fig. 12.2, the first three circles on the right-hand side of the big cycle indicate the antecedents in the goal pursuit process. Enabler 3, Explore, is aligned with the phase of pre-contemplation, while Enabler 5, Envisioning is similar to contemplation. When we prepare, it is similar to Enabler 7, Embarking. The next three circles on the left-hand side of the big cycle relate to the goal achievement phase. Here, we notice that Prochaska and DiClemente provide valuable input to the Enabler process as it addresses action, maintenance and relapse. All three of these processes are essential and should be dealt with in the Eight Enabler, Execute. The critical step that is particularly relevant to this Eighth Enabler is MAINTENANCE. Sustaining the change is possible, since new behaviour has replaced the old and even then, a relapse might occur, where one could fall back into old behaviour patterns, which of course, would hopefully lead back to pre-contemplation and a new round of the upward spiral. Learning from each relapse is required.

Podcast of Prochaska and DiClimente's Stages of Change

Listen to this podcast on the model, uploaded on 2 October 2009 and last accessed by the authors on 5 April 2018: http://socialworkpodcast.blogspot. co.za/2009/10/prochaska-and-diclementes-stages-of.html

While it is vital to ensure plans are executed, we also have to pay attention to sustainability. John Kotter (1996) of Harvard warns leadership not to declare victory too soon. This enabler relates to his principle as well as Cummings and Worley's (2015) on the institutionalisation of culture, meaning the internalisation or making the change part of the existing culture. As individuals, teams and organisation, we easily fall back into old habits. It is not easy to form new routines, and as a result, organisations find it hard to sustain the momentum and make certain that new habits form before new challenges would prompt them to lose focus. This enabler is thus about maintaining momentum until the change is part of the way we do things around here, in other words, the culture. In our lectures, we regularly point to momentum management to sustain change rather than change management. Continuous reinforcement of the reason for the change is required.

The organisation's culture acts as a fundamental constraint to the strategic reorientation of an organisation and hampers its effectiveness if an intervention around culture is not undertaken. Without leadership's dedication and patience to implement cultural transformation, an organisation is unlikely to become effective. The outcome of a culture change intervention should be a revised set of values and behaviours aligned with the strategy.

Found and Harvey (2007) stressed that cultural transformation is required across all levels of the organisation, starting from top to bottom, coupled with visionary leaders who "walk the talk". In our interviews as part of research for this volume, an interviewee was adamant that culture change starts at the top. "It depends on the leader's authenticity. If you are authentic and truly believe in the idea, you will be able to sell it. We as the leaders, need to walk the talk". Rosenberg (2003) concurs with Found and Harvey (2007) on developing a set of behavioural guidelines and ensuring leaders model these values with their behaviour as integral parts of successful change management.

Change disrupts the status quo. Price and Chahal (2006) explain that employees need to take on greater responsibilities, new functions are required and new ways of working. However, where processes and culture have been well established, employees may operate within a comfort zone. Alignment of organisational culture is thus critical to successful change. Franken, Edwards, and Lambert (2009) in this regard, advise engendering and reinforcing an organisational culture of continuous change. Organisational culture is a unique pattern of shared values and norms in an organisation that distinguishes it from another organisation, according to the classic work of Schein (1984). Higgins and McAllaster (2004) emphasise that cultural artefacts are important as they usually support the old strategy and not the new one; for example key values and norms, myths and sagas, language systems and metaphors, symbols and ceremonies, as well as physical surroundings such as interior design.

Stetler, Richie, Rycroft-Malone, Schultz, and Charns (2009) stress that a change agenda and internal efforts within the organisation influence the institutionalisation and therefore they need to be aligned. An interesting study by French and Holden (2012) revealed that a key indicator of an organisation's effectiveness in communicating bad news messages is the state of its organisational culture before the change. Cultivating a positive organisational culture prior to an acute organisational crisis can enable an organisation to buffer bad news.

Scholars like Alhazemi, Rees, and Hossain (2013) too, emphasise the ability to quickly align the culture to the new strategy as well as the coordination of all stakeholders in the change process. Hofstede (2001) demonstrates that different organisations, similar to nations, have different histories and cultures, which are products of history, communication, environment and leadership. Leaders need to be role models and shape the behaviours of employees through formal and informal mechanisms (Nilsson, 2010).

An organisation's employees look up to leadership to define and interpret the culture of the organisation and set an example of how they should behave. Therefore, leaders need to be disciplined and internalise and demonstrate commitment to organisational change through creating the right structure and environment for change and championing new behaviours that are aligned to the changes desired by the organisation (Levin & Gottlieb, 2009).

A phenomenon in the emerging markets that deserves particular attention in the discussion of this Eighth Enabler is Mergers and Acquisitions (M&As). It often results in several challenges such as job insecurity, lack of merging of cultures and low morale due to the laying off of employees (Anifowose, Genty, & Atiku, 2011). Integration during mergers and acquisitions should thus not only take place at a system level, but also more critical integration should take place at employees' level to merge different cultures. Lawlor (2013) agrees that M&As usually require a change in organisational culture, particularly of the acquired organisation. Culture differences at the top management level are most likely to influence the merging organisation's ability to realise synergies. M&A transactions are dependent on the wide-scale integration of people and cultures, including their processes, systems and practices. Smit (2007), therefore, declares that cultural compatibility issues cannot be ignored as the merging companies could face many difficulties and not meeting the anticipated purpose of the transaction. Managing change in the highly complex world of M&As is not easy, and research has found that as much as 70% of change initiatives are unsuccessful (Smit, 2007).

M&A's occur regularly between various companies. DePamphilis (2012) states that synergy is the simplistic notion that the combination of two businesses create higher shareholder value than if they were operated separately. Saunders, Altinay, and Riordan (2009) recommend that companies conduct a cultural audit, so cultural differences are diagnosed and understood to avoid cultural shocks during the post-merger stage. Some of the personal impacts employees have are anxieties about job loss and changes in salary and performance evaluation processes (Marks & Mirvis, 2001). According to Chatterjee (1986) conflict because of cultural differences between the employees of the acquiring and the acquired companies are not uncommon during an M&A, resulting in further resistance to the integration. The strategy needs to incorporate organisational socialisation in order to ensure success. The best place for this input is the organisations own employees (Stojanovic & Kessler, 2011).

A method of carrying out the operational aspects of merging the two companies and continuing operations can follow a four-stage process, which includes, formulation of the integration logic and performance goals, establishing integration planning approach and then executing the operational integration and finally executing a strategic integration (Burgelman & McKinney, 2005). The integration strategy will not always be clear, but at least a roadmap should be created to indicate where the organisation wants to go, where it is and what is expected of the integration (Barros & Domínguez, 2013).

Leaders play the roles of visionary, cheerleader, deal closer, captain and crusader in an M&A transaction (Gadiesh, Buchanan, Daniell, & Ormiston, 2002). The visionary aspect includes getting the message across on why the company is doing the M&A and what it wishes to achieve both internally and externally to the organisation and the new culture and values of the new organisation. To institutionalise these new golden rules leadership must demonstrate these in a consistent manner. As a cheerleader, leadership creates enthusiasm and obtains buy-in from the employees, investors, suppliers and customers. Closing the deal as quickly as possible ensures stability and reduces the risk of the deal not being successful. As captain, the leader owns and manages the plan to integrate the two companies and finally as crusader the leader ensures that enthusiasm and momentum for the merger are maintained.

Sonenshein (2010) identifies three responses from employees in his research on the impact an organisational change has, namely, resisting, championing and accepting. The resisting response is primarily elicited by employees' concerns about job security, a loss of identity and a change in their general level of comfort and the status quo. The championing response is of those employees who consider the change as a beneficial transformation to the business and are willing contributors to activities that will lead to the success of the change. Finally, the change-accepting response is from those employees who feel that they would be able to adjust easily to the change.

Worley, Hitchin, and Ross (1996) emphasise that integrated strategic change (ISC) involves strategy-making as an intervention rather than a decision-making process conducted in isolation. It points to the requirement to better integrate the processes of strategy formulation and strategy execution. This approach paves the way for operational planning that aligns with the overarching strategy. To improve execution, it is essential to develop a two-pronged plan (top-down and bottom-up) to communicate the vision and strategy, as well as the eliciting of feedback from the bottom. Another element to improve execution is the appropriate resourcing of change agents for the entire duration of the change and not only at the initial phases of the change. Deploying effective structures, as well as realigning roles and responsibilities appropriately will ensure execution is successful.

This executing enabler emphasises that it is essential to institute robust training interventions and implementing a retention plan to ensure critical skills are not lost during the execution. In the next enabler evaluating will be discussed, but during this discussion, it remains crucial to mention that obtaining feedback from employees regarding the perception of the success of the change process is required and to respond by reinforcing dedication to change and communicate short-term wins.

12.3   Executing in Practice

In Enabler 7, Embark we developed action plans. In Enabler 8, Execute, these plans now need to be actioned. It is the role of the change leader to monitor the delivery of these actions and the resources required to deliver the action on time and at the desired quality level. The Progress and Delivery Template below provides a framework for change leaders to monitor the execution of the change plan. We suggest copying the columns into a Microsoft Excel spreadsheet to enable ease of reviews and updating action.

It is best to schedule regular review sessions (depending on the urgency of the project, it could be weekly, biweekly or monthly) where change agents report back on progress made. The Excel spreadsheet is then kept up to date to monitor progress and to highlight potential lagging actions requiring attention.

Tool 8.1 Progress and Delivery

Tool 8.1 lists the action plans with the target dates and the accountable persons, the resources required and utilised, as well as a column to record when the actions were delivered.

12.3.1 Team Member Motivation

Tool 8.2 Team Member Motivation Sheet

From time to time, the change leader will need to review the motivation levels of the Change Agent Team members. Considering their fears and desires, their drivers and their desired "love" languages, all helps with motivation. Tool 8.2 provides a template to do this review.

12.3.2 Change Team Commitment, Readiness, Capability, Skill (CRCS)

Tool 8.3 Change Team Member Commitment, Readiness, Capability, Skill (CRCS)

The commitment, readiness, skill, capability, matrix can be used here to analyse the team members' strengths and weaknesses and the action required to ensure they are willing and able to deliver goals as agreed. Tool 8.3 provides a template to conduct such an analysis.

12.3.3 Why Do We Procrastinate?

We have all had the experience where we dread tackling a difficult task—the one we do not feel like doing, the one we must do, the one where the deadline is creeping ominously closer. Instead of tackling the task we tend to do menial, unrelated tasks to make us feel productive. We know we are not on target. It is frustrating, stressful and it can lead to feeling useless and even depressed. There could be many reasons why we procrastinate. It could be because the task we need to perform is too complicated, too boring (easy), or there might be something nicer or easier to do. Focusing on getting the job done is hard work, and there are no shortcuts.

12.3.4 Celebrate Milestones

Kotter (1996) emphasises short-term wins and encourages leaders to give recognition for small victories. It improves staff morale and lowers dissatisfaction in the long term. Celebrations do not have to be expensive but need to be of value to those who are celebrating the success.

Practical Application of Celebrating Milestones

In a change process we were involved in, celebrations were always in the form of a meal after work, or a t-shirt or a takeaway burger. Employees later complained that these celebrations meant nothing to them. This might sound

(continued)

unthankful, but we have to tune into the needs of those involved in the change. Some might not appreciate the gifts we consider to be of value. It was a lesson we had to learn the hard way. Ask, engage with the stakeholders and find out what they believe to be of value. In a similar vein, the "person of the month" photograph on the wall or the "well-done card" might also have insufficient value to those we are trying to motivate.

Tool 8.4 Milestone Celebrations

Tool 8.4 was designed to force the change leader to plan for celebrations of small wins. We suggest the change leader involves the Change Agent Team and the broader stakeholder group to determine the kind of celebration/ rewards those involved in the change consider to be of value.

12.3.5 Resistance to Change (RTC)

The RTC Tool 7.3 in Enabler 7, Embark can now be revisited to ensure resistance is dealt with effectively.

12.3.6 Implementation Tips for Executing

We would like to share the following practical tips around Enabler Eight:

- Track progress
- Track morale
- Keep your ear to the ground
- Observe what is going on
- Celebrate successes
- Compliment people doing things right
- Encourage others
- Build confidence
- Provide the means, ability, accountability

12.4   Neuroscience Insights into Executing

Practical Application of Executing

While completing this chapter, I experienced first hand how difficult it is to deliver on a goal. The goal was set. It was SMART. I was motivated and yet I found it so difficult to complete the task at hand. Yes, doing it and being busy with it was one thing, but finishing it and sending it off, knowing that it was my best work possible was an entirely different kettle of fish. It made me reflect on why so few organisational goals actually get delivered. Setting goals and agreeing on them takes time, but delivering goals is when the value is added. Only once the "product" has been delivered can one claim to have added value.

It made me think—why "just doing it" is so tricky. Why do people not deliver on their agreed SMART goals? Why am I battling so much to achieve my goal? I developed my own list of reasons why I was battling to complete this chapter? I came up with the following reasons: Fear of not doing it right, competing goals, something easier/more enjoyable to do, too difficult, being tired or even burnt out, getting distracted, hating doing it, boredom. Let us see if neuroscience can help. . .

Ps. In the end, I learned that the answer lies in focus, focus, focus—blind focus!

(Source: Author Sonja Swart's personal reflection)

12.4.1 Goal-Delivery: How to "Just Do It!"

There is no doubt that achieving goals and changing behaviour are both challenging tasks to accomplish. Berkman (2018) states, "Neuroscience can never change the fact that pursuing goals is hard, but it can provide some explanations for the difficulty as well as some new insights about how to mitigate it" (Berkman, 2018, p. 32).

Our drive to take action, achieve goals and exert effort emanates from some of our deepest and oldest brain regions. Motivation is a survival necessity, so the neural circuitry developed for it is both extensive and heavily interconnected (Vorhauser-Smith, 2011). When we are motivated to pursue something, we trigger approach mechanisms that are reinforced by the neurochemical dopamine. By activating this system, we receive biofeedback that the activity is good, rewarding and enjoyable. This enhances the positive flow, and we pursue it further.

For every milestone achieved, the body releases dopamine, creating a sense of pleasure and leading to higher concentration and inspiration to recreate the experience (Kegler, 2014; Mehta, 2013). One has to collect wins, no matter how small, to obtain the repeated release of dopamine. The levels of dopamine can also be increased by visualising fear, novelty in any form, humour, changing perspectives or expecting something positive. Dopamine secretion is diminished when we activate any other regions than the PFC (Rock, 2009b).

Success is not possible without changing the daily behaviour of people throughout the company. But change is hard, even for individuals (Rock & Schwartz, 2006).

12.4.2 Distractions

Today more than ever before, we are exposed to constant distractions. Beeping or vibrating phones remind us when we have a new message or e-mail, noise and visual pollution easily and constantly distract our attention and the ongoing pressure from multiple clients with varying and ever-increasing demands makes focusing on one task for longer than a couple of minutes nearly impossible. Social media and the Internet can both be addictive distractors and can impact profoundly on productivity. Rock (2016) reminds us that office distractions can consume as much as 2.1 h/day. It has also been found that we get distracted on average every 11 min, and we take 25 min to get back to the original task at hand—if at all. On average every 3 min, we switch between activities be it speaking to a colleague, making a call or reading a text (Rock, 2016).

Distractions occur in two main ways: sensory distractions (things happening around us) and emotional distractions (the voice in your head about yourself, others, things happening in your life or things you have to do) (Goleman, 2013). If you have ever had a highly emotive issue occupying your thoughts, you will recall that it is almost impossible to get on with the task at hand. This is because the brain is seeking a solution, so we can stop worrying about the issue. Trying to put the issue on the back burner is unfortunately not helpful, because our subconscious mind is still struggling with it, even if we are trying our best to ignore it. These emotive issues are the most powerful disruptors. Goleman (2013, p. 48) says it best when he states that it "Is not the chatter of people around us that is the most powerful distractor, but rather the chatter of our own minds". The bad news is that it appears that on average we tend to focus mostly on negative and self-centred thoughts than on anything else (Cooper, 2016).

Berkman and Rock (2014) suggest we book out dedicated, distraction-free time to work on critical novel tasks and challenges. The brain operates at its best when it performs serial tasks. So, focus on one task only but be sure to build in distractions and rewards. Another way to ensure you deliver your goal is to break the big goal down into small achievable goals and reward them often (Mehta, 2013). However, we should not set the bar too high because every time we fail, the brain is drained of dopamine preventing us from learning or concentrating (Mehta, 2013).

Goleman (2013) believes spending time in nature helps our mind relax. For example, walking down a city street does not lead to the brain relaxing as much as when we spend time in nature.

One could easily be fooled thinking that those who multitask have lots of outstanding skills. In a study by Eyal Ophir, Clifford Nass and Anthony Wagner from Stanford University in Palo Alto, California they found that people who multitask are poor performers (Ophir, Nass, & Wagner, 2009). The researchers hypothesised that people who multitask excel at filtering information, switching between tasks quickly and keeping a high working memory. However, their research proved them wrong. People who multitask are much worse at filtering irrelevant information and switching between tasks. Multitasking results in being less productive and an inability to filter out irrelevant information.

Interview with Clifford Nass

The Myth of Multitasking
https://www.npr.org/2013/05/10/182861382/the-myth-of-multitasking

Medina (2008) in the book, *Brain Rules*, states we are biologically incapable of processing attention-rich inputs simultaneously. Human beings consciously function in a serial fashion. The more demanding the task, the more we are single minded.

People who multitask are not being more productive—They just feel more emotionally satisfied by their work (Nauret, 2018).

It happens from time to time that we do things that have nothing to do with our goals or even contradict our goals. What happens in the brain then is that your goals are in your conscious and subconscious awareness and sometimes these two spheres are at odds. When these two systems are at odds, the chances are very good that the subconscious will gain the upper hand. The attention system and the amygdala both get their instructions from the subconscious, rather than the conscious and every time the subconscious perceives some progress towards subconscious goal achievement, dopamine will be released even if we might regret it later. The conscious mind will try and make a different choice, but if the goal has not been communicated to the subconscious mind, the conscious choice will not prevail. It is, therefore, critical to ensure your conscious and subconscious are synchronised.

12.4.3 Habits

In this section, we pay attention to how a habit is formed for an individual. This could help change leaders understand themselves and others better. It could also help change leaders change their own habits. They could then be role models to others and influence their teams and change agents to change their habits too. A habit is defined as a decision you made at some point, then stopped making it, but are still continuing to act on it. Habits are formed because the brain is constantly looking for ways to save energy. The brain converts a sequence of actions into an automatic routine called chunking. We rely on hundreds of behavioural chunks each day just to function. This allows the brain to focus on novel ideas and inventions (Duhigg, 2013).

Conscious effort and focused attention are needed when we want to change a habit or embed a new behaviour. This can feel frustrating and exhausting. Changing a habit requires focused attention and then we get physically tired, emotionally drained, overworked, stressed or distracted, the PFC loses its focus, and we fall back into old habits (Langley, 2018).

Duhigg (2013) proposes that habits work using a three-step loop (Fig. 12.3). It starts with a trigger (he calls it a cue) that notifies the brain to go into automatic habit mode. This is followed by a routine, which can be mental, emotional or physical. In the last stage of the process, there is a reward, reminding one that this routine was useful and beneficial and should be remembered in the future. Over time this loop becomes unconscious, the cue and the reward become entangled, and a powerful sense of anticipation and craving follows. Duhigg (2013) uses this three-step loop to explain how to manage habits (Fig. 12.3).

Any new task we take on requires our brain to exert effort. Think how hard a baby needs to work to master the skill of walking. We all walk without even giving it a second thought. The process has been fully automated. Duhigg (2013) suggests that because the three-step loop has been hard-wired into our brain, we need to use it to escape the loop.

To change a habit that is no longer required, one has to find a new habit yielding the same reward with which to replace the old habit with. For example, you want to start the process of drinking fewer cups of coffee per day. You are consuming eight

Fig. 12.3 Circular process of three steps in habit forming (Adapted from Duhigg's, 2013)

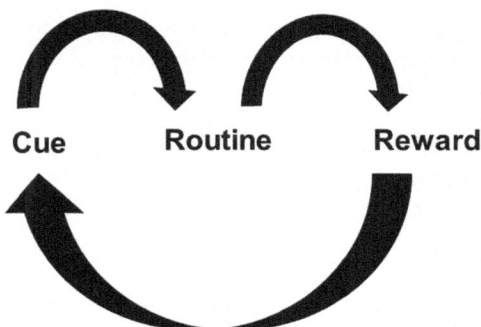

Cue   Routine   Reward

cups and would like to bring it down to three cups. The cue in this example will be "I am frustrated/bored/stressed/tired". The routine will be: you make a cup of coffee, or you treat yourself to a latté in the local coffee shop. The reward is a sense of relief, and you feel better.

To stop the habit of drinking so many cups of coffee per day, you would need to find another way of feeling better whenever you feel frustrated/bored/stressed/tired. There are in fact two rewards, the first being the break in monotony and the second the effect of the caffeine on your body. You need these rewards, but if you replace coffee drinking with something you do not enjoy such as drinking water you might be miserable.

However, we have all embarked upon change processes that have lasted for a month or two, only to fall back into old habits when we are under stress. According to Duhigg (2013), there is a missing part of the puzzle. The missing part is believing we can change and that often requires the assistance of others. Belief is the ingredient that turns a new habit loop into a permanent behaviour. Joining a group can assist with positive reinforcement and provides the support necessary to make the change permanent.

YouTube Clip: Interview with Duhigg

https://www.youtube.com/watch?v=sBpMQiMCgBE
https://www.youtube.com/watch?v=pxy8dDSHHaw
https://www.youtube.com/watch?v=szgoDIkimNU

Long-term change will not be sustainable if the goals are only set at the beginning of the project. New behaviours will only come about if they have been repeated enough for the neural networks to form new connections. That is why our New Year's resolutions regularly fall by the wayside (McAbe & Baum, 2017).

We become what we think about most of the time, and that's the strangest secret (Earl Nightingale, n.d.).

When the comment mentioned by Earl Nightingale was made in 1956, we did not yet know that neuroscience would prove this to be true. If we repeatedly think about our goals, new habits will be formed, and goals will be reached. Unfortunately, there

1. Stop: Bad habit
Ventrolateral PFC
(handbrake)

- Limited resource
- With every brake, resource diminishes

- Can only do for short periods of time
- Can only do one thing at a time

2. Start: New habit: FOCUS!
Pre-frontal Cortex (PFC)

3. Continue: REPEAT ! REPEAT !
REPEAT!

- Forms new links. With every repeat, myelin coating becomes thicker and denser and the more easily it fires

4. Becomes a new habit
Into Basal Ganglia

Fig. 12.4   Four steps to changing a habit (Authors' own, adapted from Duhigg (2013))

is no substitute for the repetition that needs to happen. Connecting the action to an intense emotion is the only way to speed up the process.

Figure 12.4 locates the area in the brain where the four steps to changing a habit take place.

Step 1: Stop the Old Habit
Stop the old habit: The Ventrolateral PFC is the handbrake of the brain helping you to stop and to say no to old habits. However, it is a limited resource, and with every brake action, the power is diminished.

Step 2: Start
To start the new habit, we need to focus for short time periods in a serial fashion, i.e. perform one action at a time. Here the PFC is involved.

Step 3: Repetition
To establish a new habit, we need to continually repeat, repeat and repeat the action. This will help form new links between neurons and create a denser myelin coating between neurons (Fig. 12.5). New neural connections are now being established. With enough attention, focus and repetition, this can result in "hard wiring" or in other words, a shifting of conscious intentions to automatic processing. It then becomes the basis for future actions and will enable us to act without too much

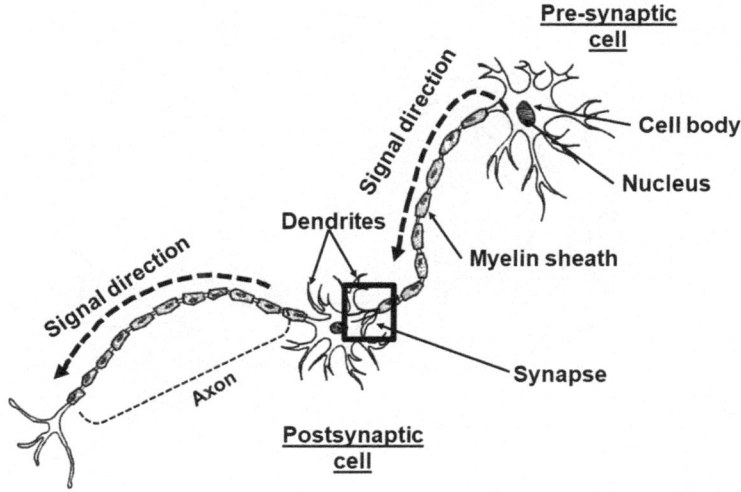

Fig. 12.5 Two neurons connecting (After many repetitions the myelin sheath becomes thicker, Authors' own)

effort (Rock & Page, 2009). Thus, a habit is formed. When we try to erase a habit, we must consider what we want to replace the habit with. This takes considerable effort to consciously redirect our attention—especially in the face of danger or when we are exhausted.

Step 4: Becomes a New Habit

The basal ganglia are a group of structures situated deep within the brain, near the brain's core and are involved in habits and routine activity (Fig. 12.6). When repeated, routine activities are practised and the basal ganglia take over these functions. Conscious thought is then freed up for new learning activities (Rock & Page, 2009). This then is another explanation why change is so difficult. Most of what we do personally or organisationally is routine. Once the basal ganglia take over, it is difficult to unlearn. The PFC consumes a lot of glucose, a metabolically expensive chemical for our bodies to produce, and therefore, cannot resist temptations for very long. Our brain prefers to use the basal ganglia, which have a higher capacity than the PFC and does not use as much glucose. The basal ganglia store our actions and memories as habits, making it easier to fall back on when we do not have the capacity to focus our attention. Figure 12.6 illustrates the basal ganglia in the human brain.

When we celebrate successes and reward people for milestones reached and displaying appropriate behaviour, the neurotransmitter, dopamine is released in the brain. It is one of the most active neurotransmitters in the brain's motivation, reward and pleasure system (Hampton, 2015).

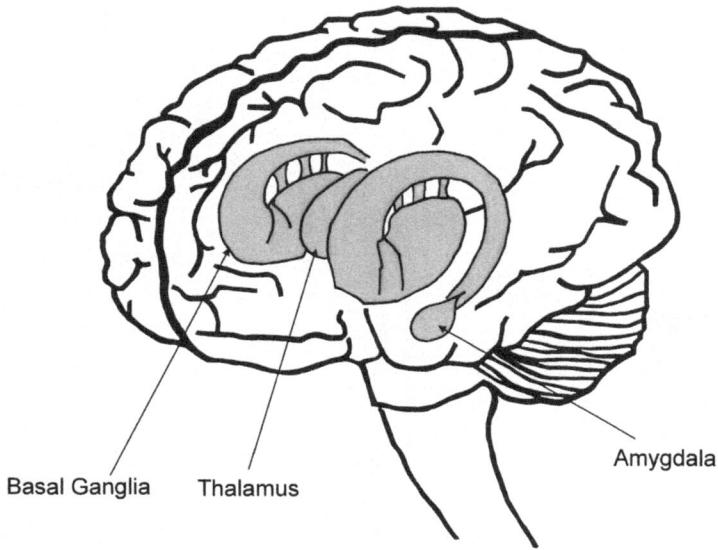

Basal Ganglia   Thalamus

Amygdala

Fig. 12.6 Basal ganglia, thalamus and amygdala (Authors' own)

12.4.4 Implications for Organisations Going Through Change

To change the culture of an organisation, one has to focus on channeling people's attention in new ways for long enough. Rock (2009a) provides three components to changing others' paradigms:

* Create a safe environment to minimise the threat response. Until people are at ease, they cannot focus their attention.
* Focus attention on the new.
* Focus the attention over and over again.

12.5   Executing in Emerging Markets

12.5.1 Case Examples of Executing in Emerging Markets Contexts

In the emerging markets, the execution of change plans is critical for successful change processes. Concerning the volatility in the emerging markets, leadership of organisations in these markets must be extra careful of moving on to the next thing, without following through on the current change process. There will be external changes, internal disruptions, etc. that will draw the attention of leadership away from their focus on the execution of change plans. Furthermore, with international competition increasing, companies in emerging markets are required to be effective at introducing change in their business models, technology, marketing, governance and operational processes, as well as human resources practices.

Pihlak and Alas (2012) point out that subsequent to the collapse of the Soviet Union, many countries, including those around the Baltic sea, namely Latvia, Lithuania and Estonia, welcomed a market economy after an extended period of a centrally-controlled economy. Pihlak and Alas (2012) observed that several organisations in these countries had to make enormous changes to cope with the environmental challenges. These scholars lament that most of the literature on change management was developed in stable Western countries and question the suitability of these theories in their contexts, especially with the cultural differences in the emerging markets.

Riga is the capital of Latvia and Vilnius the capital of Lithuania. Tallinn is the capital of Estonia.

In terms of ethnic groups: in Lithuania, more than 80% are speaking Lithuanian; with the remainder being Polish and Russian, with over 70% being Roman Catholic. In Latvia, over 60% are speaking Latvian, and most of the rest speak Russian. Lithuania was historically home to a significant Jewish community and was an important centre of Jewish scholarship and culture from the eighteenth century until the start of World War II. Of the approximately 220,000 Jews who lived in the Republic of Lithuania in 1941, almost all were annihilated during the Holocaust. The community numbered about 4000 at the end of 2009. Most of the Jews' descendants in South Africa had originally been from Lithuania. Founding of businesses, including the Bidfood Baltics, can be traced back to the family relations between the Jews in South Africa and Lithuania. MBA students from the Gordon Institute of Business Science from the University of Pretoria have been visiting Estonia annually for a couple of years and we have been involved in leading a group of students to this interesting location.

It was interesting to observe **the execution of change plans** in Estonia, especially around the e-government strategy. During the era of the Soviet Union, Estonia was earmarked as a country to develop telecommunications capability, and this legacy was serving the country. Estonia has a strong electronics and telecommunications sector and is one of the most wired countries in the world. Mobile penetration rate stood at a high of 161.9 per 100 people in 2014. There were more than 1.09 million Internet subscribers, with 85.12% of the population having access to the Internet, in 2014. The unemployment rate was 6.5%. The government was successful in bringing the unemployment rate down from 17% in 2010; through several initiatives, such as their job creation in the telecommunications sector. Interestingly, 98% of the population bank online and 93.5% of the country's tax declarations are online.

According to the World Economic Forum International Technology Index, Estonia ranked 21st among 148 countries. This is based on the level of IT use for the promotion of the country's economy. The headquarters of the European IT Agency called the Schengen visa area information system is located in Tallinn.

Their success with e-government is illustrated by 66% of the population that participated electronically in the 2012 census. During the 2015 parliamentary election, Estonian citizens from 116 different countries cast their votes online. The

Republic of Estonia is the first country to offer e-Residency—a secure digital identity available to everybody in the world interested in running a location–independent international business online (Tallinn, 2015).

12.5.2 Case Examples of Executing in Emerging Market Organisations

A company that is very interesting and straddles the three countries around the Baltic Sea is Bidfood Baltics. We were involved in conducting a case study research project on this organisation. The case study on this particular organisation can be found at www.iveycases.com and is referenced in the reference list at the end of the chapter (Scheepers & Ramsingh, 2018). For the purposes of the Eighth Enabler, the execution of strategic change in this company's case, required intense communication with the head office function that was located in Johannesburg, South Africa. The CEO Ramunas Makutenas had to travel to South Africa to influence the executive team of the global company to allow expansion in his business through capital investment in a warehouse that he wanted to be located in Lithuania. He found that the executives had difficulty in understanding the realities of his business and rationale for expansion in this emergent market. As a result, he relied heavily on face-to-face communication and Skype sessions, as well as video material that he collected to show visually what he meant, in terms of the opportunities that the fish industry offered his company, which was delivering a service to this industry. Interestingly, the software for Skype was actually developed in one of the Baltic countries, Estonia and there was a drive to develop the region as a start-up hub, which explains the focus on e-connectivity and even e-residency in these countries.

In emerging economies where institutions vary widely, especially regarding their strength and functionality, and are very different from those in developed economies, it is pertinent for companies that invest to have a clear understanding of institutions and how they work in markets in which they operate (Khanna, Palepu, & Sinha, 2005). A problem in especially frontier markets, such as countries like Malawi, is the existence of institutional voids. These include the lack of regulatory systems, the absence of contract-enforcing mechanisms and specialised intermediaries (Khanna et al., 2005). Change leaders need to have in-depth knowledge and appreciation of institutions and institutional voids to understand and operate in these emerging market environments.

A great risk for execution of change plans in the emerging markets, is thus the institutional gap or lack of infrastructure. Unlike developed markets, which have functional and predictable environments defined by their advanced institutional structures, the transaction costs in emerging economies are much higher as a result of the weakness of their institutions. Navigating the institutional environment can be complicated and unpredictable. Organisations have to adapt the execution of their plans to overcome obstacles presented by the absence or weakness of institutions (Meyer, Estrin, Bhaumik, & Peng, 2009). North (1991) defines institutions as humanly-devised constraints that structure political, economic and social interactions. Institutions comprise of formal rules such as property rights and constitutions. There are, however, simultaneously informal norms such as traditions, norms and codes of conduct (North, 1991). The role of institutions is critical in a market-based economy, and it enables individuals and firms to engage in market transactions without incurring undue risks and costs (Meyer et al., 2009).

Another interesting example from emerging markets to consider is a case of Microsoft in India. Bose and Vallurupalli (2015) published a case and distributed it through *The Case Centre*. They shared the story of the new CEO, namely Raj Biyani, who created a new vision for Microsoft IT India called MSIT. This action of his adhered to the first step in Cummings and Worley's (2015) five steps in culture change, namely formulating a clear strategic vision. The second step includes considering the values and behaviours to make it work. Applied to this case study, MSIT fully considered along the way how the culture change could affect the organisation's values and behaviours as a whole. They continuously conducted pulse checks like the polls they conducted frequently. These polls even indicated along with the implementation of the process, that their performance improved to levels never attained before.

The third step providing purpose and direction to the culture change, as Cummings and Worley's (2015) explained, was taken to by Biyani and his team by initially involving a transformation specialist to guide them on the journey. They had workshops to establish the purpose and direction of the change. They came up with the culture transformation framework to provide direction to where they wanted to take the process. MSIT, with the assistance of the transformation specialist, used the Organisation Culture Index (OCI), an assessment instrument on culture, to understand the initial As–Is or current diagnosis of what their culture was like. They used the results to establish where to go from there, for example they restructured and had driven a values intervention, based on this assessment. MSIT created a Regional Talent Hub (RTH), a pool of experts to enhance the quality of their skills and offered a clear roadmap to execute this structure.

The top management displayed their commitment (step four) by enlisting the buy-in from the head office function of Microsoft for MSIT for India's idea of a hub and a culture change process. The national culture of competitiveness worked against the idea of sharing a resource pool and collaborating across the divisional boundaries. When there was a leadership change at the top, it created confusion, since the new global Microsoft CEO, namely Satya Nadella, started a culture change on his first day as CEO on 4 February 2014. Nadella aptly declared that they had an unparalleled capacity to make an impact. Microsoft's earlier mission was about the PC on every desk and home. Their mission evolved when they welcomed Nokia's mobile devices and services into their company. They wanted to zero in on what Microsoft could uniquely contribute to the world. Nadella contended that their opportunity required them to reimagine what they had done in the past for a mobile and cloud-first world.

Microsoft was uniquely positioned to build platforms and ecosystems that create broad opportunity. Alignment was required of the global CEO and India's CEO ideas of how to achieve a culture change in the organisation, since they had to model the culture change at the highest levels, as the final step in Cummings and Worley's (2015) culture change model. Leadership used metaphors effectively, such as Nadella who used the rowing competition and the coordination of this sports team of what they need to do across boundaries in the organisation. They had to work in unison to find their swing. Biyani showed his commitment to the culture change by aligning his own behaviour and values to be passionate about transforming the organisation from solid to superb delivery. Other executives in the top team in India also demonstrated their commitment by their positive behaviour towards the flexible new structure of the experts' pool in the hub.

MSIT adapted their Human Resources (HR) practices to fit their new structure by focusing on moving towards the shared pool, such as creating value by initiating a Microsoft Academy of college hires and developing high potential employees. Other HR practices that were aligned to the strategy included the training and development at their Management Excellence Center. MSIT also restructured its business by creating three new discipline heads to create a hybrid matrix and process-based structure, which changed the reporting lines and management reporting and processes.

They selected and socialised newcomers to the organisation and terminated deviants. They indoctrinated newly hired employees to adopt the changed culture. It created new-found energy and momentum for the change. For some executives, the change was moving too fast. However, Biyani felt that they would lose momentum if they were to stop pushing for changes. Alignment in this top team was essential, prior to moving forward with more change.

With regards to the MMI case study (Scheepers & Swart, 2015), the Eighth Enabler, Execute, is illustrated through the finalisation of key merger integration decisions on system integration.

Further management layers were also populated using their Human Resources strategy and policies consistently. They finalised their business philosophy and determined their common values. MMI's divisional strategies were also implemented. A manner in which they reduced resistance was to decide not to retrench anyone. After the competition tribunal, journalists realised that 2000 people would be retrenched and the outcome was that they were not allowed to retrench. While the competition tribunal did not have any jurisdiction over this type of decision on retrenchments and MMI could probably have won an appeal court case, yet they decided for the sake of their reputation and to reduce resistance to change not to retrench anyone for 2 years, following the merger. They created a redeployment centre. The executives followed a bottom-up strategy, where the divisional strategy was first led by divisional CEO's, and they then collated these strategies to formulate the group strategy.

12.6 Measuring Eight Enabler: Execute

Reflection Questions Enabler 8: Execute

Reflection Questions Enabler 8: Execute, contains a short questionnaire to help you assess the extent to which you are practicing this enabler. You can also ask others to assess you using this instrument.

12.7 Conclusion and Outcome of the Eighth Enabler, Execute

The outcome of this enabler is that the change process delivers results, because the focus is on execution and therefore the change plan is ultimately implemented. Hopefully, new habits were formed, and the new culture had been institutionalised in the organisation.

References

Alhazemi, A. A., Rees, C., & Hossain, F. (2013). Implementation of strategic organizational change: The case of King Abdul Aziz University in Saudi Arabia. *International Journal of Public Administration, 36*(13), 972–981. https://doi.org/10.1080/01900692.2013.773036

Anifowose, B. D., Genty, K. I., & Atiku, O. S. (2011). The post consolidation of banks: Human resources management challenges and prospects in Nigeria banking sector. *International Journal of Business and Management, 6*(11), 67–75. https://doi.org/10.5539/ijbm.v6n11p67

Barros, R. H., & Domínguez, I. L. (2013). Integration strategies for the success of mergers and acquisitions in financial services companies. *Journal of Business Economics and Management, 14*(5), 979–992. https://doi.org/https://doi.org/10.3846/16111699.2013.804875. Retrieved from https://www.tandfonline.com/doi/abs/10.3846/16111699.2013.804875

Beer, M., & Nohria, N. (2000, May–June). Cracking the code of change. *Harvard Business Review*, 2–9. Retrieved from https://hbr.org/2000/05/cracking-the-code-of-change

Berkman, E. T. (2018). The neuroscience of goals and behaviour change: Lessons learned for consulting psychology. *Consulting Psychology Journal, 70*, 28–44. https://www.ncbi.nlm.nih.gov/pmc/articles/PMC5854216/

Berkman, E. T., & Rock, D. (2014, September 5). AIM: An integrative model of goal pursuit. *NeuroLeadership Journal*. https://cpb-us-e1.wpmucdn.com/blogs.uoregon.edu/dist/1/172/files/2014/09/Berkman-2014-AIM-An-integrative-model-of-goal-pursuit-2k2tp3c.pdf

Bose, I., & Vallurupalli, V. (2015). *Cultural transformation at Microsoft IT in India: Too fast or just right?* Indian Institute of Management, Calcutta, Singapore Management University, Case Centre, IIMC-CRC-2014-08. https://ink.library.smu.edu.sg/cases_coll_all/115/

Burgelman, R. A., & McKinney, W. (2005). *Managing the strategic dynamics of acquisition integration: Lessons from HP and Compaq.* Stanford GSB Research Paper Series, No. 1907. Retrieved from https://papers.ssrn.com/sol3/papers.cfm?abstract_id=804565

Chatterjee, S. (1986). Types of synergy and economic value: The impact of acquisitions on merging and rival firms. *Strategic Management Journal, 7*(2). https://doi.org/10.1002/smj.4250070203

Cooper, B. B. (2016). *The two brain systems that control our attention: The science of gaining focus*. Retrieved July 27, 2019, from https://blog.bufferapp.com/the-science-of-focus-and-how-to-improve-your-attention-span

Cummings, T. G., & Worley, C. G. (2015). *Organization development & change* (10th ed.). Cincinnati, OH: South-Western College Publishing. https://www.loot.co.za/product/thomas-cummings-organization-development-and-change/lszv-2176-g370?referrer=googlemerchant& gclid=CjwKCAjw5vz2BRAtEiwAbcVIL_ 49WYGXAaU1mrKBwWHl3ZZBiQ72sHG5Qwv5JACp9vKcDEEphNuZKhoCKWQQAv D_BwE&gclsrc=aw.ds

DePamphilis, D. M. (2012). The corporate takeover market: Common takeover tactics. In *Antitakeover defenses, and corporate governance*. San Diego, CA: Academic. https://booksite.elsevier. com/samplechapters/9780123854858/Chapter_3.pdf

Duhigg, C. (2013). *The power of habit—Why we do what we do and how to change*. London: Random House. https://www.amazon.co.uk/Power-Habit-Why-What-Change/dp/1847946240

Found, P. D., & Harvey, R. (2007). Leading the lean enterprise. *IET Engineering Management, 17* (1), 40–43. https://doi.org/10.1049/em:20070110

Franken, A., Edwards, C., & Lambert, R. (2009). Executing strategic change: Understanding the critical management elements that lead to success. *California Management Review, 51*(3), 49–73. Retrieved from http://algu.weebly.com/uploads/1/9/2/4/1924527/stra.mgtcase2.pdf

French, S. L., & Holden, T. Q. (2012). Positive organisational behaviour: A buffer for bad news. *Business and Professional Communication Quarterly, 75*(2), 208–220. Retrieved from http:// journals.sagepub.com/doi/abs/10.1177/1080569912441823

Gadiesh, O., Buchanan, R., Daniell, M., & Ormiston, C. (2002). A CEO's guide to the new challenges of M&A leadership. *Strategy & Leadership, 30*(3), 13–18. https://doi.org/10.1108/ 10878570210427918

Goleman, D. (2013). *Focus: The hidden driver of excellence*. New York: HarperCollins Publishers. https://www.amazon.com/Focus-Hidden-Excellence-Daniel-Goleman/dp/0062114964

Hampton, D. (2015). *How happy happens in your brain: The best brain possible*. Retrieved July 26, 2019, from https://www.thebestbrainpossible.com/how-happy-happens-in-your-brain/

Higgins, J. M., & McAllaster, C. (2004). If you want strategic change, don't forget to change your cultural artifacts. *Journal of Change Management, 4*(1), 63–73. https://doi.org/10.1080/ 1469701032000154926

Hofstede, G. (2001). *Cultures' consequences. comparing values, behaviours, institutions and organisations across nations* (2nd ed.). Thousand Oaks, CA: Sage. https://digitalcommons. usu.edu/unf_research/53/

Kegler, A. (2014). *What happens in your brain when you set a goal*. Retrieved February 5, 2018, from https://blog.rjmetrics.com/2014/12/16/the-psychology-of-goal-setting/

Khanna, T., Palepu, K. G., & Sinha, J. (2005). Strategies that fit emerging markets. *Harvard Business Review, 83*, 6–15. Retrieved from https://hbr.org/2005/06/strategies-that-fit-emerging-markets

Kotter, J. P. (1996). *Leading change*. Boston, MA: Harvard Business Press. Retrieved from http:// www.hbs.edu/faculty/Pages/item.aspx?num=137

Landrum, N. E., Howell, J. P., & Paris, L. (2000). Leadership for strategic change. *Leadership & Organisation Development Journal, 21*(3), 150–156. https://doi.org/10.1108/ 01437730010325031

Langley, S. (2018). *The neuroscience of change*. Retrieved from http://suelangley.com/keynote-speaker/keynote-topics/the-neuroscience-of-change/

Lawlor, J. (2013). Employee perspectives on the post-integration stage of a micro-merger. *Personnel Review, 42*(6), 704–723. https://doi.org/https://doi.org/10.1108/PR-06-2012-0096. Retrieved from https://arrow.dit.ie/cgi/viewcontent.cgi?referer=https://www.google.co.za/& httpsredir=1&article=1067&context=tfschhmtart

Levin, I., & Gottlieb, J. Z. (2009). Realigning organization culture for optimal performance: Six principles & eight practices. *Organization Development Journal, 27*(4), 31–46. https://www. semanticscholar.org/paper/Realigning-Organization-Culture-for-Optimal-Six-%26-Levin-Gottlieb/30eebf44a9e8f7dfcc13c4b130a63fb263a52c9a

Marks, M. L., & Mirvis, P. H. (2001). Making mergers and acquisitions work: Strategic and psychological preparation. *Academy of Management Executive, 15*(2), 80–92. https://doi.org/ 10.5465/AME.2001.4614947.

McAbe, J., & Baum, J. (2017, January 6). *The science of goal setting and new year's resolutions— Make your goals real with conscious/subconscious goal setting.* Retrieved from https://journal. thriveglobal.com/use-the-neuroscience-of-goal-setting-to-turn-your-new-years-resolutions-into-realities-25f853aede5b

Medina, J. (2008). *Brain rules: 12 principles for surviving and thriving at work, home, and school.* Seattle: Pear Press. https://www.amazon.com/Brain-Rules-Principles-Surviving-Thriving/dp/ 0979777720

Mehta, M. (2013). *The entrepreneurial instinct: How everyone has the innate ability to start a successful small business.* New York: McGraw-Hill. https://www.amazon.com/Entrepreneurial-Instinct-Everyone-Successful-Business/dp/0071797424

Meyer, K. E., Estrin, S., Bhaumik, S. K., & Peng M. W. (2009). Institutions, resources and entry strategies in emerging economies. *Strategic Management Journal, 30*(1), 61–80. Retrieved from http://eprints.lse.ac.uk/4217/

Nilsson, T. (2010). The reluctant rhetorician: Senior managers as rhetoricians in a strategic change context. *Journal of Organizational Change Management, 23*(2), 137–144. https://doi.org/10. 1108/09534811011031300

North, D. C. (1991). Institutions. *Journal of Economic Perspectives, 5*(1), 97–112. https://doi.org/ 10.1257/jep.5.1.97. Retrieved from https://www.aeaweb.org/articles?id=10.1257/jep.5.1.97

Ophir, E., Nass, C., & Wagner, A. D. (2009). Cognitive control in media multitaskers. *Proceedings of the National Academy of Sciences of the United States of America, 106*(37), 15583–15587. https://pubmed.ncbi.nlm.nih.gov/19706386/

Pihlak, Ü., & Alas, R. (2012). Resistance to change in Indian, Chinese and Estonian organizations. *Journal of Indian Business Research, 4*(4), 224–243. https://doi.org/10.1108/ 17554191211274767

Price, A. D. F., & Chahal, K. (2006). A strategic framework for change management. *Construction Management and Economics, 24*(3), 237–251. https://doi.org/10.1080/01446190500227011

Prochaska, J. O., DiClemente, C. C, & Norcross, J. C. (1992). In search of how people change: Applications to addictive behaviors. *American Psychologist, 47*(9), 1102–1114. Retrieved from https://www.ncbi.nlm.nih.gov/pubmed/1329589

Rock, D. (2009a). *Your brain at work: Strategies for overcoming distraction, regaining focus, and working smarter all day.* New York: HarperCollins. https://www.harpercollins.com/ 9780061771293/your-brain-at-work/

Rock, D. (2009b, October 4). *Easily distracted: Why it's hard to focus and what to do about it.* Psychology Today. https://www.psychologytoday.com/za/blog/your-brain-work/200910/easily-distracted

Rock, D. (2016). *Beat back distractions: The neuroscience of getting things done.* Retrieved from https://www.huffingtonpost.com/david-rock/beat-back-distractions-th_b_498120.html

Rock, D., & Page, L. J. (2009). *Coaching with the brain in mind: Foundations for practice.* Upper Saddle River, NJ: Wiley. https://www.wiley.com/en-us/Coaching+with+the+Brain+in+Mind% 3A+Foundations+for+Practice-p-9780470405680

Rock, D., & Schwartz, J. (2006). The neuroscience of leadership. *Strategy Business, 43*, 72–82. https://www.strategy-business.com/article/06207?gko=f1af3

Rosenberg, R. (2003, Summer). The eight rings of organisational influence: How to structure your organisation for successful change. *The Journal for Quality & Participation, 26*(2), 30–34. Retrieved from http://asq.org/qic/display-item/?item=19162

Saunders, M., Altinay, L., & Riordan, K. (2009). The management of post-merger cultural integration: Implications from the hotel industry. *Service Industries Journal, 29*(10), 1359–1375. https://doi.org/10.1080/02642060903026213

Scheepers, C. B., & Swart, S. (2015). *Momentum and metropolitan merger: Authentic transformational leadership.* Ivey Publishing, 9B15C004. https://www.iveycases.com/ProductView.aspx?id=70560

Scheepers, C. B., & Ramsingh, C. (2018). *Bidcorp baltics: Contextually intelligent leadership of entrepreneurial food services.* Ivey Publishing, 9B18C013. https://www.iveycases.com/ProductView.aspx?id=95452

Schein, E. H. (1984). Coming to a new awareness of organizational culture. *Sloan Management Review, 25*(2), 3–16. https://sloanreview.mit.edu/article/coming-to-a-new-awareness-of-organizational-culture/

Schmidt, B. (2011). Improving the operational planning process. *Fire Engineering, 8,* 118–120. Retrieved from http://www.fireengineering.com/articles/print/volume-164/issue-8/features/improving-the-operational-planning-process.html

Smit, M. (2007, November 9). *Change management in mergers and acquisitions: Making change work.* Retrieved from http://www.changewright.co.za/?p=92

Sonenshein, S. (2010). We're changing—Or are we? Untangling the role of progressive, regressive, and stability narratives during strategic change implementation. *Academy of Management Journal, 53*(3), 477–512. http://www.jstor.org/stable/25684333

Stetler, C. B., Richie, J. A., Rycroft-Malone, J., Schultz, A. A., & Charns, M. P. (2009). Institutionalizing evidence-based practice: An organizational case study using a model of strategic change. *Implementation Science, 30*(4), 78. https://doi.org/10.1186/1748-5908-4-78

Stojanovic, A., & Kessler, K. (2011). Case study: Solutions for multidisciplinary decision making. *Journal of Medical Marketing, 11*(1), 60–70. https://doi.org/10.1057/jmm.2010.38

Sujova, A., & Rajnoha, R. (2012). The management model of strategic change based on process principles. *Procedia: Social and Behavioural Science, 62,* 1286–1291. https://doi.org/10.1016/j.sbspro.2012.09.220

Tallinn. (2015). *Tallinn City Government.* Enterprise Department, Estonia Brochure. https://www.tallinn.ee/eng/Profile

Vorhauser-Smith, S. (2011). The neuroscience of talent management. *Employment Relations Today, 28,* 17–22. https://onlinelibrary.wiley.com/doi/10.1002/ert.20327

Worley, C., Hitchin, D., & Ross, W. (1996). *Integrated strategic change: How organization development builds competitive advantage.* Reading, MA: Addison-Wesley. https://www.amazon.com/Integrated-Strategic-Change-Organizational-Development/dp/0201857774

Reference List for Quotes

Nauert, R. (2018, August 8). Multitasking seems to serve emotional, not productivity, needs. *PsychCentral.* Retrieved July 26, 2019, from https://psychcentral.com/news/2012/05/01/multitasking-seems-to-serve-emotional-not-productivity-needs/38057.html

Retrieved July 26, 2019, from https://www.brainyquote.com/quotes/confucius_140908

Retrieved July 26, 2019, from https://www.goodreads.com/quotes/363836-motivation-gets-you-going-and-habit-gets-you-there

Ninth Enabler

Evaluate

If you can't measure it, you can't change it.
(Peter F. Drucker, n.d.)
The biggest room in the world is the room for improvement.
(Helmut Schmidt, n.d.)

Learning Outcomes
At the end of this chapter, change leaders will be able to:

- Evaluate the change project using self-reflection and feedback from others
- Identify lessons learned
- Evaluate the successful application of the Ten Enablers Model
- Make recommendations regarding next steps

Electronic supplementary material The online version of this chapter (https://doi.org/10.1007/978-3-030-40846-6_13) contains supplementary material, which is available to authorized users.

13.1   Orientation to Evaluating

Evaluation is the process of determining the worth, merit or value of something. Evaluating a project includes reviewing the project's operation as well as outcomes. This is done to determine or gauge the success and to identify opportunities for improvement in the future.

Figure 13.1 illustrates that change is never over. As one change process nears completion, the next wave of change commences. It also advocates that lessons need to be learned from past change processes and there needs to be a notion of building on past change processes and not starting from scratch every time a new change is embarked upon. Change leaders need to anticipate future waves of change.

Figure 13.1 illustrates that an evaluation process prevents another downturn and even provides impetus to take on the next wave of change towards a higher level of performance. Evaluation can take place during the change process or at the end.

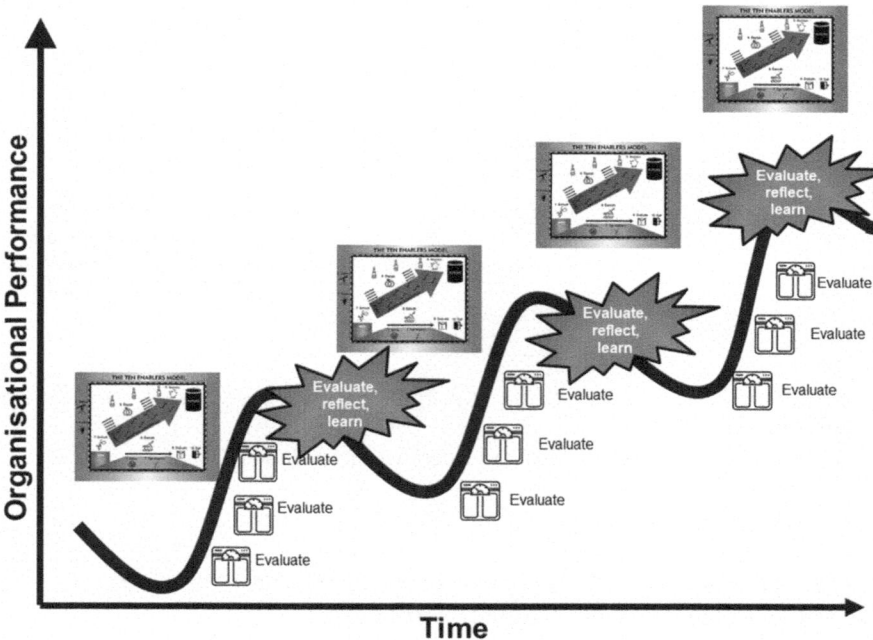

Fig. 13.1 Illustration of waves of change (Authors' own)

Practical Application of Evaluating

Caren learned the discipline of review after each wave of change, while working for Gemini Consulting. After each phase of a project, and in some instances, after each change project meeting, B's and C's evaluation would be conducted. This implied that a consultant would go and stand next to a flipchart and capture the B (Benefits), or what went well during the meeting or during this phase of the project and C (Concerns) or what could be improved upon. The way the team functioned and interacted during this phase of the project was also evaluated. When concerns were raised the next step would include an action plan to address and prevent the same mistakes in future projects. Figure 13.1 offers a visual representation of how these waves of change are practically applied.

13.2   Importance of Evaluating

Sujova and Rajnoha (2012) emphasise monitoring effects of change and specifically around the impact of the change on employee's behaviours. According to Martin (1993), troubled companies initially establish a corporate vision that informs the development of operational steering mechanisms. Unfortunately, these mechanisms then become rigid over time and cause feedback and information flow to diminish. Change leadership must examine the difference between the strategy the company adopts and the company's actual behaviour, especially with customers.

Evaluation depends on the intention of the change process when the project initially had started. For example, depending on the type of merger, strategies can be followed, including merging quickly; cutting duplication and expense and with lack of goodwill and disparity between the organisations. Alternatively, the merger could be a well-planned and prosperous merger by using incentives and ensuring retention of people, with high rate of goodwill and low disparity between the organisations (Lind & Stevens, 2004). Evaluation at the end of the change process would thus entail going back to what the initial intention was and assess against these initial intentions. Unfortunately, many M&A activities fail to create value for shareholders (Chakravorty, 2012). Luckily, there are often benefits from building synergies to create a business unit where the profits will exceed those of the two entities, had they continued to operate on their own (Shaver, 2006). A trend has emerged particularly in the pharmaceutical industry of merging to create further market power, while containing research and development costs. For example, in the case of Allergan South Africa (Scheepers & Sita, 2016), the company had experienced so many acquisitions that the analysts called it "merger-mania".

Evaluation must also be perceived as an intervention in itself, because the questions asked during the evaluation process, would prompt perceptions and make people think about whether the change process was successful or not. Saunders, Altima, and Riordan (2009), for example recommend companies to conduct a cultural audit, especially before, during and after the merger integration, so that cultural differences are diagnosed and understood to avoid cultural shocks during the post-merger stage. The audit would take the form of a collaborative effort by leadership from both companies who would interact with employees at different levels in both companies. They further propose an independent external party such as a consulting firm to assist in identifying both visible and invisible cultural elements. They suggest acculturation to develop trust between two different cultures as this can enhance cooperation between those groups. An acculturation plan should include information on dialogue, how to resolve conflict, monitoring conformity to norms and values and how to address nonconformity. Cummings and Worley (2015) advise an elimination of deviants, which is a radical action to take, when the evaluation indicates that some people are not adhering to the new value system that the change process is promoting.

13.3   Evaluating in Practice

The evaluation process is illustrated in Fig. 13.2. Evaluations are required throughout the change process, to review the progress being made, and identify how adjustments can be made to move the project forward. The final evaluation comprises an in-depth assessment of the deliverables, the change process, the change team and the change leader. We recommend a post-project evaluation date also be set at the beginning of the project, to ensure the long-term effects of the project are considered. A reasonable time frame for this evaluation is 9–12 months after the final sign-off of the project. Lessons learned should also be identified throughout the process to prevent an ongoing repetition of the same mistakes.

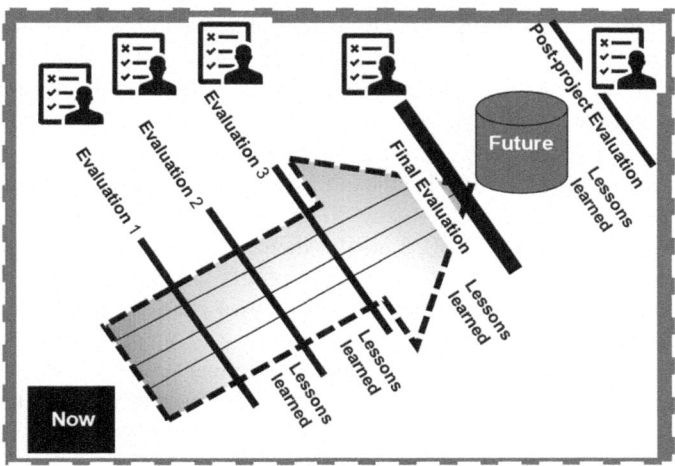

Fig. 13.2 Evaluation process (Authors' own)

13.3.1 The Evaluation Process

In addition to the ongoing reviews discussed in Enabler 8, Execute, we recommend a structured, formal and upfront planned evaluation process. The criteria for success need to be agreed upfront, the review dates need to be agreed and diarised, and the evaluation method and assessors need to be assigned.

Tool 9.1 Evaluation Process Tool

The Evaluation Process Tool helps to ensure all bases are covered. The options for "what will be evaluated?" in Tool 9.1 include, inter alia, output delivery, change intervention delivery, costs management, ethics management and timing. The "how will it be evaluated" could include interviews, questionnaires, focus groups, walkabouts, observations, discussions and presentations by change agents, etc. The "who" can include the steering committee, change leaders, change agents, external consultants, objective observers, clients, stakeholders and community members.

Evaluation criteria could include the following questions:

- Is the project delivering on outputs as planned and agreed?
- Are change interventions helping or hindering the process?
- Are change agents helping or hindering the change process?
- Is the change managed according to the Ten Enablers Model?
- Are there any unintended consequences being noticed?
- Are stakeholders satisfied?
- Are costs being managed according to the budget?
- Are resources being managed?
- What can be done differently?
- What lessons can we learn?
- What are the obstacles we need to deal with that were not anticipated?

The Post-Project Evaluation criteria could also include the following questions:

- Are the impacts from the change project still evident?
- Was the change sustainable?
- Did old habits reappear?
- Were there any unintended consequences that are only being noticed now?
- Are stakeholders still satisfied?
- Looking back, what could have been done differently?
- What further lessons can we learn?

13.3.1.1 Change Process Final Evaluation

Tool 9.2 Evaluation of Change Process

Tool 9.2 provides the reader with a template for conducting a final evaluation of the Change Process. It can be used on the three levels: the overall change process, the change leader and the change team.

13.3.1.2 Ten Enablers Model Evaluation

Tool 9.3 Ten Enablers Model Evaluation

In this tool, the ten enablers are used as a framework to help with the evaluation process. Change leaders could perform a self-assessment or could ask trusted colleagues, coaches, stakeholders, change agents and clients to help with sincere and honest feedback.

13.3.1.3 Upcoming Changes

Tool 9.4 The Next Big "Thing"

This Ninth Enabler, Evaluate, provides an opportunity for change leaders to start anticipating what the next change would be. This will be explored in more detail in the Tenth Enabler, but the process starts now. Template 9.4 gives change leaders the opportunity to identify what the next wave of change will be.

13.3.2 Implementation Tips for Evaluating

In closing off this section, we offer practical tips below for evaluating change processes:

* Do not believe your own press
* Embrace your biggest critics
* Do not take anything too personally
* Learn from negative criticism and move on
* Always be on the lookout for the next big "thing"

13.4 Neuroscience Insights into Evaluating

This enabler requires receiving feedback from stakeholders regarding the way in which the change process was implemented and how it could be improved. It also requires rational reflection on the success of the change process against the vision and goals set earlier on in the process. It also asks for rational decision-making on what the next steps might be to enhance and complete the change process.

13.4.1 Receiving Feedback from Others

We learned in Chap. 3 that a risk and reward assessment methodology governs the brain's operating system and the valuation network in the brain which constantly supplies us with information, about what will add value, or what will endanger our existence. When we ask for feedback from others, we are opening ourselves up to being criticised, and this can be perceived at a subconscious level as a threat. We need to be aware of the fact that we might tend to avoid the feedback for this reason. Here a paradigm shift is required. We need to look at the feedback as a source that will enable our success and we need to try and embrace the process.

13.4.2 Rational Reflection

During the process of evaluation, we want to use our higher-order or intellectual brain functions controlled by the cerebral cortex to reflect rationally on the successes and failures of the change process. The cerebral cortex is the tissue that covers the cerebrum (Fig. 13.3). A thick band of nerves (corpus callosum) connects the right and left cerebral cortex sides.

We learned in Chap. 3, that the cerebral cortex consists of the neocortex (90%), the hippocampus, and parts of the cingulate cortex. The neocortex contains the prefrontal cortex (PFC) in the very front of our brain, behind our forehead, involved in executive

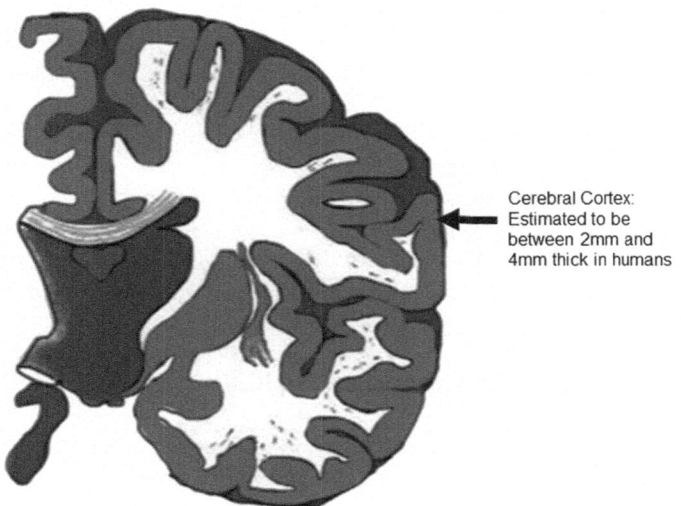

Cerebral Cortex:
Estimated to be
between 2mm and
4mm thick in humans

Fig. 13.3 Cerebral cortex (Authors' own)

functions such as planning, goals and actions. The PFC forms part of the frontal lobes. Cognitive control and evaluation happen in different regions of the PFC.

A study at the University of Iowa used data collected from 350 people over 30 years with injuries to, or lesions in regions of the frontal lobes. This study was conducted to determine the role of these different brain areas. It further helped scientists confirm the involvement of the particular regions of the brain as studies using imaging could potentially lead to erroneous assumptions, as participants could be distracted in the scanners (Neith, 2012).

A lot of distracting information (e.g. emotional and irrational perception) can flow into our awareness, so we have to take care to evaluate the change process against objective success criteria so to ensure the evaluation remains unbiased. This is not to say we should not consider the emotional and irrational perceptions of others as it can provide valuable information to deal with resistance to change.

13.5   Evaluating in Emerging Markets

13.5.1 Case Examples of Evaluating in the Emerging Markets Contexts

In this discussion, we focus on case examples from India, of a change process at a major utility and in the information technology sector.

One of our interviewees, from a higher education institution in New Delhi, observed that in reflection on consulting in a large-scale change process at a major utility in another province: the social hierarchy, within the Indian society of high power distance, made it especially difficult on the change project. The change process involved a combined committee, called the joint council, of representative members from the unions, the lower employees and management to discuss productivity issues at their respective plants, grouped together according to the region in which the plants were situated.

The interviewee learned that it was not easy to change mindsets and attitudes that had been shaped by traditional sociocultural paradigms. Grievances related issues often dominated the interactions and discussions. Human Resources played an important role in communicating the goals and objectives of the change programme and getting the top and senior management both at plant level as well as corporate level buy-in.

In evaluating whether their change programme was successful, they investigated whether there was alignment between joint councils' purposes and objectives and the corporate vision and direction. They found that there was indeed an inculcation of adherence to the corporate core values. The management at the utility developed an appreciation that employee nominees could meaningfully contribute to productivity-related issues. The project team also gauged that there was an improvement in communication across various participative forums and between nominees and their constituencies.

Another measurement that they used was the fact that the action plans from the various groups were consolidated per region and distributed amongst the participating members of the workshops. There were even follow-up workshops held with the members who participated initially at the workshop. They learned that the dependence on Human Resources caused a bottleneck with the implementation and the time lag was not ideal.

Since only a few representatives received exposure to the workshops, all employees at the plant level had not developed through the experience. However, at some plants, they initiated their own plant-level workshops to come up with productivity improvement plans.

The change agents experienced that they personally developed through the experience on the change project, through being exposed to union members and officials. They were touched by the lower-level employees' transparency, their good ideas and positive outlook and it reconfirmed their faith in these employees. The change team ensured that these employees were engaged, by reviewing the initiatives that they took in implementing the change plans at their plants. While the employees lower down were engaged, the plant level management was scared of losing power, and continuous candid communication was required with them. Management teams in some instances exhibited resistance to the change effort. In these instances, the support of top management provided legitimacy and credibility to the change effort.

Their evaluation showed that a paradigm shift was apparent from being focused on the hierarchy to equality, from competition to collaboration and working together, rather than in isolation. Interestingly, this example relates to the published case study on Microsoft in India, where a change in mindset was also required, from employees being competitive to collaborative. In this case, they also had to conduct interventions to develop team spirit and creating synergy (Bose & Vallurupalli, 2015, Cultural transformation at Microsoft IT India).

Another aspect of evaluation is how to report on progress towards the change strategy. A study in India by Murthy and Abeysekera (2008) highlights that when

Indian firms report on their Corporate Social Responsibility change initiatives, most of them will use a dual strategy in evaluating and then giving feedback by offering the impact of their actions on both their human resource internally to the organisations, as well as their social relations with the community to legitimise their activities to stakeholders. Srivastava and Mohapatra (2013) also reported on the importance of continuous evaluation on change projects in India and to involve the internal Human Resources function.

13.5.2 Case Examples of Evaluating in Emerging Market Organisations

Bose and Vallurupalli (2015) shared that Raj Biyani, CEO of the Microsoft India operation, initiated an evaluation of the design components as Cummings and Worley (2015) depicted in their diagnostic model in their seminal book *Organisational Development and Change* (10th edition). An important aspect of evaluating is determining how aligned the design components, such as technology, Human Resources (HR) systems, structure and management processes and ultimately culture, are with the strategy of the organisation.

In Microsoft's case, they were focused on prioritising innovation and empowering users and organisations to do more. Biyani at Microsoft India, in particular, had bought into this idea. The Indian operation was struggling, prior to Biyani's appointment with low morale and rising attrition rates. As a result, Biyani's strategy was to break down silos between structures and created a shared pool of talent, reinforced by his hub or Regional Talent Hub (RTH) structure. In evaluating how the design components fit the strategy, the actions to invigorate the management processes, HR systems and reporting processes had to be evaluated. Biyani initiated projects to move the company from value creators towards being game changers. They identified performance and opportunity gaps in their process of evaluating whether the design components were indeed aligned to the strategy.

Vital to the success of MSIT India's strategy was the underlying or foundational technology, which transformed the inputs in their systems, based on market and product requirements, to products and services as demanded by the market. MSIT India responded by altering its structural design to bring together engineering resources that were shared in a pool. This allowed for flexibility and breaking of silos to achieve fast responses and efficient outcomes for the design and delivery of new systems. At very short notice, internal teams could call upon the deep technical expertise of the pool to assist them with any issues they might have had. This improved their utilisation rate and fundamentally they became much more responsive to external customers.

These initiatives were clearly aligned to the design components at the organisation, focusing on strategy, technology and management processes, as well as structures. MSIT India's shared pool or hub model was heavily focused on HR systems and management processes. For example, value creation initiatives were implemented, such as an induction programme. MSIT India had an issue with a pear-shaped organisation, where there were not an adequate number of people actually conducting the work, like programming. Instead, they had many people in the middle of the organisation. This recruitment drive focused on campus hiring of university-qualified people to meet their staffing goals, and they started hiring top talent for the organisation.

They also focused on developing high-performing individuals with an end goal in mind of promoting them. The Management Excellence Centre that they created, assisted in growing the management competencies and deliver on their strategic goals.

The management processes at MSIT India were quite complex, and coordination between the teams could be quite difficult. There was initially a dual reporting structure that had been confusing to the employees and caused frustration. The hub model assisted in overcoming the frustration. Decision-making through these optimised structures improved and processing of information could happen a lot faster since the flexibility achieved through the new structure improved processes.

Alignment between the management processes and the organisational structure was crucial to optimising their efforts to achieve their strategy of becoming a great company. The new structure allowed MSIT India to make quicker decisions, improved understanding of performance and coordinate work more effectively through the shared pools focused on technical expertise and delivering value.

In evaluating the structures, Biyani's new structure of the hub offered the three discipline heads the opportunity to report directly to Biyani and thus optimised decision-making. Delayering the structure and ending up with fewer layers between the top and the bottom is a common way of restructuring and regularly offers higher efficiency. The evaluation also shows that the restructuring realised better coordination between the units. The interdependence between the units was also improved.

In evaluating the culture at MSIT India, the vision of Biyani was to create a game changer culture, where the opportunity gap was addressed by employees. A couple of initiatives assisted in creating the culture, for example through role modelling of the top executives of this proactive behaviour they communicated the change vision and reinforced the message of the ideal culture regularly. The evaluation thus indicated that the design components were closely aligned with the strategy of MSIT India.

13.6   Measuring Ninth Enabler, Evaluate

Reflection Questions Enabler 9: Evaluate

Reflection Questions Enabler 9: Evaluate, contains a short questionnaire to help you assess the extent to which you are practicing this enabler. You can also ask others to assess you using this instrument.

13.7   Conclusion and Outcome of the Ninth Enabler, Evaluate

This Ninth Enabler offered an opportunity to reflect on how well the change process has been executed and to learn from the assessment. The benefit is that lessons are learned from past mistakes, and preventative measures are implemented to ensure that mistakes are not repeated. This continuous improvement process enables an ability to implement successful changes that improve over time. Evaluating success is essential prior to the final enabler, exiting, since the timing of exiting is important. Should the evaluation indicate that the benefits that had been envisioned were still not realised, exiting has to be postponed.

References

Bose, I., & Vallurupalli, V. (2015). *Cultural transformation at Microsoft IT in India: Too fast or just right?* Indian Institute of Management, Calcutta, Singapore Management University, Case Centre, IIMC-CRC-2014-08. https://www.iimcal.ac.in/cultural-transformation-microsoft-it-india-too-fast-or-just-right

Chakravorty, J. N. (2012). Why do mergers and acquisitions quite often fail? *Advances in Management, 5*(5), 21–28. https://econpapers.repec.org/article/mgnjournl/v_3a5_3ay_3a2012_3ai_3a5_3aa_3a2.htm

Cummings, T. G., & Worley, C. G. (2015). *Organization development & change* (10th ed.). Cincinnati, OH: South-Western College Publishing. https://www.amazon.com/Organization-Development-Change-Thomas-Cummings/dp/1133190456

Lind, B., & Stevens, J. (2004). Match your merger integration strategy and leadership style to your merger type. *Strategy & Leadership, 32*(4), 10–16. https://doi.org/10.1108/10878570410547652

Martin, R. (1993). Changing the mind of the corporation. *Harvard Business Review, 71*(6), 81–94. Retrieved from https://hbr.org/1993/11/changing-the-mind-of-the-corporation

Murthy, V., & Abeysekera, I. (2008). Corporate social reporting practices of top software Indian firms. *Australasian Accounting, Business and Finance Journal, 2*(1), 36–59. Retrieved from https://ssrn.com/abstract=2601740

Neith, K. (2012). Role of the frontal lobes in reasoning and decision making. *SciTechDaily.* Retrieved July 27, 2019, from https://scitechdaily.com/role-of-the-frontal-lobes-in-reasoning-and-decision-making/

Saunders, M., Altinay, L., & Riordan, K. (2009). The management of post-merger cultural integration: Implications from the hotel industry. *Service Industries Journal, 29*(10), 1359–1375. https://doi.org/10.1080/02642060903026213

Scheepers, C. B., & Sita, D. (2016). *Allergan SA: Contextual leadership sustaining culture during mergers.* Ivey Publishing, 9B16C044. https://www.iveycases.com/ProductView.aspx?id=82246

Shaver, J. M. (2006). A paradox of synergy: Contagion and capacity effects in mergers and acquisitions. *Academy of Management Review, 31*(4), 962–976. https://doi.org/10.5465/AMR.2006.22527468

Srivastava, B., & Mohapatra, M. (2013). Legitimacy to employee voice: Role of progress intervention. *The Indian Journal of Industrial Relations, 49*(3), 197–211. https://www.jstor.org/stable/24546949?seq=1

Sujova, A., & Rajnoha, R. (2012). The management model of strategic change based on process principles. *Procedia: Social and Behavioural Science, 62*, 1286–1291. https://doi.org/10.1016/j.sbspro.2012.09.220

Reference List for Quotes

Retrieved July 26, 2019, from https://quotefancy.com/quote/888168/Peter-F-Drucker-If-you-can-t-measure-it-you-can-t-change-it

Retrieved July 26, 2019, from https://www.brainyquote.com/quotes/helmut_schmidt_756166

Tenth Enabler

Exit

Leave a legacy, not a vacancy.

(John Maxwell, 1998)

Learning Outcomes

At the end of this chapter, Change Leaders will be able to:

- Identify and appoint an appropriate, competent successor/new change leader
- Conduct a smooth handover
- Exit the project with grace
- Move onto a new change project with enthusiasm

Electronic supplementary material The online version of this chapter (https://doi.org/10.1007/978-3-030-40846-6_14) contains supplementary material, which is available to authorized users.

C. B. Scheepers, S. Swart, *Change Leadership in Emerging Markets*, Future of Business and Finance, https://doi.org/10.1007/978-3-030-40846-6_14

14.1 Orientation to Exiting

At the end of a change process geared to finalise a particular wave of change, the conclusion is psychologically a critical milestone to celebrate. Organisations sometimes fail to consolidate after a large effort of change, prior to taking on the next huge challenge. Because our organisations are in flux, the natural rhythm of making endings and then going into new beginnings is disrupted, and we expect our employees to keep going with change processes and sometimes simultaneous projects, without natural consolidation, prior to steaming ahead to the next wave. The Ninth Enabler thus focuses not only on the leaders of the change initiatives, but the actual projects that are part of the change processes, which need to end and exit, with a natural stop and consolidation, prior to a renewal of the existing ones and before brand new projects are launched. Celebrating the completed ones will offer a sense of completion and supply the energy to keep going with the next one.

Our modern globalised changing environment and economic uncertainty result in high employee turnover and regular restructurings in organisations. Due to this uncertainty, attachment during separation is an intrinsic part of organisational life. Attachments and separations are frequently experienced by leadership and employees in the organisational life cycle. Organisations would benefit from not underestimating the psychological impact of separation, as Grady and Grady (2013, p. 207) observed, "Considering the economic and social significance of work to the individual it is not surprising to find attachments that are associated within the workplace". Braun (2011) in his turn, points out that the level of complexity in organisations increases insecurity and work pressure, which increases attachment behaviour as the individual becomes more dependent on internal working models.

14.2 Importance of Exiting

Bowlby, the pioneer on attachment theory, explained already in 1969, that our internal working models of attachments develop in individuals through experience-based mental representations of attachment relationships. Dykas and Cassidy (2011) presented an integrated lifespan theoretical model explaining attachment and the processing of information and knowledge regarding attachments. The core of the model is described through "internal working models of attachments" (Dykas & Cassidy, 2011, p. 19). Interestingly, the separation from the change project or the organisation could elicit change leaders and employees' earlier issues around their separation and attachments with parents. As a result, organisations must offer support to individuals affected by the end of a project or who are separating from the organisation. Employee Wellness or Assistance (EAP or EWP) Programmes are essential in these times. Even when individuals hold secure, experience-based internal working models of attachment processes, the psychological impact could be far reaching, especially in cases of negative attachment association (Dykas & Cassidy, 2011).

The manner in which the separation takes place and the causal factors would have a huge impact on how the individual deals with the exiting of the change project or organisation. In cases where the restructuring due to the end of the change project causes layoffs, David Noer (1993) in his seminal work of survivor sickness, called *Healing the wounds*, advises that an organisation should treat the victims in this process well, such as organising redeployment processes, for example upskilling and training on CV writing and interview skills. The degree to which the victims were treated well, would influence the lack of trust or called level of survivor sickness in the organisation.

In Bluen's (2013) book on *Talent management in emerging markets*, he reports that Huawei has a strong learning and development focus and is attractive to Chinese employees. New employees receive up to 6 months' induction training at Huawei University. Organisations must take this lead time to get a new employee up and running, organisations must take this lead time into account. For example, they must consider when projects come to an end, whether new leadership and employees are required for their different types of projects going forward. In this regard, Standard Chartered Bank China developed a raw talent superhighway, where they offer professional and management development as well as training in English language skills and business etiquette. An extensive suite of e-learning programmes ensures that learning is accessible to all. Chinese high-potential employees are often moved globally, including to the company head office in London. Most importantly, the culture is nurturing and performance driven that assist in having bench strength through thorough succession planning and retaining talent for other projects, with an attrition rate of a remarkable 3% per year (Ready, Hill, & Conger, 2008).

The framework of Elliott Jacques is relevant here, in which he praises the hierarchy in his book, *Executive Leadership, a practical guide to managing complexity*, co-authored by Stephen Clement (1994), and declares that hierarchy is the most effective organisational form, where tasks vary along a continuum between simple and complex. There are jumps in levels of responsibility as leadership moves up in the hierarchy, where the time span of the longest task assigned to each managerial role increases. Accordingly the level of experience, knowledge and mental stamina required increases. At the same token, exiting an organisational change process could signal time to take on a more complex change process, perhaps with a larger programme and longer-term focus, with its relevant projects resorting under the programme. With this increased complexity of the change process, more stamina would be required and an ability to apply knowledge and experience.

In our research in the form of interviews and our experience, we observed that exiting and its emotional connotations could create huge discomfort in organisations and in leadership in particular. The succession plan is, therefore, essential, prior to the end of a change process. A proactive approach could save time and energy later.

Leadership must ensure a proper ending when enabling exiting. Bridges (1980) had an appropriate framework that consisted of an ending, transition and new beginning. See Scheepers (2012) for an application of the Bridges framework and for the purposes of this volume, it is worthwhile for individual change leaders and organisations to take time to consciously go through the process of making a definite ending to make the transition to the new beginning easier. In the spiritual realm, it is essential to take note of the impermanence of periods in our lives. This deepens our awareness of another life (some religions believe in an afterlife) and focuses our attention on how temporary the good as well as challenging times in our lives are.

Exiting also relates to a phenomenon of high turnover at the top. Moss-Kanter (2003) of Harvard in this regard point to the generally accepted principle that a new leader is appropriate for a new phase of an organisational life cycle. As the saying goes, a new broom sweeps clean. The old guard or previous change leadership thus has to exit to make space for new and perhaps more modern ideas to lead the organisation into the next phase in its life cycle. In cases where the change process is intended to bring about a turnaround in an organisation, this principle might be particularly relevant. Khumalo and Scheepers (2018) found in their research that in public sector turnarounds, in particular, a new broom was required because the transactional leadership style of retrenching people during the turnaround, was not ideal in the next phase of the turnaround, where a new vision was required, and a transformational leadership style was more relevant. It is rare that the same person would possess all these leadership styles in equal measure and thus a new person is generally required with a different style, appropriate to what the context requires.

14.3 Exiting in Practice

For leaders, the relinquishing of power is especially difficult (De Vries, 2003).

14.3.1 The Exiting Process

In this volume, we propose a seven-step process for *Exiting*. Figure 14.1 illustrates this process.

The process starts long before the project has reached its conclusion or even well before there is a need for the change leader to exit. It is an ongoing process in which the change leader identifies potential successors and ensures they are developed long before they need to step into the change leader's shoes. Next, the change leader starts

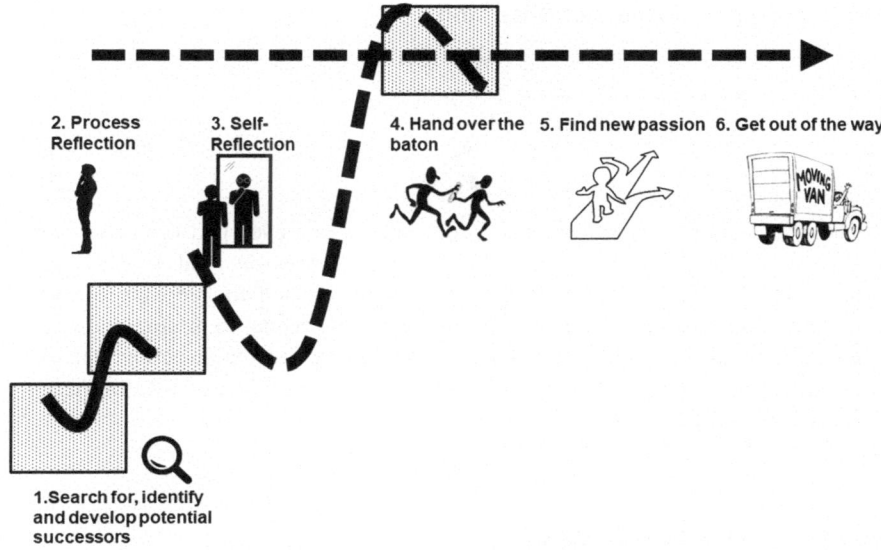

2. Process
Reflection

3. Self-
Reflection

4. Hand over the   5. Find new passion 6. Get out of the way
baton

1.Search for, identify
and develop potential
successors

Fig. 14.1   Exiting process (Authors' own)

wrapping-up the project. Here he will do the final evaluation (as discussed in Enabler 9, Evaluate) and ensure all documentation is in place to hand over to his successor.

The change leader then takes a hard look in the mirror and reflects on his role in the change process. He considers what he did well and what he could have done better. This is done to elicit what he can learn from his own functioning during the change process, in order to identify how these situations could have been avoided. Recommendations are made on how similar issues might be addressed in the future.

Next, the change leader selects a potential successor and ensures that the baton is handed over as smoothly as possible. He formally introduces his successor and ensures followers "buy" the new leader.

In the final two steps, the change leader explores his own new future, moves away and let go with grace. He can provide moral support and open doors for the new change leader but meddling in daily affairs and reminiscing with others about the "good old days" are definite taboos.

Because *Exiting* is the last enabler, it provides an opportunity to go right back to where the process started with Enabler 1, Ethos and Enabler 2, Ego Mastery. As it is a cyclical process, we can connect with the very first enablers as we progress to the next S-curve. Endings and beginnings are very similar in many regards: Strong emotions such as anxiety, rejection, curiosity, excitement, anticipation, fear, sometimes anger and loss can also be expected during the handover (Webber, 2010).

14.3.1.1 Step 1: Succession Planning

Tool 10.1 Succession Planning Template

The Succession Planner Template (Tool 10.1) was developed to encourage existing change leaders to identify potential successors and to actively approach these individuals to consider following in their footsteps or to lead other change processes. This will require the change leader to be continuously on the lookout for potential talent and to then jointly develop an action plan to ensure competencies are developed to equip these individuals to fulfil these roles at the required time.

14.3.1.2 Step 2: Project Wrap-Up

Tool 10.2 Project Wrap-Up Checklist

As the change project starts nearing its end, the change leader should encourage decision makers and stakeholders to evaluate the achievement of the Balanced SMART Vision and share comments and feedback on the progress made. The first step in the wrap-up process is to review the Balanced SMART Vision Worksheet (Tool 5.5 in Enabler 5, Envision) to check to what extent the vision was reached. Tool 10.2 enables change leaders to review delivery and record comments against each of the balanced goals. It also provides an opportunity to reflect and list general lessons learned (self-reflection and feedback from others). It also prompts change leaders to identify who contributed greatly to the success of the project, who might need to be personally thanked or recognised. Suggestions/new ideas/opportunities that could be put forward to the organisation as well as the individuals who will need to be influenced to bring these idea to fruition, need to be identified.

14.3.1.3 Step 3: Process Evaluation
Repeat Tools 9.2–9.4 here.

14.3.1.4 Step 4: Change Leader Self-reflection

Tool 10.3 Change Leader Self-Reflection Tool

In many respects, Tool 10.3 is similar to Tool 9.3 in Enabler 9, Evaluate. However, this template will help the change leader to reflect on his **personal** change leadership journey. The change leader needs to set aside quality quiet time to reflect deeply on what he can improve on in future projects. The ten enablers are used here as a framework to help the change leader with this process. Change leaders could also ask trusted colleagues, coaches, stakeholders, change agents and clients to assist with obtaining sincere and honest feedback.

14.3.1.5 Step 5: Appoint the Successor

Tool 10.4 New Change Leader Appointment Checklist

The New Change Leader Appointment checklist in Tool 10.4 can be used to help with the process of ensuring a new change leader is in place to lead new change projects.

14.3.1.6 Step 6: Personal Next "Big Thing"

Tool 10.5 My Personal Next Big Thing

This tool can help change leaders who are ready to move on, identify their personal fears, desires and emotional state regarding the progression. It also helps identify potential opportunities and networks that could be explored.

14.3.1.7 Change Leader's Personal Change Plan

Now that the handover has been done, the change leader can focus on himself and define what he wants to achieve in the next 24 months. Of course, this part of the process can be done earlier on in the process too. Following the descriptions of where he wants to be in 24 months, the change leader can now start planning what needs to happen, how, who can help, and when.

> **Tool 10.6 Change Leader's Personal Change Plan**
>
>
>
> In Tool 10.6 change leaders can describe their desired end state and develop an action plan of how to get to this desired end state.

14.3.2 Implementation Tips for Exiting

In conclusion of this enabler, we share the following tips with change leaders:

- Look out: Do not be defined by what you do. This change project does not define you. You might be needed elsewhere. Sometimes you need to move on to grow and learn new skills.
- Another leader might just be what the project needs to take it to another level.
- Do not overstay your welcome. There are always other opportunities out there.
- Do not burn bridges. You never know when you might need to tap into old networks.
- Say thank you—personally—to those who wish you well and those who contributed to your success or the success of the project.

Quitting your job can be just as heart breaking as ending a romance (Huhulea, 2016).

14.4   Neuroscience Insights into Exiting

The brain operates best when following a habit, therefore, exiting or leaving something behind can be very difficult for those leading as well as for those participating in the change. Exiting involves letting go of what is familiar. In neuroscience, this implies stopping existing neural pathways and forming new neural pathways. This is never an easy task, no matter how exciting the future might be.

The exiting process brings ambivalence as one could be ready to move on and keen to follow a new direction, yet be apprehensive and nervous about the unknown. The brain loves predictability and hates surprises and will, therefore, resist any change—no matter how beneficial it might be. Letting go is often an emotional process too. Change leaders can, therefore, become very attached to their change project.

Saying goodbye affects the pleasure regions of the brain. When humans become attached to someone or something, they derive pleasure from the attachment, and the nucleus accumbens is activated. The nucleus accumbens plays a central role in the reward system and is responsible for the dopamine and serotonin, as Fig. 14.2 illustrates.

For most people letting go is a matter of mourning intensely for a few weeks or months and then gradually moving on. For a small number of people, however, it can become a debilitating event, leading to an inability to continue functioning normally. They experience complicated bereavement. Functional magnetic resonance imaging (fMRI) has shown that grief activates regions of the brain associated with processing pain. FMRI scans displayed intense activity in pain processing areas of the brain and

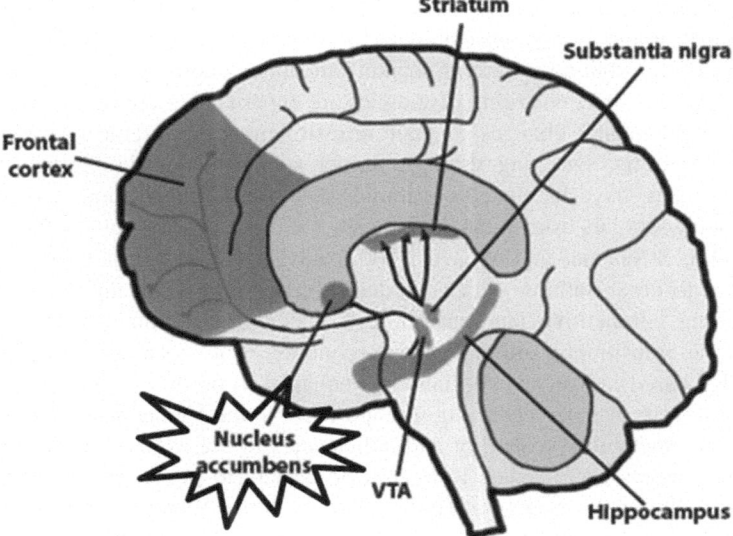

Fig. 14.2 Nucleus accumbens (Authors' own)

activity in the nucleus accumbens, a region of the brain linked to pleasure and reward of those experiencing complicated grief. At a sudden death this could mean that the brains of those with complicated grief have not adequately adjusted to the fact that their loved ones are gone (O'Connor et al., 2008). Their nucleus accumbens activation signals that those with complicated grief have a harder time accepting and letting go than noncomplicated grievers. Scientists now have a clinical marker that can help them distinguish among those with complicated and noncomplicated grief (AAAS, 2008).

As exiting also indicates having to change a direction and breaking ties with the old, we would like to refer change leaders back to the neuroscience insights of *Habits,* we discussed in Enabler 8, Execute. For more information about setting a new course and developing a personal vision and goals, we refer you to the Second Enabler, Ego mastery.

14.5   Executing in the Emerging Markets

In this discussion, the changes in Vietnam will be focused on, as well as some company examples such as an information technology company in India and a multinational, Johnson and Johnson (J&J).

14.5.1 Case Examples of Executing in the Emerging Markets Context

Enabler Ten, the Exiting Enabler highlights the link with the first enabler, because exiting implies that something new will start. It also emphasises the need to continuously improve through engaging in continuous change. As a background and focus of this volume, emerging markets are apt examples of the requirement of constant change, since emerging economies are experiencing unprecedented transition and fundamental changes in their infrastructures. The radical political and economic reforms, sweeping through former socialist countries during the last several decades, have facilitated economic growth and urbanisation, according to the following scholars from Vietnam: Nguyen, Le, Tran, and Bryant (2015). Marino, Strandholm, Steensma, and Weaver (2002) advise that this fast growth created challenges to organisations, which are doing business in these emerging markets. The shifting competitive landscape forced Vietnamese companies to innovate. Vietnam is transitioning to a market economy. The software industry as a knowledge-based industry is continuously engaged in producing innovations, and thus this industry has been growing in importance to the Vietnamese economy.

The unpredictability, volatility and deficiencies in the external environment of emerging markets urge leaders to have a propensity to pay greater heed to their companies' internal resources. These scholars from Vietnam highlighted that Vietnam is characterised by a high competitive intensity, primarily due to market pressure from foreign-invested software companies. An interesting phenomenon worth mentioning here is the finding of Malesky and Taussig (2009) that while Vietnam is transitioning to a market economy and needing a considerable amount of bank credit lending to fund entrepreneurial initiatives, banks in Vietnam were found to be ineffective, in most cases where they used connections or relationship-based lending or through the existing social structure in the society to make investment decisions. They found that "Rapid development of the domestic private sector in communist China and Vietnam has been offered as evidence against a large body of literature that claims a solid legal infrastructure is required for the financial sector to contribute to economic development" (Malesky & Taussig, 2009, p. 535). It shows that relationship-based lending has not served as an adequate substitute for legal institutions.

It seems that in Vietnam, like in China, the private sector and financial sector are expanding dramatically, but the rule of law has not kept pace. This finding points to the impact of the institutional gap in the emerging markets. Most importantly, Malesky and Taussig (2009) established that political connections were an ineffective tool for channelling bank credit to the most profitable investors and most entrepreneurs would fund their undertaking through informal loans. Expansion strategies of companies in Vietnam would thus have difficulty in getting investors to support their ideas for continuous improvement and in some cases they would need to abort or exit the initiative or project up to such time that funding is available to start a change process all over again through establishing the ethos (as with Enabler One).

14.5.2 Case Examples of Executing in Emerging Market Organisations

Another example worth mentioning here is, Johnson and Johnson (J&J), a multinational that has been in existence for more than 125 years and continues to grow its global footprint through various strategic interventions. J&J's global vision is caring for the world "one person at a time". It inspires and unites the staff members of J&J. Approximately 115,000 employees at more than 265 J&J companies work with partners in health care to touch the lives of over a billion people across the world per day. See their website for more information on their vision at https://www.jnjconsumer.co.za/our-company. The ethos of the organisation is clear by calling the business in the group a family. "Our Family of Companies comprises: The world's sixth-largest consumer health company; the world's most comprehensive medical devices business; the world's sixth-largest biologics company; as well as the world's fifth-largest pharmaceuticals company". Johnson and Johnson's baby products are known in most countries world wide.

With a strong culture such as this one displayed by their family values, an exit of a leader, even top management in the organisation, would not change the family values, since they would ensure that the successors would share the same values as their predecessors. In a study conducted by Cavallo and Brienza (2006), the standards of leadership contained in a traditional set of managerial and leadership competencies are built around the J&J credo, which embodies the company's orienting business philosophy towards responsibility, integrity and ethical behaviour. This type of strong ethos survives individuals who come and go in the organisation.

The final enabler, Exiting prompts organisations to question the sustainability of the change process. In Cummings and Worley (2015), a relevant model is offered to assess whether the change processes would be sustainable, namely the institutionalisation model. According to this model, the organisation's characteristics would need to be taken into account to ascertain the degree of sustainability or institutionalisation of change interventions. As an example, this model was applied to the case study of Microsoft India, mentioned in previous discussions. We offer the application of the model to Bose and Vallurupalli's (2015) case study on Microsoft India with their new CEO, Raj Biyani, as follows:

Regarding the organisation's characteristics, the degree of harmony between MSIT India and the head office of Microsoft in Redmond, in the United States, was an important organisational characteristic to consider, since this harmony was still developing. The country CEO, Biyani and the global CEO, Nadella had still to align their specific goals and initiatives to sustain a countrywide agenda for Microsoft.

Concerning stability, the restructuring of MSIT India into the shared pool created instability and disrupted the status quo, but apart from that change, overall it appeared to be a relatively stable period in the organisational life cycle. The case had not mentioned any union activity, which would have made the organisation more unstable and unpredictable.

With regard to intervention characteristics, the goals of the change processes were clarified. However, initially, they were quite broad and only, later on, moved to be more specific. They created an itemised plan of the culture intervention, which made the goal of culture change more specific. A translation of the implications of the culture change for every department would make the goals even more specific and relevant as well as applicable to each department. On exiting, these goals specificity would make the changes sustainable and ensure they were instituted into the organisation. The rolling out of the change processes to all departments had to be accompanied by rigorous communication processes. Biyani and his team had to specify in advance the socialisation processes, as well as the commitment and reward allocation that was required to ensure the success of the initiative.

The level of the change agent is another indicator of the degree of institutionalisation. The rollout had to include the lowest levels of the organisation at all locations throughout India. MSIT India had thus required role models, regular communication and reinforcement mechanisms through change agents on all levels in the organisation to ensure sustainability. MSIT India created multiple channels to provide support to people who wanted to understand the intervention.

Top management's passion and commitment were evident in the published case study on MSIT India. This level of sponsorship was required to ensure sustainability. The commitment from the top was, however, not adequate. A socialisation process was needed throughout the organisations, where all newcomers had to learn about the values and expectations of MSIT India. The existing employees also had to be inducted into the game changer culture that they were envisioning. There were multiple initiatives in place, and this is essential in sustaining the culture change.

Behavioural change at the top is crucial in showing commitment to the change processes in the organisation. Without reward allocation to the new behaviour, the degree of sustainability is low. In MSIT India, they linked the reward system to the required new behaviour to institutionalise the culture. For example, they identified the teams that showed initiative in becoming game changers. These quick wins had to be diffused, meaning spread throughout the organisation. These early successes were shared as examples of what a game-changing culture looks like.

Continuous monitoring of the success of the change processes assisted MSIT India to sense and calibrate behaviour that was aligned with the ideal culture of being game changers. They focused on what behaviour had to be rewarded and conducted informal pulse checks or polls to give an indication of the intervention's success. The results of these checks informed the corrective actions that had to be taken.

Regarding indicators of institutionalisation, the foundational level of institutionalisation reflects the degree to which the employees in the organisation, in this case, MSIT India has a firm knowledge of the behaviours that are required for a game changer culture. The next level of institutionalisation represents the degree to which the actual behaviour or performance is influenced by the envisioned game changer culture. In this case, there were pockets of excellence where the new behaviour was exhibited, for instance, those working in the shared pool of experts. The question remains whether the MSIT India's employees would prefer the new behaviour when exiting had taken place? So to what extent had people agreed on the appropriateness of this game changer culture for their future, in other words, was there normative consensus at the organisation? Did employees believe that the new culture would add value to the organisation?

With regards to the MMI case study (Scheepers & Swart, 2015), the Tenth Enabler: Exit is illustrated by the exiting of the two CEOs. Wilhelm van Zyl demonstrated true leadership by staying on for another 2 years when he was not appointed as MMI's group CEO. He told us that he wanted to show his commitment to making the change work by staying on and assisting his employees in dealing with the change processes. Nicolaas Kruger, in his turn, only left in 2018 and thus had seen the merger process through and only left after the integration process had been completed.

14.6 Measuring Tenth Enabler: Exit

Reflection Questions Enabler 10: Exit

Reflection Questions Enabler 10: Exit, contains a short questionnaire to help you assess the extent to which you are practicing this enabler. You can also ask others to assess you using this instrument.

14.7   Conclusions and Outcome of the Tenth Enabler, Exit

The final enabler highlighted that leadership must be prepared to exit when their time has come to move on, and the change process had been delivered. For the individual leader, exiting symbolises a new phase in their own careers, where they move on to new challenges either laterally in the organisation, or to a larger change programme with multiple change processes at the same time or another division or a start-up of a new organisation with new opportunities to add value.

For the organisation, the exiting enabler signals a time for a new wave of change, or a renewal or revitalising of an existing change process to derive more value from the change process as described throughout the ten enablers. In some instances, exiting could represent the ending of an existing process and a move to a new change process, with hopefully even greater opportunities and an enlarging scale of impact. In these instances, the First Enabler would become important and the questions around the impact that the organisation has on its environment and customers. The Tenth Enabler thus links to the First Enabler and an ongoing process with a feedback loop is required to derive value from the overall change process. It is, therefore, as if a new Sigmoid or S-curve will be signalled by this Tenth Enabler. The building of a continuous process of change through multiple change curves or S-curves calls for continuous change and a change capacity within the organisation. Building this change capacity would enable resilience to adapt to new external challenges and opportunities. Recovery or a phase of stability might be required before embarking on the new wave of change, to enable resilience in the organisation. The final chapter focuses on the adaptive change capability in the closing of this volume.

References

AAAS. (2008, June 27). *Why it's hard to say goodbye*. America Association for Advancement of Science. Retrieved July 27, 2019, from https://www.sciencemag.org/news/2008/06/why-its-hard-say-goodbye

Bluen, S. (2013). *Talent management in emerging markets*. Randburg: Knowres. http://www.kr.co.za/knowres-publishing-1/talent-management-in-emerging-markets-mobi

Bose, I., & Vallurupalli, V. (2015). *Cultural transformation at Microsoft IT in India: Too fast or just right?* Indian Institute of Management, Calcutta, Singapore Management University, Case Centre, IIMC-CRC-2014-08. https://ink.library.smu.edu.sg/cases_coll_all/115/

Braun, G. (2011). Organisations today: What happens to attachment? *Psychodynamic Practice, 17* (2), 123–139. https://doi.org/10.1080/14753634.2011.562692

Bridges, W. (1980). *Transitions: Making sense of life's changes*. Reading, MA: Addison-Wesley Publishing. https://www.amazon.com/Transitions-Making-Changes-Revised-Anniversary/dp/073820904X

Cavallo, K., & Brienza, D. (2006). Emotional competence and leadership excellence at Johnson & Johnson. *Europe's Journal of Psychology, 2*(1). https://doi.org/https://doi.org/10.5964/ejop.v2i1.313. Retrieved April 17, 2018, from http://ejop.psychopen.eu/article/view/313/221

Cummings, T. G., & Worley, C. G. (2015). *Organization development & change* (10th ed.). Cincinnati, OH: South-Western College Publishing. https://www.loot.co.za/product/thomas-cummings-organization-development-and-change/lszv-2176-g370?referrer=googlemerchant&gclid=CjwKCAjw5vz2BRAtEiwAbcVIL_49WYGXAaU1mrKBwWHl3ZZBiQ72sHG5Qwv5JACp9vKcDEEphNuZKhoCKWQQAv D_BwE&gclsrc=aw.ds

De Vries, M. K. (2003). The retirement syndrome: The psychology of letting go. *European Management Journal, 21*(6), 707–716. Retrieved from http://newsletters.isb.edu/FamilyBusiness-Newsletter/File/The-Retirement-Syndrome-The-Psychology-of-Letting-Go. pdf

Dykas, M. J., & Cassidy, J. (2011). Attachment and the processing of social information across the life span: Theory and evidence. *Psychological Bulletin, 137*(1), 19–46. https://doi.org/10.1037/a0021367

Grady, V. M., & Grady III, J. D. (2013). The relationship of Bowlby's attachment theory to the persistent failure of organizational change initiatives. *Journal of Change Management, 13*(2), 206–222. https://doi.org/10.1080/14697017.2012.728534

Huhulea, I. (2016). *Quitting your job can be just as heartbreaking as ending a romance*. Retrieved July 26, 2018, from http://qz.com/701102/quitting-you-job-can-be-just-as-heartbreaking-as-ending-a-romance/

Jacques, E., & Clement, S. D. (1994). *Executive leadership: A practical guide to managing complexity*. New York: Blackwell. https://www.wiley.com/en-us/Executive+Leadership%3A+A+Practical+Guide+to+Managing+Complexity-p-9780631193135

Kanter, M. R. (2003). Leadership and the psychology of turnarounds. *Harvard Business Review, 81*(6), 58–70. Retrieved March 31, 2017, from https://hbr.org/2003/06/leadership-and-the-psychology-of-turnarounds

Khumalo, M., & Scheepers, C. B. (2018). Leadership of change in South Africa public sector turnarounds. *Journal of Organizational Change Management* (in press). https://doi.org/10.1108/JOCM-04-2017-0142

Malesky, E., & Taussig, M. (2009). Out of the gray: The impact of provincial institutions on business formalization in Vietnam. *Journal of East Asian Studies, 9*(2), 249–290. https://www.cambridge.org/core/journals/journal-of-east-asian-studies/article/out-of-the-gray-the-impact-of-provincial-institutions-on-business-formalization-in-vietnam/A849B19C73A4874E8F3E4EF78694C239

Marino, L., Strandholm, K., Steensma, H. K., & Weaver, K. M. (2002). The moderating effect of national culture on the relationship between entrepreneurial orientation and strategic alliance portfolio extensiveness. *Entrepreneurship Theory and Practice, 26*(4), 145–160. https://doi.org/10.1177/104225870202600409

Nguyen, T. V., Le, C. Q., Tran, B. T., & Bryant, S. E. (2015). Citizen participation in city governance: Experiences from Vietnam. *Public Administration and Development, 35*(1), 34–45. https://doi.org/10.1002/pad.1702

Noer, D. M. (1993). *Healing the wounds. Overcoming the trauma of layoffs and revitalizing downsized organisations*. San Francisco, CA: Wiley. https://www.wiley.com/en-us/Healing+the+Wounds%3A+Overcoming+the+Trauma+of+Layoffs+and+Revitalizing+Downsized+Organizations%2C+Revised+%26+Updated-p-9780470500156

O'Connor, M.-F., Wellisch, D. K., Stanton, A. L., Eisenberger, N. I., Irwin, M. R., & Lieberman, M. D. (2008). Craving love? Complicated grief activates brain's reward center. *NeuroImage, 42*, 969–972. PMC2553561. https://www.ncbi.nlm.nih.gov/pmc/articles/PMC2553561/

Ready, D. A., Hill, L. A., & Conger, J. A. (2008, November). Winning the race for talent in emerging markets. *Harvard Business Review*, 1–10. Retrieved from https://hbr.org/2008/11/winning-the-race-for-talent-in-emerging-markets

Scheepers, C. B. (2012). *Coaching leaders: The 7 P tools to propel change*. Randburg: Knowres. http://www.kr.co.za/mentoring-coaching/coaching-leaders-7-p-tools-to-propel-change

Scheepers, C. B., & Swart, S. (2015). *Momentum and metropolitan merger: Authentic transforma-tional leadership*. Ivey Publishing, 9B15C004. https://store.hbr.org/product/momentum-and-metropolitan-s-merger-authentic-transformational-leadership/W15045
Webber, L. (2010). *Beginnings and endings in therapy and in life: Two sides of a coin*. Retrieved from https://counsellingresource.com/features/2010/09/29/beginnings-and-endings-in-therapy-and-in-life/

Reference List for Quotes

Maxwell, J. (1998). *The 21 irrefutable laws of leadership*. Nashville, TN: Thomas Nelson Publishers. https://www.amazon.com/21-Irrefutable-Laws-Leadership-Anniversary/dp/1480554030

Conclusion and Future Research

15

Life is a journey—not a destination
(Ralph Waldo Emerson, n.d.)

15.1 Orientation to Final Chapter

We have arrived at our destination. Thank you for joining us on this journey. Considering your change challenge: What have you realised, while learning about the ten enablers? What is the one thing that you can go and DO that will move things forward? Just take one action—today! In this final chapter, we summarise the Ten Enablers Model, discuss our future research, invite you to conduct further reading and offer our contact details for you to join the community of practice on leading change.

© Springer Nature Switzerland AG 2020
C. B. Scheepers, S. Swart, *Change Leadership in Emerging Markets*, Future of Business and Finance, https://doi.org/10.1007/978-3-030-40846-6_15

15.2   Summary of the Ten Enablers Model of Leading Change in Emerging Markets

15.2.1 Considering the Whole Process as a Summary

In Part II of this volume, we presented the Ten Enablers Model. Each of the ten enablers was designed to help you as change leader implement change successfully. As a holistic model, it can be used in its entirety and we suggest you "toggle" between enablers as the change project evolves. Any one of the ten enablers can also be used as a standalone module to help with a specific part of a change process. We leave it up to you to decide how best you want to use this book.

You will recall, we started this change process with ensuring your **Ethos** and the ethos of the team, organisation and the project, are all aligned and serve the greater good of the majority of stakeholders. In the Second Enabler, **Ego Mastery**, we proposed a Road to Personal Mastery to help change leaders ensure their egos are intact and they remain energised and balanced throughout the change process. In Enabler 3, **Explore**, we urged change leaders to look up and out to engage with the broader environment to find opportunities to take the organisation to a higher level. Next, change leaders were invited to seek **Eureka** (a-ha!) Moments where they find meaningful and unique responses to the challenges in the environment and start the process of envisioning. In Enabler 5, **Envision,** we asked change leaders to ensure that the improved future is quantified and measurable (BHAG and SMART vision). In Enabler 6, we encouraged change leaders to **Engage** with a wide variety of stakeholders, before setting goals and planning the change. In the Seventh Enabler, **Embark**, the execution process was presented as the crux of any change process. It is in this Eight Enabler, **Execute**, that movement towards the vision was generated and maintained to reach the vision. We next suggested an ongoing evaluation process (Enabler 9, **Evaluate**) during, directly after, and at least 9–12 months after the vision had been achieved. Finally, in Enabler 10, we urged change leaders to learn how to **Exit** with grace.

As mentioned in Chap. 4, when we introduced the Ten Enablers Model, we mentioned that a change process is not strictly speaking a sequential one and that it moves more like cogs and wheels. At Enabler Ten, we arrived at the point where a new change was introduced, and we therefore returned to Enabler 1, Ethos, but with a completely different focus, vision and goals.

15.2.2 Link Between Ethos and Exit: The Helix Model

The Ten Enablers Model offered steps towards the implementation of a change process. The process started with the First Enabler, Ethos. Ethos represents transcendence and includes where we have come from, where we are and where we are going. It also includes wisdom to consider when the right time to start the change process would be and when to end the process.

The Ten Enablers Model thus starts with wisdom, but then progresses towards knowledge and skills while implementing (Executing and Enhancing) and then ends

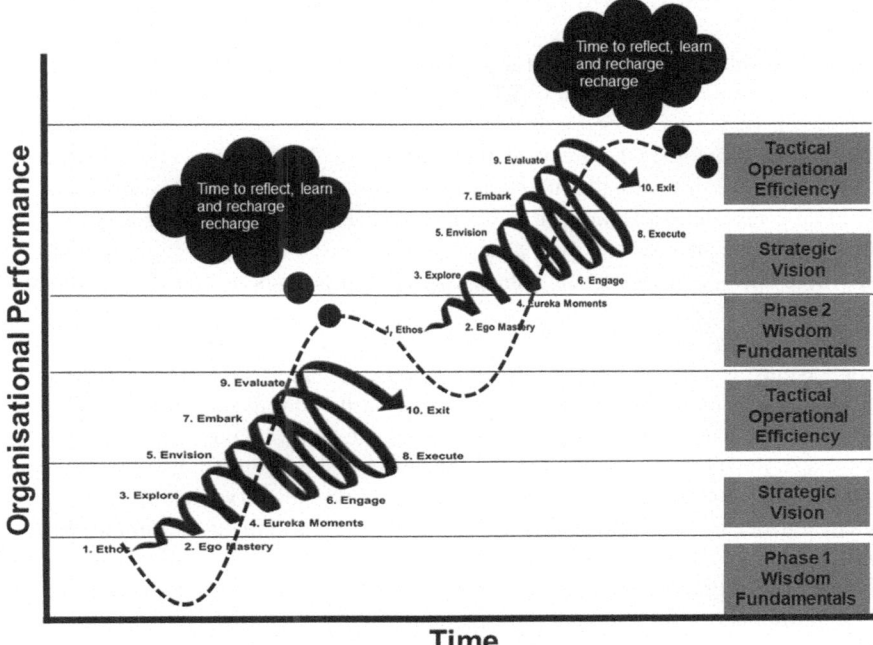

Fig. 15.1 The Ten Enablers Helix Model used over time (Authors' own)

again with wisdom when completion is celebrated in the final Enabler 10, Exit. Just to be faced again with the next wave of change.

The process therefore could be represented by a helix formation starting with a wisdom foundation, advancing into strategic visioning, followed by tactical operational efficiency and returning to a wisdom foundation as the next wave of change commences. Figure 15.1 explains the helix analogy by presenting two helix formations following each other.

If at all possible, we need to allow for an opportunity to consolidate and reflect at the end of Phase 1 to consider how to approach Phase 2. This will enable adequate planning and re-energizing before a new wave is embarked upon. In our experience, we all too often neglect this aspect of allowing the rhythm of ebb and flow and tend to jump onto the next band wagon without reflecting and learning from past experiences.

Figure 15.1 illustrates that the Tenth Enabler leads to a phase of consolidation and wisdom just to initiate the First Enabler Ethos in Phase 2 again. The ten enablers are thus meant to be ongoing and the model offers a framework to direct the phases.

As discussed above, change is continuous and as such, we too now need to move onto the next helix in our research process. The next section will consider future research suggestions.

15.3   Continuous Change as Future Research

The Ten Enablers Model does not negate the modern organisational environment's need for continuous change. In fact, as discussed above, we support the classic framework of Greiner (1998) on the phases of evolutionary change, as well as revolutionary change in the lifecycle of organisations. These phases could be likened to episodes in an individual's life cycle as described by Weiss (2004), who advised qualitative researchers to anchor semi-structured interview questions in particular episodes for the interviewee. Similarly, organisations experience specific episodes in their lifecycles of disruption or radical change and periods or episodes of relative stability (Fig. 15.2).

While change processes are by no means linear, we are able to plot or map the progression, as Greiner (1998) already advised in the 1980s. For example, an organisation is required to continuously improve its current products and services for current clients and markets. However, particularly in our connected global landscape, the threat of new entrants into the market and or digital disruption require organisations to introduce transformational or revolutionary change, that spans across current systems and processes in the business and includes a mind shift or new way of thinking, doing and being. Greiner (1998) called this revolutionary change. You might ask the question whether the Ten Enablers Model is relevant for the evolutionary or revolutionary change processes?

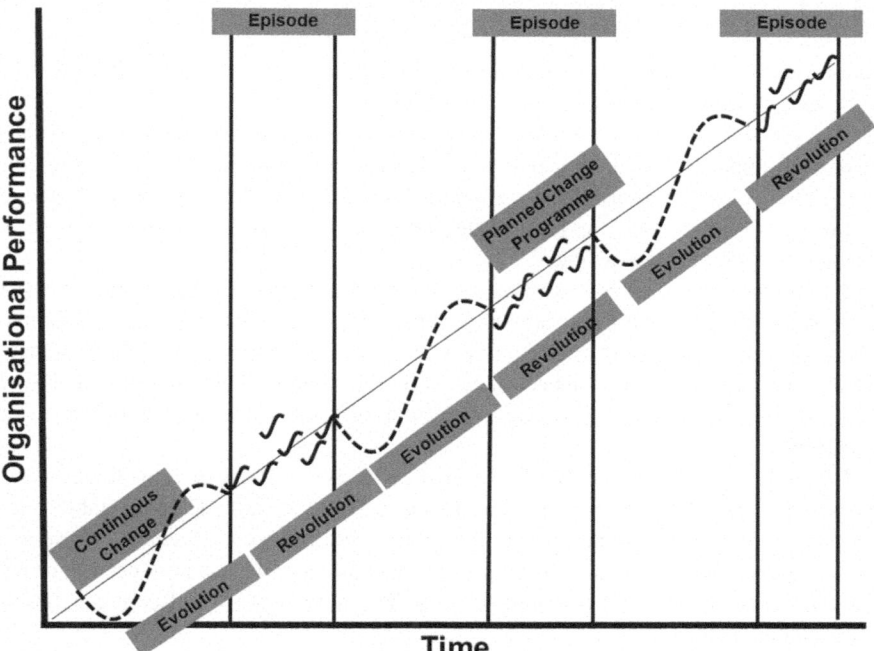

Fig. 15.2   The Ten Enablers Model applied to the evolutionary and revolutionary change processes [Authors' own concept adapted from Greiner (1998) model]

Well, the Ten Enablers Model is an Organisational Development (OD) process that generally will be used to implement a change programme, with various change projects to address either a significant threat which has to be mitigated, or capitalise on a significant opportunity, that requires extensive larger scale change or revolutionary change. While the evolutionary, continuous improvement aspect is important, it maintains the status quo and thus does not necessarily require the same amount of effort or dedicated resources than the case of revolutionary change. However, the organisation might want to introduce a culture of learning, called a learning organisation by Peter Senge (1990) or a built-to-change capability (Collins, 2001) in the organisation to enable the capability for continuous change. These OD interventions would require strategic change and introducing a new culture of sharing and collaboration that require a clear strategy or reason for the change, the engagement of organisational members and organisation-wide participation and thus the Ten Enablers Model would in these instances be relevant to continuous change processes.

Throughout the book, the Sigmoid curve is used to illustrate the requirement for organisations to continuously rethink their strategy to continuously grow and prevent decline. In the figure above, the Sigmoid curve is superimposed on the revolutionary change episode. The figure further demonstrates that organisations will likely go through more than one episode of revolutionary change in their lifecycles. The research on organisational decline, offers evidence of recurrent situations or episodes of organisations requiring turnarounds (Learn more about these episodes in Olson, Van Bever, & Verry, 2008; Reisner, 2002).

This illustrates that organisations benefit from considering both types of changes, the revolutionary as well as the evolutionary. To continuously improve, change leaders must ensure that they are leading others to be able to lead change. This implies that a leader would play the role of what we called, the change leader, or the one initiating the change and then support another leader, who we called the changee as the one receiving the change leadership support, who in turn, would transfer this skill to another leader. In this situation, the changee becomes the change leader in this particular relationship, which thus illustrates that the same person could play and actually we advise them to have to play both roles. In this way, the transfer of change leadership is possible throughout an organisation and across the levels of management. The continuous process is illustrated in Fig. 15.3.

We advise change leaders to purposefully and deliberately develop the change leadership in others and allow other leaders to invest in them and develop their change leadership. The continuous learning process is demonstrated in this Fig. 15.3. We advise leaders to open themselves up to being coached or mentored in terms of their change leadership skills and in this way, the learning always increases.

To demonstrate that we as authors practice what we preach, we had joined an international community interested in Complex Adaptive Change. This field of Complexity Science is represented by emergent change and knowledge about living responsive systems. For example, Dr. Glenda Eoyang heads up the company Human Systems Dynamics and there are 750 consultants in this network. She offers amazing adaptive change workshops and we attended them and keep on learning about the

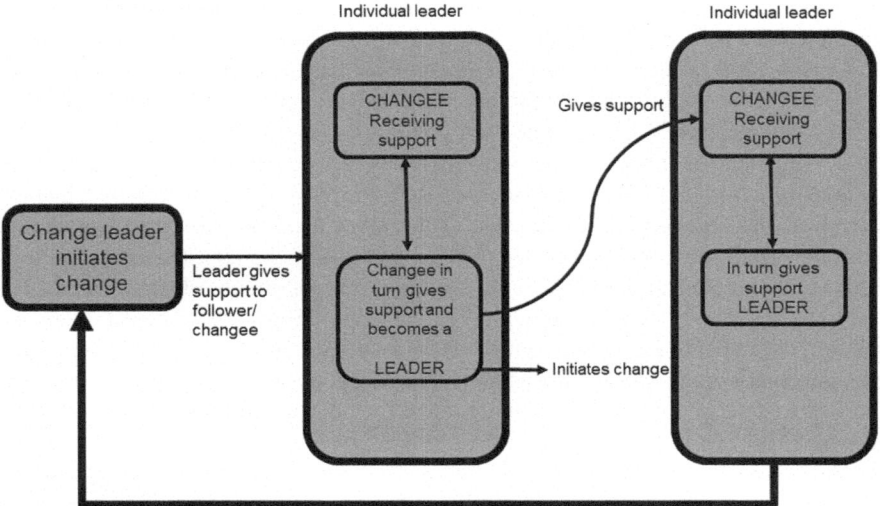

Great change leaders develop others into change leaders

Fig. 15.3 Change leaders and changees (Author's own)

next wave of knowledge in the dynamic field of OD and change. Her book, *Leveraging uncertainty in your organisation* (2013) highlights the principles of emergent change.

Dave Osborne and Jill Hinson, who are themselves gurus in the domain, had thanked Eoyang in their work. They offered practical examples of "Leading in Complex Times" in the *NLT's Practitioner's Journal* (2011). Since their work symbolises for us the next wave that we are interested in following, we offer a short summary of their article here.

In essence, they advise on leadership imperatives that enable leadership success in complex times: Increase in connectivity, due to technology advances, leads to increased interdependence and subsequently higher levels of complexity. Complexity science encourages a shift in our mindset around leadership towards influencing the speed and direction of change that naturally emerges. Leadership thus requires sensing and noticing of patterns, called contextual intelligence and leveraging self-organising.

They advise change leaders to be a disruption creator—a leader who encourages creativity and supports the exploration of ambiguity and experimentation. Since innovation happens at the edge of chaos, being too comfortable is not conducive to creating the climate for experimentation and ultimately exploring new horizons. We concur and would like to encourage change leaders to say, "Let's try it!"; "How about a pilot study?"

Another important implication of emergent change is that change leaders must become a connector—a leader who builds bridges and connection across disparate parts to increase innovation and diversity of ideas. Since the future is built on local interactions, through partnering with customers to co-develop solutions, leadership can leverage collective intelligence. Many disruptive social movements have consciously leveraged social media to connect the entire world to their mission. Crucial for change leadership in complexity is to say, "Let's collaborate"; "How about connecting and co-designing?"

Sensing strategically—a leader who, in a chaotic environment, senses the external patterns that are emerging is another important competence of change leaders in our complex world. We call this contextual intelligence and are studying this type of intelligence to be able to transfer our knowledge to our future work. Contextual intelligence includes noticing patterns, since patterns provide insight into what is currently emerging in an unpredictable environment, contextual intelligence requires ways to tap into knowledge exchanges on the context and channel people's attention to information across silos. We advise change leaders to say, "Let's attend that conference and share with other departments or divisions to seize the opportunity"; "How about we involve people from the frontline and other departments in our decision making?"

Given this body of knowledge, we developed 25 Cs of Contextual Leadership. Let us know whether you would like to engage with us in researching these to prepare for our next book. Emerging markets are growing and accelerating their growth. We would like you to share your research on emerging markets with us. We hope that this volume would urge companies operating in emerging economies to respond to the ongoing changes in market conditions. As growing emerging economies, it would be fascinating to watch the trends in the emerging economies as they transition to higher levels of market economies (Malesky & Taussig, 2009). We urge you to respond to the shifting competitive landscape.

As we had mentioned, in the unpredictability, volatility and deficiencies in the external environment of emerging markets, leaders have a propensity to pay greater heed to their company' internal resources. We would like to add, change leaders must focus on their internal resources, for example their own personal spiritual awareness and emotional grounding in who they are and what forms their identity. This anchor assists in staying grounded in times of volatility. We have high expectations for the exponential growth of emerging markets, since we have experienced the internal strength of our co-emerging markets' colleagues and clients. We hope that our book will contribute to enhancing the success of emerging markets.

15.4   Final Message

We would love feedback on how you have used the Ten Enablers Model while leading change. Network research shows that ideas are triggered at the intersection of networks. We would like to connect with you and your networks. We encourage you to be a core connector, where you connect others and even a broker connector connecting other networks with one another. In this way, we form ecosystems of interested people in change leadership.

We envision our book to form a core link to networks. Join our community of practice and stay connected to others who also want to learn more about leading change.

It has been a privilege to have an opportunity to write down the lessons that we learned and to share it with you.

Stay in touch!

Connect with us on LinkedIn or Twitter

Sonja

sonjaswart@mweb.co.za

Caren

scheepersc@gibs.co.za

References

Collins, J. (2001). *Good to great*. New York: HarperCollins. https://www.harpercollins.com/9780066620992/good-to-great/

Eoyang, G. H., & Holladay, R. J. (2013). *Adaptive action: Leveraging uncertainty in your organization*. Stanford, CA: Stanford Business Books. https://www.sup.org/books/title/?id=21971

Greiner, L. E. (1998). *Evolution and revolution as organisations grow*. Boston, MA: Harvard Business Publishing. https://hbr.org/1998/05/evolution-and-revolution-as-organizations-grow

Malesky, E. J., & Taussig, M. D. (2009). Where is credit due? Legal institutions, connections, and the efficiency of bank lending in Vietnam. *The Journal of Law, Economics, & Organization, 25* (2), 535–578. https://doi.org/10.1093/jleo/ewn011

Olson, M. S., Van Bever, D., & Verry, S. (2008). When growth stalls. *Harvard Business Review, 86* (3), 50–61. https://hbr.org/2008/03/when-growth-stalls

Osborne, D., & Hinson, J. (2011). Leading in complex times. *Practicing Social Change, NLT's Practitioner's Journal, 1*(4), 26–30. http://www.ntl-psc.org/assets/Uploads/PSC-Journal-Issue-04-Dave-Osborne-and-Jill-Hinson.pdf

Reisner, R. A. F. (2002, February). When a turnaround stalls. *Harvard Business Review*. Retrieved from https://hbr.org/2002/02/when-a-turnaround-stalls

Senge, P. M. (1990). *The fifth discipline: The art and practice of the learning organisation*. New York: Doubleday. https://www.amazon.com/Fifth-Discipline-Practice-Learning-Organiza tion/dp/0385517254

Weiss, R. S. (2004). In their own words: Making the most of qualitative interviews. *Journal of Applied Behavioural Science, 3*(4), 44–51. https://doi.org/10.1525/ctx.2004.3.4.44

Reference List for Quotes

Retrieved July 26, 2019, from https://www.goodreads.com/quotes/24142-life-is-a-journey-not-a-destination

The manufacturer's authorised representative in the EU is Springer
Nature Customer Service Centre GmbH, Europaplatz 3, 69115 Heidelberg,
Germany. If you have any concerns regarding our products, please
contact ProductSafety@springernature.com

Printed and bound by CPI Group (UK) Ltd, Croydon, CR0 4YY
29/04/2026
02099455-0007